DISCARDED

PATTERNS OF AMERICAN
FOREIGN POLICY

PATTERNS OF AMERICAN FOREIGN POLICY

Gene E. Rainey
*University of North Carolina
at Asheville*

ALLYN AND BACON, INC.
Boston • London • Sydney

Copyright © 1975 by Allyn and Bacon, Inc.,
470 Atlantic Avenue, Boston, Massachusetts 02210.

All rights reserved. Printed in the United States of America. No part of the material protected by this copyright notice may be reproduced or utilized in any form or by any means, electronic or mechanical, including photocopying, recording, or by any informational storage and retrieval system, without written permission from the copyright holder.

Library of Congress Cataloging in Publication Data

Rainey, Gene E   1934-
   Patterns of American foreign policy.

   Includes bibliographical references.
   1. United States — Foreign relations — 1945-
I. Title.
E744.R324

ISBN 0-205-04651-7

To Cheryl and Eric

Contents

Preface ix
Acknowledgments xi

SECTION 1 Introduction 1

1 *Patterns of Diplomatic Behavior 3*

SECTION 2 The Background of American Foreign Policy 17

2 *Traditional Patterns of American Foreign Policy 19*
3 *Patterns of American Foreign Policy Images and Goals 44*

SECTION 3 Domestic Sources of American Foreign Policy 65

4 *National Values and American Foreign Policy 67*
5 *The Influence of Public Opinion on American Foreign Policy 81*
6 *The Controversial Role of Mass Media in U.S. Diplomacy 99*

7 *Special-Interest Groups and U.S. Foreign Policy*   115
8 *Partisanship and Foreign Policy: The Role of Political Parties*   130

SECTION 4   Foreign Policymaking and Implementation   139

9 *New Voices in Foreign Policy Formulation: The Problem of Coordination*   141
10 *Functions of Bureaucracy: Information and Implementation*   164
11 *The President and the Bureaucracy: Patterns of Control*   186
12 *Congress, the Supreme Court, and the President: Partners in Policy Formulation*   208

SECTION 5   Issues in American Foreign Policy   231

13 *Patterns of American Military Strategy*   233
14 *Patterns of Arms-Control and Disarmament Policy*   254
15 *Alliances and Patterns of American Foreign Policy*   278
16 *Patterns of American Diplomacy in International Law and Organization*   299
17 *Patterns of Public Diplomacy*   311
18 *Patterns of U.S. Economic Assistance Policy*   332
19 *Patterns of American Foreign Trade Policy*   356

SECTION 6   Conclusion   381

20 *Patterns of American Foreign Policy: Continue or Innovate?*   383

INDEX   393

Preface

A balanced and comprehensive examination of American foreign policy should aim to achieve several objectives. First, it should be interdisciplinary, combining research and ideas from history and the social sciences. United States diplomacy is not a monopoly of political science or history: a student cannot confine himself to one discipline and comprehend contemporary developments. International trade and monetary policy are the most active, challenging, and complex issues today, demanding that economics figure prominently in the analysis of foreign policy. National values, public opinion, and mass media can be better comprehended by examining research by sociologists, anthropologists, and psychologists. Even the physical and biological sciences cannot be neglected; they now are an accepted part of the decision-making process, especially when weapon development, disarmament, and espionage are discussed.

Second, the latest scholarly trends in interpreting American foreign policy must be discussed. U.S. diplomacy has been read almost exclusively through Realist glasses for most of the post-World War II era. Readers are no longer exposed to the rich Liberal tradition that predated Realism, and Right-Wing and Left-Wing Revisionist analyses also tend to be neglected. This book attempts to present a balanced evaluation of these contending viewpoints, allowing the reader to form his or her own opinions.

Third, the policy-formulation process that occurs behind institutional walls must be analyzed. Tomes could be written about the agencies, bureaus, and departments involved in this process—their organization, function, history, and role. However, more interesting are the bureaucratic personnel who function within these institutions. American foreign policy is composed of people making decisions—not boxes, lines, and arrows on organizational charts.

Fourth, the reader should be introduced to the wide range of activities that fall under the rubric of American foreign policy. Political and economic problems obviously are part of that rubric, but so are propaganda activities, *educational and cultural affairs, tourism, "think tanks," the Supreme Court, and a host of other subjects on which this volume focuses. Believing that U.S. foreign policy has been defined too narrowly, I have attempted to redraw its parameters to include topics that are usually neglected.*

Finally, a book on U.S. diplomacy should furnish a framework to analyze events yet to happen. It is not enough to acquaint readers with past and present events without a construct to use in evaluating the future. The construct or framework used here is the concept of "patterns." Most readers will live out the remaining years of this century, which in all probability will be one of the most challenging and perilous times in the history of American diplomacy.

These were my objectives as I began writing. As I finish, I am convinced they are still valid.

G.E.R.

Acknowledgments

In an undertaking of this magnitude, I have been helped by many people whose assistance was invaluable. Professors James F. Morrison and Walter Jones read the entire manuscript and offered insightful criticisms and advice. Robert J. Patterson, Senior Editor at Allyn and Bacon, encouraged my writing with a sincere personal interest and with well-intended, prodding letters that were most effective.

Others read sections: Richard Merritt (University of Illinois) and members of the political science colloquium at Ohio State University (especially Philip M. Burgess). Bahram Farzanegan, George Stein, and Goetz Wolff (political science), Shirley Browning, Mel Stone, and John Barthel (economics), and Stan Kelley and Milton Ready (history)—all at the University of North Carolina at Asheville—also read sections.

Students both in Columbus and Asheville offered ideas for improvement. Douglas Dearth, Ohio State graduate student, was supportive with his research assistance.

My wife, Dorma, proofread all revisions and offered suggestions that increased the depth and clarity of the book as it grew from an idea to a fruition. Ms. Una Phillips, my efficient secretary, shepherded the manuscript through various stages of preparation. And Ms. Cynthia Hartnett, who served as production editor, saved me from occasional vagueness, inaccuracies, and inane statements. They cause me to regret even more the unfortunate requirement of formal writing which dictates the constant use of male pronouns in this book.

PATTERNS OF AMERICAN FOREIGN POLICY

SECTION 1

Introduction

The concept of "pattern," the framework around which the analysis of this text is built, is introduced and defined in chapter 1. Many of the terms presented in this chapter are basic to an understanding of international relations in general, and they are essential to the study of patterns of American foreign policy. The patterns approach equips a student with the background and concepts of American diplomacy that are useful for analyzing past, present, and future U.S. foreign policy. American diplomatic behavior is dynamic and multifaceted: to comprehend its diversity and breadth, a conceptual framework is needed to organize the vast amounts of factual information about past events and to incorporate the many theories that purport to explain U.S. diplomatic behavior.

1

Patterns of Diplomatic Behavior

Before launching this study of American foreign policy, several concepts that are used in this book should be defined. For some readers, this exercise will be a brief review of international politics. For others, who are entering for the first time into a concentrated study of world politics, this chapter will furnish a knowledge of basic concepts to use in evaluating American foreign policy.

THE CONCEPT OF "PATTERN"

The organizing framework of this study of American foreign policy is the concept of patterns in diplomatic behavior. A *pattern* is defined here as a series of related policies occurring over a period of time. Diplomacy, within a historical framework, assumes a shape or a form based on the interrelation of events. Present positions are built on past commitments, and most contemporary pronouncements echo former themes. As a result, current events or policies possess a relationship or a consistency with those embedded in history.

For the student of American foreign policy, the patterns approach implies that events *qua* events will not be focused upon because events become dated and are overshadowed by later developments in diplomatic history. The patterns approach attempts to analyze a series of diplomatic events—treaties, wars, foreign policy programs, or international conferences—in terms of their relationship to each other. Thus, a pattern may be composed of episodes that share a common stimulus; that are based upon a similar assumption; or that are aimed at accomplishing similar objectives.

Certain diplomatic events may also represent an aberration of past patterns that could signify a new pattern developing in American foreign

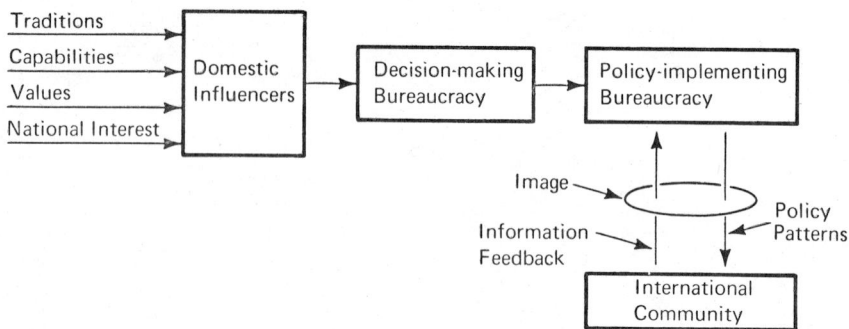

Figure 1-1. Model of American Foreign Policy Patterns.

policy. However, a period of time must pass before it can be ascertained whether a new policy pronouncement is an innovative trend or a unique occurrence bearing no relationship to previous events.

Chronology and Relationships

A pattern is not the result of a unique event in American diplomacy, which occurs, by definition, only once. This fact does not relegate a unique event to a scholastic limbo because it may be of such impact that it serves as a benchmark in the chronological development of a nation's diplomacy. Only one civil war has occurred in American history, for example, but its effect on American diplomacy was profound; it served as an end point for one period of U.S. diplomacy and the beginning of another, as the next chapter will show. The Monroe Doctrine, on the other hand, was a source for a pattern because it stimulated related events in American diplomatic history.

A new chronological pattern often is initiated by a single event. Washington's Farewell Address, which warned against "permanent alliances," stimulated a series of policy positions on alliances and the balance of power, resulting in an isolationist posture for the U.S. in the world. The American government for a century and a half scrupulously avoided alliances with any other state. In 1949, with the signing of the North Atlantic Treaty, American foreign policy radically changed, and the United States in the 1950s frenziedly began to build alliances.

The patterns approach also permits a degree of confidence in predicting American behavior in the future, although a healthy amount of caution should be used in this area. However, discernible trends in American foreign policy do serve as indicators of probable future diplomatic behavior.

REASONS FOR PATTERNS

Why do patterns occur in diplomacy? Several explanations, all of which will be discussed in this book, are suggested: national interest and goals; national values; past traditions; contemporary domestic influences; and regularities in the decision-making process. These possible explanations are illustrated in Figure 1–1, which shows the relationship between influencers in society and the decision-making bureaucracy. National traditions, values, and interests condition the reaction of domestic influencers. After a decision is reached, the bureaucratic policy implementers are charged with putting it into effect, thus affecting the behavioral pattern of the international community. All policy decisions are conditioned by an image or perception that national leaders have of their world environment and the type of feedback or response received from previous policies.

National Interest and Goals

As many definitions exist of national interest as there are analysts of international relations. Here, *national interest* refers to the diplomatic goals that American decision makers attempt to achieve. *Goals* are long-term, broadly gauged projections of the composition of the international system that policymakers perceive to be the most favorable to their nation. Since the decision maker's perception of what should constitute a goal is involved, the image concept, with its values, also is important. Although goals are broadly defined and are future, not immediate, projections, they cannot border on the utopian (i.e., too broad and too far removed from reality) or they will result in frustration when they cannot be attained.

The function of goals is to establish priorities in foreign policy. Depending on the goals considered to be the most important, a nation will make subsidiary and related decisions. Not all goals can be treated as of equal importance, nor can they be shifted radically from period to period. In chapter 20 the question of whether American foreign policy has failed to order priorities among its goals is explored.

Survival. The first goal of foreign policy is national survival, or an independent status free from encroachments by other nations. It can be described in other words: self-preservation, military security, and political security. Survival may mean more than erecting defenses to protect boundaries. National leaders may view expansion or aggression as necessary to maintain national integrity. The goal of survival figures prominently in discussions of whether or not the United States has followed an expansionist policy since 1945.

The intermediate objectives in American diplomacy to ensure United States self-preservation revolve around military strategy (discussed in chapter 13) and alliances, such as the North Atlantic Treaty Organization.

At the same time, another contemporary objective is to negotiate a reduction of armaments vis-à-vis other nations that will thereby permit American military expenditures to be reduced without endangering American survival. This topic is the focus of chapter 14.

Economic Well-Being. Nations attempt to maintain and to improve their economic position in the international system. Although this goal can be viewed as secondary to the primary goal of survival, in the case of the European Economic Community, economic well-being has been placed before maintenance of national sovereignty. The EEC members have been willing to delegate some of the traditional areas of decision making to a regional organization in return for economic benefits.

Chapter 19 surveys the rise and fall of the American international economic position from a status of dominance in world trade to an unstable position reflecting chronic imbalances in both trade and payments. While the goal of economic welfare and prosperity remains, the procedures for implementing them have undergone a transformation as the international economic environment has changed.

National Prestige. Another major foreign policy goal is national prestige, or the reputation that a state possesses among other states in the international system. Although reputation can be tied to the military and economic position of a state, there are occasions when less powerful and less wealthy nations are held in esteem. India under Nehru (1945–1960), for example, was a recognized leader of the Third World nations.[1]

The search for national prestige often involves propaganda or information programs. The role of these programs in American foreign policy is discussed in chapter 17. The desire for prestige is also a motivating force behind foreign-aid programs (the subject of chapter 18) and behind policy positions assumed by international organizations, such as the United Nations (discussed in chapter 16).

National Values

National values are concepts and behavioral traits that characterize a majority of the population. National values, analyzed in chapter 4, are important because they color the interpretation of events occurring in our environment. Facts do not have a wholly objective existence because they are interpreted (sometimes reinterpreted in different historical periods) as they are filtered through national values. Since each nation's values differ, events will seldom be interpreted uniformly by national leaders.

Values are deeply ingrained in the national fabric and therefore do not change radically over a period of time. Traumatic experiences, such as wars, revolutions, and economic depressions, have their impact on molding new clusters of values; sometimes the changes are substantial and perceptible.

Past Traditions

No nation can ignore its past patterns of diplomatic behavior because they contain commitments still considered binding (such as treaties). In some cases, revolutions in a nation may result in the new leaders' rescinding the ousted government's commitments; however, this act itself becomes part of the historical record of the new regime. As the revolutionary government adds to that record, it begins to create traditions that restrain and condition its own future decisions.

On another level, some traditional patterns of behavior can never be ignored or rescinded. Geopolitical considerations are not blotted out by the fires of revolution. The American Revolution begun in 1776 did not change the opportunity to expand westward, nor did it change the existence of a declining colonialist neighbor to the south, Spain. The 1917 Bolshevik Revolution neither obviated Russia's need for warm-water ports nor divested the new government of the nation's extensive mineral wealth.

Traditional modes of thinking or problem solving are seldom changed. Americans continue to be practical and non-doctrinaire in their approaches to political, economic, and social problems. The similarities between the tsars and Soviet leaders again illustrate that revolutions sometimes effect only superficial breaks with traditional patterns of behavior. The Russian obsession with secrecy in dealing with other states, for example, is a characteristic of both tsarist and Soviet foreign policy.

The next chapter will trace behavioral patterns as they developed in U.S. diplomatic history. Although the primary focus of this book is U.S. diplomatic patterns since World War II, traditions that developed during the previous 150 years need to be delineated. Some traditions were modified in the post-1945 era, some were dropped, and new patterns were developed in their place.

Capabilities

Capability is here defined as a nation's potential to influence the behavior of other states. Aspects of capability include both tangible and intangible factors, many of which readily come to mind. Among the tangible components are military strength, industrial–productive capacity, agricultural productivity and availability of raw materials. These major components generate other needs; for example, military strength might require possession of nuclear weapons, a varied delivery system for these weapons, and devices that warn of an enemy attack in sufficient time for the President to order a retaliatory strike.

Intangible capabilities include the skills of the labor force, the morale of the public, the quality of leadership, and the efficiency of the government in making rapid and accurate decisions in a crisis. These components are more difficult to measure. In 1973, for example, it was relatively simple to count the number of Americans under arms and the quantity of U.S. nuclear submarines, but it was more difficult to access American morale after the Nixon administration was beset by scandals.

Capability changes over a period of time. In the next chapter, the American transformation from a small state with limited capability to a nation of "superpower" status will be discussed. However, American capabilities are being threatened in the 1970s. The "energy crisis" and a deteriorating international economic position (discussed in chapter 19) portend a restricted capability base for the United States.

Because capability is relatively static, changing slowly over a period of time, it influences the regularities and patterns of American foreign policy. U.S. leaders cannot push American diplomatic initiatives beyond the tether imposed by economic and military factors. Changes in capabilities permit shifts in policy; but these changes have been gradual and stretched over a span of years. In the post-World War II era, the pace of change affecting American capabilities has increased. The period of time needed to develop nuclear weapons is much shorter than the years required to build a modern navy, for example.

Domestic Influencers

Foreign policy patterns in an open society such as the United States are conditioned by domestic influences. The impact of the several influencers — public opinion, political parties, interest groups, and mass media — varies, as chapters 5 through 8 show. These chapters focus on the question: How do domestic influencers affect the decision-making process?

Domestic influencers tend to be a stable source for American foreign policy formulations, contributing to its patterns of behavior. American public opinion has rarely vacillated between polar extremes; no major shifts in American voting behavior have been noted in the post-World War II era, no restructuring of the instruments of mass media has occurred (except that television has come more into its own), and the two majority parties appear to be as viable as ever. Assuming that domestic influencers do affect the decision-making process, patterns in U.S. foreign policy can be explained, in part, by the lack of radical upheavals in these sectors of American society.

Domestic groups also become important in "transnational" relations, as distinguished from "international" relations. Figure 1–1 illustrates the bilateral aspects of world relations: governments exchanging ambassadors, sending messages, and issuing pronouncements. Another dimension of world politics exists in which the societies of all nations become involved, having relationships with another society's government, with groups in foreign nations, and with international and regional organizations. These activities are transnational and are seldom noticed because they do not attract the publicity that international or bilateral governmental activity attracts. In chapter 17 transnational relations are discussed as public diplomacy.

The Foreign Policymaking Machinery

Perhaps the primary source for regularities in American diplomacy is the foreign policymaking machinery which has undergone no radical change in the history of the United States. Discussion of this machinery in this book is divided into two areas: the elected (or appointed) officials and the career bureaucracy.

The Elected Officials. The route that the President and members of Congress take to attain national prominence has not experienced much transformation since 1789, when the American Constitution was adopted. Changes have occurred peacefully and have been readily absorbed: the demise of the Electoral College and the rise of the convention as the nominating instrument for the President; woman, black, and youth suffrage; and direct election of senators are a few examples of modifications that have been absorbed without upsetting American diplomatic patterns. The roles of the President and Congress in the decision-making process are analyzed in chapters 11 and 12.

The Bureaucracy. Bureaucracy refers to the complex organization of government staffed by career personnel skilled in handling administrative problems. The term is a technical one, and should not be used in a pejorative sense. In chapter 10 the two primary functions of the bureaucracy, information input and implementation of policy, will be discussed.

The bureaucracy has a longevity of its own. It is usually longer than the period of service that the elected or appointed official engages in; the bureaucracy outlives the elected decision makers. The bureaucracy's longevity, in part, also explains the presence of patterns in American foreign policy; it tends to approach a new problem in much the same way and with many of the same values as it used in handling past problems. However, the career bureaucracy does experience some turnover of personnel. Chapter 9 examines the new voices formulating policy that have emerged since the end of World War II. For the most part, these new voices have been absorbed without a major break in the patterns of American diplomacy.

Stages in the Decision-Making Process

One of the first myths that a student of American foreign policy must bury is: The President makes policy. The President, and other elected members of American government, make *decisions,* some of which may coalesce into *policy.* The term "policy" is too loosely employed and misapplied to a variety of stages in the decision-making process. Primarily, "policy" is used to describe a public statement by a national leader. Or it is applied to a directive, memorandum, or instruction written by the leader's assistant or assistants in the bureaucracy to operationalize the leader's public statement. And finally, it is used to refer to the implementation of the written instructions in the field.

Because something often is lost in the translation of a policy statement into policy in the field, policy is more accurately used to designate the outcome of the *total* decision-making process, i.e., the implementation stage. *Decisions* are made at every stage of the definition–evaluation–selection–implementation process, but only *policy* appears as the final outcome. Since a large-scale bureaucracy develops its own behavioral patterns to define problems, evaluate and select alternatives, and implement decisions, its traditional procedures and values contribute to the regularities that are found in American foreign policy. Policy, then, takes on different meanings wherever it appears in the stages of decision-making process. However, for our purposes, "policy" shall refer to what emerges from the implementation stage; i.e., the form that a President's decision takes in the field is *policy*.

The Definition Stage. The diplomatic situation must first be defined; that is, the issue or crisis must be recognized as existing, and more importantly, as constituting a problem vital enough to merit the decision maker's attention. Some crises are of such obvious magnitude that they present no ambiguity at the definition stage. Others may represent threats to the decision maker *if* the facts are interpreted as such, while other events may be completely ignored even though their presence under normal conditions would constitute a crisis.

In defining a crisis, it must be remembered that facts do not speak for themselves. For example, the attack on an American destroyer on the high seas in the Gulf of Tonkin in August 1964 by a small ship of the North Vietnamese Navy can be interpreted as a highly significant threat to American honor and security. While other events, such as the capture of an American spy vessel in 1968 on the high seas by North Korea can be interpreted as not worth a fight. Facts do not have a separate existence in policymaking; their significance depends on the image that the decision maker has of his environment. The North Vietnamese commander who thought that he could sink a destroyer with machine-gun fire may be interpreted as a threat to American security or simply as a lunatic who never should have been given the command of a ship. The interpretation depends on the values that are built into the image of the decision maker; or it can depend on whether the event is interpreted in such a way as to support policy initiatives already decided on independently of the event itself.

An image is the decision maker's cognitive map of his environment. It is his window through which he views the world. Figure 1–2 illustrates the function of an individual's image in relation to an event or to the facts. Some facts (F_1) might be so antagonistic to the policymaker's values that they could never be accepted as existing or "real" and would be rejected. Other facts may be in keeping with the decision maker's view of the world, and therefore would be accepted. Yet a third group of facts (F_3) might be allowed to pass through the policymaker's image, but are distorted in the process. For example, if an American leader considers the Soviet Union aggressive, any action by the U.S.S.R. aimed at reducing tensions either

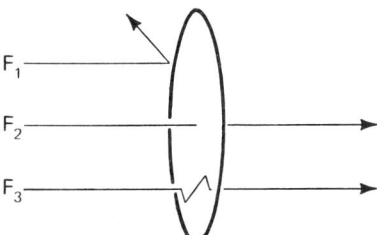

Figure 1-2. The Decision Maker's Image.

will be screened out (F_1) or distorted (F_3) to mean something different. Thus, facts can be defined as problems or crises — or they can be ignored, in which case, a decision-making problem does not arise.

The concept of the image held by the decision maker is important in understanding how some facts can be interpreted as threats and others interpreted as friendly maneuvers. In chapter 3, the four major images that are held by American leaders who decide on U.S. foreign policy and by academicians who write about these decisions are examined.

Evaluation of Alternatives. The second stage of the decision process involves evaluation of all the alternatives available to solve a problem as defined by the decision maker's interpretation of the facts. The effective policymaker will always attempt to maximize his alternatives; he will avoid being caught with only one avenue of action left open to solve his problem. Normally, a policymaker with but one alternative has failed to prepare himself and his nation for a problem, even though he recognized that it might arise. A decision maker must avoid, as best he can, those situations in which he is left with the choice of using force to solve issues. Of course, there are situations in which the use of force is the only alternative to loss of independence; in these situations an opponent will not permit rational consideration either by negotiation or by continuing the status quo. Except for choose among to solve the problem. Furthermore, the effective decision these situations, the decision maker should have a variety of alternatives to maker will be careful to consider options that permit his opponent to select alternatives that do not involve the use of force. During the October 1962 Cuban missile crisis, President Kennedy chose the option of a pacific blockade of Cuba, but announced the blockade in sufficient time to permit Premier Khrushchev to order different courses for Russian vessels sailing toward Cuba. An effective policymaker does not force his opponent into a corner, where his only choice is to fight or to be humiliated.

Selection of Alternatives. Often the policymaker has access to several alternatives; however, they may all be, to some degree, unattractive. In these situations, the decision maker will try to make the most of a difficult and embarrassing situation.

The final choice among the options available depends primarily on the policymaker's calculation of the cost involved, the odds that failure may be the outcome, and the amount of national benefits or payoff to be derived if the decision is the right one. Table 1-1 illustrates this calculation, using

Table 1-1. The Cost-Risk-Payoff Calculation in Selecting Alternatives

	Cost	Risk of Failure	Payoff if Successful
U-2 flights over U.S.S.R. in 1955	Low	Low	High
American involvement in Vietnam in 1965	High	Low	Medium

"high," "medium," or "low" to characterize the amount of the cost of each policy initiative, the probability that failure may occur, and the amount of the payoff if the policy is successful.

In the first example, the U-2 flights over the U.S.S.R. during the mid-1950s involved the small cost of developing a high-flying aircraft to photograph Soviet military installations. Because of the altitude at which the U-2 operated, the risk of failure was calculated as low. (Although one pilot, Francis Gary Powers, discovered that this judgment was in error.) The payoff was quite attractive: invaluable photo intelligence. This type of matrix presents no problem to the American decision maker. If at least one of his many options showed a "low-low-high" calculation, he would have no trouble choosing the policy alternative to follow.

The second example in the matrix presents a decision maker with more of a challenge. The cost of pursuing a military solution in Vietnam reached 30 billion dollars a year before President Nixon's "Vietnamization" program. The risk that the United States would suffer an ignoble defeat as the French did in 1954 was low; it was doubtful that the North Vietnamese and the Viet Cong could drive the Americans, with their superior fire power, out of the country. The payoff expected from the conflict is difficult to assess because it depended primarily on American goals, which were never clearly stated during the conflict.

Goal-setting is a crucial activity for the decision maker when selecting alternatives or objectives. The policy alternative that appears to best accommodate the long-range goal envisioned by the policymaker will be chosen. The objectives formulated after a goal is decided upon should be framed in specific, non-ideological terms. An objective to gain photo intelligence of Soviet missile sites by U-2 flights is quite different from "halting the spread of International Communism" in Vietnam. The first objective is specific, which means that achieving it can be plotted with some measure of success. The second objective is too amorphous, pregnant with too many underdefined values, and lacking precise benchmarks to ascertain whether it has been or will be achieved.

Implementation. The official and public declaration of intentions by the decision maker does not constitute *policy.* Often the policy declaration and the policy outcome are different for several reasons. The policymaker, to begin with, may have misjudged capabilities on hand to carry out his stated purpose. A political leader may possess a distorted perception of his environment, believing that his nation is stronger and wealthier than is the case. He may assume, as President Monroe did, that his nation's military and economic strength is sufficient to discourage other countries from staking claims on neighboring lands. The Monroe Doctrine enunciated objectives that required capabilities beyond those possessed by the United States.

Policy statements and policy outcomes implemented in the field may diverge from each other for a second reason: the implementing bureaucracy may disagree with the stated policy and may attempt to sabotage its execution by either ignoring the leader's wishes, by delaying tactics, or by projecting a different image than the one intended by the policymaker. W. H. Page's interpretation of Woodrow Wilson's protests to the British over Great Britain's repeated violations of American neutrality is an example. Page, as ambassador to Great Britain, tended to soften the blow at each point, convincing the British that Wilson's protests were for domestic consumption and therefore should not be taken seriously.

Yet a third factor may explain the difference between stated and implemented policy. The President and Secretary of State, in enunciating policy, usually address several audiences, domestic and foreign; this tends to encourage speaking in general terms. As directives trickle down through the bureaucracy, they must be honed and polished to fit actual situations, rather than the broad abstractions that decision makers have in mind. A Country Director for Poland, for example, will have to apply the President's desires for more friendly relations with the East European nations to everyday problems that arise with tourists, businessmen, and students.

People Make Decisions. Foreign policy is made by individuals, not nations. This statement must be emphasized because we have a tendency to anthropomorphize the United States. We are inclined to say that the United States "believes," "declares war," or "sends troops" when actually a group of individuals, interacting with one another and subjected to separate pressures and motivations, make the decisions. It is *people,* both officials and citizens, who create, sustain, and change patterns. People aspire to goals, hold values, and follow interests. We should not divorce concepts, patterns, programs, and policies from identifiable and actual individuals. Consequently, the tendency to say that nations make policy should be resisted. Often, we use this terminology as a short-hand method to describe American foreign policy, but it is an unfortunate habit.

International Stimuli

Not all the stimuli that encourage regularities in a nation's foreign policy are internal. Some are external, emanating from the international system itself.

In the model in Figure 1-1, this aspect is labeled "information feedback."

The United States is part of an international system that has been evolving since the 16th century. As a result of almost 500 years of systemic evolution, behavioral norms, encompassed either in international law or unwritten customs, have developed. These requirements are filtered through the American image, as Figure 1-2 shows; thus, what the rest of the world considers a legal norm may not be similarly regarded by the American government. Many of the legal stimuli, however, are not ignored and make for stable patterns in American foreign policy. For example, American leaders honor the requirements of international law on the exchange of diplomatic representatives.

National leaders and publics sometimes reject some of the customary methods of doing business in the international system because these customs are at odds with national values. For example, the balance of power, a behavioral pattern that began to develop in the latter part of the 17th century and was written into the Treaty of Utrecht in 1713, was openly rejected by American decision makers for a century and a half. As will be shown in chapters 2 and 15, American reluctance to accept the balance of power as a concept and a diplomatic procedure has diminished in the post-World War II era.

International and regional organizations, such as the United Nations and the North Atlantic Treaty Organization, also impose regularities on American diplomacy. Allies expect certain behavioral patterns from their friends in a coalition. The United States, playing the role of an alliance leader, exhibits a consistency of behavior; irregular behavior confuses alliance partners.

STIMULI FOR IRREGULARITIES

Not all factors in international relations contribute to the development of patterns. When the United States matured and moved through small-, medium-, great-power, and superpower levels (*see* chapter 2), its behavioral patterns tended to undergo a transformation. Each level of capability brought about new opportunities and new challenges. But the new patterns tended to be variations of the regularities contained in the previous period.

Previously weak nations that became strong (e.g., Germany, Japan, and the People's Republic of China after World War II) and nations previously strong that lost strength (e.g., Great Britain after World War II) also introduced breaches in the patterns of diplomacy. Old relationships erode and new ones are forged. Again, these new patterns will not be complete severances with the past, but modifications of past patterns.

Despite these stimuli and others that will be mentioned later in this book, discernible patterns are present in American foreign policy. The reader should not accept patterns that survive stimuli for change as somehow sacrosanct. In chapter 20 some of these age-old patterns are singled

chapter 1   Patterns of Diplomatic Behavior   15

out as no longer viable as the United States becomes two centuries old and moves toward the year 2000.

ADVANTAGES OF THE PATTERNS APPROACH

To affirm that patterns of diplomatic behavior exist in American foreign policy may appear to be a relatively simple task. To ferret out the reasons for the development of patterns is a little more difficult; this chapter offers the reader only a sampling of reasons that are developed in greater detail in this book.

What are the peculiar benefits to be gained from using the concept of patterns to analyze diplomatic behavior? First, a wealth of data and an abundance of events can be organized, many of which are difficult to find time to study on an individual or case basis. The United States is a superpower with worldwide interests touching every issue of a complex world. Most of these issues have never entered our consciousness because American foreign policy is often conceived of in terms of foreign aid, anti-Communism, nuclear weapons, and the President. U.S. diplomacy is too variegated for simplifications.

Second, by using the patterns concept, some important questions about American foreign policy can be broached: What are the prospects for a particular pattern continuing? What innovations should be introduced that might divert American foreign policy into a different channel and perhaps begin a new pattern? What are the rigid and fixed factors that maintain the status quo? What are the obstacles to changing to a more attractive and progressive behavioral response?

And finally, the patterns approach permits us to speculate about the future. An identified behavioral pattern can be used to predict the response of the American government to a future event, such as a war between the Soviet Union and the People's Republic of China. We can organize our study of U.S. foreign policy around patterns to determine the direction of contemporary American diplomacy and to judge whether or not that direction should be changed.

NOTES

1. "Third World" is a term that contemporary writers employ without much attempt at precise definition. Its origin is traced back to the East–West conflict, or in other terms, the United States, leader of the Western "world," versus the Soviet Union, leader of the Eastern "world." The Third World then refers to the non-Western nations largely located in Africa and Asia, although Latin America, which sometimes has been identified with the Western world, also has been included.

SECTION 2

The Background of American Foreign Policy

This section offers the reader two general approaches to the analysis of American foreign policy patterns: historical and conceptual. In chapter 2, the historical backdrop that precedes the present era in American foreign policy is examined. Diplomatic patterns of behavior are traced through the small-, medium-, great-power, and superpower eras in the history of the United States.

In chapter 3, the four images or worldviews that have been held by most American decision makers are analyzed. Every imageholder proposes goals and objectives for American foreign policy based on assumptions and values imbedded in his perception of the international system.

2
Traditional Patterns of American Foreign Policy

Nations are not captives of their history, but previous successes and failures form a context within which decision makers evaluate current initiatives under consideration. Past incidents tend to become hallowed traditions in national folklore, sometimes long after the stimulus for the original action is past. Washington's Farewell Address and the Monroe Doctrine, for example, created honored traditions in American foreign policy that continue to serve as behavioral cues for U.S. leaders in a modern world.

This chapter divides the chronology of the American experience into four periods: the era of a small power (1789–1865); a medium power (1865–1898); a great power (1898–1945); and a superpower (1945 to the present). Within these four eras, four major patterns of behavior, based on four underlying concepts, are discernible: unilateralism, expansionism, legalism, and moralism.

THE UNITED STATES AS A SMALL POWER (1789–1865)

A small power is a nation with interests in its immediate neighbors and with capabilities to pursue foreign policy goals identified with its immediate world neighborhood. A small power, then, has the military and economic capacity to handle effectively foreign policy problems that appear on its borders. Conflicts or challenges beyond its immediate boundaries involve resources that a small power does not possess.

The United States experience as a small power lasted from the inception of the American nation in 1789 until the end of the Civil War in 1865.

During this period, the U.S. began to develop four behavioral patterns of unilateralism, expansionism, legalism, and moralism. At the same time, the infant United States, at least on two occasions, exhibited behavior unbecoming to a small power.

Unilateralism

The earliest behavioral pattern that emerged in American foreign policy was unilateralism, or an inclination toward independent action in solving international problems. The early American government attempted to maintain the widest possible latitude in decision making; it refused to become allied with or even beholden to other states. At times this approach pushed the infant U.S. into positions that required more resources than the American nation possessed, such as entry into the War of 1812 and the enunciation of the Monroe Doctrine.

Distrust of the European Powers. A unilateralist stance in foreign policy is rooted in the American colonial experience and watered by their first encounter with European diplomacy. In European conflicts of the 18th century, American colonists usually found themselves deeply involved in wars, the cause and purpose of which they seldom understood. For the Americans, these conflicts were fought for desiderata embedded in British foreign policy and not for the political and economic interests of the North American colonies.

The Seven Years War in Europe (1756–1763) illustrates the basis for colonial distrust of British diplomacy. The colonists suspected that London was using colonial resources and lives to achieve goals unrelated to life in the New World. The war was instigated by a coalition of France, Russia, and Austria for the purpose of punishing Prussia for its diplomatic behavior growing out of an earlier conflict, the War of Austrian Succession. The British government supported Prussia for a variety of reasons, not the least being that Prussia was important to maintaining the balance of power. The colonists dutifully fought the French in the New World (after all, the Austrians and Russians had no colonies there). As a result of the war—but not necessarily because of American victories—the French lost their holdings in the Western Hemisphere and the Mississippi River was made the western boundary of the English colonies.

Other conflicts carried the same hallmarks of a European-based war with an ancillary impact on the colonies: The war's rationale was never explained and often misunderstood by the colonists. The colonial historians and newspaper publishers assigned the war a different name than it was known by in British dailies. And the outcome of the conflict was an increase in British holdings and prestige. The colonists' dissatisfaction was mirrored in their tendency to christen the wars after the ruling monarch's name; thus, in the New World, the War of Spanish Succession was called Queen Anne's War and the War of the League of Augsburg, King William's War.

The Revolutionary War. The experiences of the Revolutionary War reinforced the American predilection for avoiding the machinations of European politics.[1] The Americans were impressed by the deviousness of European diplomacy, and they received an education in the sophisticated diplomatic practices carried on by their allies, Spain and France. They also learned quickly that the French and Spanish governments supported the American revolutionary effort for reasons of their own national interest, rather than for love of such concepts as "freedom" and "democracy." The French viewed the colonial conflict as a way to reduce the power of Britain, which had reached a position of near hegemony in the international system. The French were cautious; they refused to give overt and massive support to the American cause until Washington's armies had won a major victory in the field. France lent encouragement to the revolutionaries whenever the Americans took a policy tack that the French viewed as inimical to their interests. When the Americans appeared to be settling for less than complete severance from the crown, for example, the French successfully urged the colonial leaders to fight on.

Spanish policy, with its separate goals and objectives, quickly became a breeding ground for American suspicions of European diplomacy. Spain had her own score to settle with the British, particularly in regard to Gibraltar and the Floridas, which England had won in previous conflicts. Spain appeared to be more interested in reclaiming former territories than in establishing an independent United States. Since a strong United States would constitute as much of a threat to Spanish holdings in the Western hemisphere as the British presence, the Spanish government did not savor a large and strong United States emerging from the war. For this reason, the Spanish government attempted to dissuade the revolutionaries from claiming the Mississippi River as the western boundary of their new nation. The Spanish would have preferred an America with the Appalachian chain as its western border.

Spain profited from the Revolutionary War. Although Madrid did not repossess Gibraltar, Spanish rights to the Floridas, Louisiana, and Texas were recognized by the British. In the long run, this result benefited the United States because it meant that Spain—and not England—would be its major neighbor to the south and west. Spain was hardly a military power in the late 18th and early 19th centuries and presented less of a threat to the new nation than the British.

The Balance of Power. The American distrust of traditional diplomacy, fed by experiences during the colonial and revolutionary periods, early surfaced as a suspicion of the balance-of-power concept. The concept of a balance of power had developed as the Western state system matured. The essential core of the concept was that a coalition formed by nations interested in maintaining the status quo pitted themselves against nations with revisionist foreign policies. Hopefully, a coalition or alliance was strong enough to deter the aggressor and thus ensure the system's stability.

U.S. leaders rejected the balance of power as an instrument for maintaining stability in the international system; rather, they viewed it as an instigator of conflict and a concept considered foreign to the new diplomacy practiced by the American republic. "Separated as we are from Europe by a great Atlantic Ocean," wrote James Monroe in his 1824 annual message, "we have no concern in the wars of the European governments nor in the causes which reproduce them. The balance of power between them, into whatever scale it may turn in its various vibrations, cannot affect us." When a series of conflicts greatly enlarged the United States in the 1840s, European diplomats discussed the possibility of applying the balance of power to contain American expansion. James K. Polk observed that American growth had attracted "the attention of the powers of Europe, and lately the doctrine has been broached in some of them of a 'balance of power' on this continent to check our advancement." He refused to concede that the balance of power, an Old World technique, was applicable to New World conditions.

While the early American decision makers associated the balance of power with the cause of wars, their nation rapidly matured during the 19th century, one of the most peaceful in the history of the state system. The balance of power, which the American leaders distrusted, contributed to a hundred years of peace, lasting from the Congress of Vienna (1815) to the outbreak of World War I (1914). Only one conflict occurred that involved more than two major powers during this period, the Crimean War.

The Monroe Doctrine. The Monroe Doctrine conformed perfectly to the diplomatic pattern of unilateralism, illustrating the American desire during this period to "go its own way" in international politics without help from other nations.[2] The doctrine also underscored the observation that the policy goal of unilateralism was the security of the American nation in the light of the United States perception of attempts by the European states to reassert their hegemony over Latin America.

During the Napoleonic wars, when the French occupied Spain, the Spanish colonies had revolted and declared their independence. President James Monroe stated in his State of the Union message in 1823 that the United States would consider Spain's intent to reassert its control over its former colonies an unfriendly and hostile act. After the defeat of Napoleon, the Holy Alliance leaders (France, Russia, Austria, and Prussia) talked of restoring the old regime, the world system that was present prior to the French Revolution. President Monroe declared in 1823 that the Western Hemisphere was not open for further colonization by European powers. In return for European abstinence from interfering in Western Hemisphere affairs, the American President pledged not to interfere in European matters, a rather hollow gesture because the U.S. had shown no inclination to meddle in the European system nor possessed the capability for doing so.

The Monroe Doctrine is an example of an American desire to maintain the widest possible latitude in foreign policymaking. The Americans could have collaborated with England, since the British government had proposed earlier that both Washington and London jointly discourage the Holy Alliance from undertaking any attempt to restore the Spanish colonies to the Spanish monarchy. The American government refused because, as Secretary of State John Quincy Adams declared, the Americans did not wish "to come in as a cock-boat in the wake of the British man-of-war." The British foreign ministry, in spite of the American rebuff, informed the Holy Alliance nations that they should not undertake the restitution of the Spanish colonies. The Holy Alliance heeded the British message rather than Monroe's, whose navy was hardly capable of enforcing the President's doctrine.

Although the Monroe Doctrine fit the policy pattern of unilateralism, it was clearly outside the predictable behavior of a small power, which the United States was. The American President overreached U.S. capabilities by asserting American protection over a *region*, a characteristic behavior of a medium, but not of a small power. Since the United States lacked the necessary capability to translate the doctrine into policy in the field, it remained for the British navy to effect the American President's declaration. The Monroe Doctrine, therefore, was one of the most pretentious declarations in the history of the state system.

While clearly not in keeping with the policy patterns of a small power, the Monroe Doctrine did express a goal—hegemonic control over a region—that remained a part of American diplomacy. When the U.S. finally gained medium-power capability after the Civil War, the American government began to replace the British, Spanish, and French as the paramount nation in Latin America. While a small power, however, the United States leaders stood aside while their own doctrine was violated repeatedly. The British claimed the Falkland Islands and blockaded Latin American ports at will to collect on defaulted debts.[3] The French went even further and set up a puppet regime in Mexico in the 1860s under Maximilian.

The Monroe Doctrine, requiring a capability beyond the pre-Civil War strength of the United States, enunciated a utopian goal for a weak, but growing, nation.

The War of 1812. The American desire for the widest possible latitude in policymaking, in addition to the lack of sophistication of the United States leaders, led to a series of foreign policy mistakes culminating in the War of 1812.[4] On their way to their first major conflict after independence, the Americans, led by President Madison, eventually blundered into a war with Great Britain, the state system's most powerful actor. In brief, the scenario involved a tug-of-war between the effective British blockade of Napoleon's Europe and Napoleon's paper blockade of England: "paper," because the French lacked the navy to enforce it. The United States, a declared neutral intent on trading with both sides and highly dissatisfied with the restraints and harrassment that both blockades presented, was caught between them. President Madison, pushed by the war hawks of the hinterland states (not the seaboard areas that supposedly were the most damaged by the two blockades), announced that the United States would declare war on the state that did not lift its blockade against the other belligerent. The British refused, since their blockade was an important weapon against the French. Napoleon, on the other hand, graciously lifted his blockade, which was ineffective anyway. The Americans, caught in the web of their own making, declared war on Britain.

Soon after their decision to join the hostilities, the Americans suggested that peace negotiations begin. The eventual peace settlement in 1815, based on a return to the *status quo ante bellum,* was eagerly accepted by the U.S. The British were more concerned with European problems than they were with the upstart Americans.

Although the War of 1812 inaugurated the tradition that the United States never lost a war, it served as a reminder that the U.S. does not win them all, either. It also represented the first major threat to American independence, a threat that was turned aside by political difficulties in Europe—not by U.S. military strength.

Expansionism

For a small state, the American nation proved especially vigorous in extending its borders. In 1789, at its inception, the United States was already the second largest geographical state in the world, exceeded only by Russia. Within sixty years the United States more than doubled in size. Expansionism, in the form of the acquisition of territory, was indeed a behavioral pattern of the new United States.

First Phase: The Indians. The initial impression that continental expansionism sent Americans into vast, empty spaces is a misperception. The hinterland was occupied by Indian nations, many of whom, such as the Cherokees, controlled large areas of territory and had developed a high degree of civilization. The continental expansion was based on the assumption that the Indian had no international rights to the land that he occupied. Since the British government had not recognized any rights, and the Americans had defeated the British, the Indian nations existed only as nomadic tenants on land that now belonged to the United States.

The subjugation of the Forest Indian nations east of the Mississippi began almost immediately. The first presidents in their State of the Union messages emphasized the need for security along the frontier. By the time of the Civil War, the political and social structure of the Forest Indians had been destroyed.

The subjugation of the Indian nations of the plains began in earnest in the 1840s with the massive emigration of Americans into territories added during the decade and with the discovery of gold in California. (The Civil War briefly interrupted the process.) The Plains Indians proved more formidable fighters than the Forest Indians; able leaders, sophisticated alliances, and the capability to maneuver on the vast stretches of the western plains gave the Indians an advantage in battles with settlers and soldiers. The continued onslaught of Americans with their superior weaponry eventually wore down the diminishing Indian power.

Expansion and the Europeans. Since the Forest and Plains Indians possessed no legal status in the eyes of the American government, all land to the north, west, and south of the United States was titled to a European nation. Spain, at the moment of American independence, occupied territory to the west and south, and the British recognized Spanish claims in these regions as a result of the Revolutionary War. England, of course, still remained predominant in Canada.

Spain was a weak nation and growing weaker at the end of the 18th century and the beginning of the 19th century. The British in Canada were strong, but the Americans were fortunate to have a weak neighbor to the south and west, and a preoccupied neighbor to the north. The British, after the French Revolution and the rise of Napoleon, paid more attention to the European continent than they did to the Western Hemisphere.

When Napoleon gained control of Louisiana, the Americans were faced with a different security problem because a strong neighbor had replaced a weak one. Napoleon needed money for his continental enterprises and not an overseas territory to protect and to administer, especially since the British navy stood between him and his possession. When the opportunity arose in 1803 to purchase the Louisiana territory from France, President Jefferson accepted. Again the United States benefited from Europe's problems.

The U.S. purchase of Florida in 1819 represented Spain's bowing to the inevitable.[5] American settlers had infiltrated across the Florida border and the American military had made incursions into the Spanish-held territory on the pretext of protecting settlers from Indians. These were portents of U.S. pressure to come. The Spanish government chose to exit with the best possible deal rather than to hold on for reasons of honor.

American imperialism, inactive for two decades after the Florida purchase, began again in the 1840s, the golden decade of American expansion. By 1840, a weak Spain had been replaced by an even less formidable opponent, Mexico. In 1845, Texas, which had defeated Mexico in its own war for independence, was annexed by the United States. And in 1848 a Mexican–American military confrontation ended in victory for the United States with the acquisition of the California territory. Sandwiched between these Mexican–American conflicts was the settlement of a dispute with England over the Oregon territory. The final addition to American continental expansion was the purchase of the Gadsden territory in 1853 to obtain a more favorable route for railroad building.

At the beginning of the 1860s, therefore, the United States had grown to its farthest continental limits. Its position was favorable in almost every respect: to the north, relations with Canada were improving and to the south, Mexico posed no threat to the security of the United States. Mexico was so weak, in fact, that penetration by external powers was more of a threat, as the Maximilian affair illustrated.

It may appear strange that a nation at such a moment of strength would slide within one decade into one of the bloodiest civil conflicts in history. Perhaps expansionist activity postponed the Civil War; or perhaps the additional land and capabilities were too much for the American political system to digest readily, producing fissures that contributed to a major fratricidal conflict. Whatever the reasons for the Civil War, it ended the first period of American diplomatic history and elevated the United States to medium-power status.

Moralism

Realistic Federalists. The moralistic overtones in American foreign policy did not appear until after the two Washington administrations. The Federalists, under Alexander Hamilton's influence, were realistic about American capabilities and the problems that the new nation faced. Beginning with Thomas Jefferson, however, several moralistic themes began to appear in policy pronouncements by American decision makers.[6]

The North African "Pirates." The North African pirate episode best illustrates the moralistic behavioral pattern of the United States as a small power.[7] The "Barbary pirates," as they came to be called in American history, were Arab clans that controlled sections of the northern coast of Africa. While possessing no military power, they did constitute a nuisance to shipping in the Mediterranean. Most of the European nations, including Great Britain, paid tribute or "protection money" to the clans to ensure safe passage for their merchant vessels. Although paying tribute was onerous, it was far less expensive than providing naval escorts. The Federalists under Washington and Hamilton, being realistic about the problem and realizing that American trade in the region was minimal, also paid tribute.

President Jefferson felt differently and dispatched naval vessels to teach the North African Arabs to respect the American flag. After the American vessels and marines had left, the Arabs went back to their traditional vocation. But the young United States had stood for principle and protected its integrity and honor—a behavioral pattern that would repeat itself many times in the future.

Legalism

Legalism, the fourth pattern, refers to the American belief that international behavior, both their own and that of others, should be in accordance with legal norms. In some areas of state behavior, legal norms were not developed or lacked specific application to the problem at hand. On these occasions, the U.S. government interpreted the dictates of international law to conform to its own interests.

Legalism and Foreign Trade. The overriding concern for the United States in its weakened, small-power status was its own survival. Central to that survival was international trade, especially since independence from England also meant that the United States was severed from many of the mother-country and sister-colony markets that American businessmen had access to prior to 1776. New markets had to be found.

The Napoleonic wars created new markets on the continent of Europe and at the same time introduced dangers for the nation that tried to take advantage of them. The American position was simple: the U.S. flag was a neutral flag and therefore any goods sailing under it should be protected from confiscation by the British blockade, except for articles of warfare (i.e., contraband).

Friction early developed over two points, one minor, the other one major. The minor point of dispute was the British inclination to widen the contraband list. The American merchants, for obvious reasons, wanted the list kept brief. The major point of friction was the British practice of confiscating French goods carried in American ships (or bottoms, to use the nautical language) that had originated from French shippers and that were destined for French markets. The British believed that these goods were not technically neutral goods: they were not owned by Americans and the Americans were being used only as transhippers to avoid the blockade. For the United States government, "neutral ships make neutral goods except for contraband of war" became an often stated principle in American foreign policy during its small-power period. The British obviously disagreed.

Neutrality and Invasion. For the United States during its small-power status, neutrality not only had its rights but also its duties. Early presidents were officially concerned with the propensity of American citizens for meddling in other nations' internal affairs. Such actions violated principles of international law. The prospect of American citizens invading Canada to spread the gospel of revolution would not be viewed very kindly by London. Neutrality was an indispensable ingredient for the survival of the United States.

Consequently, the American government found occasions to halter the crusading spirit of its citizens bent on spreading democracy to the rest of the world. The danger of involving the United States in a conflict larger than American capabilities could handle was very real.

American Goals During the Small-Power Era

During this period, the American government pursued three broad goals: security, economic well-being, and prestige.

Security. During its period as a small power, the primary goal of American foreign policy was survival. For this reason, the U.S. expanded rapidly into territories as opportunities arose, afraid they might fall into the hands of more powerful European states.

As small states have tended to do in the post-World War II era, the United States used international law as a basis for building its claims in the world community. The American navy would have been no match for the British navy should the U.S. government have decided to enforce its claims to neutral rights. The American government instead appealed to international law to validate its claims.

Unilateralism helped to achieve a measure of security by providing the

United States government with the widest possible latitude in formulating its own policy without encroachment or dictation by other nations. Washington's advice in his Farewell Address to avoid "permanent alliances" (Jefferson later called them "entangling alliances") was one indication of the young nation's intention to remain clear of Europe's problems.[8] United States diplomats did not attend any multilateral conferences until the 1860s, or the end of the small-power era, when an American delegation showed up at an international meeting on postal exchange. American diplomatic exchanges during this period were bilateral, not multilateral.

One brief entangling alliance dots this early period: the Franco-American alliance signed in 1778 in a moment of fraternal feeling generated by French assistance during the Revolutionary War. Following France's own revolution in 1789, the American government found itself allied with a nation that had quarrels with every state in Europe. The treaty ended in 1800 by mutual agreement after it became obvious that the U.S. would not honor the treaty's provisions as faithfully as the French thought that the Americans should.

Economic Well-Being. Neutral rights were also important in pursuing the goal of economic well-being. Throughout this period the United States imported more than it exported, with the difference made up by investments from European, and principally British, sources. The need for new markets for American industrial and agricultural production introduced business considerations into American foreign policy. Concern for U.S. business ventures abroad became one of the primary foci of the young American government—a focus that has never diminished.

Prestige. The goal of national prestige was partially achieved through the grandiose declaration of the Monroe Doctrine, the North African "pirate" episode, and the periodic pronouncements of the uniqueness of the American nation. As a small power, the United States had little to point to with pride, except its own perceptions of its own experiences as being new and different from any other nation in the world.

THE UNITED STATES AS A MEDIUM POWER

The United States emerged from the Civil War a medium power, i.e., a nation with regional interests and regional capabilities. At Appomattox the American army was not only well trained and battle tested, but was the largest in the world. But the new-found American position was based on more than military power, which was allowed to contract after the war: the economic development that followed the Civil War laid the foundation for the United States to become a major industrial power. The date for the end of the medium-power status was the Spanish-American War in 1898.

Each of the four behavioral patterns identified with the United States as a small power continued, but with significant shifts in emphasis.

Expansionism

Seward's Expansionism. The Civil War ushered in an introspective period in American history. Except for the purchase of Alaska and Midway Island no active expansion was undertaken as the United States attempted to recover from the Civil War and to develop its continental resources.

The Spanish-American War. The Spanish-American War in 1898 was the beginning of a new wave of expansionism characterized by a new navy, a revised ideology, and increased domestic interest in obtaining new territory.[9] The new navy dated from the early 1880s, when the American government found itself enjoying treasury surpluses, which were spent to build modern vessels. The process was slow, but the new navy appeared at the beginning of the 1890s ready to be used as an instrument of policy.[10]

In the 1890s most Americans appeared to be infected by expansionist fever. With the newly developed power of a modern navy and a "just" cause for war with Spain over Cuba, the United States launched its first expansionist surge since the 1840s. The Spanish-American War became more than a war: it became a crusade.

In the treaty that ended the war, the United States gained Puerto Rico, Guam, and the Philippines. These additions, plus the annexation of Hawaii in 1900, gave the United States government insular interests in the Far East. In contrast, United States expansion as a small power was on a continental basis.

Unilateralism

U.S. and Latin America. In Latin America especially, the unilateralist pattern was apparent. As a medium power with regional interests, the United States possessed the capability to implement its policy pronouncements in Latin America. In 1879 Viscount Ferdinand de Lesseps, the builder of the Suez Canal, signed an agreement with Colombia to dig a canal across the isthmus of Central America. Secretary of State William Evarts informed the French that the American government considered the project an unfriendly act, and the French decided to drop the idea.

The British also occasionally ran aground on American unilateralism in Latin America. One such incident was a dispute concerning the boundary line between Venezuela and British Guiana, which the Venezuelan government wanted the United States to mediate. When the British government rejected the mediation agreement and negotiation failed, American public opinion became aroused and in 1895 Secretary of State Richard Olney accused the British of violating the Monroe Doctrine. He argued that the

British had given their assent to the doctrine and should now respect it in the boundary controversy. The dispute was finally submitted to arbitration.

Legalism

The emphasis on international legal norms shifted when the United States moved from small-power to medium-power status. As a small power, the American government was concerned with its own citizens committing aggressive acts against other nations in attempts to spread the spirit of 1776. The United States as a small power also appealed to international law to protect its trade with belligerents.

During the medium-power era, the United States leaders began to develop a more positive view of international law. Rather than emphasizing international law as a shield, the American government now sought to use international law as an instrument for solving thorny political issues. In particular, differences between the British and Americans that grew out of the Civil War were solved through arbitration.

British Neutrality in the Civil War. The British paradoxically were farsighted in their interpretation of neutral rights, but extremely nearsighted on neutral duties during the Civil War.[11] On neutral rights, the British wanted to create precedents which might be used later by London in its conflicts against the Americans. Consequently, the British respected "paper" blockades, or blockades that were decreed but unpatrolled by American vessels. On other occasions, England permitted the North to interdict shipping between British ports. On the basis of the "doctrine of continuous voyage," the North seized vessels carrying goods bound for the South before they reached Nassau, a British port. The ships were released but the cargo was condemned on the ground that the ultimate destination was the South, even though its immediate destination was a British port.

The British refused, then, to claim all their legal rights as neutrals. They were farsighted, thinking that the precedents could be used in future conflicts. Indeed, the Americans found them resurrected during World War I, between 1914 and 1917, before the United States entered the conflict.

The British and Neutral Duties. On the subject of neutral duties, the British were shortsighted. Since the South was outmanned and outgunned by the Northern navy, the Confederate states sought foreign shipbuilders to provide both long-range wooden ships suitable for destroying commerce on the high seas and iron-clad, heavily armed warships for naval engagements in Southern waters. England and France had the facilities to build both types of vessels for naval duty. While the French respected their neutral duties, the British were lax.[12] The *Alabama,* built and commissioned by the British, destroyed 57 prizes alone and contributed to driving unescorted Northern merchant vessels from the seas. At the end of the conflict, Washington presented to the British a listing of financial losses by American businessmen as a result of the commerce destroyers built for the South. In 1871 the British and Americans agreed to submit the dispute to arbitration, and the United States was awarded 15 million dollars in damages.

Moralism

The doctrine of Manifest Destiny, which in extended form contributed to American involvement in the Spanish-American War, was an example of the moralist self-image possessed by Americans. Reverend Josiah Strong, a Congregationalist clergyman, preached that the Anglo-Saxons were divinely commissioned to give leadership to the rest of the world. His book, *Our Country,* published in 1855, stated that the United States represented "the largest liberty, the purest Christianity, the highest civilization"; as well, it possessed "peculiarly aggressive traits calculated to impress its institutions upon mankind." He quoted, with approval, Charles Dickens, who said that an American would be reluctant to enter heaven until assured that he could move further west in his celestial home. Some Protestant denominations became interested in the "large policy," a term ascribed to the view that it was time to expand the American experience overseas. Not all churches felt this way: the Quakers, Catholics, and Unitarians, for example, opposed the war.

President McKinley, in an address to a Methodist delegation, declared that he had prayed fervently over the decision to go to war. The divine answer was in the affirmative, he said, and included a directive "to educate the Filipinos, and uplift and civilize and Christianize them." It was America's destiny to bring the benefits of a civilized world to a backward people and to make them into good Protestants as well.

U.S. Goals and Medium-Power Status

Security. American security and independence was never threatened during its medium-power period. The nation that the Americans viewed as a threat, Great Britain, began to appear less hostile. While arbitration agreements helped, Britain's growing suspicion of Germany's foreign policy was the primary generator of good will. The British government customarily refused to take on more than one major enemy at a time. With growing German power augmented by alliances with Austria and Russia, the British felt obligated to reduce areas of friction with the United States and other nations (e.g., France). At the same time, American leaders were beginning to share British suspicions of Germany.[13]

Economic Well-Being. Economic well-being was one goal toward which the United States made giant strides as a medium power. Foreign investors continued to help finance industrial development after the Civil War, but only for a short period of time. The depression of 1873, the United States' first major economic downturn, signaled two developments: the American economy was now industrialized, and thus subject to economic cycles, and European investors were now reluctant to further underwrite American growth. Since foreign investors had been hurt by the 1873 depression, they were hesitant to pour money into the American economy at their previous pace.

The United States began its medium-power era by importing more goods than it exported; toward the end of the period, the American economy turned around and exported more than it imported. While the American businessman exported more to his overseas customers, the U.S. economy in general remained an international debtor until World War I. Foreign loans made during the 19th century, especially by British investors, remained to be paid off; this process meant that more capital continued to flow out of the U.S. than was returned through the sale of exports.

Prestige. The American yearning for prestige led to the building of the new navy and to a conflict with a European nation, which on paper appeared militarily stronger than it really was. As a result of the Spanish-American War, the United States became an empire with holdings sprawled across the Pacific. Ironically, the U.S., born from a revolt against an empire, and dedicated to fighting the subjugation of nationalities, now was an imperial power itself, ruling over non-Americans without their consent.

THE UNITED STATES AS A GREAT POWER (1898–1945)

A great power has worldwide interests and worldwide capabilities. All regions are of interest to a great power, but not all regions are assigned the same priority. Some regions, those contiguous to the great power's heartland, are "spheres of interest" and are more sensitive to foreign intrusion. The United States government traditionally has reacted strongly to any threat that it perceived in the Caribbean area, its "sphere of influence."

Unilateralism

An "Associated" Power. In World War I, the United States fought with Great Britain, France, and Russia, but refused to be allied with them. Thus, the term often appearing in World War I history to describe this relationship was "allied and associated powers." The United States was an "associated," not an "allied" power.[14] Even in war, the American nation wanted to maintain its independent policy.

A vivid illustration of American unilateralism and independence from its "allies" in World War I is Woodrow Wilson's personal negotiations with Germany to end the war. As the German military and economic situation became more and more hopeless, the German government opened negotiations with Wilson on a truce agreement. Four exchanges of telegrams took place between the two governments. Wilson did not consult with Britain and France in making major demands, such as the abdication of the Kaiser, on the German government. Both London and Paris knew of the exchanges and their content, so efficient were their monitorings of German message traffic. It was only after Wilson was satisfied with the German sincerity and commitment to a bona fide settlement that he turned the correspondence over to his allies.

American Isolationism. The isolationist impulse in American foreign policy usually is identified with American diplomacy in the interwar period following the 1920 election, which brought the Republican Harding–Coolidge ticket to the White House. The election campaign was fought partially on foreign policy issues and signaled the end of American interest in the League of Nations and the beginning of isolationism.

American isolationism during the interwar period was an odd mixture of attitudes of quietude and disquietude toward world problems. In reality, the United States government was unconcerned about Europe while troubled with Japanese actions in the Far East. Washington also was ambivalent about its role in providing world leadership for peace. While refusing to join the League, thus weakening that organization's capability to act, the American government took the lead in the Washington disarmament conferences and in negotiating the "Paris Peace Pact" that outlawed war. The three acts of neutrality passed in the 1930s did more to stamp American foreign policy as isolationist than did the alternating hot-and-cold policies of the 1920s.

Monroe Doctrine Modified. The military capability that the United States possessed as a medium-range power ensured that the Monroe Doctrine could be implemented. As a great power, not only could U.S. decision makers more effectively protect the cardinal provisions of the Monroe Doctrine, but they could freely reinterpret it, a process that first swung in one direction with the 1904 Roosevelt Corollary to the Monroe Doctrine and back in the opposite direction with the Good Neighbor Policy of 1933.

Theodore Roosevelt's reinterpretation of the doctrine was stimulated by events in the Dominican Republic. Foreign holders of Dominican bonds were unhappy over the Republic's inability to pay as a result of internal chaos. In 1904 the Dominican government asked Washington to take over customs houses and collect money to pay the debts. Roosevelt complied.

Roosevelt's justification for his actions began with the assumption that the United States desired to see stable, orderly, and prosperous nations as neighbors. These nations were obligated to keep order within their own borders; but if disorder occurred, a "civilized" nation would be required to act as policeman. If domestic instability infected any nation in the Western Hemisphere, even though American interests were not involved, the United States government would shoulder the burden and intervene. If the American government failed to do so, other nations might be tempted to intervene, a prospect unacceptable to Roosevelt.

With the Roosevelt Corollary the United States government became the chief enforcer of law and order in the Western Hemisphere. American behavior after World War II as the "policeman of the world" was a logical extension of the policy pattern introduced by the Roosevelt Corollary.

Expansionism

Reluctance to Add Territory. Prior to World War I, the United States added the Panama Canal Zone in 1903 and the Virgin Islands in 1917. After the war ended in 1919, the American nation refused territorial acquisitions offered to it; rather, U.S. expansion took the form of economic penetration. German holdings in the Pacific, islands that were eventually given to the Japanese and were the sites of some of World War II's bloodiest battles, and Ottoman lands in the Middle East were offered to President Wilson as mandates, but he refused them.

While declining to enlarge its territorial borders, the United States was not as reluctant to extend its economic influence, as the Open Door Notes and interwar economic behavior illustrate. The Open Door Notes were written in 1899 and 1900 by Secretary of State John Hay on the subject of China. The United States asked the various nations with interests in China, then in the last years of a tottering Manchu dynasty, to extend to American citizens the same treatment accorded to their own nationals. The Open Door Notes expressed the desire of the United States to compete on equal footing with other nations for the trade of the world.[15]

A Far Eastern Power. While the United States added no significant territory during its great power period, American leaders did extend U.S. influence and presence into other parts of the world, especially into the Far East. The Spanish-American War gave to the United States possessions in East Asia, but additional growth and maturity had to occur before American leadership could be exerted in that region. In 1905, President Roosevelt extended American good offices to the belligerents in the Russo-Japanese War. His offer was accepted and the negotiations that ensued resulted in the Treaty of Portsmouth. Although the United States added no new territory, its growth of economic power and prestige was significant during this period.

A Creditor Nation. The United States emerged from World War I as a creditor nation for the first time in its economic history primarily because of trade relations during the three years of neutrality (1914–1917) that the United States enjoyed before entering the war as a belligerent. During this period the warring nations, especially Great Britain and France, purchased large amounts of food, natural resources, and other materials, first by paying gold and then by buying on credit.

Following the war, the United States became the prime source of international credit for European nations intent on rebuilding from the ravages of conflict. While receiving large sums of American money for investment purposes, the European nations also found the United States aggressively competing for markets that before 1914 were largely monopolized by the Germans, French, and British. The American government insisted that the "open door" approach worked out earlier in China should be universally applied. The American businessman, therefore, should be accorded the same status in trading as other nationals.

The United States government was insensitive to the economic needs of Europe during this period of time. The French and British argued unsuccessfully that the money that they borrowed prior to the American entry into the war should be considered a part of the price for fighting aggression. Hence the French and British contended that the American government should forgive some debts. The American government saw it differently: the money had been borrowed and it was up to the French and British to repay it.

While two attempts were made to find a solution to the war debt problem, nothing came of them as the depression of 1929 sent the international economic system reeling. The United States must bear a major part of the responsibility for the depression since American policy on the wartime debts and the decision by President Franklin Roosevelt to emphasize national—rather than international—solutions contributed to the continuing economic chaos. The American Congress passed the high, prohibitive Smoot–Hawley Tariff in 1930, and other nations retaliated. When the United States turned to economic nationalism, other nations followed.[16]

Moralism

The moralist approach to foreign policy, which has become identified with American diplomacy in the 20th century, was the most obvious behavioral pattern during this period. Theodore Roosevelt and Woodrow Wilson contributed to the moralistic tone. In addition to personages, events were important indices to the presence of moralism, especially during the interwar years.

The Peace of Righteousness. One of the most interesting moralistic concepts was Theodore Roosevelt's "Peace of Righteousness."[17] No counterpart to it exists prior to Roosevelt's time, nor does any later presidential pronouncement parallel it. Nevertheless, this theory was propounded on numerous occasions by a President of the United States who ushered in a period of American history when moralism was a dominant characteristic.

Roosevelt's concept of peace was built around a virile America whose heart was attuned to the ways of righteousness. He saw the United States playing a larger role on the international scene, and possessing sufficient military strength to bring about peace in the world.

Roosevelt divided the nations of the world into two categories: the civilized, enlightened countries and the uncivilized, barbaric states. He believed that wars to discipline uncivilized people were justified. In his 1901 annual message he stated that wars with "barbarous or semi-barbarous peoples" were a "most regrettable but necessary international police duty which must be performed for the sake of the welfare of mankind." The self-appointed policemen of the world to ensure a peace of righteousness were the civilized nations with military strength, led by the United States.

Virility was the necessary ingredient to lead the world, according to Roosevelt. Peace would result from an aggressive and fearless policy pursued by a just nation. A nation had to be courageous in facing up to its responsibilities in the world. If the solution required a war, then the nation must be willing to engage in conflict, provided its motives were "just." There are occasions, he wrote in 1905, when war is preferable to peace because a "just war is in the long run far better for a nation's soul than the most prosperous peace obtained by acquiescence in wrong or injustice."

Roosevelt's Peace of Righteousness is without precedence and progeny in American foreign policy. It represented in its day the most extreme application of the moralist pattern of diplomacy. The United States, to Theodore Roosevelt, should be right and virile.

The Pledge System. Another indication of the moralist behavioral pattern was the "pledge system" approach to world politics. The Open Door Notes, it may be recalled, simply asked for a pledge from other nations to respect the rights of Americans to trade in China. The naval disarmament treaties of 1922 were also part of the pledge system. No provisions for inspection of the Pacific islands to ensure that the Japanese were not fortifying them were written into the treaties.

The most famous offspring of the pledge system was the Kellogg–Briand Agreement of 1928.[18] Sometimes referred to as the Paris Peace Pact, this agreement contained a prohibition against using war as an instrument of policy. After the French and Americans signed it, numerous other states acceded to the agreement. Again, no provisions for enforcement were written into the treaty.

Legalism

The Rule of Law. During the great-power period, the emphasis on legalism shifted to the "rule-of-law" concept. In the small-power era, legalism focused on neutral rights and duties and during the medium-power period on arbitration. During the great-power era, American decision makers tended to frame their view of world law in broad, nebulous terms. The specificity that characterized the two previous eras dissipated into generalizations that sometimes bordered on the meaningless.

Two explanations exist for this development. First, the American government ignored one possible source of a more realistic and practical basis for international law, the League of Nations. The League, after a decade of checkered successes (1919–1929), began a decade of checkered failures (1929–1939). It should have generated legal norms for international society, but did not, in part because of its "empty chairs": two major powers, the U.S. and U.S.S.R., were not members at the beginning, although the Soviets later joined. After the 1929 depression set in, economic hardships made the international system more akin to a jungle than to a sophisticated trading community.

A second explanation for the rule-of-law approach lies in the crass law of the jungle that prevailed during the interwar period. Since there was little agreement on the basic assumptions for a legal society, the high-sounding phrases of the rule of law permitted the international system to maintain a symbolism of legality while anarchy actually prevailed.

The ultimate impotence of the nebulous rule of law was demonstrated by the Stimson Doctrine of Nonrecognition. The U.S. refused to recognize Japan's conquest of Manchuria after the Mukden incident in 1931. While the Japanese were cut off from American money markets for developing Manchuria, they continued to expand without showing much concern for the Doctrine of Nonrecognition.[19]

U.S. Goals as a Great Power

Security. Ironically, the American nation felt more secure as a small and medium power than as a great power with all the military might at its disposal. The United States had matured during the hundred years of European peace between 1815 and 1914, lulled into complacency by the absence of major European conflicts. Indeed, one of the most belligerent nations of the post-Napoleonic era was the United States, which fought two wars with foreign nations (Mexico and Spain) and one with itself.

The United States as a great power faced entirely different prospects. First came the cataclysmic World War I, followed by a turbulent twenty years of economic, political, and social instability, and finally, in 1939, another total conflict. If the collective American psyche entertained any idea that peace was the norm of international society, it was dispelled in the 20th century.

In the 19th century, threats to the United States as perceived by American decision makers were primarily specific and related to certain nations. Hence, the French and British were American enemies in the first part of the century and the Germans were in the last. In the great-power stage, however, the enemies tended to be ideas or concepts rather than nations. Even a form of government (autocracy) or an ideology (Communism) could be viewed as a threat to the peace. "The evidence before us clearly proves," Franklin Roosevelt stated in his 1936 State of the Union message, that "autocracy in world affairs endangers peace and that such threats do not spring from those nations devoted to the democratic ideal." While the American leaders still perceived nations as a threat, they also began to perceive forces or concepts as constituting a danger to their security.

During the interwar period the fear of Communism resulted in a public hysteria known as the "Red Scare." In 1919 agitation by Communists and socialists in the United States, who occasionally employed terror tactics, reached a peak. These conditions led the Attorney General to raid Communist and alleged Communist groups, deport Russian citizens, and arrest thousands of "sympathizers." The domestic feelings, plus the affront to the Soviet

Union administered by deporting Soviet diplomatic agents, affected U.S.–U.S.S.R. relations during this period.[20]

As the United States gained great-power status, American leaders began to perceive concepts, ideologies, and environmental conditions as threats more frequently than when the United States was a small or medium power. One explanation for this development is that the American leaders tended to classify ideas as hazards as the United States began to project its own values more frequently into the world. As a result, American values, heretofore circumscribed because the U.S. was only a neighborhood or regional power, began to come in contact with values considered foreign and antithetical. American leaders then viewed these foreign values as dangerous to United States traditions, and therefore a "threat."

Economic Well-Being. Just as security proved to be an elusive goal, economic well-being was first achieved and then lost in the 1898–1945 period of great-power status. Although the United States emerged from World War I a creditor nation, the American government was unprepared to be a world economic manager. American experience in managing international economic problems during the interwar period was a major contributing factor to the Great Depression of 1929. Of all the errors in judgment that American leaders were guilty of after 1919, the most harmful were those mistakes connected with economic policy: they emphasized the United States' lack of comprehension and paucity of experience to be, in reality, a "great power."

Prestige. The first part of this period witnessed the high-water mark in prestige for the United States. The American nation emerged from the Spanish-American War as an insular nation with colonies in Latin America and the Pacific. Theodore Roosevelt's activities contributed to an increase in American prestige: he sent the Great White Fleet (as the U.S. navy was called) around the world to show the flag, and he offered his good offices to end the 1904–1905 Russo-Japanese War. Woodrow Wilson's triumphant arrival in Europe in 1919 stimulated near adulation for him and for his nation. These incidents illustrate the prestige generated by American diplomatic behavior during this period.

After Wilson's visit to Paris in 1919, the race for prestige produced a series of losses. U.S. refusal to join the League, intransigence over the interallied debts, and a nationalistic approach toward solving the depression's problems were benchmarks in the downward drift of prestige. American participation in World War II provided the opportunity to recoup losses and rebuild the esteem bestowed upon the United States prior to the Versailles Peace Treaty.

In the final analysis, security, economic well being, and prestige could all have been achievable goals if the United States had behaved as a great power should have during the interwar period. A great power traditionally commits its power to maintain stability in the system. Instead of assuming the responsibilities of a great power, the United States played the role of a great-power-withdrawn, leaving a vacuum in the world's security and economic system.[21] Unfortunately, because the United States either misunderstood the role of the great power or because it chose to ignore that role, the span between two major conflicts was the shortest and most turbulent on record.[22]

THE UNITED STATES AS A SUPERPOWER

A "superpower" is a great power with sufficient military capability to destroy the international system. It is a term that was coined to describe the position that the United States and the Soviet Union held after World War II. Since United States behavior as a superpower is the focus of this volume, this section will only sketch the general characteristics of the post-war era and relate them to the traditional patterns examined thus far.

Traditional Patterns Continued

American diplomacy after World War II continued many of the behavioral patterns developed over the previous century and a half. Expansionism, lying relatively dormant during the great power era, was rekindled with the acquisition of Japanese holdings in the Pacific and occupation of Italy, Japan, and Germany. The American presence was everywhere, except in Eastern Europe where the Soviet Union carved out its own sphere of influence. The economic thrust of U.S. businessmen reached into almost every marketplace except the planned economies of the Communist states.

The threat that American leaders and the masses previously had perceived in classical Marxism, mutated by Lenin and Stalin, increased in intensity after 1945. The apparent subjugation of Eastern Europe to Soviet hegemony, the victory of Mao Tse-tung's forces in China, the emergence of Third World leaders who applied too much (in Washington's eyes) of Marx's teachings to their own problems gave rise to new fears of Communism in official and public thinking.

New Revolutions

As the United States was crossing the threshold from a great power to a superpower and was experiencing internal transformations in its capabilities, the international system itself was changing. These changes contained their own trauma and can be classified as "revolutions" without too much presumption. In turn, these revolutions worked their influence on America's traditional patterns of behavior.

Nuclear Weapons. The invention of awesome nuclear weapons revolutionized thinking about military strategy and doctrine. Although only two nuclear devices have been employed in active combat—against Japan in the closing days of World War II—their impact furnished political and military leaders with a prophetic image of the nature of World War III. Chapter 13 will develop in detail the import of this revolution.

Third World Nationalism. With the post-World War II disintegration of colonial empires, the number of independent states in the world system increased to approximately 145, creating another revolutionary impact on the international system. Arab nationalism was stimulated by events in World War I, and Afro-Asian nationalism began to flourish after World War II. Most of these states were economically underdeveloped. The patterns of U.S. policy that emerged in response to the challenge of inducing industrial and agricultural growth in the Third World are discussed in chapter 18.

World Trade Realignments. United States leaders remembered the economic lessons learned from World War I and did not repeat their mistakes during World War II. Instead of selling war materiel to its allies, the American government "lent" or "leased" it, sometimes on terms of reciprocity.[23] Consequently, no interallied debts plagued the post-World War II era as they did after 1919.

The United States' enviable trade position after World War II was largely built on the lack of competition and on markets claimed before the war by the Germans, French, British, and Japanese. The decline of the American position, the reasons for it and Washington's attempts to reverse the process, are discussed in chapter 19.

Statecraft. In addition to substantive changes induced by nuclear weapons, world trade realignments, and Third World nationalism, procedural changes in how the nations of the world carry out their diplomacy also have occurred since 1945. The two traditional instruments for carrying out foreign policy decisions were the diplomatic corps and the military. Intelligence, while a long-time component of statecraft, did not reach a high level of sophistication until after World War II. Science, propaganda, cultural exchanges, and economic assistance now supplement the traditional instruments of statecraft.

REVOLUTIONS AND PATTERNS

The revolutionary changes in the contemporary international system have forced American leaders to reconsider their traditional ways of diplomatic behavior and to seek new approaches to current problems. Thus, the four revolutions described above have engendered a transformation in some areas of American foreign policy. The United States joined the United Nations, formed its first alliance since the Franco-American coalition of 1778, and committed troops to foreign soils for extended periods of time—all these signify a change in U.S. foreign policy.

The magnitude of these revolutions in American foreign policy is the subject of this book. Some of the changes have been more subtle, such as the transition from one ideological image to another (to be discussed in the next chapter). Whether subtle or bold, our task is to analyze them and to determine what responses should be undertaken by American leaders in the immediate decades to come.

As the United States entered the post-World War II era, the four revolutions produced strains on the traditional way that American policy is made, on the domestic influences that have participated in the policy formulation process, and on the policy outcomes themselves. Changes came rapidly after 1945, almost too rapidly to be effectively absorbed into the American decision-making process.

Since the remainder of this book examines in detail the factors that go into the patterns and development of the United States as a superpower, final observations on both patterns and goals are reserved for chapter 20. Do the patterns of expansionism, unilateralism, legalism, and moralism continue? Some patterns disappear or drastically change; others undergo transformation and redirection; and a few remain untouched by the trauma of world politics since 1945.

NOTES

1. Samuel F. Bemis, *The Diplomacy of the American Revolution* (Bloomington: Indiana University Press, 1957); William C. Stinchcombe, *The American Revolution and the French Alliance* (Syracuse, N.Y.: Syracuse University Press, 1969).
2. Donald M. Dozer, *The Monroe Doctrine: Its Modern Significance* (New York: Alfred Knopf, 1965); David Green, *Containment of Latin America: A History of the Myths and Realities of the Good Neighbor Policy* (Chicago: Quadrangle Books, 1971); W. Raymond Duncan and James N. Goodsell (eds.), *Quest for Change in Latin America: Sources for a Twentieth-Century Analysis* (New York: Oxford University Press, 1970); Jose Yglesias, *Truth About Them* (New York: World Publishing, 1971).
3. James F. Rippy, *Rivalry of the U.S. and Great Britain over Latin America, 1808–1830* (New York: Octagon Press, 1964).
4. Bradford Perkins, *Prologue to War: England and the U.S., 1805–1812* (Berkeley: University of California Press, 1968); Alfred LeRoy Burt, *The U.S., Great Britain, and British North America from the Revolution to the Establishment of Peace after the War of 1812* (New York: Russell and Russell, 1961).

5. Charles C. Griffin, *The U.S. and the Disruption of the Spanish Empire, 1810–1822* (New York: Octagon Books, 1968).
6. Adrienne Koch, *Power, Morals, and the Founding Fathers: Essays on the Interpretation of the American Enlightenment* (Ithaca, N.Y.: Great Seal Books, 1961); Paul A. Varg, *Foreign Policies of the Founding Fathers* (Lansing, Michigan: Michigan State University Press, 1963). Cecil B. Currey, *Code Number 72: Ben Franklin, Patriot or Spy?* (Englewood Cliffs, N.J.: Prentice-Hall, 1972). For excerpts of the views of American leaders on foreign policy, see Arnold Wolfers and Laurence W. Martin (eds.), *The Anglo-American Tradition in Foreign Affairs* (New Haven: Yale University Press, 1956).
7. R. W. Irwin, *The Diplomatic Relations of the United States with the Barbary Powers, 1776–1816* (Chapel Hill: University of North Carolina Press, 1931); L. B. Wright and J. H. McLeod, *The First Americans in North Africa: William Eaton's Struggle for a Vigorous Policy against the Barbary Pirates, 1799–1805* (Princeton, N.J.: Princeton University Press, 1945).
8. Felix Gilbert, *To the Farewell Address* (Princeton, N.J.: Princeton University Press, 1961).
9. Julius W. Pratt, *Expansionists of 1898: The Acquisition of Hawaii and the Spanish Islands* (Chicago: Quadrangle Books, 1964); Foster Rhea Dulles, *America's Rise to World Power, 1898–1954* (New York: Harper & Row, 1955); Theodore P. Greene, *American Imperialism in 1898* (Boston: D. C. Heath, 1955).
10. Allan F. Westcott, *American Sea Power since 1775* (Chicago: J. B. Lippincott, 1947).
11. Ephraim D. Adams, *Great Britain and the American Civil War* (New York: Russell and Russell, 1958).
12. Lynn M. Case and Warren F. Spencer, *The U.S. and France: Civil War Diplomacy* (Philadelphia: University of Pennsylvania Press, 1970).
13. Otto Stolberg-Wernigerock, *Germany and the U.S. during the Era of Bismarck* (Reading, Pa.: Henry Janssen Foundation, 1937); Lionel M. Gelber, *The Rise of Anglo-American Friendship: A Study of World Politics, 1898–1906* (Hamden, Conn.: Anchor Books, Doubleday & Co., 1966).
14. Clinton H. Grattan, *Why We Fought* (Indianapolis: Bobbs-Merrill, 1969); Warren I. Cohen, *The American Revisionist: the Lessons of Intervention in World War I* (Chicago: University of Chicago Press, 1967).
15. Paul H. Clyde, *U.S. Policy Toward China: Diplomatic and Public Documents, 1839–1939* (New York: Russell and Russell, 1964); Alfred W. Griswold, *The Far Eastern Policy of the United States* (New York: Harcourt, Brace, and World, 1938).
16. Herbert Feis, *The Diplomacy of the Dollar* (New York: W. W. Norton, 1966).

chapter 2   Traditional Patterns of American Foreign Policy   43

17. Howard K. Beale, *Theodore Roosevelt and the Rise of America to World Power* (Baltimore: Johns Hopkins Press, 1961); Theodore Roosevelt, *Fear God and Take Your Own Part* (New York: George H. Doran, 1916); Thomas A. Bailey, *Theodore Roosevelt and the Japanese-American Crises* (Gloucester, Mass.: Peter Smith, 1964); Raymond A. Esthus, *Theodore Roosevelt and Japan* (Seattle: University of Washington Press, 1967).

18. Lavis E. Ellis, *Frank B. Kellogg and American Foreign Relations, 1925–1929* (New Brunswick, N.J.: Rutgers University Press, 1961).

19. Robert H. Ferrell, *American Diplomacy in the Great Depression: Hoover–Stimson Foreign Policy, 1929–1933* (New Haven, Conn.: Yale University Press, 1957).

20. George F. Kennan, *Soviet–American Relations, 1917–1920* (Princeton, N.J.: Princeton University Press, 1960); Peter G. Filene, *Americans and the Soviet Experiment, 1917–1933* (Cambridge, Mass.: Harvard University Press, 1967); Robert P. Browder, *The Origins of Soviet-American Diplomacy* (Princeton, N.J.: Princeton University Press, 1953).

21. For an examination of the isolationist policies of the United States, consult: Manfred Jonas, *Isolationism in America, 1935–1941* (Ithaca, N.Y.: Cornell University Press, 1966); Selig Adler, *The Uncertain Giant: 1921–1941: American Foreign Policy Between the Wars* (New York: Macmillan, 1965); William L. Langer and S. Everett Gleason, *The Challenge of Isolation: The World Crisis of 1937–1940 and American Foreign Policy* (New York: Harper & Row, 1964).

22. American policy immediately prior to World War II is examined in Charles A. Beard, *President Roosevelt and the Coming of the War, 1941: A Study in Appearances and Realities* (New Haven, Conn.: Yale University Press, 1962); William L. Lanzer, *The Undeclared War, 1940–1941* (New York: Harper & Row, 1953); Forrest Davis, *How War Came, An American White Paper: From the Fall of France to Pearl Harbor* (New York: Simon and Schuster, 1942); Herbert Feis, *The Road to Pearl Harbor* (Princeton, N.J.: Princeton University Press, 1950); Stephen E. Ambrose, *Rise to Globalism: 1938–1970* (New York: Penguin Books, 1971); Harry L. Feingold, *The Politics of Rescue: The Roosevelt Administration and the Holocaust, 1938–1945* (New Brunswick, N.J.: Rutgers University Press, 1970); Bruce M. Russett, *No Clear and Present Danger* (New York: Harper & Row, 1972).

23. Under the Lend-Lease program, the American government gave 50 destroyers to the British navy in return for control over British naval bases in the North Atlantic and Caribbean. President Roosevelt feared at the time that these British territories might fall into German hands. The American government also assumed control of French possessions after France fell to the German armies and the Vichy regime was established.

3

Patterns of American Foreign Policy Images and Goals

Along with the unfolding behavioral patterns in U.S. diplomatic history, American decision makers have developed patterns of official viewpoints or images. These images, defined in chapter 1, are the policymaker's cognitive map of the international system in which he operates. An image is based on salient assumptions that a national leader makes about his political and economic environment. Thus, the image is a mental framework for interpreting events in world affairs.

An image can change over a period of time, as it has in American foreign policy. In U.S. diplomatic history, the Realist image that characterized the Washington–Hamilton administration gave way to the Liberal worldview that lasted almost a century and a half until 1945 when Realism again came into vogue. To what extent American policymaking has—or should have—departed from Realism in the face of the contemporary transformation of the international system is a topic covered in chapter 20.

The image serves as a blueprint or model for American foreign policy. Among its functions is the ordering of national priorities: Which goals are more important? To what regions of the world is the national government more sensitive? Which nations are considered the greatest threat? A blueprint should function further to designate the preferred method for solving specific problems or situations in which the United States finds itself: Should a regional organization (such as the Organization of American States) or the United Nations be used? Is military force needed to solve the problem?

Goals are conditioned by the imageholder's assumptions about the international system. If it is presumed, for example, that the international environment is hostile, then it must be concluded that American leaders should give priority to developing national military strength. The opposite assumption—that the world community consists of friendly, non-threatening states—may result in a government that emphasizes the goals of disarmament and the development of the United Nations into a stronger, more viable institution. Assumptions, then, are crucial to an understanding of policymaking because they have an impact on goals and orientation.

In this chapter the four major images that have appeared in two hundred years of American diplomacy as ideal types are discussed. Classifying American leaders or even the American public in one or the other of these broad ideal types should be approached with a healthy amount of caution. After examining the content of these images, it will be determined whether or not specific decision makers can be categorized as an adherent to one of them.

THE LIBERAL IMAGE

Liberalism has been the most influential image for most of the life of American diplomacy. Although the Founding Fathers, especially Alexander Hamilton, were Realists, most American leaders of the 19th and 20th centuries were imbued with the Liberal tradition that characterized Western political thought after the Napoleonic Wars ended in 1815. Liberalism was expounded in the writings of Thomas Paine, Thomas Jefferson, and later, by Woodrow Wilson, on one side of the Atlantic, and by Adam Smith, Richard Cobden, and John Stuart Mill on the other. Liberalism has been given other names, such as idealism, moralism, and utopianism, all of which reflect aspects of the Liberal image when applied to American foreign policy.[1]

The Liberal and Economics. Individuals influenced by the Liberal view begin with the assumption that man is a rational animal, that he can perceive his own best interests, and that his behavior for the most part will be motivated by his rational perceptions. On the basis of this rather naive assumption, the Liberals argue that man's political activities are seldom irrational or insane and that conflicts between individuals can be resolved peacefully by reason, discussion, and negotiation. Conflicts occur when one person's interests are at odds with another's; however, man can be taught to subjugate his personal, selfish interests to the common interest of a group or community, thus eliminating conflict. The most effective approach to building common interests is economic intercourse. Individuals profit from exchanging surplus goods for supplies that they lack. Conflict is avoided because each person profits from mutual exchanges and because conflict will destroy the economic ties that bind together the community of interests. Law is also important because it guides citizens in a common pursuit of peace.

The application of Liberalism to international relations results in an emphasis on trade and on building worldwide institutions to control conflict. States do have national interests, but international trade will draw nations together into a world community of common interests. Conflict is diminished as nations realize that their self-interest is served by peace, rather than by wars that disrupt economic bonds.

Other Conditions Necessary to Build a World Community. While the Liberals tend to emphasize the economic prerequisites for world community, other conditions are often mentioned as important, although not as crucial. A sound communal development must have an efficient communication network. Misunderstandings can result when nations fail to talk over or negotiate their difficulties. Moreover, nations should be willing to take the high road in dealing with each other. Petty, selfish, ethnocentric, and national interests should be repressed and statesmen should place more emphasis on humanitarian or worldwide objectives that transcend national borders. National leaders should look to the future and not succumb to the shortsighted and more primitive motivations of power politics.

The Liberals and War. Wars occur when national leaders ignore the common interests of international society and fail to listen to the voice of the people. The common man wants peace, whatever the desires of his rulers. Democracy is the best form of government because it permits the voice of the people to be heard, while autocratic governments are prone to start armed conflicts because the wishes of the people are silenced. Democracy and the republican form of government encourage a reign of peace in the international system. The Liberals assume that the public is inherently peaceful; war results, then, from special interests, such as munitions manufacturers who pursue their own selfish goals, and from the secret agreements made by professional diplomats. The ultimate objective of diplomacy is to implement the national values held by the body politic, not only by the elites.

The Liberals frown on the use of the balance of power to bring about peace. The balance of power causes wars; it does not prohibit them. It applies power to the international system when law and reason should be used. The common bonds of economic intercourse are disrupted when force is employed to obtain goals that satisfy the interests of a few states, and not the interests of the community of nations.

Liberalism and American Nationalism. The Liberal tradition, when coupled with American nationalism, produces a vision of a better world with the United States as the prime executor of that world. The American destiny is to bring peace to the world; no other nation possesses the physical and spiritual resources to accomplish this as well as the United States. In the end, it becomes difficult to distinguish between the traditions of Liberalism and the utopian–idealist–moralist principles that American spokesmen advocated in the 19th and early 20th centuries.

The philosophy of Woodrow Wilson illustrates the wedding of Liberalism to the self-image of the United States as a unique nation in the world. In his 1914 State of the Union message, Wilson said that his nation's greatness lay in the fact that the Americans were "champions of peace and concord." The United States should be jealous of "this distinction," he declared, for they faced "an opportunity such as has seldom been vouchsafed any nation, the opportunity to counsel and obtain peace in the world and a healing settlement."

He further expressed his faith in the basic Liberal creed that trade would build a world community. In his 1915 annual message, he called merchant vessels "not ships of war, but ships of peace, carrying goods and carrying much more: creating friendships and rendering indispensable services to all interests on this side of the water." Wilson's views on trade and the balance of power were echoes of other American presidents. In 1842, John Tyler called trade "that great civilizer."

American leaders were nurtured on the concepts of Liberalism, combined with a perception of the United States as the unique nation in the world. Both Liberalism and this self-image seemingly provided satisfactory answers to the foreign policy problems as the United States matured during the century of peace (1815–1914). World War I, however, ended the placid era and ushered in a half-century of war. The assumptions of Liberalism—that man is rational, that trade builds a world community, that law solves disputes—were discounted by events in the 20th century.

Liberalism and Foreign Policy Goals. On the basis of its assumptions, the Liberal critique propounded goals for American foreign policy. First, the U.S. government should do everything within its diplomatic power to expand foreign trade, not for reasons of profitmaking, but to forge a world of common interests. Trade could bind the world's nations together and find a common ground for national interests. As a result, all areas of the world should be open to trade, as the Open Door Notes requested in China.

A second goal was to build an effective international organization to protect the security of individual nations. Since the "community of power" had replaced the evil balance of power, a world organization was needed to house the new relationship among states. The League of Nations, as Wilson envisioned it, would be composed of republics who eschewed the ways of war and were devoted to the paths of peace. The American Liberal emphasized an international organization, since a world institution, such as the League, would generate legal norms either by fiat or as a result of customs and traditions associated with its behavior. Law also was necessary to solve disputes that might disrupt the economic cords that bound states together. Since political man is rational, so the Liberals argued, an institution for peaceful settlement of disputes had a logical place in the world community.

Disarmament was a fourth goal emanating from the Liberal's assumptions about the state system. This goal was especially propounded during the interwar period (1919–1931) and eventually was implemented in the 1922 Washington naval conferences. Prior to World War I, however, the American reaction to disarmament proposals was ambivalent. While applauding attempts to set in motion disarmament proposals, American presidents contended at the same time that such proposals did not apply to the United States. After World War I, interwar presidents who eschewed Wilson's desire to join the League pushed his disarmament policy.

A final goal expounded by the American Liberals was that the United States should set a pattern of rectitude for the rest of the world to follow. The prestige of the American nation should flow from its moral leadership and proper example and not from its wealth and military power. If following the moral path in world politics meant walking alone, then the United

States should be prepared to unilaterally act to enforce peace when other nations choose to follow their own national interests. The American nation must choose to place moral precepts above the selfish interests of the nation.

The Transformation of Liberalism. In addition to developments within the international system which led to disillusionment over the type of world that the Liberals were building, the Liberal worldview was challenged by Realism. Realism did not deal Liberalism a crippling blow; that would be ascribing too much credit to the Realists and would underestimate the impact of the 20th-century political environment on Liberalism. Rather, the Liberal image was no longer applicable after World War I. It well served the American decision maker in the 19th century by giving him a model of the international system which, for the most part, corresponded to reality. Beginning with World War I, however, reality changed, and the Liberal blueprint did not adjust to the new alignment of international political forces. Liberalism offered adequate policy prescriptions to a United States that was a small or medium power protected by two oceans and with few quarrels with the rest of the world. In the 20th century, however, the United States emerged as a major power, a creditor nation, and in contact with parts of the world that had been safely ignored during the 1800s.

The Liberal image, therefore, suffered from its own unfulfilled prophecies of a better world. The golden age of Liberalism in the 19th century did not survive the pessimism of the 20th century, brought on by two major wars, a depression, a Cold War, and two limited armed conflicts in Korea and Vietnam. Liberalism has not disappeared, but it has been displaced by another worldview with a different set of assumptions and prescriptions—Realism.

THE REALIST IMAGE

The Realist worldview appeared in strength after World War II at a time when Liberalism had reached its nadir of influence in American foreign policy. Realism supplied a conceptual framework for policymakers that promised better solutions to post-World War II problems than the liberal program which was discredited by the turn of world events. The publication of Hans Morgenthau's *Politics Among Nations* in 1949 marked the beginning of the training of a generation of political scientists in the Realist model.[2] Realism moved into the vacuum left by Liberalism.

The burden of Realism during the immediate post-World War II period was to educate American leaders to apply United States power to international political problems. The danger, as the Realists saw it, was that the United States would lapse again into an isolationism similar to that of the 1930s or continue the Liberal foreign policy ideals personified by Woodrow Wilson. To the Realists, the United States should now behave as an international leader and use its considerable strength to defend its national interest and to shape the world into a stable framework.

The Realist's Theory of Human Nature. The Realists begin with a set of assumptions about the nature of man quite different from those of the Liberals. Man is basically selfish, motivated by a desire to gain power. Some possess the "will to power" more than others; these highly motivated individuals must be halted or they will eventually attempt to establish their hegemony over all people.

In *Scientific Man versus Power Politics,* published in 1946, Hans Morganthau argued that man is motivated by a desire to dominate others.[3] Reinhold Niebuhr, on the other hand, began with a different premise but reached the same conclusion: he attributed man's will-to-power to the existence of original sin.[4] Man is possessed of a moral flaw and cannot do otherwise than engage in conflict and conquest. Although not all Realists probe the nature of man, Morgenthau and Niebuhr do, and they illustrate the relationship between basic assumptions and policy prescriptions.

Power and the Revisionist State. Moving from the human to the international level, the Realists point out that the contemporary international system is populated by independent nations; hence, the singular guiding principle of world politics is national interest. Foreign policy goals should be formulated in terms of national interest and supported with the necessary power to achieve them. The primary responsibility of foreign policy is to manage power. A decision maker should not postulate foreign policy goals that require increments of power beyond his national resources. His goals, therefore, must be realistic and not tied to utopian, moral, or idealistic principles.

A few of the states in the international system are "revisionist," that is, they are intent on unilaterally revising or changing their economic, geographical, or political position. Revisionist states are dissatisfied with their status in the world and seek to improve their standing by aggression. The foreign policy objectives of revisionist states, therefore, must be countered with sufficient force by nations satisfied with the status quo.

In the late 1940s, the Realists viewed the Soviet Union as the major revisionist state to be opposed by the United States. Major Realist writers arrived at this conclusion through separate routes. Niebuhr and Walter Lippmann (a journalist whose column "Today and Tomorrow" was widely distributed in newspapers)[5] argued at length against the authoritarianism of the Soviet regime, while George Kennan warned that the geopolitical position of an expanded U.S.S.R. would pose an unacceptable threat to American security.[6] All deplored the propensity to paint the Soviet Union in moralistic hues of malevolence and to ascribe to the United States only the purest of motives. Power is amoral and should be employed against any state that attempts to change its position without the consent of others. If the Soviet Union were opposed by American power, it would eventually evolve into a less aggressive and less revisionist state. Russian foreign policy would "mellow" and its more militant behavior would be mitigated.

International Law and Change. The Realists do not hold the status quo sacrosanct. Changes in the international system are necessary, but they should be accomplished through diplomatic agreement among all the parties involved. Compromises through diplomatic negotiations can facilitate change and keep it within the bounds of stability. To rely on legal procedures to bring about change is to make the status quo rigid and unyielding to rapid developments within the international system. International law, therefore, does not create periods of stability; in fact, world law develops because stability is present in international relations. American decision makers, the Realists argue, have been too legalistic in their approach to world problems, emphasizing legality rather than traditional diplomacy as an instrument to bring about peace and stability.

Realism and the Third World. The major Realist writers are Europe-oriented, and unlike the Liberals, they tend to neglect the Third World. The European nations are industrialized and possess respectable military establishments; thus, military alliances with them will deter Soviet aggression. On the other hand, alliances with small Middle Eastern, Latin American, African, and Asian nations saddle the United States with too many commitments from which it derives too few benefits. The military strength of Iran, for example, is too meager to add much to a coalition, while a pledge to protect Iran spreads American military power. The Realists also oppose American involvement in land wars in Asia, such as the Korean and Vietnamese conflicts. Asian land wars only bleed American military strength.

Realism and Foreign Policy Goals. For its primary goal, the U.S. must learn to use the balance of power to halt the expansionist tendencies of an imperialist state. Aggression, the Realist would argue, cannot be stopped by invisible cords of trade that bind states, by international organization and law, or by moral example. The Realists would place the emphasis in American foreign policy on *national* survival and *national* security, rather than on world community interests. In order to survive, the United States must be willing to employ its power to balance the strength of a revisionist state. Conflict sometimes cannot be avoided, especially on the grounds that it might disrupt a mythical "community of nations."

Since the Realists begin with the assumption that the international community is divided into two types of states—status quo and revisionist —the first goal of American foreign policy is to identify the revisionist nation and build an alliance against it. They see at work in the international system forces that motivate a state to expand until it is either satiated by its gains or stopped by force. In 1946–1947, the Realists perceived in Soviet behavior the characteristics of a revisionist state, and argued that Russian expansion must be met by American power. The balance-of-power principle dictated that the weakened Western European states should be protected by forming an alliance to "contain" the Soviet Union and dissuade it from a revisionist foreign policy. Imperialism, however, was not considered a permanent, congenital characteristic of Soviet foreign policy. Eventually, the Russian state would learn to live in a stable world order.

In summary, the all-encompassing goal of the Realists is survival, ensured by the effective use of the balance of power. Security is threatened by the aggressor state, identified in the post-World War II period as the Soviet Union. These assumptions, as well as those of the Liberals, have come under heavy attack by the Left Wing and Right Wing of the political spectrum.

RIGHT-WING REVISIONISM

Realism has been the most common image held by decision makers and analysts of American foreign policy since the end of World War II; however, advocates of the Liberal school remain. In the post-World War II period, two worldviews or images have developed which question the Realist and Liberal perceptions of international events since 1945. These worldviews are called "revisionist" because they offer a revised interpretation of historical events since World War II. The term should not be confused with the Realist's designation for an aggressive nation: a *revisionist state* and a *revisionist critique* are conceptually very different.

Right-Wing Revisionism is not new to the American political scene; its themes of anti-Communism and isolationism are found in the period between the two world wars.[7] After 1945, isolationist sentiment surfaced briefly, only to be overwhelmed by a strong Realist argument which convinced United States leaders that an American world presence was indispensable to a stable international system. Although Right-Wing Revisionism failed to attract a following in the early post-war period, crucial events in 1948–1949 offered new opportunities for different viewpoints on American foreign policy. Between February 1948, when the Communist *coup* occurred in Czechoslovakia, and October 1949, when Mao Tse-tung's forces were victorious in China, events stimulated alternative interpretations to those offered by the Liberals and Realists.

Right-Wing Classifications. The Right-Wing Revisionists range from moderates to radicals on a political spectrum. They include respected academicians engaged in the study of international political behavior and Soviet foreign policy and individuals in the mass media and government. Radicals, who carry the tenets of Right-Wing Revisionism to extremes, are disowned by more moderate theorists and represent a small minority of Right-Wing Revisionist writers.

The Right-Wing imageholders, as a group, disagree among themselves, as do Liberals and Realists. They do agree, however, that Communism is a menace, that American foreign policy should be aggressive in fighting Communism, and that the naive (or treasonous) views of some American government officials have aided the Communist threat.

The Menace of Communism. The major theme of Right-Wing Revisionism is that the American enemy is Communism in the form of a Soviet or Chinese state.[8] The emphasis, therefore, is placed on the presence of an ideological, rather than national, threat. Soviet leaders are motivated by ideological goals, such as world revolution; any deviation from these goals is deceptive since the Russians are unwaveringly committed to Communism. Western leaders must understand the intensity of this commitment and guard against direct or indirect aggression by Communist states to fulfill their ideological goals. Every Communist policy is aimed at the eventual destruction of the capitalist nations.

Because the enemy is Communism with its goal of world revolution in all capitalist countries, U.S. citizens should anticipate an extended period of conflict at the end of which one ideology triumphs over the other; either Communism or democracy will win. The United States government must follow an aggressive foreign policy during this period of protracted conflict. Simply "containing" the Soviet Union until it "mellows," as the Realists propose, is a negative response to the Communist menace. As long as Communism exists, the West will be in danger. American decision makers, therefore, must jettison any "containment" policies and substitute a more positive policy of "forward strategy."[9]

Communism is a monolithic force with no significant ideological variances, according to the Right-Wing advocates. Since Communist nations are bound by a common ideology, differences in policy caused by conflicting national interests are illusory. Right-Wing Revisionists, therefore, were reluctant to accept the sincerity of the Sino-Soviet split in the 1960s or the reality of Yugoslavian President Marshall Tito's break with the Soviet Union in 1948.

Forward Strategy and American Foreign Policy. In the Right-Wing Revisionist policy of forward strategy, the United States would apply persistent pressure to the Soviet bloc for the purpose of either reforming the Communist governments or eradicating Communism. The goal of an aggressive American foreign policy, therefore, is victory.[10] Peace in the world will come only when democracy triumphs over Communism: the only other alternatives for Americans are slavery or death.

Not only must the United States get on with the job of winning victories over the Communists, but the American government must be quick about it. The longer that the democratic nations wait to counter aggressively Communist designs, the greater the danger that the Soviet bloc will grow too strong. A foreign policy of hesitation, passivity, and peaceful coexistence with Communism can lead only to the ultimate defeat of the United States and the "free world." Further delays will work to the Russian advantage since time is on the side of Communism. The Right-Wing Revisionists, especially the radicals among them, are pessimistic about the Cold War ending in a victory for the American nation.[11]

Right-Wing advocates recognize the existence of Soviet military strength, but they argue that it is partly the result of Western aid rendered during World War II. The radicals further contend that Western treason and duplicity contributed to Russian strength. To counter Soviet military might, the Right-Wing Revisionists have advocated a strong American military establishment augmented by alliances with other non-Communist states.

The Right Wing also has advocated an integrated Europe, allied with the United States, as a deterrent to the Soviet Union.

Despite Soviet strength, the Right-Wing Revisionists seem assured that aggressive American policy will not provoke the Russians into a general, nuclear war. Although they do not discount the possibility of nuclear war, they feel that the U.S.S.R. would retreat rather than fight. If the Russians chose to take up arms, they would face a hostile indigenous population as well as American armed might, for the Right-Wing Revisionists believe that the Russian people would welcome an opportunity to revolt during a general war.

It should be emphasized that most Right-Wing Revisionists recommend the use of military force against the Soviet Union as a last resort. In their image, the Communist world is replete with "internal contradictions" that can be exploited by United States policy. The Right-Wing imageholders assume that these "contradictions" exist (such as conflict between the people and their government and weaknesses in centralized economic planning) and are fatal if properly exploited by constant American pressure short of military force.

The Right Wing and Domestic Sources of Foreign Policy. Past American foreign policy failures are explained in part by domestic weaknesses. To the radical Right Wing, the American government has been influenced by Communist agents or well-meaning "liberals" who adhere to the Soviet foreign policy line. To the moderates, American decision makers have misunderstood the true nature of the Communist menace. In Right-Wing literature, "liberalism" is quite different from the Liberal image previously discussed.[12] Realists are considered victims of "liberalism"; indeed, the Right-Wing writers see little difference between the Liberalism of Woodrow Wilson and the Realism of Hans Morgenthau.

The Right-Wing adherents assume that the American man-in-the-street is basically conservative in his politics, motivated by patriotism, and interested in winning the Cold War. American politics, however, have been dominated by the "liberals," who are intent on accommodating the Communists, rather than defeating them. If the American people could speak effectively, they would choose leaders who would prosecute a vigorous forward-strategy foreign policy.

In 1964, this assumption about American politics was tested when the Republicans nominated Senator Barry Goldwater of Arizona to head their presidential ticket against Lyndon Johnson, the incumbent Democratic President. Goldwater, identified with the Right-Wing image, was overwhelmingly defeated by President Johnson, apparently dispelling the belief that the American people were innately conservative and would opt for a candidate espousing Right-Wing policies.

Right-Wing Revisionists and Foreign Policy Goals. To the Right-Wing Revisionists, the major goal of American foreign policy should be the defeat and reformation of the Soviet Union. "Defeat" is not enough; beyond that, the Communist ideology embraced by the U.S.S.R. must be eradicated in order for the continued existence of the American nation to be assured. In the Right-Wing Revisionist image, there is no doubt that the Soviet Union can be vanquished politically, economically and, if it chooses to fight, militarily.

The agenda for Right-Wing goals focuses on internal American reform as well. United States foreign policy has largely been a failure because of domestic weaknesses, which include liberal and socialistic tendencies that hinder the working of the traditional American economic and political system. These weaknesses must be shorn up before the United States collapses from within. The more radical Right-Wing ideologies argue that the Trojan Horse of Liberalism and socialism represents more of a danger than the external threat of Soviet aggression.

To the Right-Wing Revisionists, the domestic and foreign policy goals for the United States are clear-cut. An aggressive, all-out attack on the ideological enemy—Communism—eventually will bring victory.

LEFT-WING REVISIONISM

Left-Wing Revisionism is the most recent foreign policy image to develop a sizable body of literature and a large number of adherents.[14] It is also a radical minority voice, as is Right-Wing Revisionism. The Left-Wing blueprint has had an impact on American diplomacy in the 1960s through its reinterpretation of Cold War events. It has been active in three areas: first, reinterpreting Soviet foreign policy after World War II; then redefining the motivations of American diplomacy; and finally, reexamining the relationship between domestic influencers and the outcomes of United States diplomacy. The most potent impetus for Left-Wing development was the Vietnam War which engendered public protest demonstrations, although opposition to the Indochina war did encompass groups other than those who subscribed to the assumptions of the Left-Wing image.

Soviet Weakness and the Cold War. While the Soviet Union's strength in 1945 is the starting point for the Right-Wing image, the Left-Wing Revisionists use the same date to emphasize Russian weaknesses. Left-Wing imageholders point to Russian manpower and economic losses from the German invasion. The retreating German army executed its own form of vengeance on the Russian countryside, destroying villages, collective farms, cattle, factories, and crops. Consequently, the U.S.S.R. was weakened by the war to the extent that the Soviet government sought, and expected, Western aid to rebuild the Russian economy. In addition to economic weaknesses, the Soviet Union faced an American government that possessed a monopoly over nuclear weapons. Negotiating from a position of economic and military strength, the United States sought to force Stalin to accept the American program for a post-war world.[15]

The roots of the Cold War, according to the Left Wing, were embedded in Soviet unwillingness to make concessions to a more powerful United States on vital issues. The Cold War, then, is as much an American as it is a Russian responsibility.[16]

The Open Door Strategy. The Left-Wing Revisionists view American policy after World War II as a continuation of ingrained patterns repeated over a number of years and not as a departure from traditional American behavior. The disappearance of the American frontier at the end of the 19th century caused American businessmen to turn to foreign markets as outlets for domestic production. The United States government supported the business interests and agreed that underdeveloped nations were open to investment and sales. The Open Door policy, first applied to China, became the primary consideration of American diplomacy in the 20th century.[17] The Open Door strategy did not envision the application of military power to win victories, since "victory" would come through peaceful, economic competition. In the Cold War era, the Left-Wing Revisionists argued that "victory" is synonymous with remolding the Soviet bloc, as well as the Third World, into the American image. The ultimate purpose of American foreign policy is to convert all Communists into capitalists.

American industry gradually accumulated a world empire through the Open Door strategy. It was not an empire of colonies, but an economic empire built on infiltration of foreign economies by American capital. Hence, one of the issues of the East–West conflict, if not the basic issue, is the aggressive out-reach of American economic power. American expansion has come, not by armies, but by marching businessmen who have expected and received the protection of their government for overseas enterprises. The United States government since 1945 has sought a world in which to carry on its capitalist endeavors which the Soviet Union, a Communist nation, has opposed. The result has been a struggle rooted in competing economic systems.

Domestic Conditions and American Foreign Policy. If American foreign policy is to reject its Open Door strategy, there must be a transformation of the internal economic structure of the United States. The Left-Wing Revisionists argue that foreign policy is the continuation of a nation's domestic economic system. If a nation's economic structure breeds injustices, its expressions of foreign policy will be aggressive and violent. Not only does U.S. foreign policy mirror the aggressive qualities of the American economy, but other aspects of American society as well: racism, class distinctions, myths purporting that Americans are God's chosen people, and a technocratic society that has dehumanized personal relationships. The more radical Left-Wing prescriptions border on nihilism; it appears that they are advocating that the entire American culture be made over in order to have a peaceful world.

The more moderate Left-Wing worldviewers have allied themselves with groups in society that they consider "progressive." Their program for change has advocated means short of force, employing confrontation politics to bring attention to changes that should be made in the social fabric. Protests and demonstrations are ordinarily employed. Although it is difficult to assess their impact on decision makers in changing a policy direction, the Left-Wing's accomplishments in organizing and supporting opposition to the Vietnamese conflict in the late 1960s is a political fact that cannot be ignored. Similar activities were organized with apparent success against businesses and universities that held large contracts with the Department of Defense for supplying war materiel and conducting research.[18]

The Left-Wing Revisionists express supreme confidence in the *people*. The slogan, "power to the people," heard often during the late 1960s and early 1970s, illustrates the Left-Wing's belief that the common man either has been neglected or covered with layers of special interests and governmental bureaucracy to the point that his voice is no longer listened to by decision makers. The common man must become active politically and voice his interests as effectively as other groups in society.

The Left-Wing Revisionists have misjudged the political orientation of the American people as much as their Right-Wing counterparts. While Senator Goldwater's defeat in 1964 punctured the Right-Wing Revisionist assumption that the American voter was innately conservative, Senator George McGovern's candidacy in 1972 confirmed that the American voter was not innately liberal either. McGovern was nominated by a Democratic Party that had instituted far-reaching internal party reforms; these reforms reduced the power of the "old guard" Democrats and opened the party more to youth, minorities, and women. Senator McGovern's overwhelming loss to President Richard M. Nixon indicated that a left-of-center view of the world was not shared by the American common man.

The Left Wing and Foreign Policy Goals. Based on their assumptions about international relations, Left-Wing Revisionists propose three foreign policy goals for American diplomacy. First, a more balanced approach should characterize U.S. diplomatic behavior toward the Soviet Union. The Russians have been misrepresented and maligned by American decision makers, who were either naive or were purposefully hateful toward the Soviet Union.[19] To view the U.S.S.R. as an aggressive nation, as the Realists do, is an absurd misperception that generates mistrust and discord. The United States should take the lead in burying the Cold War since American diplomacy bears part of the responsibility for it.

The second goal of the Left-Wing Revisionists is to restrain American business interests, which have been too aggressive and expansive. It is not important that American manufacturers have an "open door" to developing nations because the purpose of diplomacy is to generate stability, not to ensure a profit for multinational corporations with headquarters in New York or Detroit. Since some of these U.S. industries are larger than most nations' industrial production, the small states are not in a position to bargain with them on a basis of parity. It is the responsibility of the American government to restrain U.S. business from exerting undue influence in the Third World nations.

A third goal is to correct domestic flaws. The Left-Wing Revisionists perceive foreign policy to be flowing out of the injustices and inequalities of domestic American politics. If the United States is to regain its prestige in the world community, it first must clean its own house. The American government cannot preach racial equality to the Republic of South Africa or social justice to the Soviet Union, if it condones or tolerates such behavior within its own borders. An effective foreign policy can only be rooted in moral and just principles that must be reestablished in American life.

LINKING IMAGES TO FOREIGN POLICY

It is necessary to link the four images or conceptual frameworks that appear in the history of American foreign policy either to the decision makers who formulate policy or to the American public that influences the policy-formulators. In chapter 5, the second of these relationships will be examined; here, the problems encountered in linking decision makers to a particular image will be focused upon. The problem of establishing relationships also can be applied to other areas in the study of foreign policy: national values, political party identification, and interest-group activities.

Aside from considering Woodrow Wilson as a Liberal and Secretary of State Dean Acheson a Realist, no general consensus exists that would link American decision makers to a specific image.[20] Senator J. William Fulbright is quoted often by Realist writers, but he has undergone a metamorphosis of his own views that makes categorizing him difficult.[21]

In order to develop a relationship between an image and a decision maker, it is necessary to construct rigorous models of each image, and then proceed to analyze a policymaker's views to determine whether or not they correspond to the model.

Model construction is the less difficult of the two tasks, and centers on translating into rigorous hypotheses the general description of each image contained in this chapter. Since words are slippery, definitions of crucial terms must be included in the analysis. The Realist's "national interest," the Liberal's "community," the Right-Wing Revisionist's "victory," and the Left-Wing Revisionist's "U.S. imperialism" must all be defined precisely.

After precision has been achieved, the image model must then be *operationalized*, i.e., applied to the beliefs of specific decision makers. If one could determine the authorship of a particular policy and then ascertain that author's image-type, the linkage problem would be solved. The Realist's containment theory, first proposed by George Kennan in his famous "Mr. X" article, is an example of this approach, but it also illustrates the pitfalls encountered.[22] Although Kennan's containment proposal eventually was translated into policy, he later argued that American decision makers never fully understood the thrust of his argument in 1947 and misinterpreted it to include a prolonged state of siege between East and West.[23]

Content-Analysis Approach

A second approach is to apply the rigors of established social science research methodologies to the task of identifying the models and the decision makers whose views correspond to them. One research technique is content analysis, which systematically classifies verbal symbols contained in written or spoken statements. The researcher develops categories to analyze symbols (e.g., words or concepts) and their frequency of appearance or intensity of feeling expressed. Reliability of the findings is strengthened by using two coders who must agree on their selection of symbols for categories, or by using a computer to do the coding.

An example of the application of content analysis to evaluate systematically a decision maker's view of the world is Oli Holsti's study of the image held by John Foster Dulles, Secretary of State from 1953 to 1959.[24] Dulles's image, Holsti found, contained three value dichotomies: (1) the Russian people were "good" while their leaders were "bad"; (2) Russian national interest was "good" while Communist ideology was "bad"; and (3) the Russian state was "good" while the Communist party was "bad."

Using these values, Dulles placed his own interpretation on Soviet policies that the Russian government thought reduced the level of hostility between the U.S. and U.S.S.R. For example, he failed to perceive any friendliness in the Soviet announcement of a reduction in Russian armed forces. Dulles thought that the armed forces reduction increased, rather than decreased, Russian military capability. "I would rather have them standing around doing guard duty than making atomic bombs," he stated.

Nor did Dulles's image permit him to prescribe motivations to the Soviet Union other than those associated with selfishness and duplicity. Acts of negotiation that might bring about a reduction of tensions were interpreted as signs of weakness on the part of the Russians, rather than as indications that the U.S.S.R. was willing to engage in the process of building a peaceful international system. During the Geneva Summit in 1955, Dulles expressed the view that the Russians were willing to negotiate because they occupied a position of weakness.

The Operational Code

Another approach to ascribing relationships between images and decision makers is the Operational Code proposed by Alexander L. George.[25] The Operational Code lists the assumptions that subconsciously intrude into the policymaker's decisions or those that he consciously calls on to guide him in making decisions. Philosophical assumptions about the nature of man and his control over his own environment would be included. A decision maker with a fatalistic attitude, for example, would tend to doubt that he could do much to shape the course of his nation's history.

The Operational Code approach also uses the decision maker's view of the contemporary international political environment, which touches on many of the topics covered in this chapter: Is harmony or conflict the characteristic of the contemporary international system? Is war inevitable or is coexistence possible? What are the prospects for change in the system? Who are our enemies?

Finally, the Code asks questions about the decision maker's attitude toward the instruments of policy. What is his personal style in selecting alternatives? Does he possess a "sense of timing" in making decisions, hoping to make a policy correspond to the most propitious time? How does he select tactics to implement his decisions? For example, a President who believes that a decision to go to war should involve Congress is expressing an instrumental assumption about American foreign policy and the American Constitution.

The Operational Code approach necessitates a comprehensive search of the artifacts of a decision maker's life to find clues to his assumptions about his environment. A researcher must construct the detailed background of a President, Secretary of State, or congressman to evaluate the individual's decisions.

ADVANTAGES OF THE IMAGES

The efficacy of linking images to specific decision makers must await more research of the type that Holsti undertook on John Foster Dulles or of the type advocated by George. It may be, given these studies, that the researcher will discover key decision makers with hybrid or mutated images, rather than individuals who correspond to the ideal models. Some of Dulles's values, for example, fit the Realist image, while others fall within the Right-Wing framework.

Despite difficulties in establishing relationships or linkages, the images are useful analytical tools. They permit us to classify much of the literature written about American foreign policy. With the introduction provided in this chapter, the reader should be able to wade through contemporary literature on the United States in world affairs with a knowledge of the assumptions of each approach.

The student should be cautioned that it is relatively easy to assume that the Realists must be accurate in their assessment of international relations because we are constantly bombarded with their views. The encouragement of a critical attitude about assumptions long held sacrosanct is another advantage to studying these images. A student of American foreign policy should subject his own assumptions about U.S. diplomacy to a self-examination process.

Finally, by examining the images early in this study, the patterns of U.S. foreign policy that lie beyond the ideological debates of the image-advocates can be concentrated upon. Questions such as the following are important: "Should public opinion influence foreign policy?" "Should we blame the U.S.S.R. for the Cold War?" "Should the U.S. get out of the UN?" However, these questions point only to the threshold of the study of U.S. diplomacy. We should pause at the threshold, but we should also be anxious to enter into a deeper, more meaningful analysis of the patterns of American foreign policy.

NOTES

1. The following writers describe the basic tenets of Liberalism: Frank Tannenbaum, *The American Tradition in Foreign Policy* (Norman: University of Oklahoma Press, 1955); Thomas I. Cook and Malcolm Moos, *Power Through Purpose: The Realism of Idealism as a Basis for Foreign Policy* (Baltimore: Johns Hopkins Press, 1954); Harlan Cleveland, *The Obligations of Power: American Diplomacy in the Search for Peace* (New York: Harper & Row, 1966); John C. Bennett, *Moral Tensions in International Affairs* (New York: Council on Religion and International Affairs, 1964); and Herbert C. Butterfield, "The Scientific versus the Moralistic Approach in International Affairs," *International Affairs* 28 (October 1951): 411–422.
2. Hans Morgenthau, *Politics Among Nations*, 5th ed. (New York: Alfred A. Knopf, 1972). Analysis of Morgenthau's theories are contained in Kenneth E. Boulding, "The Content of International Studies in College: A Review," *Journal of Conflict Resolution* 8 (March 1964): 64–71; and Robert W. Tucker, "Professor Morgenthau's Theory of Political 'Realism'," *American Political Science Review* 46 (March 1952): 214–224.
3. Hans Morgenthau, *Scientific Man versus Power Politics* (Chicago: University of Chicago Press, 1946). Other writings by Morgenthau include: *Dilemmas of Politics* (Chicago: University of Chicago Press, 1958); *In Defense of the National Interest* (New York: Alfred A. Knopf, 1951); *The Purpose of American Politics* (New York: Alfred A. Knopf, 1960); *Vietnam and the United States* (Washington: Public Affairs Press, 1965); and *A New Foreign Policy for the United States* (New York: Praeger, 1968).
4. For Niebuhr's views consult: *Beyond Tragedy: Essays on the Christian Interpretation of History* (New York: Scribner's, 1937); *The Children of Light and the Children of Darkness* (New York: Scribner's, 1944); *Christianity and Power Politics* (New York: Scribner's, 1953); *Christian Realism and Political Problems* (New York: Scribner's 1953); *The Irony of American History* (New York: Scribner's, 1952); and *The Structure of Nations and Empires* (New York: Scribner's, 1959). Evaluations of Niebuhr's views are found in: David R. Davis, *Reinhold Niebuhr: Prophet from America* (New York: Macmillan, 1948); Harry R. Davies and Robert C. Good (eds.), *Reinhold Niebuhr on Politics* (New York: Scribner's, 1960); Gordon Harland, *The Thought of Reinhold Niebuhr* (New York: Oxford University Press, 1960); Charles W. Kegley and Robert W. Bretail, *Reinhold Niebuhr: His Religious, Social, and Political Thought* (New York: Macmillan, 1956).
5. In addition to his newspaper column, Lippmann's writings include: *The*

Cold War: A Study in U.S. Foreign Policy (New York: Harper & Row, 1947); *The Coming Tests with Russia* (Boston: Little, Brown, and Co., 1961); *The Communist World and Ours* (Boston: Little, Brown, and Co., 1959); *Isolation and Alliances: An American Speaks to the British* (Boston: Little, Brown, and Co., 1952); *U.S. Foreign Policy: Shield of the Republic* (Boston: Little, Brown, and Co., 1953); and *Western Unity and the Common Market* (Boston: Little, Brown, and Co., 1962). Two compilations of his writings are Marquis Childs and James Reston (eds.), *Walter Lippmann and His Times* (New York: Harcourt, Brace, and World, 1959); and Clinton Rossiter (ed.), *The Essential Lippmann* (New York: Random House, 1963). A thorough critique of Lippmann's views is contained in Anwar Hussain Syed, *Walter Lippmann's Philosophy of International Relations* (Philadelphia: University of Pennsylvania Press, 1962).

6. For Kennan's views of American foreign policy, see *American Diplomacy, 1900–1950* (Chicago: University of Chicago Press, 1951); *On Dealing with the Communist World* (New York: Harper & Row, 1964); *Realities of American Foreign Policy* (Princeton, N.J.: Princeton University Press, 1954); *Russia and the West under Lenin and Stalin* (Boston: Little, Brown, and Co., 1961); *Russia, the Atom and the West* (London: Oxford University Press, 1958); *Soviet–American Relations, 1917–1920* (Princeton, N.J.: Princeton University Press, 1956); *Soviet Foreign Policy, 1917–1941* (New York: Van Nostrand, 1960).

7. For a general discussion of Right-Wing Revisionism, see Seymour M. Lipset and Earl Raab, *The Politics of Unreason: Right Wing Extremism in America, 1790–1970* (New York: Harper & Row, 1970); James McEvoy III, *Radicals or Conservatives? The Contemporary American Right* (Chicago: Rand McNally, 1971).

8. The Right-Wing Revisionist views of Communism are contained in Stefan T. Possony, *A Century of Conflict: Communist Techniques of World Revolution* (Chicago: Henry Regnery, 1953); Robert Strausz-Hupé and Stefan T. Possony, *International Relations in the Age of Conflict Between Democracy and Dictatorship* (New York: McGraw-Hill, 1950); and Thomas A. Lane, *America on Trial: The War for Vietnam* (New Rochelle, N.Y.: Arlington House, 1971).

9. Robert Strausz-Hupé, William R. Kintner, and Stefan T. Possony, *A Forward Strategy for America* (New York: Harper & Row, 1961), and Robert Strausz-Hupé, William Kintner, James Doughty, and Alvin Cottrell, *Protracted Conflict: A Study of Communist Society* (New York: Harper & Row, 1959).

10. Barry Goldwater, *Why Not Victory? A Fresh Look at American Foreign Policy* (New York: McGraw-Hill, 1962), and Stefan Possony and J. E. Pournelle, *The Strategy of Technology: Winning the Decisive War* (New York: Dunellen, 1971).

11. See Curtis E. LeMay with Dale O. Smith, *America Is in Danger* (New York: Funk and Wagnalls, 1968), and James Burnham, *The Struggle for the World* (New York: John Day, 1950).

12. William F. Buckley, *Up from Liberalism,* rev. ed. (New York: Arlington House, 1968), and James Burnham, *Suicide of the West* (New York: John Day, 1964).
13. For views of the radical Right Wing on the internal threat of the Communist party, *see* W. Cleon Skousen, *The Naked Communist* (Salt Lake City: Ensign Publishing Co., 1961); Fred Schwarz, *You Can Trust The Communists (To Be Communists)* (Englewood Cliffs, N.J.: Prentice-Hall, 1960); M. Stanton Evans, *The Politics of Surrender* (Old Greenwich, Conn.: Devin-Adair, 1966); and Robert Welch, *The Blue Book of the John Birch Society* (John Birch Society, 1961).
14. For a survey of the Left-Wing Revisionist image, *see* Christopher Lasch, *The New Radicalism in America (1889–1963)* (New York: Alfred A. Knopf, 1965), and "The Cold War, Revisited and Revisioned," *New York Times Magazine,* Jan. 14, 1968, pp. 24–7; 44–59; Irwin Unger, "The 'New Left' and American History: Some Recent Trends in United States Historiography," *American Historical Review* 72 (July 1967): 1237–1264; and Robert W. Tucker, *The Radical Left and American Foreign Policy* (Baltimore: Johns Hopkins Press, 1971).
15. Gar Alperovitz, *Atomic Diplomacy: Hiroshima and Potsdam* (New York: Simon and Schuster, 1965).
16. Denna F. Fleming, *The Cold War and Its Origins, 1917–1960,* 2 vols. (Garden City, N.Y.: Doubleday, 1961); David Horowitz, *The Free World Colossus: A Critique of American Foreign Policy in The Cold War* (New York: Hill and Wang, 1965); and John Lukacs, *A History of The Cold War* (Garden City, N.Y.: Doubleday, 1961).
17. William A. Williams, *America and The Middle East: Open Door Imperialism or Enlightened Leadership?* (New York: Holt, Rinehart, and Winston, 1952); Harry Magdoff, *The Age of Imperialism: The Economics of U.S. Foreign Policy* (New York: Monthly Review Press, 1969); David Horowitz, *Empire and Revolution: A Radical Interpretation of Contemporary History* (New York: Random House, 1969).
18. *See* Daniel C. Kramer, *Participatory Democracy: Developing Ideas of The Political Left* (Cambridge, Mass.: Schenkman, 1972).
19. Staughton Lynd, *The Other Side* (New York: New American Library, 1966).
20. Several books have been written by Dean Acheson, among them: *A Citizen Looks at Congress* (New York: Harper & Row, 1956); *Power and Diplomacy* (Cambridge, Mass.: Harvard University Press, 1959); *Morning and Noon* (Boston: Houghton Mifflin, 1965; *The Korean War* (New York: W. W. Norton, 1971). For an analysis of Acheson, *see* Ronald J. Stupak, *The Shaping of Foreign Policy: The Role of the Secretary of State as Seen by Dean Acheson* (Indianapolis: The Odyssey Press, 1969).
21. Books written by J. William Fulbright on American foreign policy include: *The Arrogance of Power* (New York: Random House, 1966); *Old Myths and New Realities* (New York: Random House, 1964);

Prospects for the West (Cambridge, Mass.: Harvard University Press, 1963); and *The Crippled Giant: American Foreign Policy and Its Domestic Consequences* (New York: Vintage Books, 1972). Analyses of Fulbright's views are contained in Tristram Coffin, *Senator Fulbright: Portrait of a Public Philosopher* (New York: E. P. Dutton, 1966), and Haynes Johnson and Bernard M. Gwertzman, *Fulbright: The Dissenter* (Garden City, N.Y.: Doubleday, 1968).

22. George Kennan, "The Sources of Soviet Conduct," *Foreign Affairs* 15 (July 1947): 571–582. Mr. Kennan at the time of publication of this article was with the State Department. His article was published identifying only "X" as the author in order to protect Kennan's identity.

23. Edmund Stillman, "Twenty Years After 'Mr. X' Proposed It, 'Containment' Has Won, But. . . ," *New York Times Magazine*, May 28, 1967, pp. 23; 73–76.

24. Ole R. Holsti, "The Belief System and National Images: A Case Study," *Journal of Conflict Resolution* 6 (1962): 244–252. Writings on Dulles include: Herman Finer, *Dulles Over Suez: The Theory and Practice of His Diplomacy* (Chicago: Quadrangle Books, 1964); Roscoe Drummand and Gaston Coblentz, *Duel at the Brink: John Foster Dulles' Command of American Power* (Garden City, N.Y.: Doubleday, 1960); and Benjamin Nimer, "Dulles, Suez, and Democratic Diplomacy," *Western Political Quarterly* 12 (September 1959): 784–798.

25. Alexander L. George, "The 'Operational Code': A Neglected Approach to the Study of Political Leaders and Decision-Making," *International Studies Quarterly* 12 (June 1969): 2. George did not originate the Operational Code approach, but his work has resulted in its extensive application to American foreign policy decision makers by political scientists who have presented papers at the annual meetings of the American Political Science Association and who have written Ph.D. dissertations.

SECTION

3

Domestic Sources of American Foreign Policy

This section attempts to answer the question, "To what extent is the American public a source of behavioral patterns in American foreign policy?" Five possible domestic sources are evaluated: national values, public opinion, mass media, interest groups, and political parties.

In this analysis, the four worldviews or images discussed in chapter 3 will be related to the American public. Each of the images embodies a concept of the role that the public should play in foreign policymaking. In addition, studies of domestic behavior conducted by researchers using social science methodologies (such as interviews, content analysis, and roll-call analysis) are analyzed. Often, the assumptions embedded in these images distort the actual role of the domestic influencers. The various social science methodologies furnish us with a more accurate evaluation of the function of domestic influencers than do the image-holders, who tend to prescribe—rather than describe—these functions. The images focus on *what ought to be* the role of domestic influencers. We are more concerned with *what is*, in reality, that role.

4

National Values and American Foreign Policy

Images are built on assumptions which in turn are composed of values. National *values* are concepts and traits that characterize a majority of the population.[1] Concepts are verbal symbols that express ideas and ideals venerated in American history. "Due process," "self-determination of nations," "justice," and "separation of powers" are examples of concepts that are revered. Traits, on the other hand, are behavioral patterns that Americans display in applying these concepts to problems (otherwise known as "operationalizing" the concepts).

Values are instilled at an early age through socialization and the absorption of dominant cultural mores and taboos. While Americans differ individually, their common values and traits compose a basic personality structure, formed as they mature in the American cultural environment.[2]

Values have become the basis for analyzing complex clusters of policies. Often these values are cited as existing *a priori* and then described as the motivating force behind a behavioral pattern. Several examples of this line of analysis exist. (1) One congressman, who opposes foreign aid, attributes the motivation for U.S. economic assistance programs to the behavioral trait of "check grabbing":

> We are historically a nation of check grabbers. I do it myself. You go into a restaurant with a party and all the men reach for the check. We think that it impresses people to pick up the bill. What we do as individuals we usually do as a nation.[3]

(2) Another commentator perceives two values predominating American behavior: a desire for quick and simple solutions and an inclination to make judgments on the basis of personalities rather than issues. Diplomacy is thereby avoided because the negotiation process requires patient dialogue on complex problems. Moreover, failures in our foreign policy have been

blamed on individual statesmen; Prime Minister Nehru, for example, was held responsible for India's failure to join the Southeast Treaty Organization, and President Charles de Gaulle was viewed as the chief obstacle to a healthy North Atlantic Treaty Organization.[4]

(3) Another writer singles out the double standard in American foreign policy. The United States does not consider as objectionable its own use of force because American power is always employed with reluctance. Yet the use of force by other states is excoriated. Americans then judge others by their *actions,* but want to be judged on the basis of U.S. *intentions,* which are always assumed to be pure.

These three examples illustrate the use of national values as shortcuts to explaining American behavioral patterns. Before this line of analysis can be engaged in, the concepts and traits that are most characteristic of Americans must be identified and then linked to specific policy decisions. Both tasks are not easy, and some analysts judge them to be impossible on the basis that behavioral traits on a national level actually do not exist.[6]

Questions should be raised about using analytical shortcuts to explain American diplomacy: Are most Americans check grabbers, and if they are, can check grabbing be linked to the Turkish foreign-aid program? Do Americans dislike diplomacy, and if they do, can this dislike be linked to the five years of negotiations (1968–1973) to end the Vietnam War? Does an American double standard exist, and if it does, what impact did it have on the decision to devalue the dollar in 1972–1973? A large amount of groundwork must first be laid before these apparent shortcuts can be employed with any confidence.

THE FOUR IMAGES AND NATIONAL VALUES

The debate between the Realist, Liberal, Right-Wing, and Left-Wing imageholders seldom touches on the identification of values and their relationship to policy decisions. The dialogue is on a grander scale and involves a subjective judgment: Should American national values be taken into consideration in the decision-making process? The Liberals and both Revisionists answer in the affirmative; the Realists alone say "no."

The Realist's View of Values

The Realists believe that the American man-in-the-street is too idealistic and tends to overestimate the influence that his nation's values can have on improving the world and bringing about peace.[7] They argue that the American does not appreciate the role of power in the international system. He considers war an aberration from normal world behavior, explaining the presence of conflict in the world as the result of evil rulers who force their inherently good citizens into war for selfish reasons. Because peace is the rule, rather than the exception of world politics, the average American does not take foreign policy seriously; in fact, he relegates it to a secondary position, placing domestic politics first. When he attends to international problems, he approaches them with an impatient "let's get this job done in a hurry" attitude so that he can return to his domestic business endeavors in peace. The American views foreign policy as an end in itself, rather than a means to an end; the Realists would reverse the order.

The Realists further contend that the American approach to international problems is akin to the zeal of a missionary. Each problem is unique and threatens a basic belief of Western civilization, such as "democracy," "freedom," and "justice." Each problem requires the wholehearted application of American military power to achieve uncompromising, ideological, moralistic, and utopian goals. Hence, the American is willing to apply the full force of United States power to shape the world in a way that he believes is best.

Because the Realists disapprove of the traits that they see ingrained in American character, they are presented with a dilemma. For the United States to pursue a successful foreign policy ("successful" from the Realists' point of view), the decision makers must possess different values, and they must ignore traditional American behavioral patterns. The emphasis should be on electing or recruiting and training leaders who hold concepts and exhibit traits different from the American body politic. In effect, the Realists advocate a foreign policy under the guidance of leaders selected because they possess values unlike those of the people who will be affected by the foreign policy eventually implemented.

Values and the Liberals

The Liberals applaud the American behavioral patterns that the Realists deplore.[8] The Liberals perceive concepts and traits of character in the American public which they want translated into policy preferences for United States diplomacy. For example, the theory that "all men are created equal" is transformed at the international level into a belief that all states are equal; belief in domestic law and order leads to faith in international law; and emphasis on the role of domestic public opinion surfaces at the international level as emphasis on world public opinion. In each case, American domestic behavioral patterns dictate an international response.

Both Realists and Liberals, reading the same historical record, are impressed with divergent American behavioral patterns. To the Liberals, United States foreign policy has been free from utopian, dogmatic, and fanatic moralizing and characterized instead by a highly pragmatic approach. To the Realists, the same record reveals an emphasis on those traits that the Liberals say are either missing or of minor consequence. Both Realists and Liberals examine the historical record through glasses tinted by the biases of their models. The Realists argue that the problems in American foreign policy are caused by values which the Liberals believe have been neglected too often in contemporary American diplomacy.

The Revisionists

Both Left-Wing and Right-Wing Revisionists feel that traditional American values are neglected, which accounts for the mistakes in United States diplomacy. If traditional American values have been undermined, Communist ideology brought in by welfare programs is the cause. The Right-Wing position would sympathize with Theodore Roosevelt's "Peace of Righteousness" discussed in chapter 2; that is, the concepts of morality and virility should be implemented as the United States furnishes aggressive leadership to the Western world in its conflict with Communism.

The Left-Wing Revisionist position has no historical counterpart in American traditions, unless it be the periodic populist movements that elevated the common man. The government, in its domestic policy as well as its foreign policy, is a disappointing extension of society because the values of the most powerful and most wealthy groups are reflected in decisions. Values should play a role in American foreign policy, but they should be the values of the people and not those of the dominant business and financial interests.

IDENTIFICATION OF AMERICAN VALUES

The debate between the Realists, Liberals, and Revisionists over values contributes little to the search by students of American foreign policy for a rationale for cultural concepts and traits in the foreign policymaking process. Before a final judgment can be passed on the role of values, they must first be accurately identified. Although the Realists and Liberals do not disagree over the existence of specific values, they do profess divergent views on the place values should hold in policymaking. The Revisionists, on the other hand, have their own views as to what values exist in the first place. They especially take exception to those cited by the two orthodox critiques.

Two groups of observers, foreign visitors and introspective Americans, have attempted to identify and catalog American values. Both groups have their analytical strengths and weaknesses.

Evaluation by Foreign Observers

Early Observers. The most famous foreign visitor to record his observations of American national values was Alexis de Tocqueville, a Frenchman who toured the United States in the 1830s.[9] Tocqueville commented on the American propensity to form associations or groups; on his inattention to philosophy; on his concern for physical well-being; and on a host of other subjects. Tocqueville was not the first foreign observer; J. Hector de Crèvecoeur, who predated him by forty years, asked "What then is the American, this new man?" He cited industriousness, good living, selfishness, pride, litigiousness, and political orientation among the characteristics of the new American man. Despite the presence of some unflattering traits, he concluded that the United States was "the most perfect society now existing in the world." Other foreign visitors throughout the 19th and 20th centuries also recorded their observations.[10] Tocqueville has become the best known and the most often quoted by American writers who remain to this day impressed by his insights into early American behavior.

Two Notes of Caution. The foreign visitor, viewing American behavior from a different cultural background, may provide new perspectives overlooked by citizen observers. The foreign observer can compare American values with those that are dominant in his own nation's behavior. However, he has his limitations. In the first place, American society is highly complex; it is doubtful that one or a few visits to the United States can furnish an observer with sufficient experiences on which to base valid judgments. Present-day observations of American behavior are only partial accounts of one or more segments of a multifarious society. Perhaps when American society was more simple, in Tocqueville's time, for example, the foreign observer's notations were a worthwhile addition to knowledge about American values.

The second cautionary note is a reminder that national values can change.[11] A nation's behavior is conditioned by traumatic experiences, such as defeats in war, economic depression, or revolutions. Moreover, migrations of people—from farms to cities and from foreign countries—and changes in the educational level of the population have an effect on the concepts held and ways of solving problems. Consequently, Tocqueville's observations, though interesting, may no longer apply. The dominant American values of the 1830s may have been risk-taking, self-reliance, and independence, but the traits of an industrialized, urbanized 20th-century America are vastly different from those found in a frontier society. The views of the foreign observer should not be discounted, but they must be qualified, since he, at best, has only a partial and dated view of American behavior. Perhaps the foreign observer's conclusions tell us more about his country than about the United States, since he might use American culture as a foil for observations about his native land. To conclude, as did Crèvecoeur, that the United States was the world's most perfect society is more a commentary on his dissatisfaction with French society.

American Introspection

The Problem of Objectivity. Although foreign observers are not closely bound to American culture and can view behavior from a different perspective, they may be criticized for a lack of substantial knowledge of the intricacies of American society. American observers, on the other hand, may have a detailed knowledge of their own culture, but they are submersed in it; thus, their objectivity can be questioned.

The literature of American introspection is extensive. It may be divided into historical and behavioral analyses. The historical approach emphasizes trends in behavioral patterns as the American nation developed, relying on historical artifacts, such as public and private presidential papers, for data to substantiate these trends.[12]

The Behavioral Scientists. Behavioral scientists include psychologists, sociologists, social psychologists, and anthropologists who have brought their skills to the subject of American national character. For example, anthropologist Margaret Mead believes that American values are geared to success rather than status; thus, the American is never satisfied. This attitude is instilled in children, who soon learn that parental affection corresponds to achievement. Although this orientation to success produces aggressive citizens, they shun violence and keep their aggressive drives within the bounds of domestic law. Karen Horney, a psychologist, also singles out aggressive behavior as a trait of American character. Although competitiveness is primarily confined to the economic sphere, it extends to all aspects of society. Competition and rivalry produce hostile tensions within individuals, which, in turn, engender fear of failure and fear of rivals. A social psychologist, David Riesman, characterizes the American citizen as motivated to conform to the habits and thinking of his peers, a condition which Riesman calls "other directedness." Riesman believes that national behavior changes as the national environment changes. The American citizen in the 19th century was "inner directed"; that is, he developed a set of fixed principles to guide him in response to different stimuli. These principles may be instilled in individuals by parents or by religion. Mead, Horney, and Riesman are only three examples of the behavioral scientists who have compiled lists of traits of American national character and who relate national character to cultural environment.[13]

The differences between the historical and behavioral introspective approaches lie in the author's frame of reference. The historian's observations are based on the verbal and written record; the behaviorist focuses on the human act (if he is a psychologist), or the social act (if he is a sociologist), or a combination of both. Both the historian and behavioral scientist have offered subjective insights into American national character. Being subjective, they are open to the question of whether an American can analyze his own culture any more than a psychiatrist can psychoanalyze himself.

The Question of Differentiation

The question of differentiation is a question of whether or not each nation possesses a topology of values different from other nations. Do preferred concepts and traits vary from state to state? Although the answer to this question may appear to be an obvious affirmative, two alternative explanations for the existence of national values must first be dealt with. First, American values may be universal characteristics and not limited by national boundaries. Thus, "idealism" or "industriousness" are not uniquely American values, but they are innate human characteristics expressed in most societies, although they may be stressed more in one society than in another.

A second explanation makes the existence of values more a projection of subjective judgments of friends and enemies. We ascribe "good" values to ourselves and our friends and "bad" values to our enemies. Some evidence exists for this position: the shift in the American perception of Soviet national character between 1944, when the U.S. and U.S.S.R. were allies fighting a common enemy, and 1948, when the Cold War began in earnest with the Communist take-over in Czechoslovakia and the Soviet blockade of Berlin. During World War II, Americans responding to public opinion polls ascribed favorable traits to the Russians; after the war, Russian behavior was described in unfavorable terms.[14]

The description of American values in the Latin American press demonstrates conflicting foreign opinion.[15] While most foreign visitors to the United States were writing nice things about American values, the most frequently mentioned characteristics of American life in the Latin American press were sometimes different. Values most frequently occurring in Latin American dailies were that the United States was democratic, Europe-oriented, ignorant of Latin America, affluent, and anti-intellectual. Occurring less frequently: the Americans were arrogant, friendly, and supportive of dictators.

Certain values, no doubt, are shared by all nations, and national friendship and hostility do affect the way that nations perceive each other. Beyond these explanations, and not contradicting them, is the idea that values also exist in a national framework, unique to that nation and not dependent on subjective perception by friends or enemies. That value differentiation exists among nations is confirmed by a study of five cultures, the United States, United Kingdom, Germany, Italy, and Mexico, using in-depth interviews.[16] One of the conclusions of the study was that the American valued participation in the political process, believing that his participation could have a positive effect on the government. On the other hand, the Germans were politically detached, the Italians were alienated from their government, and the British were deferential toward theirs.

A List of Values? The preceding analysis does not end with a precise list of values because none exists. Those who have explored the concepts and traits that Americans profess to hold cannot agree on a catalog of values. This circumstance does not discredit values as an analytical concept or tool for the social scientist; rather, it is a commentary on the paucity of research that the social scientist has allocated to the concept. The need is for more systematic research into the composition of the American value profile, research of the type conducted by Lee Coleman and by a Canadian group headed by Carl L. Kline.

Coleman employed the research technique of content analysis to identify themes in books written by foreign and American observers describing "Americanism" or the "American way."[17] He divided the literature into four periods according to their publication dates: pre-Civil War (1789–1860); post-Civil War to World War I (1866–1917); World War I to the depression (1918–1929); and the depression to 1941, when results of his study were published. Coleman found eleven concepts mentioned in all periods, including association activity, belief in democracy, individual equality and freedom, local government, practicality, Puritanism, and uniformity and conformity. In addition, forty-six traits were mentioned in three of the four periods, such as bragging and boasting, idealism, optimism, desire for peace, and dominance by women. Unfortunately, no attempt has been made to catalog systematically the concepts and traits of American character in the post-World War II period.

Kline and his associates offer an interesting view of American values through a study of young men who fled to Canada to escape the draft during the Vietnam War.[18] The values that these expatriates (as the authors call them) espouse are contrasted with the values of their parents. The young expatriates are self-reliant, introspective, with a strong moral outlook on life in general and the Vietnamese conflict in particular; they are individualistic, non-conformist, antipathetical to authoritarianism, and willing to carve out a new life for themselves in a different country. Their parents, on the other hand, are described as patriotic, worried about the effect of their son's action on their own social standing and reputation, and conformist. Ironically, the values that the expatriates exhibited were those of the 19th-century American frontiersman, an individual whose characteristics are idolized by most American adults. When these values were found in expatriates, however, they were viewed with hostility and suspicion.

If more research of the Coleman and Kline variety is undertaken, progress will be made toward identifying the values that make up the American character. Identification of dominant concepts and traits, however, is only the first and perhaps the easiest step in finding a place for values in the foreign policymaking process. Linking these values, once identified, with specific policies is the second, more difficult step.

LINKING NATIONAL VALUES TO FOREIGN POLICY

The absence of an agreed-upon list of concepts and traits that comprise the American value profile complicates any meaningful research on linking national values to foreign policy decisions.[19] Some general observations can be posited, however, using the concept of *political socialization*.

Political Socialization

Political socialization is the process by which political attitudes and behavioral patterns are acquired by members of a political system. One of the vehicles for this socialization process is the family; political attitudes may be passed from parent to child. Another vehicle is the school system in which American history is uniformly taught in a way that perpetuates national myths and national heroes. Peer-group pressure—whether expressed at work, in the residential neighborhood, or in voluntary associations (such as churches or civic clubs)—is another important vehicle for inculcating political attitudes.

Other vehicles for political socialization are institutional expressions of social differences. Americans are divided into social classes, ethnic and religious groups, and by sex. Differences in values exist between the middle- and upper-classes, among Jews, Protestants, and Catholics, between blacks and whites, and between men and women. People are socialized by the specific values of the social groups to which they belong. White, Anglo-Saxon, Protestant, middle-class, and male values predominate in American society; they have tended to become institutionalized in literature, in political decision-making positions, in executive business positions, and in social and civic club elites. The government itself can become a vehicle for formulating political attitudes. A later chapter examines the government's attempt to manipulate mass media, but there are other government vehicles. The armed forces socialize recruits or volunteers, and government bureaucracy develops its own set of attitudes.

Consequently, values held in common exist as a result of a shared political socialization process. However, there are enough differences to caution making generalizations about these values. A possible interpretation of American society in the 1970s is that common values are in the process of fragmenting. The political socialization process may have run aground because social groups are becoming more cognizant of common *group* values than common national values. It would be naive to assume, then, that American leaders possess the same values as all citizens simply because they have gone through a political socialization process.

Decision Makers and Values

Perhaps by moving to another level in our analysis—to that of the decision makers themselves—we can more readily discover values that enter into the process of formulating foreign policy. Thus we move from a focus on aggregate values to individual values found in the personalities of American leaders.

The presidency, as might be expected, has been the focus of psychological and psycho-historical studies on the personality of leadership. The personality of Woodrow Wilson has attracted the most research.[20] He is described as idealistic, unwilling to compromise, and supercilious in his relations with other people. He had faith in his own considerable political instincts, and on occasion he rejected the counsel of advisers which, if followed, would have permitted him to avoid some of his more fatal political mistakes.

Other political leaders have been the subject of psychological studies.[21] Richard Nixon, a more contemporary President, stimulated a small body of psychological literature on his decision-making style.[22] Mr. Nixon's approach to major decisions or crises was to withdraw into quiet contemplation and shut himself off from advisers. One of his tendencies was to respond quickly and decisively, sometimes losing control of his temper, to challenges that brought intense pressure and criticism.

The personality traits of these two presidents can be linked to specific foreign policy decisions. Wilson's unwillingness to compromise with Republican senators on the Versailles Treaty ending World War I led him to instruct his own party, the Democrats, to vote against the agreement. Mr. Nixon ordered massive bombing of North Vietnam in December 1972 after secluding himself at his Camp David retreat. His decision was reached without consulting the secretaries of State and Defense and the Joint Chiefs of Staff.

The correlations between presidential behavioral traits and foreign policy decisions offer a measure of confidence in the use of values as analytical tools for understanding American foreign policy. It is necessary, however, to correlate the aggregate traits of the majority of adult Americans with the foreign policy orientation of the United States. Personality studies of American leaders do not provide us with data on which to base conclusions about the values of the majority of Americans.

Correlation between Values and Foreign Policy

The best-known attempt to link national values to policy outcomes is Gabriel Almond's *The American People and Foreign Policy*.[23] Almond formulates "psycho-cultural hypotheses" about American values from the behavioralist literature, especially the writings of Riesman, Mead, and Horney. He concludes that "mood," or mental disposition, conditions the American response to foreign affairs stimuli. The American reacts to stimuli on the basis of his disposition, rather than on the basis of factual information or any analytical process. Since the American body politic may reflect several moods at the same time, it is difficult to predict how the public will react to a given issue.

Almond believes that the public's moods are unstable and subject to rapid and radical change. The dominant public outlook for peace may be optimistic at one time, but may shift to pessimism in response to an external stimuli. The public's volatile disposition explains the different readings that various observers obtain in their study of American values.

Almond's hypothesis of changeable moods has been both confirmed and unsubstantiated by researchers. Klingberg analyzed presidential State of the Union addresses, political party platforms, and naval expenditures, and found that American policies have reflected an alternation between introverted and extroverted moods.[24] During periods of extroverted moods, annexations, expeditions abroad, and strong diplomatic pressures characterized American foreign policy. These politics were followed by isolationist behavior during periods of introverted or withdrawn moods. Other researchers have not found support for Almond's mood theory.[25]

IDENTIFICATION OF COMMON AND IDIOSYNCRATIC VALUES

The concept of national values has been employed so often to explain American diplomatic behavior that the reader may be surprised at the difficulty encountered in analyzing these values. Real or imagined values are convenient crutches to be employed when addressing a specific policy or an era of diplomacy. To argue that the United States leaders failed at Versailles in 1919 and in Vietnam in the 1960s because of their idealistic bent may be accurate, but first it must be established that Americans are idealistic, that their leaders reflect this idealism, and that their idealism is a resource for making policy.

The primary problem is to separate the common or aggregate behavioral traits from the idiosyncratic. An individual decision maker, whether he or she be the President or the newest intelligence officer in the bureaucracy, may possess the values held by a majority of American adults. He or she may have participated in the national political socialization process. But until one can more rigorously identify the aggregate behavioral traits and link them more confidently to policy decisions, the concept of national values should be used judiciously.

NOTES

1. This definition of national values is influenced by Inkeles and Levinson's definition of national character. See Alex Inkeles and Daniel Levinson, "National Character: The Study of Modal Personality and Sociocultural Systems," in Gardner Lindzey (ed.), *Handbook of Social Psychology,* vol. 2 (Reading, Mass.: Addison-Wesley, 1954), p. 973. Other definitions are offered by Sir Ernest Barker, *National Character* (London: McThuer, 1948), p. xi, and Frederick Hertz, *Nationality in History and Politics: A Study of the Psychology and Sociology of National Sentiment and Character* (New York: Oxford University Press, 1944).
2. The concept of a "basic personality structure" is developed by David M. Potter, *People of Plenty: Economic Abundance and the American Character* (Chicago: University of Chicago Press, 1962), chapter 1.
3. Congressman Otto E. Passman, Chairman of the House Appropriations Committee, *New York Times,* March 15, 1970, Sec. 4, p. 5.
4. Stanley Hoffmann, *The State of War* (New York: Praeger, 1966), p. 175.
5. David S. McLellan, "Style and Substance in American Foreign Policy," *Yale Review* 48 (Autumn 1958): 41–57.

6. The comment by Fred A. Shannon, contained in his review of David Potter's *People of Plenty* in the *Mississippi Valley Historical Review* 41 (March 1955): 733, is typical of those who doubt the existence of national character: "I can envision 162,000,000 different American characters, perhaps divisible into 327 categories with wide divergencies in each, but I cannot see an American national character." *See also* Henry Hamilton Fyfe, *The Illusion of National Character* (London: Watts and Co., 1940); Monroe Berger, "'Understanding National Character' and War," *Commentary* 11 (April 1951): 375–386; and Maurice L. Farber, "The Problem of National Character: A Methodological Analysis," *Journal of Psychology* 30 (1950): 307–316.

7. For the Realist's views of national character and American foreign policy, *see* George Kennan, *Realities of American Foreign Policy* (Princeton, N.J.: Princeton University Press, 1954), pp. 18; 35–36; and 93; and J. William Fulbright, *Arrogance of Power* (New York: Viking Press, 1966), pp. 198–200. Most textbooks on American foreign policy accept and build their analyses around the Realist view of U.S. national values. *See* Cecil V. Crabb, Jr., *Foreign Policy in the Nuclear Age*, 2nd ed. (New York: Harper & Row, 1965), pp. 21–41, and Charles O. Lerche, Jr., *Foreign Policy and the American People*, 3rd ed. (Englewood Cliffs, N.J.: Prentice-Hall, 1967).

8. *See* Frank Tannenbaum, *The American Tradition in Foreign Policy* (Norman: University of Oklahoma Press, 1955), pp. 3–37.

9. Alexis de Tocqueville's *Democracy in America* has undergone many translations into English since it first appeared. J. Hector de Crèvecoeur's *Letters from an American Farmer* first appeared in 1782.

10. Observations by numerous foreign visitors have been recorded. Among them are Harriet Martineau, *Society in America* (1837), reprinted 1970 by Da Capo Press, New York; James Fullerton Muirhead, *America, Land of Contrasts: A Briton's View of His American Kin* (1898), reprinted by Da Capo Press, New York; Hugo Munsterberg, *The Americans* (New York: McClure, Phillips, 1904); Issac Fidler, *Observations on Professions, Literature, Manners, and Emigration in the United States and Canada, Made During a Residence There in 1832* (New York: J. and J. Harper, 1833); Harold J. Laski, *The American Democracy* (1948), reprinted by Augustus M. Kelley, Clifton, N.J.; Simone de Beauvoir, *America Day by Day* (New York: Grove Press, 1953); Hans Habe, *The Wounded Land: Journey Through a Divided America* (New York: Coward-McCann, 1964); Geoffrey Gorer, *The American People: A Study in National Character*, rev. ed. (New York: W. W. Norton, 1964); D. W. Brogan, *The American Character* (1944), reprinted by Peter Smith Publishers, Gloucester, Mass.; Jane L. Mesick, *English Traveller in America, 1785–1835* (1922), reprinted by Scholarly Press, St. Clair Shores, Mich.; Max Berger, *The British Traveller in America: 1836–1860* (1922), reprinted by Peter Smith Publishers, Gloucester, Mass.; Robert W. Smuts, *European Impressions of the American Worker* (New York: King's Crown Press, 1953); Andrew J.

Torrielli, *Italian Opinion on America as Revealed by Italian Travelers: 1850–1900* (Cambridge, Mass.: Harvard University Press, 1941); and Luigi Giorgio Barzini, *Americans Are Alone in the World* (1953), reprinted in 1972 by Library Press, Freeport, N.Y.

11. Kluckhohn argues that there have been discernible shifts in American national character in only one generation's time. *See* Clyde Kluckhohn, "Have There Been Discernible Shifts in American Values During the Past Generation?" in Elting E. Morrison (ed.), *The American Style: Essays in Value and Performance* (New York: Harper & Row, 1956), pp. 145–217.

12. Examples of introspective literature written primarily by historians include: John M. Blum, *The Promise of America: An Historical Inquiry* (Boston: Houghton Mifflin, 1966); Daniel J. Boorstin, *The Americans: The National Experience* (New York: Random House, 1965); Henry Steele Commager, *The American Mind: An Interpretation of American Thought and Character Since 1880's* (New Haven, Conn.: Yale University Press, 1950); Hans Kohn, *American Nationalism: An Interpretative Essay* (New York: Macmillan, 1957); Seymour M. Lipset, *The First New Nation: The United States in Historical and Comparative Perspective* (New York: Basic Books, 1963); Robert E. Spiller and Eric Larrabee (eds.), *American Perspective: The National Self-Image in the Twentieth Century* (Cambridge, Mass.: Harvard University Press, 1961); and Max Lerner, *America as a Civilization* (New York: Simon and Schuster, 1957).

13. For the views of Mead, Horney, and Riesman, *see* Margaret Mead, *And Keep Your Powder Dry: An Anthropologist Looks at America* (New York: William Morrow, 1942); Karen Horney, *The Neurotic Personality of Our Time* (New York: W. W. Norton, 1964); and David Riesman, *The Lonely Crowd* (New Haven, Conn.: Yale University Press, 1950). *See also* Riesman's article: "Some Observations on the Study of American Character," *Psychiatry* 15 (1952): 333–338. Additional observations by behavioralists are found in John Gillin, "National and Regional Cultural Values in the United States," *Social Forces* 34 (December 1955): 105–113; Robin M. Williams, *American Society: A Sociological Interpretation*, 2nd rev. ed. (New York: Alfred A. Knopf, 1960); and Cora DuBois, "The Dominant Value Profile of American Culture," *American Anthropologist* 57 (December 1955): 1232–1239.

14. William Welch, *American Images of Soviet Foreign Policy* (New Haven, Conn.: Yale University Press, 1970).

15. Wayne Wolf, "Images of the United States in the Latin American Press," *Journalism Quarterly* 41 (1964): 79–86.

16. Gabriel A. Almond and Sidney Verba, *The Civic Culture: Political Attitudes and Democracy in Five Countries* (Princeton, N.J.: Princeton University Press, 1962).

17. Lee Coleman, "What is American? A Study of Alleged American Traits," *Social Forces* 19 (May 1941): 492–499.

18. Carl L. Kline, Katharine Rider, Karen Berry, and J. McRee Elrod, "The Young American Expatriates in Canada: Alienated or Self-defined?" *American Journal of Orthopsychiatry* 41 (January 1971): 74–94.
19. Several writers have addressed themselves to the problem of linking decisions with a decision maker's personality traits. *See* Herbert McClosky, "Personality and Attitude Correlates of Foreign Policy Orientation" in James Rosenau (ed.), *Domestic Sources of Foreign Policy* (New York: Free Press, 1967), pp. 51–109; J. David Singer, "Man and World Politics: The Psychological Interface," *Journal of Soviet Issues* 24 (1968): 127–156; and Bjorn Christiansen, *Attitudes toward Foreign Affairs as a Function of Personality* (Oslo: Oslo University Press, 1959). Two of Harold D. Lasswell's books deal with politics, power, and personality on a more general level: *Psychopathology and Politics* (Chicago: University of Chicago Press, 1930) and *Power and Personality* (New York: W. W. Norton, 1948). *See also* Fred I. Greenstein, *Personality and Politics: Problems of Evidence, Inference, and Conceptualization* (Chicago: Markham Publishing Co., 1969), chapter 5.
20. Alexander and Juliette L. George, *Woodrow Wilson and Colonel House: A Personality Study* (New York: John Day, 1956), and Sigmund Freud and William C. Bullit, *Thomas Woodrow Wilson, Twenty Eighth President of The United States: A Psychological Study* (Boston: Houghton Mifflin, 1967).
21. Arnold Rogow, *James Forrestal: A Study of Personality, Politics and Policy* (New York: Macmillan, 1963); and L. Pierce Clark, *Lincoln: A Psycho-Biography* (New York: Scribner's, 1933).
22. James David Barber, *The Presidential Character: Predicting Performance in the White House* (Englewood Cliffs, N.J.: Prentice-Hall, 1972), and Bruce Mazlish, *In Search of Nixon* (Baltimore: Penguin, 1973).
23. (New York: Praeger, 1960), pp. 26–28. This book first appeared in 1950.
24. Frank I. Klingberg, "The Historical Alternation of Moods in American Foreign Policy," *World Politics* 4 (January 1952): 239–273.
25. William R. Caspary, "The 'Mood Theory': A Study of Public Opinion and Foreign Policy," *American Political Science Review* 64 (June 1970): 536–547.

5

The Influence of Public Opinion on American Foreign Policy

Of the five domestic sources of influence on American foreign policy (national values, public opinion, mass media, political parties, and interest groups), public opinion has gained the most attention, and it is currently being extensively researched by several disciplines. Political scientists, sociologists, and psychologists have exhibited a continuing interest in the public's expressions on issues, as well as the opinion of individuals who comprise the public. Despite all of this scholarly attention, none of the domestic sources is more replete with popular misunderstandings, myths, and blatant inaccuracies than public opinion. Although proponents of the four images of American foreign policy have debated extensively the role of public opinion, they have failed to answer questions on its composition, role, and actual impact on policymaking.

THE IMAGES AND PUBLIC OPINION

The Realists

The Realists do not express much confidence in public opinion as a guide to making foreign policy decisions. Their approach, rather, is to place the formulation and implementation process in the hands of those who are professionally competent; thus, their approach can be labeled *professional diplomacy*.[1]

The Realists assume that the most effective diplomacy is secret diplomacy. Diplomatic endeavors conducted in the full glare of publicity, such as summit conferences, result in rigid negotiating positions because the negotiators are seldom inclined to depart from their publicized positions. Consequently, diplomacy should be carried on without publicity so that negotiators can compromise without the humiliation of retreating from original policy positions and without the fear of losing public support.

The Realists further point out that the public is most often uninformed, and sometimes misinformed, on issues of contemporary foreign policy because decisions must be based on intelligence reports which usually cannot be revealed to the public. Even if the public possessed sufficient information to take a position on an issue, it would be difficult to tap their views. Their responses to public opinion polls are too simplistic to fit the realities of contemporary foreign policy. Foreign policy alternatives seldom correspond to answers of "yes," "no," or "no opinion." Policy formulation and implementation are replete with nuances of meaning that cannot be captured by a polling question.

Foreign policy is dynamic and must change to meet new challenges; the views of the body politic cannot be consulted readily whenever events demand a change in policy. Mass opinion is slow to crystallize, the Realists contend, and the decision maker cannot wait for the public to be apprised of new circumstances, make up its mind, and then state its preferences.

The Realists also argue that public opinion is malleable and can be molded to fit the policy decision after the national leader makes up his mind. Public opinion should be the result, not the initiator, of foreign policy decisions. An adept President can persuade the public to support policy alternatives that he has chosen on the basis of intelligence reports and professional advice.

The professional diplomacy approach of the Realists can be criticized for assuming a monolithic public when in fact there are three groups: a small elite group, a knowledgeable and concerned public, and the masses. The masses may be uninformed and lethargic, but the elite and knowledgeable publics usually are aware of international developments. Moreover, the professional diplomacy approach assumes that the most common decision-making situation is a crisis, when events develop rapidly. Crises may occur with regularity but not always in the same region of the world. There are periods of reasonable calm between political storms when the public opinion can crystallize and be identified by decision makers.

The Liberals

The Liberals, on the other hand, posit a *citizen diplomacy* approach to foreign policy; i.e., the citizen's opinion should influence American policy.[2] The citizen diplomacy approach assumes that the public is inherently peace loving, as pointed out in chapter 3. War results from selfish special interests, such as munitions manufacturers, and from the secret agreements made by professional diplomats without consultation with the public. If the voice of the people were heard, peace would result. Since the goal of diplomacy is to implement the *national* interest, not a *group* or *elite* interest, American foreign policy should be an extension of the beliefs of the total population.

The citizen diplomacy hypothesis about the cause of war can be seriously questioned. Wars occur for a complexity of reasons, and not only because leaders fail to heed the voice of the people. No evidence exists that national leaders are more inclined toward martial behavior than private citizens.

The Revisionists

Both Left-Wing and Right-Wing Revisionists logically extend their arguments made in connection with national values. Both feel that the people more accurately reflect the views embedded in their critiques. The Revisionists, however, express the concern that the voice of the people may be manipulated by predominant forces in society. The Right-Wing advocates would point to liberal influences in American colleges and universities that mislead young minds in their opinions about government. Other liberal influences exist as well, such as the press and other instruments of mass media.

The Revisionists of the Left also see a manipulation, if not control, of the people's voice, but they identify the culprit as the capitalist orientation of American society. The business interests may not own newspapers, but the local press is dependent on advertising from community business. Thus, editorial policy is dictated by the need for advertising revenue. The public is fed a menu of news and views that will not alienate advertisers.

The Revisionists, therefore, have their own version of citizen diplomacy. The citizen's voice, even if heard, does not have a potent public forum from which to accurately state its views.

The Actual Influence of Public Opinion

The debates between the proponents of the four images center around a normative judgment of the role of public opinion. They focus on the question, "What *should* be the role of public opinion in the American foreign policymaking process?" This question is important, but the student of contemporary U.S. diplomacy must choose another anchor point: "What is the role of public opinion and does it influence policy?" The image-advocates bog down their analysis in a morass of value judgments built upon deep-seated assumptions which, as polemicists, they seldom question. We have at our disposal a plethora of studies on public opinion which help to determine the extent to which public opinion does in fact influence American foreign policy.

THE COMPOSITION OF PUBLIC OPINION

Types of Publics

The initial error committed by the image-holders is to conceive of public opinion as a monolithic structure when actually three distinguishable publics contribute to public opinion.[3] Each public is composed of different segments of American society and each segment possesses identifiable views on American foreign policy.

The Influential Public. The influential public (or the elite or opinion-making public) is composed of individuals who hold positions of leadership in society. They occupy managerial, official, or proprietary positions; they tend to be well-educated, wealthy, white, male, Protestant, and Anglo-Saxon; and they have access to channels of communication to disseminate their views to the other two publics and to the decision makers. Because of their financial, political, and social status, the influentials have an impact on other members in society. They are looked up to, perhaps respected, perhaps feared.

The influentials play a pivotal role in the flow of information from the government to the public and from the public to the government. The other two publics, especially the knowledgeables, usually take their cue from positions on foreign policy articulated by the influentials. The influential public's pivotal position is largely due to their access to the instruments of mass media. An influential member may be the editor of the local newspaper, the mayor, the head of a labor union, a prominent minister, or a friend with whom the President or congressmen will occasionally consult. Individuals belonging to the influential public sector either have direct access to the instruments of mass media or have control over the distribution of an in-house communication (such as a newsletter) or have informal access to the decision maker. Other members of the public will look to the influentials for guidance on contemporary political issues.

The influential public is a variegated public. They disagree among themselves over the best course for American foreign policy, and they compete with one another to mobilize the knowledgeables and the masses to adopt their position. Individuals in key media roles, in positions of leadership of major groupings, and in personal contact with important decision makers must mobilize support to confirm the fact that they are, indeed, influential. On any issue of concern, the influential will have his following express themselves to the decision makers, taking a prescribed, united position.

The Knowledgeable Public. The knowledgeables are acquainted with many of the contemporary policy positions in U.S. diplomacy. They tend to be businessmen with a wide range of international experiences, leaders of organizations that deal with world affairs (such as the United Nations Association), and local politicians, educators, lawyers, and journalists who have developed an interest in foreign affairs. Some white-collar and skilled workers are found among them. "Attentive" and "opinion-holding" are other terms used to refer to the knowledgeable public.

The General Public. The general public rarely has crystallized views on international affairs. Its opinions of foreign policy are conjured up on the spur of the moment in the midst of an important national event; thus, the general opinion often vacillates between intense interest and total apathy. The general public is populated primarily by high school graduates, unskilled and skilled workers, and farmers; they possess little information about international affairs and tend to be pessimistic about the outcome of world problems.

Size of the Publics. How large is each of the three publics? The influentials compose a small segment of the population, perhaps 3 to 5 percent. The knowledgeables are estimated as comprising 20 to 30 percent. Finally, the general public is quite large, representing an overwhelming 65 to 75 percent of the adult population. These percentages will vary from state to state; larger general publics exist in the South and Midwest and larger knowledgeable publics live in the coastal states. The size of the influential public probably remains the same in all regions.[4]

Divergent Opinions of the Three Publics

Differences between the three publics are not confined to their composition.[5] Because of the educational, occupational, and social distinctions between the three groups, their views on foreign policy issues also are divergent.

Positions on Issues. The more knowledgeable a citizen is about foreign policy, the more flexible and analytical he is in his approach to issues; the less knowledgeable public is more vague and obtuse in its response. The better-informed citizen often will assume positions that are unpopular with the mass public, such as advocating in the 1950s and 1960s that the People's Republic of China delegation replace the delegation representing the Republic of China at the United Nations.

Differences also exist on specific issues. People who are better-informed about world affairs support the United Nations more strongly than those who are less informed; those who are knowledgeable about the Soviet Union are more optimistic about Russo-American relations; and, surprisingly, the better-informed a citizen is, the more likely he is to advocate the use of military power to solve foreign policy problems. The knowledgeable citizens were more inclined to support the Korean war and to favor escalation of America's military commitment during the Vietnamese conflict.[6]

Foreign Affairs Literacy. Since "more informed" and "less informed" are relative categories, it is necessary to establish a basis for classifying the foreign affairs knowledge quotient for the American public. This task is complicated by the variety of tests employed by researchers to determine a subject's knowledge of foreign affairs. Free and Cantril classified 25 percent of the American public as "well informed," 35 percent as "moderately informed" and only 40 percent as "uninformed."[7] Although the "uninformed" category is alarmingly large, the "well-informed" group is portrayed as larger than the influential or elite public. This implies that some members of the general public are at least "moderately informed," since the general public constitutes 65 to 75 percent of the American population. If we accept Free and Cantril's statistics, there are individuals in the general public that know about foreign affairs even though they are motivated to express their opinions only rarely. Other studies, however, have higher standards for classifying "informed" and "uninformed" citizens.[8]

Isolationist Attitudes. Despite the relatively large percentage of uninformed citizens who are traditionally thought to advocate isolationism, American public opinion has avoided the temptation to withdraw into an isolationist shell. Throughout most of the post-World War II era, less than 10 percent of the American public has embraced isolationism. Most Americans are either satisfied with their country's current level of involvement or want the United States to play an even larger role in world affairs. The citizen in the general-public category may be frustrated and confused over foreign policy issues, but he does not believe that the United States should hide its collective head in the sands of isolationism. The Gallup Poll in recent years has reflected a new trend toward isolationism developing among the American people.[9]

Individual Classification

These observations about public opinion are based on studies using aggregate data to compile a composite of the three publics. Where an individual citizen fits into these ideal classifications depends on his or her education, occupation, economic status, and position in professional or civic organizations. As products of aggregate data, these classifications may appear to be violated in specific cases, e.g., by individuals who because of education and economic status are considered knowledgeables, but who are disinterested in international events. Other factors that influence opinions of the occupants of these three broad classifications must be considered. Party identification has an impact as do the instruments of mass media. These influences will be discussed in following chapters.

ARTICULATION OF PUBLIC OPINION

To influence the decision maker's selection of policy alternatives, the publics must articulate their opinions.[10] The influential, knowledgeable, and general publics use different methods of articulation and are effective in reaching the decision maker with varying degrees of success.

The Influentials' Articulation. The influential public usually will have direct, face-to-face access to both executive and legislative decision makers. Only a few members of the elite will have direct access to the President personally, and the choice of these elites will depend on the President's preferences for advisers, the strength of the group that the influentials represent, and whether or not a crisis exists. A President, for example, who does not consult with AFL-CIO leaders may be forced to listen to labor elites if their support is needed in a current crisis.

If congressional hearings are held on an issue (e.g., foreign aid or subsidies to shipbuilders), the influentials will represent their group's views to representatives or senators. Sometimes these appearances are made by individuals other than the president or chairman of the group, such as lobbyists. In chapter 7, the functions of the special interest group will be discussed.

The local influential public also has access to civic, professional, educational, and political organizations to express their views. The most influential businessmen, for example, will be active in the Chamber of Commerce, Jaycees, National Association of Manufacturers, and a host of lesser known groups. These organizations often host receptions for the congressman representing their district and articulate their views on contemporary political problems, some of which are foreign policy issues. The same format is duplicated by local physicians, ministers, school teachers, ethnic minorities, and women (through the League of Women Voters and American Association of University Women, for example), as well as local political party leaders.

The Knowledgeables' Articulation. The knowledgeable public possesses fewer channels through which to express its opinions. The knowledgeables do have occasion to hear congressmen and sometimes senators when these representatives appear before general audiences for speeches. Opportunities to reach representatives during question-and-answer periods or during receiving-line ceremonies are obviously quite limited. The knowledgeables write letters to decision makers, but otherwise they must depend, as members of groups, on their elites to express faithfully their opinions to the policymaker.

The General Public's Articulation. The general public has no potent medium through which to express its articulations—infrequent though they may be—except through occasional letters or in response to public-opinion polling. These polls, which also sample influential and knowledgeable opinions, are taken by established national organizations on a regular basis; they may also be contracted for a special purpose by a member of the legislative or executive branch.

Letterwriting. Although writing letters to decision makers is one method for expressing opinions that is available to all three publics, it is resorted to by only a small segment of the total public, and this segment tends to be ideologically motivated. A study of the 1964 elections found that approximately three percent of the population wrote letters to newspaper editors, the President, and congressmen. The letterwriters were largely advocates of Right-Wing Revisionism, and the extreme conservatives were the most prolific authors. In one comparison of letterwriting and non-letterwriting publics, both groups favored negotiating with the Soviet Union, but the letterwriting group was less favorable.

Letterwriting is an example of the difficulties encountered in assessing public opinion's influence on political leaders. Congressmen, the President, and cabinet secretaries are attentive to communications that they receive and they will attempt to answer every one. But decision makers also declare that they do not formulate policy on the basis of the content of their mailbag. In effect, the incoming mail offers an opportunity for the policymaker to explain his position to the interested citizen in a personal reply. Mail received that is critical of the policy currently pursued often motivates the political leader to work harder to convince people of his position; it seldom influences him to change his mind on the issue itself. President Gerald Ford's pardon of former President Nixon in 1974 attracted mail from the public that was generally critical. Despite this public response, Ford continued to defend his decision.

Influence and the Influentials. Although the influentials articulate their opinions to policymakers, it does not necessarily mean that they influence the selection of an alternative under consideration. The influential public is composed of elites who may be vocal in their views but may not affect the behavior of executive and legislative decision makers in Washington.

The problem in analyzing the impact of public opinion on foreign policy is the amorphous word "influence," which is used often but without a precise definition. While the word "influential" refers to a segment of the public, "influence" refers to the active "capability to change behavior." The question, then, is whether or not public opinion *in any form*—visits by important people, opinion surveys, editorials—has influenced a decision maker to choose one policy over another, to undertake a policy he was reluctant to accept previously, or to desist from endorsing an unpopular policy.

The Decision Maker's Attitude toward Public Opinion. Part of the problem in assessing the extent to which public opinion influences policy selection is the attitude of the decision makers themselves. Most policy leaders claim that they are seldom guided by public-opinion polls or letters from constituents on foreign policy matters. Although most decision makers might not display Harry Truman's bluntness, they would subscribe to his judgment that "a man who is influenced by the polls or is afraid to make decisions which may make him unpopular is not a man to represent the welfare of the country." Truman did not listen to the ill-informed general public whose opinion might have changed overnight. He also wrote that polls did not represent a cross section of the nation: "I do not believe that the major components of our society, such as agriculture, management, and labor, were adequately sampled."[11] To Truman, agriculture, management, and labor were important voices in his decision-making patterns. Since each decision maker brings to his position his own pattern of communication with the influential public, certain groups have access to him on foreign policy issues, while the voices of others are blocked out.

The question raised by Truman's remarks is whether or not the testimony of a decision maker on public opinion's effect on him during the policy process should be taken at face value. Since a President must play a role of formulating policy "above politics," acting in the "national interest" (rather than in a "group interest"), and being his "own man," he might be reluctant to admit that he had yielded to domestic pressure in his policy choices. Or he may not be conscious of pressure from political factions while making a decision; he may, for example, identify the elites with whom he consults as "advisers," rather than as spokesmen for a segment of the influential public.

The President or a congressman may not recognize public opinion's influence on his decisions because he is thinking in terms of polls, letters, or editorials. Public opinion still reaches him, but in a form that may be disguised. For example, a policy decision is frequently made with an eye toward upcoming elections; an election is an expression of public opinion, too. One of the reasons that President Johnson in 1968 decided to build a limited anti-ballistic missile system was Republican pressure to make the ABM a campaign issue.[12]

Past campaign promises may also enter into a President's decision, and again, he may not consider them particularly responsive to public opinion. John Kennedy, while campaigning during the 1960 election, criticized the Republican Party for its laxity in responding to Fidel Castro's revolution in Cuba. Although he had serious misgivings about the Bay of Pigs plan to invade Cuba in 1962, one reason he approved it was his campaign promise to take a firm stand against Communism in Cuba.[13]

Two Case Studies. The Vietnam War during the 1960s and the Quemoy and Matsu crisis of 1958 are two events that offer some insight into the effect of public opinion on decision making. These two events in the history of contemporary foreign policy represent instances of the influence—or lack of influence—of public opinion on governmental decisions.

In 1958, the People's Republic of China appeared to be planning an invasion of two islands off the Chinese coast, Quemoy and Matsu, which were held by the Taiwan government of Chiang Kai-shek. Secretary of State Dulles declared that it was the intention of the American government to defend Chiang Kai-shek's government, and any attack on these islands would be considered a prelude to an invasion of Taiwan. Dulles' policy was both praised and criticized in the press, but public-opinion polls reported that a majority of those sampled opposed war over the offshore islands.

Later that year, Secretary Dulles began to change the thrust of American policy. Although the U.S. government would protect Chiang Kai-shek's government, Washington did not feel as obligated to protect the offshore islands. Did the lack of public support influence Dulles to relent? It is "doubtful," one researcher reported, that the "intense and voluminous" public opinion during the Quemoy crisis "in any way affected the substance of American policy." In fact, she concludes, public opinion might have overreacted to a crisis that was not a crisis at all: "Perhaps the American press was overexcited and the American people underinformed. . . ."[14] The decision maker may not have changed his policy in the first place, or the American public was excited over an issue that did not exist.

The Vietnam War provides another case study of public opinion and foreign policy. Opposition to the war began to build during the Johnson administration and was expressed largely through the campaigns of senators Eugene McCarthy and Robert Kennedy for the Democratic nomination for President. Frequent demonstrations were held against the war, adding a new vehicle for the expression of public opinion.

One study of public opinion during the Vietnam War found that the American people were very confused.[15] Only blacks and women in the late 1960s began to form definite views, both in opposition to American involvement in the fighting. Black leaders, such as Rev. Martin Luther King, were sensitive to these views and began to express their disapproval of American behavior in Indochina. While a majority of the American public continued to voice support of the Vietnam War, this support was gradually eroded toward the end of the 1960s and the beginning of the 1970s.

Did American public opinion influence the U.S. government to reduce its commitment to Vietnam? This case study found that President Johnson was faced with as much pressure to escalate the American involvement as he received from groups that wanted withdrawal. As a result, he tried to steer a middle course, satisfying neither those favoring escalation nor those demanding deescalation. The majority of the American public was befuddled about the issues involved in the conflict, about U.S. foreign policy goals, and about the guerrilla military tactics that characterized the fighting.

In addition to the public's possible overexcitability, they can also be confused; neither one of these conditions offers any guidelines with which to assess the influence of public opinion on foreign policymaking. When public opinion does influence foreign policymaking, its impact may be subtle, amorphous, contradictory, and inconclusive, as these case studies illustrate.

MOBILIZING PUBLIC OPINION

While the three publics, especially the elites, attempt to articulate their views and focus them on the decision makers engaged in formulating policy, the decision makers also are mobilizing the publics to support their own positions. The President is usually the chief mobilizer because he is the single individual who can command all of the instruments of mass communication to explain his position. Opinion mobilization is especially necessary when he orders unpopular initiatives that he considers in the national interest, or when he undertakes tasks that are open to misinterpretation and misunderstanding.

Mobilizing the Three Publics

Because the three publics are different in composition and attitude, each is mobilized by different approaches.

Mobilization of the Influentials. Since the influentials directly converse with those individuals who make policy, the decision makers in turn use face-to-face meetings to mobilize support among the influentials. In 1958, the Eisenhower administration invited leaders of various political, social, economic, educational, and cultural groups to Washington to explain the foreign-aid program to them and to mobilize support for a specific policy.[16] Other vehicles for informing public leaders and gaining their assistance are the citizen advisory committees that liberally populate the governmental structure. Examples are the Trade Expansion Act Advisory Committee, the Advisory Committee on International Educational and Cultural Affairs, and the Maritime Advisory Committee. Almost every major governmental activity in foreign affairs has an advisory commission which periodically brings together influential American citizens and the decision makers, and which serve as two-way channels of articulation and mobilization.

Mobilization of the Knowledgeables. Since the knowledgeable public is attentive to international developments, it follows closely the policy statements made by decision makers. The knowledgeables are responsive to policy changes and usually are aware of shifts in the government's positions. Government spokesmen also attempt to keep the knowledgeable public informed through speeches before social groups. Of the policy statements printed in the 1966 *Department of State Bulletin,* over 30 percent were delivered before domestic audiences. Academic groups were most often addressed, followed by mass media, business, and foreign policy study organizations. The knowledgeable public may not converse directly with the decision makers, but it does have opportunities to hear them speak before group audiences.[17] Thus, mobilization of the knowledgeable public is an on-going process. Government officials, especially those at the sub-cabinet level (e.g., assistant secretaries of state), accept speaking engagements as a means of mobilizing the knowledgeable public to support government policy.

While letterwriting is one channel of articulation for the ideologically motivated, it also represents a channel of mobilization for the decision maker. In 1951 Department of State personnel sorted the mail received during the period that the Senate was considering the Japanese peace treaty.[18] The letters were divided into two categories: letters that were general, inaccurate, and even irrelevant to the issue, and letters written at length on letterhead stationery or carrying symbols that identified the writers as occupying an uncommon position within the social structure. John Foster Dulles, who in 1951 was an adviser to Secretary of State Dean Acheson, answered personally and in detail most of the letters from the latter group. Letterwriting, therefore, became an instrument to mobilize opinion among the knowledgeable public, as well as a means through which the knowledgeables could articulate their position.

Mobilizing the General Public. Mobilizing the general public is a task for the President.[19] A presidential address delivered over nationwide radio and television during prime time alerts the general public to a major policy initiative; it is also used to explain the rationale behind the government's present policy. Since general public opinion responds radically to external stimuli, the President may speak to reassure, as well as to mobilize. His target is not to inform the influential and knowledgeable publics; the majority of these groups already know about international events, although there is no guarantee that they will agree with the President's proposals.

Effectiveness of Mobilization

How effective are the government's attempts to mobilize public opinion? The knowledgeables do not present a difficult mobilization task because they tend to endorse the government's policy.[20] The major mobilization task is directed toward the general public whose attention must be shifted from daily activities central to their thinking to foreign policy matters which seem peripheral to their lives. The general public cannot be mobilized to fever pitch too often, or the technique will lose its effectiveness. Nor can the mobilization drive be sustained for a long period of time. Kennedy mobilized the general public for twelve days during the October 1962 Cuban missile crisis, but Truman was unable to mobilize it for two-and-one-half years during the Korean conflict (June 1950 to January 1953). The President also pays a price for mobilizing the general public: he sacrifices flexibility of alternatives in order to focus the public's attention on one goal, and he irreparably commits his nation to a specific course of action. His appeal tends to be on ideological and emotional grounds.

Mobilization from Without

In addition to the mobilization activities of the national government, foreign governments and groups outside the United States also undertake mobilization attempts. International sources of mobilization include the governments of other nations, international organizations (such as the United Nations), regional groupings (such as the European Economic Community), revolutionary groups out-of-power who need American support, and multinational private actors (such as religious groups, General Motors, and the Ford Foundation). The public, as well as the American government, reacts to events in the international system, which can range from wars, civil strife, and revolutions, on one end of the spectrum, to an international beauty contest, the Olympic games, or a grand-master chess match, on the other end.

Effect of External Events on the Publics. After a policy decision has been made, most of the members of the influential and knowledgeable publics are aware of it, while the general public is not. An external stimulus from another country (a threat, for example) also will have divergent effects on the three publics. The general public will react most mercurially to the stimulus, and the influential public will take note of it with little disequilibrium. The knowledgeable public will react with less instability than the general public, but not with the equilibrium of the influentials. Furthermore, the effect on the general public will be transitory: polls show that general public opinion usually slips back to its pre-event position. Although the influentials respond least in the beginning, the effect of the event remains in their memory. Again, the knowledgeables are midway between the general and influential publics in their return to a pre-event position.

Foreign Evaluation of U.S. Public Opinion. It is risky diplomacy for foreign governments to rely on their own evaluation of American public opinion, contrasting it to government policy, and attempting to find areas of conflict. Public expressions may exist which contradict official policy, but a foreign government may not be able to accurately distinguish between "in-group" and "out-group" influentials. For example, criticism of the Vietnam War in 1967-68 came from influentials whom President Johnson, in the main, ignored. The Hanoi government probably noted with interest the President's dilemma, but the North Vietnamese evidently did not base their policy decisions on these public buffetings. Nor did all the public demonstrations of protest carry as much weight in presidential decision making as did the defeats inflicted by the North Vietnamese and Vietcong troops during the February 1968 Tet offensive. As a result of that offensive, the American military requested 200,000 more troops for Vietnam, a 40 percent increase in strength, which President Johnson was not willing to grant.[21] Attempts during the Johnson and Nixon administrations to describe critics of U.S. policy in Vietnam as "unpatriotic" and an "encouragement to the enemy" were based on the assumption that Hanoi's policy put more emphasis on American internal division than on Communist strength in the field.

Public Opinion, Congress, the President, and the Bureaucracy

The views of the public are a more potent influence on the congressman than on the President for a number of reasons that will be developed in later chapters: the instruments of mass media are more significant as a source of information for Congress than for the presidency; the entire House of Representatives and one-third of the Senate face election every two years (which brings public opinion into Congress, not in terms of polling, but through the ballot box); and the President has another source of views and information not largely available to Congress—the federal bureaucracy.

Any discussion of the influence of public opinion on foreign policy must take into account the bureaucracy, which is largely insulated from pressures of the knowledgeable and general publics. The elites, especially influential leaders of interest groups, may have access to personnel in the bureaucracy, as will be discussed in chapter 7. The bureaucracy is largely immune to public opinion, except as it is interpreted by the elected President and Vice-President and the appointed cabinet and subcabinet individuals. The career bureaucrat's position does not depend on satisfying any segment of the public—influentials, knowledgeables, or general. His position raises the question of to what extent is a democracy's foreign policy truely democratic.

ORIGIN OF POPULAR SUPPORT

Mobilization–articulation activities create the problem of distinguishing the stimulus from the response: Are the publics merely articulating views that the government has converted them to? If the President initiates a popular policy—one that is supported by a majority of the American public—has he listened to the voice of the people or have they listened to him? A combination of both these factors may exist in policy formulation. The elected decision maker may keep his ear tuned to the public's articulation to determine if the people have understood the current policy pronouncements. If the public misinterprets the current policy, then the political leader may conclude that a new mobilization program is needed to jell support. Or the President may allow subordinates to announce new policy tacks, especially those that are not considered to be of prime importance. Policy explanations and justifications can come from the President's press secretary, Secretary of State or Defense, or the President's Special Assistant for National Security Affairs.

If public opinion articulations—polls, letters, editorials, demonstrations—do not register the degree of approval of foreign policy that the President would like to see, he may decide that a personal statement is needed to channel public opinion in the direction that he believes it should be headed. The elected official often may appear to be listening to the "voice of the people" by monitoring their opinions, when actually he is auditing their reactions to determine if additional mobilization efforts should be undertaken to educate and to propagandize the American public.

No elected official, especially the President, should place his continuation in office above the interests of the American nation. If the President believes that he should formulate diplomatic objectives on the basis of the public's views in order to stay in office, he runs the risk of basing his country's foreign policy on premises that are seldom well developed and may oscillate. No President can retain his popularity in the manner that Speaker of the House Cannon characterized President McKinley. The President, Cannon observed, kept "his ear so close to the ground he got it full of grasshoppers."[22]

It is difficult to be optimistic about the role of public opinion as a domestic influence on the foreign policy process after perusing the data from studies presented in this chapter. Obviously, the American public in general is not sufficiently informed on issues of diplomacy. Improvement in public opinion, in terms of more interest taken in foreign affairs, will come slowly, if at all. Opinion is related to educational level, economic status, and social position, all of which help to create a conglomeration of internal values. Through these values the citizen views the world and its problems. If the priority of values places foreign affairs below personal and domestic concerns, then the populace will be apathetic and ignorant about events in the international system and what the American government does about them.

NOTES

1. Some Realist writers focus in particular on the defects of public opinion. Geoffrey Chandler believes that consideration of American public opinion retards and inhibits effective decision making. See his "American Opinion and Foreign Policy," *International Affairs* 31 (October 1955): 447–458. One of the themes of Thomas A. Bailey's *The Man in the Street: The Impact of American Public Opinion on Foreign Policy* (New York: Macmillan, 1948) is that popular sovereignty is responsible for many of the irrational demands placed on the American decision maker. Max Beloff's *Foreign Policy and the Democratic Process* (Baltimore: Johns Hopkins Press, 1955) identifies three dynamic elements in American foreign policy: the Soviet challenge, the public mood, and the expert's assessment of the international situation. He bemoans the fact that the public mood has taken precedence over the expert's viewpoint.
2. For additional information on citizen diplomacy, *see* James Marshall, "Citizen Diplomacy," *American Political Science Review* 43 (February 1949): 83–90, and Elmer Davis, *"Vox Populi* and Foreign Policy," *Harper's* 204 (June 1952): 66–73. Department of State spokesmen have often attempted to convince their audiences that public views are important in the policymaking process. *See* John W. Hanes, Jr., "The Citizen and Foreign Policy," *Department of State Bulletin* 42 (May 16, 1960): 791–797, and H. Schuyler Foster, "Role of the Public in U.S. Foreign Relations," *Department of State Bulletin* 43 (Nov. 28, 1960): 823–831. One outspoken supporter of citizen diplomacy is Dexter Perkins. *See* his collection of essays, *Foreign Policy and the Democratic Spirit,* edited by Glyndon G. Van Deusen and Richard C. Wade (Ithaca, N.Y.: Cornell University Press, 1957).
3. The earliest study of public opinion and foreign policy to appear in the post-World War II period was by Leonard S. Cottrell, Jr. and Sylvia Eberhart, *American Opinion on World Affairs* (Princeton, N.J.: Princeton University Press, 1948). The two most significant works on the relationship of foreign policy to public opinion are Gabriel A. Almond, *The American People and Foreign Policy* (New York: Praeger, 1950), whose approach was explained in chapter 4, and James N. Rosenau, *Public Opinion and Foreign Policy* (New York: Random House, 1961).

4. Calculations on the size of the three publics began with Bernard C. Cohen, "The Military Policy Public," *Public Opinion Quarterly* 30 (Summer 1966): 200–211, who reported that 32 percent of his sample comprised a "foreign policy public" (or knowledgeable public). Other studies listed above in Note 3 also touch upon this topic. Admittedly, estimates of size are tenuous.
5. Differences in beliefs and life style among the influential, knowledgeable, and general publics are discussed in: Kenneth P. Adler and Davis Bobrow, "Interest and Influence in Foreign Affairs," *Public Opinion Quarterly* 20 (Spring 1956): 89–101; Paul Smith, "Opinions, Publics, and World Affairs in the United States," *Western Political Quarterly* 14 (September 1961): 698–714; William C. Rogers, Barbara Stuhler, and Donald Koening, "A Comparison of Informed and General Public Opinion on U.S. Foreign Policy," *Public Opinion Quarterly* 31 (Summer 1967): 242–252; Eugene J. Rosi, "Mass and Attentive Opinion on Nuclear Weapon Tests and Fallout, 1954–1963," *Public Opinion Quarterly* (Summer 1965): 280–297; M. Brewster Smith, "The Personal Setting of Public Opinions: A Study of Attitudes Toward Russia," *Public Opinion Quarterly* 11 (Winter 1947): 507–523; Milton J. Rosenberg, "Attitude Change and Foreign Policy in the Cold War Era," in James N. Rosenau (ed.), *Domestic Sources of Foreign Policy* (New York: Free Press, 1967), pp. 111–159; Donald J. Devine, *The Attentive Public: Polyarchical Democracy* (Chicago: Rand McNally, 1970). In most of these studies, the influential and knowledgeable publics are usually grouped together as "well informed" and their views are contrasted with the larger, less informed general public.
6. Edward A. Suchman, Rose K. Goldsen, and Robin H. Williams, Jr., "Attitudes Toward the Korean War," *Public Opinion Quarterly* 17 (Summer 1953): 171–184; Richard F. Hamilton, "A Research Note on the Mass Support for 'Tough' Military Initiatives," *American Sociological Review* 33 (1968): 439–441; John E. Mueller, *War, Presidents and Public Opinion* (New York: John Wiley and Sons, 1973). One study, however, found an increasing anti-war attitude among students generated by the Vietnam War. Vietnam may be the beginning of a new pattern of attitudes for the knowledgeables. See Roger B. Handberg, Jr., "The 'Vietnam Analogy': Student Attitudes on War," *Public Opinion Quarterly* 36 (Winter 1972–73): 612–615.
7. Lloyd A. Free and Handley Cantril, *The Political Beliefs of Americans: A Study of Public Opinion* (New Brunswick, N.J.: Rutgers University Press, 1967), p. 61.
8. Alfred O. Hero, *Americans in World Affairs* (Boston: World Peace Foundation, 1959), p. 6. Hero uses four continua: interest, information, realistic analysis, and action. He estimates that only one percent of the adult population would approach the upper reaches of each continuum. He would make the general public much larger than the figure suggested in this chapter.
9. Statistics on attitudes of isolationism versus attitudes of internationalism

expressed by the American public are given in Elmo Roper, "American Attitudes on World Organization," *Public Opinion Quarterly* 22 (Winter 1958): 464–472, and Lloyd A. Free and Handley Cantril, *The Political Beliefs of Americans: A Study of Public Opinion* (New Brunswick, N.J.: Rutgers University Press, 1967), p. 65. Their data undermine Graebner's argument that the American people tend to slip into isolationism periodically. See Norman A. Graebner, *The New Isolationism: A Study in Politics and Foreign Policy Since 1950* (New York: Ronald Press, 1960).

10. Decision makers' attitudes toward mail and public-opinion polls have been examined in L. E. Gleeck, "96 Congressmen Make Up Their Minds," *Public Opinion Quarterly* 4 (March 1940): 3–24; Rowena Wyant, "Voting via the Senate Mailbag (I)," *Public Opinion Quarterly* 5 (Fall 1941): 359–382; Rowena Wyant and Herta Herzog, "Voting via the Senate Mailbag (II)," *Public Opinion Quarterly* 5 (Winter 1941): 590–624; Louis A. Dexter, "What Do Congressmen Hear: The Mail," *Public Opinion Quarterly* 20 (Spring 1956): 16–26; Winston Allard, "Congressional Attitudes Toward Public Opinion," *Journalism Quarterly* 20 (1941): 47–50; Martin Kriesberg, "What Congressmen and Administrators Think of the Polls," *Public Opinion Quarterly* 9 (Fall 1945): 333–337. Kriesberg found that polls were considered "helpful" more by executive officials than by congressmen. The study of the 1964 elections of people who wrote letters was conducted by Philip E. Converse, Aage R. Clausen, and Warren E. Miller, "Electional Myth and Reality: The 1964 Election," *American Political Science Review* 59 (June 1965): 321–336. Sidney Verba and Richard Brody examine various "message" channels, including letterwriting, used by concerned citizens during the Vietnam War in their article, "Participation, Policy Preferences, and the War in Vietnam," *Public Opinion Quarterly* 34 (Fall 1970): 325–332.

11. These two quotes from Harry Truman are from his *Memoirs, 1946–1952, Years of Trial and Hope,* vol. 2 (New York: New American Library, 1956), pp. 208 and 228. Clearly Truman was writing about a cross section of politically powerful individuals. Most polls assume that democracy and majority rule prevail and that the response of an individual in the general public is equal in political power to that of an influential citizen.

12. Morton H. Halperin, "The Decision to Deploy the ABM: Bureaucratic and Domestic Politics in the Johnson Administration," *World Politics* 25 (October 1972): 83.

13. Thomas Halper, *Foreign Policy Crises: Appearance and Reality in Decision Making* (Columbus, Ohio: Charles E. Merrill, 1971), p. 41.

14. Marian D. Irish, "Public Opinion and American Foreign Policy: The Quemoy Crisis of 1958," *Political Quarterly* 31 (April–June 1960): 162.

15. Sidney Verba, Richard A. Brody, Edwin B. Parker, Norman H. Nie, Nelson W. Polsby, Paul Ekman, and Gordon S. Black, "Public Opinion

and the War in Vietnam," *American Political Science Review* 61 (June 1967): 317–333. *See also* Milton J. Rosenberg, Sidney Verba, and Philip E. Converse, *Vietnam and the Silent Majority* (New York: Harper & Row, 1970).

16. James N. Rosenau, *National Leadership and Foreign Policy: A Case Study in Mobilization of Public Support* (Princeton, N.J.: Princeton University Press, 1963).
17. Gene E. Rainey (ed.), *Contemporary American Foreign Policy: The Official Voice* (Columbus, Ohio: Charles Merrill, 1969), pp. 13–16.
18. Bernard C. Cohen, *The Political Process and Foreign Policy: The Making of the Japanese Peace Settlement* (Princeton, N.J.: Princeton University Press, 1963).
19. Ithiel de Sola Pool, in "Public Opinion and the Control of Armaments," *Daedalus* 89 (Fall 1960): 984–999, argues that public opinion can be mobilized and controlled by the President, a position that has wide acceptance and need not be documented extensively.
20. Support for the conclusion that the knowledgeable public tends to follow the government's position is found in Donald N. Michael, "The Beginning of the Space Age and American Public Opinion," *Public Opinion Quarterly* 24 (Winter 1960): 573–582, and Gabriel A. Almond, "Public Opinion and the Development of Space Technology," *Public Opinion Quarterly* 24 (Winter 1960): 553–572.
21. "The Vietnam Policy Reversal of 1968," *New York Times*, March 6 and 7, 1969.
22. Quoted in Theodore C. Sorenson, *Decision-Making in the White House* (New York: Columbia University Press, 1963), p. 50.

6

The Controversial Role of Mass Media in U.S. Diplomacy

In the 1960s and 1970s the instruments of mass media caused a great deal of political controversy and piqued some presidents. The Truman, Eisenhower, Kennedy, and Johnson administrations occasionally berated reporters, columnists, and broadcasters for alleged distortions created by them in covering foreign policy decisions. With President Nixon, these occasional tiffs escalated into open hostility.

The most expressive critic during the Nixon tenure was Vice-President Spiro Agnew, who criticized the press and especially, the television media. He singled out television commentators who, he said, subjected President Nixon's speeches to the nation to "instant analysis and querulous criticism." "Obviously," he charged, "their minds were made up in advance" of a speech; the commentators, said Agnew, acted as self-appointed "judge and jury" of what the American public should think about foreign policy.[1]

Criticisms of television reporting were leveled by Nixon's Director of Telecommunication Policy, Clay Whitehead, who accused TV reporters and executives of "ideological plugola." The term, "plugola," is used when a disc jocky is rewarded by a recording company for playing the company's records in order to increase their popularity. "Ideological plugola" occurs, Mr. Whitehead contended, when reporters "stress or suppress information in accordance with their beliefs."[2]

After Mr. Agnew resigned his office in 1973 as a result of a conviction for income tax evasion, the President himself expressed his irritation over the way his administration had been treated by the mass media. During an October 1973 news conference, Nixon blamed "outrageous, vicious, distorted reporting" by the television networks for the public's plummeting confidence in his administration. In response to a reporter's question as to why the President was angry with TV newscasters, Mr. Nixon replied that he was not angry because "one can only be angry with those he respects."[3]

By the mid-1970s, mass media relations with the President had reached their most acrimonious point in contemporary American history.

PERFORMANCE OF THE MASS MEDIA

Before the controversy of mass media's bias (or lack of it) is explored, a general picture of the performance of mass media is required. By examining the structure of the American press and by comparing its output with newspapers of other nations, opinions can be formed about its relative performance. The structure of the press includes the number and type of training of foreign correspondents who report the news as well as techniques of writing and publishing, which affect the content that finally reaches the printed page. Unfortunately, most of the studies of mass media have focused on the press and neglected radio and television.[4]

The Structure of American Mass Media

The Foreign Correspondent. Approximately 500 American correspondents are assigned abroad by press, radio, television, and news magazine agencies; they are supplemented by over 700 foreign reporters who work for U.S. companies. The regional distribution of this small number of foreign correspondents is very uneven. Europe is best represented; Asia and Latin America are vying for a distant second position; and the Middle East and Africa are most neglected.[5]

These data engender an uneasy feeling that world events abroad are not adequately reported by the thin ranks of American foreign correspondents. In addition, the correspondent assigned abroad is not specifically recruited for the job nor is he given special training. He can rarely speak exotic languages (e.g., Hindi, Japanese, Swahili). Because he is an adequate reporter of domestic American politics, the assumption is made that he can also interpret Ghanian or Egyptian politics. By the time that he has learned enough about the country, his assignment ends and he is rotated back to the United States.[6]

Editing from the Field to the Newspaper. Not only is news gathered by thinly manned foreign stations and handled by professional newsmen without special qualifications for foreign affairs reporting, but the details are deleted during the process of getting the news from the field to the newspaper. Foreign news is "cut" more than domestic news as it is being transmitted from the field to the editor's desk.[7] Also, the mechanical or technical requirements imposed on news reporting affect the type of foreign news reported in most American newspapers. The "lead paragraph" approach attempts to relate the essence of a story in the opening paragraph, with the details supplied in the body of the story. This technique tends to make each international event a crisis situation in order to catch the reader's eye.

Moreover, small dailies often print only the first part of a report; thus, the reader knows that an important event has occurred, but he does not have access to the details.

Prestige Papers and Also-Rans. The American press is characterized by the presence of a few prestige papers and many other dailies of uneven quality. Dailies with respectable reputations for reporting foreign news are few: *The New York Times, Christian Science Monitor, St. Louis Post-Dispatch,* Chicago *Tribune, Washington Post, Los Angeles Times,* and *Philadelphia Inquirer* are often mentioned. The mass of dailies report a modicum of international events and give space primarily to national, state, and local news. They tend to depend on one of the wire services, Associated Press or United Press International, leading to standardized reporting of international events in most American dailies.

This picture of the national distribution of prestige papers, all located in large cities in northern or coastal areas, can be related to the geographical distribution of the interest and attitudes among the three publics discussed in the last chapter. The South tends to be the most isolationist and the least informed about world affairs. The absence of any prestige paper in the South, no doubt, contributes to this condition.

National Comparisons. These observations on the structural problems of reporting foreign news are meaningless unless comparisons are made with other national presses. These problems may be ubiquitous and may prove to be insurmountable in whatever culture mass media operate. A comparison between U.S. and South American dailies reveals that South American papers carry more than twice as much foreign news as American dailies.[8] One American newspaper stands apart: *The New York Times* prints twice as much foreign news as Latin American papers.

American prestige papers fare better in comparison with British prestige dailies. When *The New York Times* and *Washington Post* are compared with the *Manchester Guardian* and *London Daily Express*, the total space alloted to foreign news is approximately the same, although each nation's papers differ in emphasis.[9] The American papers give attention to more world areas than the British dailies. The English papers print more stories on West European and African events than does the American press, while the U.S. papers devote a larger proportion of print to the Far East and Southeast Asia. However, overall comparison between two very good American newspapers and two British papers of parallel quality reveals that both publics have access to approximately equal amounts of foreign news.

Geographical location and size of a nation may account for the poor showing of American dailies when compared with foreign newspapers. When determining foreign news as a percentage of the total news that a newspaper carries, American papers do not compare favorably with insular areas such as Japan, the Philippines, and Hong Kong.[10] Continental nations, such as the United States and India, generate a large amount of internal news, while small, island nations do not have a variety of news stories on domestic developments. Large, continental nations also have less of their national economic activity tied to international trade. These factors may also explain why American papers do not compare favorably with dailies in Japan and Southeast Asia in ratio of foreign-to-domestic news stories.

The verdict of these comparative studies is a mixture of praise and indictment. The prestige newspapers publish a depth of foreign news. Their stories originate from their own foreign correspondents as well as from the press services. The mass of American dailies, on the other hand, print a modicum of foreign news, almost all of it bought from the wire services. A foreign correspondent does not ensure a more accurate report; on the other hand, the wire services tend to produce standardized and capsulized reports of foreign events.

The Problem of Bias

The images largely ignore the instruments of mass media as a source of domestic influence on American foreign policy. When they do get involved, one of their concerns is biased reporting. The Right-Wing Revisionists, in particular, have expressed negative views of the press, arguing that news reporting is biased in favor of the "liberal" viewpoint. The Left-Wing Revisionists argue that the bias is in the opposite direction: mass media reflects the wishes of conservative businessmen who supply the advertising for radio, newspapers, and television.

Although the danger of bias is always present, most studies have absolved mass media of biased reporting. News reporting does not have a monolithic system where reporters and broadcasters are organized to present a united interpretation; rather, it is diverse, decentralized, and uncoordinated. Nevertheless, the suspicion persists, especially among the Revisionists, that news is twisted to favor one particular viewpoint. One researcher argues that television broadcasting in 1968 favored the Democratic candidate, Senator Hubert Humphrey, over Richard Nixon, who won a very close race for the presidency.[11] In a more rigorous examination of treatment of presidential candidates by the Columbia Broadcasting System, no discrepancy was found in the favorable and unfavorable statements made in covering each candidate.[12]

Not all of the accusations of bias have come from the Revisionists and presidential spokesmen: one of the more frequently leveled criticisms originates with Arab leaders who contend that the American press is pro-Israeli. Also, individuals acquainted with a foreign nation or region often have expressed their dismay at the biased coverage of other nations that Americans are subjected to by their foreign correspondents.[13] Area specialists accuse news reporters of misinterpreting a foreign country's political behavior, thereby misinforming the American people. In many cases, only crises, or events interpreted as crisis situations, are reported. A reporter with a superficial knowledge of a foreign nation's history and culture is prone to misinterpret the significance of an event, although he may describe faithfully the event itself. Or the reporter will relate quaint, exotic, and unusual situations as "human interest" stories, contributing little to the interpretation of world events.

The problem of bias is inherent in the training (or lack of it) of the American correspondent abroad. A reporter not conversant in the native language must rely on English-speaking informants who may not reflect the attitudes of the foreign population. During the 1956 Suez crisis, *New York Times* reporters in France and England filed stories in which they observed that the populations of both countries overwhelmingly supported their government's invasion of Egypt. Public opinion polls, however, revealed that these observations were inaccurate.[14] *Times* reporters had talked with British and French government officials who thought (erroneously) that their nation was solidly behind them. Perhaps the officials had refused to express their own misgivings about their governments' decisions in the midst of a crisis.

Perhaps the best approach to the problem of bias is to admit that it is present and to compensate for it by tapping several sources of news. This approach would work well for the elite and knowledgeable publics who have the income and education to undertake such an approach, but the general public would find it difficult to do so.

INFLUENCE OF MASS MEDIA ON FOREIGN POLICY

Obviously, the decision maker who believes that the mass media are biased (especially against him) will not enthusiastically listen to or read the ideas and information that the instruments of the media present. However, the decision-making process in Washington involves individuals who are not all up for reelection: bureaucratic, cabinet, and sub-cabinet officials also formulate policy on the basis of incoming information. Also, members of Congress are involved in developing patterns of diplomatic behavior, and they may not share the President's distrust of news reporting.

Mass Media and New Ideas

New ideas and fresh approaches suggested by editorial writers and columnists may exert an impact upon foreign policy formulation. Political leaders reading the daily fare of respected columnists may gain insights into policy problems and apply the suggested solutions. No evidence exists, however, that either editors' or columnists' observations have been original or have been translated into policy. In fact, one example implies that the opposite is true. During an April 1947 cabinet meeting, Navy Secretary James Forrestal referred to one of Walter Lippmann's articles which warned of economic disaster in Europe unless steps were taken by the U.S. government to furnish financial support. Under Secretary of State Dean Acheson informed him that a committee of State, War, and Navy personnel already was working on a study and soon would have recommendations—a study that eventually led to the Marshall Plan.[15] Lippmann's warnings may have prepared the way for acceptance of the Marshall Plan, but he did not suggest an original foreign policy idea to the government.

Mass Media and Information

If the instruments of mass media do not furnish new ideas, do they serve as a source of information for decision makers? Upper-echelon decision makers are usually informed of foreign events through diplomatic and intelligence reports from the field before domestic audiences learn about them through radio, television, or newspapers. At one time, the press and radio were a faster source of information than government channels, primarily because reports from the field had to be first coded, then sent, then decoded before the President or Secretary of State received them. Today, the encoding and decoding processes are instantaneous, thanks to electronic data machines that "scramble" a message as it is sent and "unscramble" it as it is received in Washington. However, the instruments of mass media occasionally win the information race, as they did in 1968, when a reporter informed Secretary of State Rusk that the Russians had moved troops into Czechoslovakia before the Secretary's office could relay the message to him.

For the lower-echelon personnel in the government, their first knowledge of a crisis is generally acquired from the press. Their initial reaction to the problems is influenced by the factual information relayed by mass media.

Investigative Reporting

Mass media may have an impact on American diplomacy by finding skeletons in foreign policy closets that administrators hoped would remain undisturbed. Investigative reporting of misspent foreign aid or an inefficient ambassador may not have a lasting effect on American diplomatic behavior, but the press can stimulate the government to keep a clean house. The impact on the administration in the White House is embarrassment.

The impact of exposé reporting on the American public, on the other hand, is a loss of confidence in the administration in power. During the 1972 presidential campaigns of President Nixon and Senator George McGovern, individuals paid by the Committee to Re-Elect the President planted electronic surveillance devices within the headquarters of the Democratic National Committee. This incident was vigorously investigated by reporters, particularly those of the Washington *Post,* whose stories of possible White House involvement led to televised Senate hearings on the Watergate scandal in 1973. Public confidence in President Nixon fell as mass media evaluated Watergate developments in one of the best examples of investigative reporting in American journalism.[16] This incident eventually led to President Nixon's resignation in August 1974.

In finding and exposing mistakes, corruption, and omissions of an administration in power, the instruments of mass media are performing their traditional role as a check on overweening governmental power.[17] Much of the controversy over the mass media's reporting described at the beginning of this chapter indicates that recent presidents, and especially Mr. Nixon, have experienced difficulty in accepting this traditional role. In the interests of an open, democratic society, the mass media must not become apologists for the current administration's policy.

Because of the lack of foreign correspondents and the greater capability of U.S. representatives abroad to hide mistakes, exposé reporting is most effective at home. Military commanders operating in war zones can more easily conceal their own or their subordinates' misjudgments. Atrocities committed in Vietnam, such as those at My Lai, were finally reported by witnesses who talked to reporters after their discharge from the armed services and their return to the United States.[18]

The ultimate result of exposé reporting is a "credibility gap," i.e., a disinclination on the part of the public to accept the administration's explanation of the mistake. The Watergate scandal widened the "gap" to include other government activities that were outside the initial scandal's parameters. As a result, the "credibility gap" became wide enough in late 1974 for the House of Representatives to conduct hearings on the impeachment of President Nixon.

Finding skeleton's in government closets is the function of investigative reporting. The fact that skeletons exist is not the fault of news reporters. To expect mass media to be silent when skeletons are discovered is to undermine the free flow of information, an important characteristic of a democracy.

NEWS MANAGEMENT: GOVERNMENTAL CONTROL OF MASS MEDIA

The function of a news reporter is to faithfully reproduce an event and to interpret its significance within the contemporary scene. Often his search carries him into areas that cannot be reported for reasons of national security. Instances of government-imposed secrecy raise the question of "managed" news.[19]

Levels of News Management

The "Handout." Of the four most common attempts to influence what is published or spoken on the airwaves, the "handout" is the simplest and least effective. Usually written by one of the many public relations personnel that populate the federal bureaucracy, the "handout" is a news release phrased the way the government wishes to see it printed. But the "handout" is rarely printed as distributed; the reporter usually looks for more information to supplement the story. The "handout" is most effective when the reporter is in no position to confirm its story by other, more reliable sources. An example of an unconfirmable release was the U.S. government's story in 1960 that the aircraft flown by Francis Gary Powers and shot down inside the Soviet Union was collecting weather information; actually, it was an intelligence-gathering airplane. Newsmen could not confirm the release until the Soviet Union issued their own "handout." Since most "handouts" on foreign events cannot be confirmed immediately, the reporter is faced with the dilemma of publishing the administration's version or publishing nothing.

Privileged Briefings. Another method of news management is the privileged briefing in which elite correspondents and analysts are given the government's version on foreign policy issues. The Secretary of State, for example, invites selected newsmen to dinner, after which he explains, "off the record," the government's policy. The purpose of these meetings is to see that newsmen do not stray too far from international realities as perceived by the decision maker. The decision maker reduces confusion over his policy by informing a select group of writers who are influential within the corps of newsmen. Since these "off-the-record" sessions are looked upon as a symbol of status, the guests—if they are to be invited again—will not be hasty to betray their source or to contradict the decision maker's assessment. The stories filed after privileged briefings usually describe the source of information as "a highly placed individual in the administration" or "a source close to the President."

Diplomacy by Press Conference. A third method of control is to use the public press conference as an instrument to apply diplomatic pressure. On one occasion, Dulles informed reporters that the Anglo-American negotiations on the Japanese peace treaty were in extreme difficulty. This announcement generated pressure on the British to make concessions. In this case, by releasing information of questionable veracity, a decision maker consciously used mass media to improve the American diplomatic position. Obviously, it is this last form of news management that presents serious problems to the free press in a democratic society — and to the public's need for accurate information on which to base its opinions about its government's foreign policy behavior. Should the instruments of mass media be fed inaccurate information to pass along to the public? This question became especially pertinent in the late 1960s during the Vietnamese conflict.

Freedom of Information. A final news management technique is the classification stamp applied to documents considered too valuable to be given extensive distribution. The tendency in government agencies (e.g., the departments of State and Defense or the Central Intelligence Agency) is to stamp "Confidential," "Secret," or "Top Secret" on reports from embassies and other units in the field, on all diplomatic correspondence, on minutes of meetings, on studies made of past decisions, and on a host of other pieces of paper floating around Washington.

By the beginning of the 1970s, it became obvious that the classification process had become arbitrary. Documents largely written from public sources (magazines for technical audiences, such as petroleum engineers or aircraft manufacturers) were being stamped "confidential." The declassification process was moving at a slow pace since a document, once classified, tended to remain in the government's files long after any danger existed that release would harm the national interest. And the suspicion was always present that the classification stamp was used to hide mistakes; thus, not "national" interest but personal and sometimes the administration's interest motivated the use of the classification stamp. Both reporters and scholars were effectively barred from these files.

In 1972, President Nixon signed an executive order that modified the classification process. It reduced the number of individuals who could decide on what was to be considered classified material, reduced the number of years that most material could remain classified, and set up an Interagency Classification Review Committee to manage the executive order's provisions. Although this new classification procedure may not appreciably help the reporter, it will aid academic researchers in obtaining material heretofore kept from public view. For the reporter, the classification stamp remains the most effective barrier to keeping news out of the papers and off the airwaves.

Managed News and Vietnam

One of the more frustrating aspects of the Vietnam War was the evident success of the Kennedy, Johnson, and Nixon administrations in managing the news about the conflict. In part, this success was the fault of the reporters covering the war; few were in Vietnam long enough to master the language and to develop independent and trustworthy sources of information. In part, the administration's success was the result of the fact that the conflict in Vietnam *was* a war (although undeclared), and therefore, news management could be justified on the basis of "national security." Newsmen in Saigon had little opportunity to check stories about battlefield casualties or rumors of atrocities.

These problems are illustrated by two news-management practices used during the Indo-China war; one involved the withholding of vital information previously released to newsmen and the other involved outright deception.

In December 1972, after initial peace talks between Washington and Hanoi broke down, President Nixon ordered renewed bombing of North Vietnam, using B-52 bombers for the first time in the conflict. Several of the large bombers were shot down, along with other aircraft, and almost 100 pilots were lost in the first week of the attacks. The government decided to no longer announce the extent of American air losses, the types of planes used in the raids, or the types of targets hit. The Christmas Eve edition of the *New York Times* reported:

A briefing officer, fencing with a reporter at a briefing Wednesday, denied there was a news "clampdown," terming it "protection of information." Asked if he were "trying to protect it from the American people," inasmuch as the North Vietnamese knew what was going on, he refused to "debate the rationale" of the news policy.[20]

The second illustration is the Nixon administration's policy in 1969–70 to bomb Cambodian targets under a cover story that American planes were attacking enemy positions in Vietnam. Since the Cambodian Khmer Rouge guerrillas knew about the bombs, it would again appear that the government's action was to deceive the American public rather than to protect national security. The deception was carried to the point that Secretary of State William P. Rogers in April 1970 told the Senate Foreign Relations Committee: "Cambodia is one country where we can say with complete assurance that our hands are clean and our hearts are pure."[21]

The problem that every reporter faces is whether to keep pushing for information when the red lights of "national security" continue to flash warnings. The ethics of his profession demand that he do so; a sense of values that places nation (as defined by his government) above profession asks that he hold back.

News Leaks

Since unauthorized leaks and premature disclosures of policy choices are a common occurrence in governmental activities, it is sometimes difficult to understand why administration officials become dismayed over them. There are instances when the official and the press representative will disagree on the timing of a news release. In these cases, the decision maker will eventually release the story, but he does not care to have premature speculation about it, especially while negotiations are underway. For example, a problem was created by leaks during the 1972 disarmament negotiations when an American "fall-back" proposal that was to be presented to the U.S.S.R. was published by *The New York Times*. The Nixon administration argued that the leaked story undercut current negotiations because the Russians refused to seriously negotiate proposals on the table, waiting for the more attractive "fall-back" position.

In most cases, the White House has encountered difficulty in proving that leaks actually hurt the formulation of American policy. The Nixon administration's contention about the *New York Times* leak during the disarmament negotiations in 1972 has been disputed.[22]

The most famous leak in the contemporary period is the publication of the *Pentagon Papers,* which should be more accurately classified as a flood because of the volumes of information released.[23] The *Pentagon Papers,* a history of the Vietnam War with documents relating to decisions, were released by Daniel Ellsberg and Anthony Russo, two government researchers. The Nixon administration contended that publication of these papers, which were classified, revealed state secrets harmful to the national interest, and that they undercut other nations' confidence in the ability of the U.S. government to keep important matters confidential. Neither of these charges was proven, but it was obvious that the leak had engendered official chagrin, which in turn, stimulated the Nixon administration to undertake extensive countermeasures. The telephones of individuals suspected of leaking information were "tapped" (i.e., electronic surveillance mechanisms were attached), lie-detector tests were administered, and a White House counterintelligence unit was established to discover the source of the leaks and ordered to plug them. Quite suitably the unit came to be called "The Plumbers." The Plumbers' activities included burglarizing the office of Ellsberg's psychiatrist and executing the break-in of the Watergate headquarters of the Democratic Party during the 1972 presidential campaign.

Not all leaks are weapons *against* the government; an administration can be helped by timely releases of information that support its policy. A situation illustrating this point occurred in October 1973 during the renewed outbreak of Arab–Israeli fighting. The President received a note from the U.S.S.R. Party Secretary Leonid Brezhnev, leading President Nixon to place American forces on a low-level alert. The note was never released, but Senator Henry Jackson was allowed to see it and to characterize its contents as "brutal" and "tough." Since other political leaders were not allowed to read the note and give their impressions, the American public had only Senator Jackson's characterization, justifying the President's action.

MASS MEDIA AND THE PUBLIC

A Case of Neglect

One of the more disconcerting research findings on mass media is that average readers and viewers seldom give their attention to foreign news. The average newspaper reader spends less than twenty minutes a day reading the newspaper; only two to three minutes are devoted to international news.[24] Newspapers, however, are a source of information available to the average reader; the impact of mass media on the "above-average" reader, such as the influential public, is also important. Most of the influentials' information from the mass media about foreign affairs is gained through the printed page: books, prestige newspapers, and news magazines. Influentials prefer the printed page to the airwaves as a source of information.

The government's attempt to control foreign affairs news, then, is aimed more at the knowledgeables and elites. Since these publics also will be most likely to be aware of news management—and to resent it—it would appear that any administration attempt to control reporting and editorial functions of mass media will be counterproductive.

The Impact of Radio and Television

It was previously noted that only a few newspapers could be singled out as outstanding in their presentation of foreign news to their readers. The mass of Americans read dailies that rely on wire service reports about international events and that devote only a small percentage of their newsprint to foreign affairs. For the general public, without access to adequate foreign news reporting in local newspapers, radio and television are more frequently used as sources. In small towns and rural areas, radio and television reporting has become the single most important source of foreign news for the general public. Farmers, who tend to be avid radio listeners, have remained informed despite the absence of a good newspaper.[25]

The impact of television reporting, especially nightly news programs, is yet to be evaluated with research as extensive as that given to the printed page. Since the average TV viewer spends in excess of four hours each day before his set, television possesses a potential of informing audiences in the general public who ignore newspapers. The TV viewer can ignore programs focusing on international issues, however. Most of the inhabitants of the general public (and a few knowledgeables and influentials) would have little trouble deciding between "Meet the Press" and a professional football game.

One can only speculate about the impact of television on public attitudes. For example, the Vietnam War was the most extensively covered conflict in the short history of TV reporting.[26] What effect did continuous viewing of the carnage of war have on the American public? Only extensive research can answer this question.

Mass Media as a Transmission Belt

The instruments of mass media can influence readers, viewers, and listeners by suggesting new viewpoints, mainly through the editorial page, and by serving as a transmission belt for information. As a transmission belt for information, mass media are the primary sources of data for the public. The public is therefore informed, but exposure to mass media *per se* may not influence opinions. Does knowledge of an event or policy change reader or viewer attitudes toward that event or policy? The answer depends on a number of factors, beginning with the nature of the policy itself, whether or not a majority of reporters and commentators support the policy, and the success of the government's mobilization efforts.

One instance in which all three factors were operating was the Marshall Plan in 1948.[27] The State Department's economic recovery program for Europe was complex and technical, its economic and political motivations not easily capsulized for readers, and the bill to be funded by U.S. tax dollars not very palatable to the American public. Yet most mass media opinion makers were convinced of the Marshall Plan's necessity. Working with the President and his subordinates, they were successful in converting a majority of the public to the idea. Secretary of State George Marshall later commended the reporters for their support, stating that without it, the program would never have been enacted.

In 1963 when the Nuclear Test Ban Treaty was proposed, the mass media and government leaders again worked together to present a policy program to the public. At the beginning of President Kennedy's drive to negotiate a treaty with the Russians, public opinion polls showed little support. As the President mobilized support for the treaty through major addresses and news conferences, citizen groups hired a public relations firm to provide "filler" stories for local newspapers and radio stations, which emphasized the need for the treaty.[28]

These success stories combine an administration willingness to work with and respect the role of mass media, and a cooperative mass media elite convinced of the policy and willing to serve as a transmission belt for the administration's mobilization efforts. Not all policy initiatives, however, have this ending. Various attempts have failed, for example, to convince citizens that they should build fall-out shelters. The American public failed to respond, but the reason was *not* that mass media refused to be a transmission belt for the Eisenhower and Kennedy pleas. Two studies suggest that attitudes already ingrained into an individual's thinking are more important as predictors of behavior than the knowledge of the fall-out shelter issues themselves.[29] Home owners who built fallout shelters, and home owners who did not, posssesed similar economic and educational characteristics. The attitude of the shelter-builders was different, however; they tended to endorse the "hard line" approach to relations with the Soviet Union and looked on their shelters as improving the American military position. The non-shelter-builders, on the other hand, were optimistic about the prospects for diplomatic settlement of differences in Russo-American relations. The assumption that the shelter-builders had studied the dangers of nuclear war or were more avid readers of Russian history and diplomacy was not accurate.

MASS MEDIA: AN ASSESSMENT

The picture of the foreign news operations of the mass media is not overly attractive: readers supplied with stories by too few foreign correspondents with too little training, reporters accused of bias, foreign news largely ignored by the general public, and the harsh governmental criticism of the mass media. If the ability to attract controversy is any indication of success, then the mass media qualifies for many awards. Attacks on it by government officials are attempts at intimidation. The danger inherent in these attempts is that the reporter or broadcaster will pause before making any statements critical of the government's policy.

However, the inclination to protect the instruments of mass media from official intimidation must not obscure the fact that a need exists to upgrade the quality and quantity of foreign news reporting, especially the training of reporters and the techniques of getting news from the field to the newspaper. The instruments of mass media themselves constitute a bureaucracy, and they practice their own brand of politics.[30] These weaknesses can be strengthened by recruiting correspondents with college degrees in political science and international relations, or by sending promising reporters back to school to supplement their skills with substantive courses in academic areas. More reporters should be assigned to international posts, rather than to institutions (e.g., the White House or Congress) that combine foreign *and* domestic events. Foreign policy is a specialized subject; it requires specialists in the news corps to report and to interpret it.

Finally, more extensive research on the role of television as a transmission belt for information is needed.[31] Television reporting has replaced the printed page as the single most important source of foreign news in some sections of the U.S. Television may be ignored by the influential public, but it supplies the general public with foreign news that escapes the front pages of the vast majority of American newspapers. Television has introduced a nation-wide, standardized fare of foreign news that compensates for the local newspaper's lack of coverage.

NOTES

1. Speech delivered to the Mid-West Regional Republican Committee, Des Moines, Iowa, Nov. 13, 1969. Reprinted in *Vital Speeches* 36 (Dec. 1, 1969): 98–101.
2. Speech delivered in Indianapolis, Indiana, Dec. 18, 1972. Reprinted in *Vital Speeches* 39 (Feb. 1, 1973): 230–232.
3. *New York Times,* Oct. 27, 1973, p. 1.
4. Three general books that analyze the press and foreign policy are Bernard C. Cohen, *The Press and Foreign Policy* (Princeton, N.J.: Princeton University Press, 1963); Douglass Cater, *The Fourth Branch of Government* (Boston: Houghton Mifflin, 1959); and James B. Reston, *The Artillery of the Press: Its Influence on American Foreign Policy* (New York: Harper & Row, 1967).
5. John Wilhelm, "The Re-Appearing Foreign Correspondent: A World Survey," *Journalism Quarterly* 40 (Spring 1963): 147–168.
6. Bernard C. Cohen, "Mass Communication and Foreign Policy," in James N. Rosenau (ed.), *Domestic Sources of Foreign Policy* (New York: Free Press, 1967), pp. 195–212.
7. Scott N. Cutlip, "Content and Flow of A.P. News: From Trunk to TTS to Reader," *Journalism Quarterly* 31 (Fall 1954): 434–446.
8. James W. Markham, "Foreign News in the United States and South American Press," *Public Opinion Quarterly* 25 (Summer 1961): 249–262. Obviously, events in the U.S. would be reported as foreign news in South American dailies and as local news in American newspapers,

chapter 6   Role of Mass Media in U.S. Diplomacy   113

and vice versa for events in South America. Since more newsworthy events tend to occur in North America, a bias is introduced into the study. Markham eliminated the bias and still found that South American dailies reported more foreign news than did American dailies.

9. Jim A. Hart, "Foreign News in the U.S. and English Daily Newspapers: A Comparison," *Journalism Quarterly* 43 (1966): 443–448.
10. John Hohenberg, *Between Two Worlds: Policy, Press and Public Opinion in Asian-American Relations* (New York: Praeger, 1967), pp. 48–90.
11. Edith Efron, *The News Twisters* (Los Angeles: Nash Publishing Co., 1971).
12. Robert L. Stevenson, Richard A. Eisinger, Barry M. Feinberg, and Alan B. Kotok, "Untwisting *The News Twisters:* A Replication of Efron's Study," *Journalism Quarterly* 50 (Summer 1973): 211–219.
13. A specialist on Japan and a former ambassador to two African nations find fault with American foreign affairs reporting: George R. Packard III, "Living with the Real Japan," *Foreign Affairs* 46 (October 1967): 193 and William Attwood, *The Reds and the Blacks* (New York: Harper & Row, 1967), pp. 327–328. *See also* John W. C. Johnstone, Edward J. Slawski, and William W. Bowman, "The Professional Values of American Newsmen," *Public Opinion Quarterly* 36 (Winter 1972–73): 522–540.
14. Jean Owen, "The Polls and Newspaper Appraisal of the Suez Crises," *Public Opinion Quarterly* 21 (1957): 350–354.
15. Walter Millis (ed.), *The Forrestal Diaries* (New York: Viking Press, 1951), p. 261.
16. Lewis H. Lapham, "The Press as Sacred Cow: After Watergate: The Perils of Self-Congratulations," *Harper's* 247 (August 1973): 43–54.
17. William L. Rivers, *The Adversaries: Politics and the Press* (Boston: Beacon Press, 1973).
18. Seymour M. Hersh, *Cover-up: The Army's Secret Investigation of the Massacre at My Lai 4* (New York: Random House, 1972).
19. Lester Markel, *What You Don't Know Can Hurt You* (Washington, D.C.: Public Affairs Press, 1972); Hillier Krieghbaum, *Pressures on the Press* (New York: Thomas Y. Crowell, 1972).
20. *New York Times,* Dec. 24, 1972, Sec. 4, p. 1. For a discussion of problems that the press faced in Vietnam, *see* Dale Minor, *The Information War* (New York: Hawthorn Books, 1970); Peter Braestrup, "Covering the Vietnam War," *Nieman Reports* 23 (December 1969); and Malcolm W. Browne, "Vietnam Reporting: Three Years of Crisis," *Columbia Journalism Review* 3 (Fall 1964): 4; and Edwin Emery, "The Press in the Vietnam Quagmire," *Journalism Quarterly* 48 (1971): 619–626.
21. Quoted in the *New York Times,* July 29, 1973, Sec. 4, p. 2.
22. Seymour M. Hersh, "The President and the Plumbers: A Look at Two

Security Questions," *New York Times,* Dec. 9, 1973, Sec. 1, pp. 1 and 76.

23. Several editions of the Pentagon Papers have been published, one being the Senator Gravel edition published in four volumes by Beacon Press of Boston. Several newspapers, including the *New York Times* and the *Washington Post,* also published excerpts of the Pentagon Papers.
24. International Press Institute, *The Flow of the News* (Zurich: International Press Institute, n.d.), p. 62.
25. Television and radio are prime sources of international news in small towns and rural areas. *See* Urban Whitaker and Bruce E. Davis, *The World and Ridgeway, South Carolina* (Columbia, S.C.: University of South Carolina, Institute of International Studies, 1967), p. 23, and Ralph O. Nafziger, Warren C. Engstrom, Malcolm S. Maclean, Jr., "The Mass Media and an Informed Public," *Public Opinion Quarterly* 15 (Spring 1951): 104–114.
26. Michael J. Arlen, *Living-Room War* (New York: Viking, 1960); Frank D. Russo, "A Study of Bias in TV Coverage of the Vietnam War," *Public Opinion Quarterly* 35 (Winter 1971–72): 539–543. Russo did not find evidence of an anti-Nixon administration bias nor did he find evidence that Vice-President Agnew's attacks on TV coverage influenced CBS and NBC to be less critical of the President's handling of the war. *See also* Benjamin D. Singer, "Violence, Protest, and War in Television News: The U.S. and Canada Compared," *Public Opinion Quarterly* 34 (Winter 1970–71): 611–616.
27. Harold L. Hitchens, "Influences on the Congressional Decision to Pass the Marshall Plan," *Western Political Quarterly* 21 (1968): 51–67.
28. Mary Milling Lepper, *Foreign Policy Formulations: A Case Study of the Nuclear Test Ban Treaty of 1962* (Columbus, Ohio: Charles Merrill, 1971), pp. 52–55.
29. F. K. Bernien, Carol Schulman, and Marianne Ameral, "The Fallout-Shelter Owners: A Study of Attitude Formation," *Public Opinion Quarterly* 27 (Summer 1963): 206–216, and Sidney Kraus, Rouben Mehling, and El-Assal, "Mass Media and the Fallout Controversy," *Public Opinion Quarterly* 27 (Summer 1963): 191–205.
30. Leon V. Sigal, *Reporters and Officials: The Organization and Politics of Newsmaking* (Lexington, Mass.: D. C. Heath, 1973), examines the organization of the *New York Times* and *Washington Post.*
31. Robert Shelby Frank, *Message Dimensions of Television News* (Lexington, Mass.: D. C. Heath, 1973) is an example of the type of research needed.

7

Special-Interest Groups and U.S. Foreign Policy

A special-interest group is composed of individuals who share common goals and who are organized to influence government policy in the direction of these goals.[1] A group can propose policy initiatives to decision makers or work to defeat or to discourage the implementation of policy already formulated. Usually a special-interest group is intent on moving American foreign policy into channels that will bring financial or other rewards to the group's members. "Other rewards" may be intangible payoffs, such as a desire to see U.S. diplomacy adopt a more ideological orientation. In this chapter, the Zionists and United World Federalists are examined as examples of groups motivated by ideological, rather than financial, rewards.

Theoretically, *special* interests should never override *national* interests. No policy decision should bring more advantages to one group or party than another, nor should international relations with allies or opponents be worsened for the benefit of a domestic group. For example, it may be to the benefit of domestic wool producers to impose a high import duty on wool, but the economic advantages accrued to this group should be weighed against the adverse affect of the duty on U.S.–Australian relations, since Australia is a wool-producing nation and an ally as well. American steel producers criticized the formation of the European Coal and Steel Community, an integrated organization that the American government supported because it contributed to the solution of thorny political and economic problems in Europe.[2] United States steel companies thought, with good reason, that merging French and German steel-producing resources would present them with more competition. American foreign policy rarely can serve special interests without harming the interests of the entire nation.

THE IMAGES AND THE GROUPS

The Left Wing and Economic Motivations

An important contribution of the Left-Wing Revisionists to the study of American foreign policy is their emphasis on the economic motivations that often propel U.S. diplomatic behavior. Although these economic motivations enter the decision-making process as values molded by a capitalist society, as David Riesman, Karen Horney, and Margaret Mead contend (see chapter 4), they also are part of the pressures that industrial, commercial, banking, import–export, and investment businesses bring upon the government.

Among the most active interest groups are those composed of members of the business community, as well as large, individual firms which operate with a special relationship to the government. A mammoth firm, such as International Business Machines or General Motors, can bring its own pressure on the administration in power, a situation that is explored further in chapter 18. Businesses that compete on the open market also form groups to represent their collective wishes to the government. These special-interest groups hire lobbyists and staffs whose function it is to influence Congress, executive officers, and the federal bureaucracy to take foreign policy directions that the groups' clientele support.

Right-Wing and Radical Groups

Right-Wing Revisionists see no danger in economic groups adding their voice to policy formulation. They do object to "liberal" groups, some of which are accused of being "fronts" for Communist activities. The government must assume responsibility for exposing "front" groups so that the American people will not be duped into supporting the Communist program. There is also a racial flavor to the more radical Right-Wing Revisionist indictments against American policy decisions in the Middle East and Africa. They claim that Zionist influence has pressured U.S. diplomacy to take a pro-Israeli and anti-Arab stance. Right-Wing Revisionists charge that American relations with the emerging African nations have been influenced by domestic black groups, many of them controlled by Communists or "fellow travelers."

The Realists and Liberals

The more orthodox images have tended to neglect special-interest groups. The Realists, in line with their belief in professional diplomacy, consider special-interest groups on a par with public opinion — i.e., their influences should not be brought to bear upon decision making. Foreign policy leaders should make their judgments on the basis of professionally gathered and integrated intelligence data, not on the articulations of group elites.

The Liberals omit special-interest group activities from their citizen diplomacy model. They tend to believe that group interests represent the seamy side of politics and should not be considered in formulating foreign policy. The values of the people should be translated into policy; by adding a layer of institutional values between the public and decision makers, the people's voice becomes muffled.

Shortcomings of the Images

As was the case with public opinion and mass media, the advocates of the four images fail to provide many of the answers to questions about the role of groups in formulating American foreign policy. None of the images describes the characteristics of a successful group. Nor is a description given of the methods used in reaching the decision maker. The image-holders further ignore the fact that groups can be mobilized by the government as well. Differentiation among the various groups is missing: What happens if the Chamber of Commerce opposes a policy of which the National Association of Manufacturers approves? To answer this and other questions, the analysis in this chapter attempts to avoid the ideological and sometimes emotional tenor with which special-interest groups are often discussed.

GROUP INFLUENCE ON FOREIGN POLICY DECISIONS

The Successful Groups

The first concern in analyzing group activities is to identify the special-interest groups that are successful in bringing pressure to bear on the foreign policymaking process. The groups that score foreign policy successes have an interest in the issue under discussion, motivation to express that interest, an open channel to the key decision maker, and final acceptance by the decision maker of the group's position.

Position. A pressure group will formulate policy positions on issues within its special field of interest and will ignore issues of little concern to itself (for example, the Independent Petroleum Association of America will have no position on the question of import duties for Japanese dolls). Usually, a group's position does not represent an original foreign policy proposal; in most cases, the group audits the several proposals already under discussion within the government, chooses the one in harmony with its traditional beliefs, and works to veto the alternatives. The group, in these cases, does not approach the government with an original proposal of its own.

Motivation. Assuming that the group has a policy position, its leadership must be motivated to express its views. A group will be reluctant to expend resources on issues that are of secondary importance at the moment. Although the group takes a position on a policy proposal, it may not be motivated to channel its views to the government.

Channel. The goal of interest-group activity is to channel its message to the government official responsible for policymaking. Channels open to interest groups can be public, such as testimony before a congressional committee; channels provided by lobbyists who carry the group's message personally to the individual decision maker are private.

Reception. Assuming that the group has a position, the motivation to express its views, and a channel for conveying its wishes to the government, it must, in addition, have a receptive decision maker to complete the circuit. Government officials who politely give audience to the group's message, but do not act on the message's recommendation, are not "receptive." Receptiveness is a function of the decision maker's political values. He may value one group's support or views above another's, and he may ignore other groups altogether. A businessman in government, for example, will tend to be more receptive to positions taken by the National Association of Manufacturers or by the Chamber of Commerce than by the AFL–CIO.[3]

Types of Issues for Successful Group Activity

All special-interest groups, whether possessing the four characteristics of success or not, attempt to influence governmental decisions on a variety of issues. The type of issue under consideration conditions the success of a group.

Technical Issues. Interest groups are more active on specific and technical issues than on policies that attract wide public attention. For example, maritime shipping is a technical subject and does not attract the public's interest; the lobby for maritime companies is one of the most active and influential interest groups affecting American foreign policy. A similar situation exists with tariffs on specialized items, such as textiles. Contrariwise, a host of interest groups will be active on general foreign policy topics, such as disarmament and arms control. On issues of general interest, a single group's efforts are dissipated in a sea of other domestic influencers or are counterbalanced by groups with opposing views.

Issues Requiring Bureaucratic Coordination. Interest groups are more active on decisions that are coordinated among several units of the government than on decisions made by the President and Department of State. Foreign policy decisions that require coordination by several federal departments, such as Agriculture or Defense, permit interest groups to exert their influence. Farm lobbyists may not have access to the President or the Department of State on the Food for Peace Program, but they have an open door to the Department of Agriculture. Labor unions' views will be voiced by the Department of Labor on international labor problems. A foreign policy issue that requires congressional approval evokes group activity because groups have easier access to the legislature than to the executive.

Issues Lacking Executive Initiative. Issues where executive initiative is lacking will generate more interest-group activity than issues where presidential leadership is present. Lack of presidential direction permits Congress and other executive officials a wide latitude in decision making. They are, therefore, more susceptible to pressures from groups.

Drawn-Out Issues. Issues that remain before foreign policy decision makers for a long period of time will attract more interest group activity than issues that must be quickly decided. Policies that require weeks or months to hammer into final form furnish groups with more opportunities to mobilize support and influence the outcome. Hence, interest groups were active on foreign-aid bills, but were left out of the 1961 Bay of Pigs and 1962 Cuban missile crises. After World War I, Henry Cabot Lodge, Chairman of the Senate Foreign Relations Committee, purposely prolonged hearings on the Versailles Treaty to permit opposition groups to generate pressure on the government.

Issues at Election Time. Interest groups are more influential on decisions that must be made during an election campaign than on policy that must be decided at other times. The decision maker seeking office will feel compelled to be responsible to interest groups whose support, financial as well as verbal, is viewed as necessary to win an election. For this reason, a congressman who faces reelection every two years is more vulnerable to special interests than a senator or the President.

Multiple Points of Contact

The successful special interest group, in addition to having the capability of bending the decision maker's ear and operating in an arena of issues that are subject to influence, must have multiple points of contact with the government. These "points" include not only the President or his chief advisers, but congressmen and key policymakers in the bureaucracy. A group with several points of access is more likely to have its voice heard.

A prime illustration of a group or groups with multiple points of contact is the "military–industrial complex," a phrase that first appeared in President Eisenhower's farewell address in January 1961. "In the councils of Government," Eisenhower stated, "we must guard against the acquisition of unwarranted influence, whether sought or unsought, by the military–industrial complex." What the retiring President exactly had in mind is not clear, but the phrase has come to designate the economic alliance forged between industries holding large defense contracts, the Department of Defense, and special-interest groups whose policy positions they support.

The military-industrial complex is a maze of contact channels through which influence can flow. The veteran groups are vocal in their views on the type of defense system that the United States should maintain. Retired armed forces officers, especially admirals and generals, are employed by these groups or are in executive positions with corporations interested in obtaining defense contracts. Congressmen whose districts have industries with large defense contracts are open to the pleas of groups that advocate increased defense spending.

It would be difficult to single out the most influential aspect of the military–industrial complex. Special-interest groups make up a segment of the complex, and they cannot be evaluated in isolation. The influence of special-interest groups must be related to industries, units of bureaucracy that have a hand in foreign policy decisions, and elected officials.

Case Studies of Group Activities

The analytical problem encountered in analyzing group activities is similar to that in studies of images, values, public opinion, and mass media: relating the group's activities to the adoption or defeat of a specific policy. Only a handful of case studies that attempt to link a group's activities with specific decisions are provided here.

Labor and the American Legion. In case studies of the AFL–CIO and the American Legion, the official program adopted by each group has been compared with foreign policy decisions.[4] Most of the analyses focus on laws passed by Congress that affect U.S. diplomacy or national security policy. When the program and the law corresponded, researchers concluded that the Legion or the AFL–CIO was influential in the government's decision. The American Legion, for example, claimed that its fight for "Americanism" led to passage of the 1950 Internal Security (or McCarren) Act. A group's adoption of a platform that eventually was made into law is not altogether convincing of its impact on public policy. Other factors may have entered into the government's decision or the government may have initially sympathized with the group.

This type of study is interesting, but it does not show that a group's efforts were crucial to the policy's acceptance or rejection. Relationships cannot be established absolutely by simply quoting group leaders who claim victories whenever the government adopts a policy that the group advocated. These studies are inclined to pass over policies advocated by the group that are never enacted.

The Recognition of Israel. The Israeli case represents an occurrence of an efficient organization with multiple points of contact coming on the political scene when the conditions were favorable to effective group activity.[5]

American foreign policy on the issue of a homeland for the Jews was formulated after World War II under conditions that permitted the Zionists to influence the outcome. The issue was specific, but represented one aspect of a broader Middle-Eastern policy. It involved units of the government other than the President and Department of State: Congress had gone on record by resolution early in the 1920s as approving the concept of a national homeland for the Jews. The Department of Defense was involved because of strategic military interests in the Middle East. In addition, it was an issue that lacked presidential leadership. Truman did not inherit a

Palestinian policy from Roosevelt, and he vacillated among the policy possibilities open to him. In the absence of firm executive leadership, the Zionists were able to bring pressure to bear on decision makers who were left on their own to carve out a position. The issue also spanned a long period of time. It remained before the public from the end of World War II until 1948 when the British left Palestine. Finally, and perhaps most importantly, the issue came to a head as the 1948 presidential election approached. The Democratic and Republican parties' need for campaign money and the Jewish vote resulted in more attention to the Zionist plea than would otherwise have been the case.

The Zionist organization possessed the four characteristics of an effective interest group. The Zionists had a position and were highly motivated to express it, and they had many channels to carry their message to governmental officials. Secretary of Defense James A. Forrestal, in his diary, recorded a meeting in October 1947 between Truman and Bob Hannegan, the Democratic National Chairman:

> Hannegan brought up the question of Palestine. He said that many people who had contributed to the Democratic campaign fund in 1944 were pressing hard for assurance from the administration of definitive support for the Jewish position in Palestine. The President said that if they would keep quiet he thought that everything would be all right, but that if they persisted in the endeavor . . . there was grave danger of wrecking all prospects for settlement. Hannegan tried again to press him on this matter but he was adamant.[6]

Forrestal also noted another channel of Zionist support. In January 1948, Loy Henderson, a State Department official, told him that Justice Felix Frankfurter had approached the Philippine delegate to the United Nations to solicit his vote for partition of Palestine into Jewish and Arab communities.[7]

This case study of Israel also suggests that the successful group must propose policy initiatives that can engender broad public sympathy. The issue in this case was phrased in terms that the man-in-the-street could comprehend: democratic Israelis versus the monarchical Arabs, a return to the biblical "promised land," and the terrible suffering of the Jews under the Nazis in World War II. The general public did not grasp the deeper political issues involved; it responded emotionally to the issue.

The Foreign Lobbyist

Another political actor involved in pressure-group attempts to influence American foreign policy is the foreign lobbyist, or non-diplomatic representative.[8] He represents a foreign group, but his lobbying techniques are similar to those used by a domestic group.

Functions of the Non-Diplomatic Representative. Foreign governments, businesses, groups out of power, and individuals seeking special dispensations from the American government hire non-diplomatic emissaries to represent their cause. The non-diplomatic representative is usually from a reputable American firm that specializes in public relations, furnishes economic or legal advice, or acts as a consultant on a variety of areas of concern to the foreign government. A foreign government recognized by the United States and with an embassy staff in Washington may hire a non-diplomatic representative to supplement its normal diplomatic endeavors. Emerging nations without an extensive Foreign Service or the expertise to understand the complex American scene may seek the service of American firms. World trading partners sometimes need technical advice on American import, export, and banking laws supplied by non-diplomatic representatives. A firm may also be retained to launch an advertising campaign to attract American tourists to a foreign country. These are some of the less controversial activities of the non-diplomatic representatives of foreign countries.

The Problem of Recognition. Two aspects of non-diplomatic representation have raised considerable concern: the non-diplomatic representative who works for governments in exile or governments in power not recognized by the State Department, and the activities of foreign lobbyists to influence Congress on laws that touch on specialized economic issues. An example of the first concern occurred in 1966 when the Rhodesian government procured the services of a non-diplomatic representative. Since Rhodesian independence was not recognized at the time, its non-diplomatic representative filed a statement under the Foreign Agents Registration Act. Through its *Bulletin*, the State Department declared that registration "in no way implies U.S. approval of the activities of the registered agent or recognition of the political faction or regime which the agent represents or purports to represent."[9] In 1967, insurgent Biafra, the eastern province of Nigeria, hired a New York public relations firm to tell its story to the American people since the United States government refused to recognize its declaration of independence. In these instances, a foreign group sought to influence American foreign policy indirectly, despite the fact that its legal existence was not recognized by the State Department.

Congress and the Foreign Lobbyist. A foreign government's lobbyist may attempt to influence the United States Congress, which is the second concern related to the non-diplomatic representative. Since the traditions of diplomacy stipulate that a foreign diplomat represents the views of his sovereign to the host sovereign, he usually does not engage in attempts to influence the host country's legislature, although history records successful, as well as unsuccessful, attempts to do so. The modern practice, then, is to retain the services of a lobbyist to represent the foreign government's case to the legislature. Foreign lobbyists are especially active in areas involving tariffs and quotas. For example, a quota is set on the amount of sugar imported from each sugar-producing nation into the high-priced American market. When the United States government decided in 1960 to embargo all Cuban products, and thus to prohibit Cuban sugar from entering the

American market, quota agreements with other nations had to be renegotiated. Foreign lobbying by sugar-producing nations to receive a larger share of the discontinued Cuban quota was intense.

Are Foreign Lobbyists a Threat? The primary instrument to control the excesses of foreign lobbyists is the Foreign Agents Registration Act, passed in 1938 in response to activities by Nazi Germany's agents. It requires that non-diplomatic representatives of foreign governments register with the Department of Justice, account for their activities, and identify propaganda circulated on behalf of their employer. Approximately 500 non-diplomatic agents are currently registered under the provisions of this act.

George Ball, Under Secretary of State in 1963, told the Senate Foreign Relations Committee that the "experience of the State Department would seem to suggest that *under proper circumstances* foreign agents can serve a useful role. Whether acting for foreign governments or other foreign interests, a foreign agent can often serve as an interpreter of systems and habits of thought—as a medium for bridging the gulf of disparate national experiences, traditions, institutions, and customs."[10] The question is, then, what are the "proper circumstances?" Non-diplomatic agents who perform technical services (legal or economic counseling) must be differentiated from those who attempt to move the course of American diplomacy into policy channels that benefit their special interests. It is necessary to permit the former activity while controlling the latter.

GOVERNMENT MOBILIZATION OF GROUPS

Departmental Links to Groups

Departments of the federal government have ill-defined links to special interests: the departments of Agriculture, Commerce, and Labor, the Maritime Commission, and the Federal Aviation Agency are the most obvious examples. Each represents the viewpoint of a cluster of farming, labor, business, shipping, and aviation groups on foreign policy issues. The groups may not agree on a common response to an issue, but they do expect the department or agency to represent their generic attitudes whenever foreign policy is coordinated with the State Department. Some groups, then, have a built-in access to departments that must be consulted whenever policy decisions impinge on their specialized area of interest. The agricultural interest groups may have little opportunity to present their case to the Department of State, but they expect the Department of Agriculture to argue as their surrogate on issues that they consider important.

Quite often Department of State personnel describe themselves, with some pride, as the only federal agency without a domestic clientele to which to cater. The implication is that the State Department can then formulate foreign policy immune from pressure of specialized groups. However, the

Department of State receives the messages of interest groups from indirect and oblique sources (i.e., other federal agencies).

Departmental Co-Optation

On the other hand, a group may not be better off if it has a department channel because departmental bureaucracy may filter out group influence or mold it to fit a policy already proposed. What appears on the surface as a group successfully achieving a reception in the department is, in reality, co-optation. Co-optation occurs when the federal department enlists a group's (or groups') support for a policy initiative already decided on; it gives the appearance that the group or groups have influenced the government to adopt the policy in the first place. The federal bureaucracy decides on a course to follow, searches among the various interest groups for those who will advocate this policy, and then enrolls the group's support.

Co-optation is possible because interest groups are usually disunited. Group disunity permits the decision maker to maintain a wide latitude of choices when it appears that he is being subjected to substantial pressure.

The President and Interest Groups

The President seldom ignores interest groups. He, as well as the Vice-President and members of the President's cabinet, cultivates a group's good will, appearing at their national conventions with speeches tailored to fit the audience. The groups usually are consulted on key appointments in departments that immediately concern them. It would not be wise for the President to appoint his secretaries of Commerce, Labor, and Agriculture without consulting with business, labor, and agriculture group leaders. The President may not follow their advice, but he does not ignore them.

GROUP INFLUENCE ON PUBLIC OPINION

Instruments for Reaching the Public

Thus far, this evaluation has focused on the relationship between interest groups and the government. Any group intent on mobilizing public opinion faces a difficult task. No group has a monopoly on the means of communication, nor can it command the public's attention as the President does when he delivers a major policy statement. No interest group, no matter how large and wealthy, can compete with the communication resources and the image of credibility of the federal government. The government can muster a larger barrage of propaganda to defend its position than can any group.

Group leadership can, and does, mobilize its own members readily and within a short period of time. A national interest group can be in immediate communication with its fifty state organizations which, in turn, can contact their local leaders and members. In this way, an interest group can generate a large number of letters, petitions, delegations, and even demonstrations to impress the government, as well as the public, on the issue under consideration.

The techniques and instruments for influencing public opinion are well-known; an organization may publish a national newspaper or magazine, produce movies, broadcast radio programs, hold national conventions, and maintain a speaker's bureau to carry its message on foreign policy issues to the public. In addition to groups that have positions on many issues, *ad hoc* committees have been formed to educate the public on a single issue. The Committee of the One Million, an *ad hoc* group, opposed American diplomatic recognition of Communist China and its admission to the United Nations. The Committee attempted to mobilize support for its position from the public as well as from government officials.

Case Studies of Group–Public Relationships

The China Lobby: A Case of Successful Mobilization. If a group's efforts to mobilize public opinion are effective, one salient feature will characterize the political scene: an information vacuum will exist following an unexpected, traumatic experience that confuses and divides the American public and contributes to political partisanship. During this vacuum, a group with a plausible explanation for the event will enter, tell its story, and eventually sell its version to the minority political party (or the party that does not control the White House). Included in the group's version, of course, is the government's responsibility for the event, which is interpreted as a failure of American foreign policy. The fall of China to the Communists in 1949 is an incident that apparently fulfills these requirements. The American public was unprepared for the Communist victory, and the Truman administration failed to produce a credible explanation for it other than placing the blame on Chiang Kai-shek and the Nationalists. The China lobby, composed of several groups sympathetic to Chiang Kai-shek (such as the American China Policy Association), entered this vacuum and, blaming the American government, effectively propounded an alternative version of the Far Eastern events.[11]

World Federalists: A Case Study of Success and Failure. Whenever an information vacuum does exist, the first governmental group to gain the public's attention is not necessarily the one that eventually influences public opinion. The United World Federalists were formed in 1947 at a time when the American government had not formulated a policy on the shape of the world beyond establishing the United Nations.[12] Within two years, the United World Federalists' local chapters were instrumental in influencing twenty-five state legislatures to pass memorials or resolutions calling for initial steps toward a world federalist government. Most of the resolutions asked that a constitutional convention be convened to discuss amendments that would permit a world federation of nations. Other groups, such as the American Legion and the Daughters of the American Revolution, opposed world federalism and began mobilizing public opinion that eventually countered the World Federalists' gains. Dissension within the World Federalists' group also contributed to its decline in influence.

INTERNATIONAL ACTIVITIES OF GROUPS

Target: Foreign Governments

Not all interest-group activity in the U.S. is aimed at the American government. Whenever longshoremen decide that they do not like the diplomatic patterns of a foreign country and refuse to unload cargo off that nation's vessels in American ports, a labor union, in effect, formulates American foreign policy entirely on its own. In the post-World War II period, the longshoremen have boycotted Russian, Polish, and Australian vessels because they disapproved of their respective foreign policies at the time. When Australian dock workers refused to unload American vessels in late 1972 and early 1973 in protest over American bombing of North Vietnam, the American longshoremen retaliated with similar treatment of Australian ships in American ports.

Cross-National or Transnational Groups

The International Non-Governmental Organization. Specialized groups with cross-national ties number approximately 400. These groups establish bonds with related organizations in other countries in arrangements called international non-governmental organizations (or INGOs). The groups attend worldwide conferences and communicate with each other on common problems. The World Trade Union Federation, the National Confederation of Free Trade Unions, and the World Council of Churches are examples of INGOs.

INGO and Dual Allegiance. Theoretically, American groups that are part of an international non-governmental organization face a problem of dual allegiance; in reality, the conflict of allegiance seldom occurs. When national survival is threatened, domestic groups tend to support their own government since INGO ties among national groups are relatively weak. On the other hand, international groups do serve as a forum for communication exchanges. A Tunisian labor leader, who attended an international labor conference in the United States, returned with the heartening news (for Tunisian revolutionaries) that the American labor movement supported Tunisia's drive for independence from France. He seemed to think that it was a matter of time before the American government yielded to pressure from American labor leaders to oppose French policy in North Africa. American labor unions may not have changed the course of U. S. diplomacy toward France, but this incident illustrates the impact of an American group's position and its Tunisian counterpart on politics in Tunisia.[13]

Ethnic Minority Groups. Although not technically defined as INGOs, ethnic minority groups in the United States, who identify with foreign countries of their national origin, sometimes develop strong cross-national ties. The Irish–Americans were vocal in their hostility toward England during U.S.–British spats in the 19th century.

In the post-World War II period, the American black's attitude toward Africa illustrates the tie of national origin and its impact on American foreign policy. The American black community and Africa have reinforced each other's interests. Leaders of the American black community helped stimulate the rise of African nationalism, and African nationalism had its impact on the black community. Segments of the American black community identify with the new African states and share pride in the international and national accomplishments of African leaders.[14]

ARE GROUPS A THREAT TO A DEMOCRATIC FOREIGN POLICY?

On occasions when interest groups have gained access to the decision maker or to the public, they have left a lasting impression on the patterns of American foreign policy. The decision to recognize Israel caused a realignment of political forces in the Middle East. The repercussions from U.S. policy toward Israel will continue throughout this century and probably into the next. The China lobby's successes contributed to the rigidity of relations and lack of diplomatic recognition between the United States and the People's Republic of China until President Nixon's trip to mainland China in 1972. When groups are effective in influencing foreign policy, they move into an area of governmental affairs where the decisions cannot be recalled or corrected as easily as they can be in domestic politics.

The greatest danger is the formal and informal alliances that are sometimes forged among a special-interest group, a department or agency, and individual congressmen who hold powerful positions. The President in all probability would not reject a proposal supported by the American Legion, the Department of Defense, and the House and Senate Armed Services committees. At the same time, the most influential force in this triangular relationship might be difficult to determine. What may appear as the American Legion's suggestion could be a Department of Defense proposition that the President and the Department of State originally axed. For example, a Defense Department proposal to increase military assistance to

Third World nations might run into strong opposition from other bureaucratic agencies, as well as the President. Defense could then mobilize support from the American Legion, whose lobbyists might convince the chairmen of Senate and House Armed Services committees to consider the proposal. If this example constitutes a threat to foreign policymaking in a democracy, the danger may come from the bureaucracy, and not the special-interest group, a point that will be returned to in chapter 10.

Consequently, more research is needed on group relationships to policy decisions; on the relationship of groups to the multiple-contact points within the federal government; and on the relative strength of special-interest groups. This last area for study is especially important if we are to accept the contentions of the Left-Wing Revisionists who place heavy emphasis on economic groups as policy determiners. Little is known about the relative power that special-interest groups in American society have to influence foreign policy. Every group does not have the same clout; some can be ignored by the government, while others cannot.

Another area demanding more attention from social science researchers is the function of special-interest groups as vehicles for recruiting individuals for government positions. No group illustrates this function better than the Council on Foreign Relations, a highly prestigious organization that has provided many well-known decision makers for both Republican and Democratic presidencies of the post-war period. The Council publishes the *Foreign Affairs* quarterly and numerous books on diplomatic issues, reaching a wide distribution of influentials and knowledgeables with its ideas on American foreign policy. Other groups perform essentially the same function of providing personnel and ideas, but the specifics of their patterns of behavior await identification and analysis in further studies.

NOTES

1. In addition to the case studies cited in this chapter, the reader may consult a handful of general analyses: Bernard C. Cohen, *The Influence of Non-Governmental Groups on Foreign Policy-Making* (Boston: World Peace Foundation, 1959); Lester W. Milbrath, "Interest Groups and Foreign Policy," in James N. Rosenau (ed.), *Domestic Sources of Foreign Policy* (New York: Free Press, 1967), pp. 248–251; Sumner Wells, "Pressure Groups and Foreign Policy," *Atlantic Monthly* 180 (November 1947): 63–67; and Donald Blaisdell, "Pressure Groups, Foreign Policy, and International Politics," *Annals of the American Academy* 319 (September 1958): 147–157.
2. Max Beloff, *The United States and the Unity of Europe* (Washington, D.C.: Brookings Institution, 1963), p. 60.
3. David S. McClelland and Charles E. Woodhouse, "Businessmen and Foreign Policy," *Southwestern Social Science Quarterly* 39 (March

1959): 283–290, and Raymond Bauer, Ithiel de Sola Pool, and Louis A. Dexter, *American Business and Public Policy: The Politics of Foreign Trade* (New York: Atherton Press, 1963).

4. Roscoe Baker, *The American Legion and American Foreign Policy* (New York: Bookman Associates, 1954); John P. Windmuller, *Foreign Affairs and the AFL–CIO* (Ithaca: New York State School of Industrial and Labor Relations, 1954) and "The Foreign Policy Conflict in American Labor," *Political Science Quarterly* 82 (June 1967): 205–234.

5. Earl D. Huff, "A Study of a Successful Interest Group: The American Zionist Movement," *Western Political Quarterly* 25 (March 1972): 109–124, and Richard P. Stevens, *American Zionism and U. S. Foreign Policy* (New York: Pageant Press, 1962).

6. Walter Millis (ed.), *The Forrestal Diaries* (New York: Viking, 1951), p. 323.

7. *Ibid.*, pp. 357–358.

8. Senate Foreign Relations Committee, *Activities of Nondiplomatic Representatives of Foreign Principals in the United States*, 88th Congress, 1st Session (Washington, D.C.: U.S. Government Printing Office, 1963); Douglass Cater and Walter Princus, "The Foreign Legion of U.S. Public Relations," *The Reporter* 23 (Dec. 22, 1960): 15–22; and "Foreign Lobbyists: The Hidden Pressures to Sway U.S. Policy," *Newsweek* 60 (July 30, 1962): 18–22.

9. *Department of State Bulletin* 54 (Feb. 28, 1966): 318.

10. Mr. Ball's testimony was delivered before the Senate Foreign Relations Committee on Feb. 4, 1963. Emphasis is added.

11. Ross Y. Koen, *The China Lobby in American Politics* (New York: Macmillan, 1960).

12. Bernard Hennessy, "A Case Study of Intra-Pressure Group Conflicts: The United World Federalists," *Journal of Politics* 16 (February 1954): 76–95.

13. Dwight L. Ling, *Tunisia: From Protectorate to Republic* (Bloomington: Indiana University Press, 1967), pp. 156–157; and Charles F. Gallagher, *The United States and North Africa* (Cambridge, Mass.: Harvard University Press, 1964), p. 239.

14. Rupert Emerson and Martin Kilson, "The American Dilemma in a Changing World: The Rise of Africa and the American Negro," *Daedalus* 94 (Fall 1965): 1055–1084.

8

Partisanship and Foreign Policy: The Role of Political Parties

Primarily because it has been an accepted part of policymaking for most of United States history, the role of the political party in foreign policymaking generates the least controversy. Party considerations are no more dangerous than special-interest groups, but they are so ingrained in American politics that their presence is viewed as a natural part of the decision-making process. Political party activity permeates the federal system, especially in executive–legislative relations, so the subject of political parties will be returned to on several occasions in this volume. For this reason, this analysis of political parties as domestic influencers of foreign policy will be brief.

PARTIES AND PARTISANSHIP

Foreign policymaking has been subjected to interparty squabbles throughout most of U.S. diplomatic history.[1] In more recent years, Republican congressmen criticized Lyndon Johnson's reluctance to escalate American bombing of North Vietnam during the mid-1960s. Democratic congressmen doubted that the Nixon administration's detente with the Soviet Union in the early 1970s was more than a diplomatic facade and questioned whether or not it brought any tangible benefits to the United States. These instances raise the question of whether or not foreign policy should be removed from the arena of political partisanship.

The Case for Partisanship

A case can be made for a partisan approach to foreign policy. Partisanship is a primary characteristic of domestic politics, so it then is only natural for the opposition party to include foreign policy issues in its criticism of the party in power. In a partisan approach to international problems, congressional members support their party's stand; there is little crossing of party lines. This enables the minority party to hold the majority party responsible for policy fiascos; however, the party in power can also claim credit for policy successes. The dialogue between parties will also present the voting public with alternatives at election time. The result will be a better-informed public, since leaders of both parties will debate their disagreements on the issues.

The Case for Bipartisanship

One of the strengths of bipartisanship is that it presents a united front on American foreign policy issues to friend and foe alike. American allies are assured that policies will continue if the next election brings a change of government. Since the party out of power already is committed to past decisions through the bipartisan process of consultation and support, a change of government probably will not result in a wholesale revision of foreign policy. To international opponents, American diplomacy gives an appearance of unity at home with no prospect that the policy will change drastically because of domestic opposition or new elections.

A bipartisan foreign policy is characterized by joint participation of congressional leaders of both parties in the foreign policy formulation process. Whenever the President consults with the congressional members of his own party, he also invites the opposition leaders. In a bipartisan situation, leaders of the opposition party are consulted *before* the President has reached a final decision. Otherwise, the President presents the party out of power with a *fait accompli* and attempts to win the opposition party's support for a decision already made, a procedure hardly in the spirit of true bipartisanship. Joint decisions must be made by recognized leaders of both parties. After the decision process is completed, opposition party leaders are then obligated to rally support for the policy among their group. The President should not expect the party out of power to support his policy if its leaders were not brought into the decision process at an early stage.

There will be occasions when the President consults no congressional leaders, not even of his own party; he simply briefs them on decisions already made and solicits their support. In such cases, partisanship has little to do with executive behavior because leaders of both parties are ignored equally.

Impediments to Bipartisanship

The nature of the American constitutional and political systems presents an obstacle to a truly bipartisan approach. Constitutionally, the separation-of-power principle makes the President the head of state and gives him certain prerogatives in the foreign policymaking process. Presidential decisions may be based on secret information that cannot be circulated widely among the legislators; decisions of this sort also must be made quickly. In this case, congressional leaders of both houses of necessity will be briefed after the fact, rather than consulted during the decision process. Moreover, the President cannot seek consultations on all foreign policy decisions; an arbitrary line must be drawn between the more and less important matters; congressional leaders often disagree over the location of that line. Leaders of the President's opposition may feel especially slighted on issues that they consider important enough to be included in the bipartisan process.

Furthermore, the American political process works against a bipartisan approach to foreign policy. The President usually selects foreign affairs personnel, including the Secretary of State, from his own party. George C. Marshall was an apolitical Secretary of State who engendered Republican support, while Dean Acheson was a thoroughly partisan Democrat. Opposition party leaders may go along with the President's foreign policy and tolerate his choices for foreign affairs subordinates, but they may not be able to control the maverick members of their group. Senator Joseph McCarthy saw the Democrats as a party of traitors, and his attacks on Democrats contributed to a breakdown in bipartisanship in 1949–50.

The political process also dictates that partisan mileage should be extracted from foreign developments that are unpopular with the public. During a Democratic administration, the fall of China to Mao Tse-tung in 1949 and the Korean War in 1950 were issues on which the Republicans were reluctant to assume a benign, nonpartisan attitude. The Republicans feared the political repercussions of becoming identified with policy failures, and they sought to capitalize on their out-of-power position.

The demise of bipartisanship in foreign policymaking (occurring after Secretary Marshall's tenure and especially marked in the Eisenhower administration) has not resulted in a rancorous partisanship in foreign policy debates. Presidents, whether or not their party is the majority in Congress, have attempted to build a winning coalition of supporters on each issue. If the opposition party's support is needed to husband a foreign-aid bill through the House or a treaty through the Senate, the President will consult with opposition leaders and make compromises to build his winning coalition. He will tend to ignore the opposition on issues on which the votes of the party out of power are not needed. This strategy of compiling a new alliance of votes on each issue as it arises appears to work well. It would seem that the days of bipartisan foreign policy are over. In its place is an ad hoc approach to issues where the opposition party is included in the decision process only when its support is needed by the executive.

PARTY IDENTIFICATION WITH FOREIGN POLICY ISSUES

Formulation of Positions on Issues

Whether partisanship or bipartisanship characterizes the formulation of American diplomacy, the process by which parties arrive at positions and the effect of these positions on the public's thinking are important ingredients in the foreign policy process. In the past, parties have been identified with policy positions that have shifted as the composition of the party has undergone transformation. In U.S. trade relations, the Republicans traditionally were advocates of high tariffs and the Democrats, of low tariffs. Since the 1950s the Republicans have supported tariff reduction while the Democrats have modified their traditional free trade position. As southern states, usually Democratic strongholds, gradually became industrialized, their congressmen showed more interest in protective tariff legislation. The Republicans, on the other hand, were converted to Eisenhower's "moderation" and began to modify their protectionist stand. As a result, a "tariff revolution" occurred in 1955 with the emergence of a new alignment in Congress on tariff questions.[2]

All parties thus possess the machinery to construct policy positions on international issues. The three most important aspects of this machinery are the party platform, the party's elected officials, and the congressional party structure.

The Platform. Parties in the American system of government are organized at the state, and not the federal, level. Rather than one Republican or Democratic party, fifty exist. Although state parties focus on local and national issues, they are increasingly turning to international concerns. For example, many states send delegations abroad to drum up trade for the state's industries.

Every four years the fifty state parties of each national party meet in convention to frame a platform and to nominate presidential and vice-presidential candidates. The goal of the party platform and convention is to unite divergent elements of the party and to elect men and women to political offices. Foreign policy differences rarely divide the party, although an exception occurred at the 1968 Democratic Convention with the debate over the platform position taken on Vietnam. The foreign policy planks of the platform are usually broad and nebulous. At times they can be specific as in 1948 when both Republican and Democratic platforms called for a national homeland for the Jews. The platform does not provide detailed guidance to the party on foreign policy issues because it is drafted at four-year intervals (and thus an issue unforeseen by the party's leadership may arise in the interim), because it is a political instrument designed to bring about party unity, and because its provisions are not detailed statements of goals and strategies.

The National Candidates. As a campaign gets under way, the candidates' positions on foreign policy issues may contribute to the party's orientation toward international problems. The presidential candidate, especially if he is elected, is the head of the party, and he may stamp his personal foreign policy views on the party's thinking. The losing party, on the other hand, is set adrift without a central source of leadership to formulate policy positions. Cynicism is a common reaction to position papers issued with fanfare during elections and to the rhetoric that abounds over issues of minor importance. Most of the campaign discussion of foreign policy is too superficial to contribute to a thorough examination of existing foreign policies. Although some contribution to the party's positions on diplomatic issues may be made during the campaign, the patient construction of a foreign policy framework cannot be accomplished without securing office.

Campaign promises are not the best predictive device for a presidential victor's post-election behavior. In 1964, the Republican nominee, Senator Barry Goldwater, advocated a more aggressive stance toward the Vietnam War, while the Democratic incumbent, President Johnson, countered with a more moderate position. Johnson's overwhelming victory was attributed at least partially to the electorate's fear that Goldwater would widen the war. During the following year, the Johnson administration began a massive buildup of men and materiel in the conflict that eventually committed over 500,000 American troops to the fighting.

Presidential campaigns employing rhetoric that promises much but does not reveal the means of achieving a goal contribute little to the public's discrimination. Richard Nixon, before his narrow presidential victory in 1968, criticized the Johnson administration's inability to end the war but never revealed his own plan to terminate the conflict. His "secret plan," he argued, must not be stated in public because it would damage the U.S. negotiating position. Whether a "secret plan" actually existed is open to question since the Vietnam War did not end during Nixon's first term. Rhetoric, then, rarely serves as a vehicle for the party to formulate policy during an election year.

Not all campaign rhetoric is devoid of specifics. In 1962, John Kennedy declared his intention to establish the Peace Corps, and in 1952, Dwight Eisenhower promised to visit Korea if elected. Both ideas proved to be very popular with voters and both eventually were implemented.

The Party Machinery in Congress. The majority and minority leaders, party whips, committeemen, and party caucuses comprise the party machinery in Congress. There is little evidence that party machinery contributes to foreign policy positions.[3] Congressional machinery has failed to become a source of foreign policy leadership because party discipline is lacking in the legislative branch.

Majority and Minority Party Formulations. Where, then, does the party formulate positions? The party occupying the White House has a recognized leader supported by extensive resources in the executive branch for making foreign policy. Party positions on foreign policy problems are the result of a fusion of electoral success, which places the party's nominee in the White House, and the built-in, on-going policies advocated by the bureaucracy. The President may bring new directions and fresh ideas to American foreign policy, but he is also saddled with previous commitments made by his predecessors.

The party with limited access to the federal bureaucracy has fewer resources with which to collect and evaluate data and to propose new directions for American foreign policy. The party not occupying the White House may not be the minority party; presidents Nixon and Ford, for example, had to work with a Congress in which both houses were controlled by the Democrats. The Democrats, although a majority party, were cut off from the vast bureaucratic resources, which included classified information about world events.

All too often, the primary role of the party locked out of the White House is that of a critic. Policy failures, real or alleged, offer opportunities to blame the President's party for neglect and misjudgments. Seldom does the opposition party initiate proposals; it can approve, modify, or reject the executive's initiatives (assuming that the President's party is in the minority in Congress). The party out of power, then, is reduced to a reactive role, responding to ideas generated by the foreign policymaking bureaucracy of the federal government. With disorganized leadership, with limited resources to formulate reasonable alternatives to the party in power's policies, and normally with insufficient strength to demand transformation of the President's position, the party out of power must await policy blunders or embarrassing incidents to gain the public's attention.

The role of the party occupying the White House is usually more constructive. Its congressional leaders are taken into the President's confidence, they are shown classified information, and their opinions are sought before a final decision is made. The party out of power speaks with several (usually congressional) voices, and the President or the public can listen to any one of them. At this point, this analysis is impinging on executive–legislative relationships, discussed in more detail in chapter 12.

Thus far, the established political process has been focused upon as a source of foreign policy patterns. The newly elected party in the White House inherits a vast governmental bureaucracy committed to previous patterns. The President-elect may bring fresh ideas with him, but his primary source of innovative diplomatic patterns is the new cabinet and subcabinet-level members that he recruits for the bureaucracy.

The Maverick Politician

There is yet another source of innovative foreign policy proposals: the maverick politician who begins an apparent crusade outside the established party system and uncovers popular support that most political leaders have overlooked. In 1968, Senator Eugene McCarthy announced his candidacy for the Democratic party's presidential nomination. Although his campaign was based on several issues, opposition to President Johnson's Vietnam War policies was McCarthy's central theme. Most political observers expected McCarthy's efforts to fizzle, but his unexpected strength in the early primaries of 1968 encouraged other entrants, including Senator Robert Kennedy, and no doubt contributed to President Johnson's decision not to seek reelection.

This scenario illustrates the danger that a party in power faces when its leadership runs dry on ideas or when it refuses to listen to voices inside its own party that advocate innovative approaches considered too radical by the bureaucracy. The Democratic party was pulled asunder in 1968 by the "hawk" and "dove" factions. After Senator McCarthy's support faded and Senator Kennedy was assassinated, the party nominated Vice-President Hubert Humphrey, who lost in a close race to Richard Nixon. In 1972, Senator George McGovern capitalized on the support generated by the McCarthy and Kennedy campaigns four years earlier and was nominated by the Democratic Party. He lost overwhelmingly to Nixon, running for his second term.

In 1964, Barry Goldwater broke with the traditional pattern of Republican nominees for the presidency in the post-war years. Goldwater brought proposals to the campaign that had not been seriously suggested in the rhetoric of previous presidential elections. He also galvanized support among segments of the political spectrum that had not lent their energies to party activities in the past. Thus far, the maverick has been successful in party politics but has failed to carry the public with him.

Party Identification and the Citizen

Party identification has been one of the most influential factors in molding the citizen's opinion about foreign policy. A 1951 study found that party identification accounted more for a citizen's response to questions about foreign policy issues than any other variable, such as religion, income level, knowledge about international affairs, and place of residence.[4] In other words, when world events need interpretation, the citizen tends to look to leaders in his political party for guidance. An individual reacts to an issue by taking his behavioral cue from the party's position, waiting for a leader in the party that he respects to respond. Of course, that leader is the President, if the individual identifies with the party in power.

The 1951 study's findings appear to be eroding as a result of the surge in independent and crossover voting. The number of independent voter registrations has increased to the point that they outnumber Republicans. Independent affiliations have increased especially among the young voters. The decline of straight-ticket voting also indicates that party identification may not be as strong a force as before.

The emergence of maverick politicians in 1964 with Goldwater, in 1968 with McCarthy and Robert Kennedy, and in 1972 with McGovern also suggests that party identification is declining. In these three elections, voters traditionally inactive in politics were drawn into the presidential campaigns. Citizens who had been disinterested in the established parties were stimulated by the maverick politician. It remains to be seen in future elections if the maverick politician phenomenon is now a pattern that will regularly reappear in American politics.

THE PARTY: A TRANSMISSION BELT FOR PERSONNEL

What, then, is the role of the party in the foreign policy formulation process? Since the machinery of the party rarely churns out ideas, and since the public's identification with one party is eroding, the party's role becomes more puzzling. It is difficult to distinguish between the party machinery and the federal bureaucracy to determine the source of foreign policy ideas and proposals. The hypothesis suggested here is that the party is not the source.

The party appears to function primarily as a transmission belt for personnel, i.e., it is a vehicle for men and women who aspire to power. They may take either the conservative route and work within the established party system, or they may seek grass-roots support outside the party as mavericks have done. Once in power, the elected officials then use the party as a means of recruiting personnel for cabinet and subcabinet positions. The maverick politician, although he has not won a presidential election, has captured his party's nomination, illustrating the openness of both party structures to new faces. The ease with which George Wallace moved in and out of the Democratic Party, and then back again during his campaigns for the presidency is a case in point. Wallace, the governor of Alabama, ran well as a third-party candidate in 1968, but he decided to work within the Democratic party in 1972. Before he was forced to withdraw as a result of an assassination attempt which left his legs paralyzed, he had won one major primary and was on his way to winning another.

If the party contributes innovations to the foreign policy decision-making process, it does so through the recruitment of elected or appointed officials. Excluding the maverick politician, there appear to be few ideas put forth by the established parties. The party controlling the White House may suggest new proposals, but it has to cooperate with the federal bureaucracy whose function it is to propose ideas. The bureaucracy, however, is recruited from channels other than the party; the largest bloc of foreign policy decision makers does not originate in the political party. The party is primarily a transmission belt for talent in Congress and the highest echelons of the executive branch. Most policy initiatives, however, come from the vast bureaucracy presided over by the party faithful.

NOTES

1. Partisanship in American foreign policy has received considerable attention. H. Bradford Westerfield, *Foreign Policy and Party Politics: Pearl Harbor to Korea* (New Haven: Yale University Press, 1955) has influenced the analysis presented in this chapter. See also Cecil V. Crabb, Jr., *Bipartisan Foreign Policy: Myth or Reality?* (Evanston: Row, Peterson, 1957); Martin Shapiro, "Bipartisanship and the Foreign Policy-Making Process," in Carl J. Frederich and Seymour Harris (eds.), *Public Policy, 1960* (Cambridge, Mass.: Harvard University Press, 1960); Ernest A. Gross, "What is a Bipartisan Foreign Policy?" *Department of State Bulletin* 21 (Oct. 3, 1949): 504–505; Benjamin H. Williams, "Bipartisanship in American Foreign Policy," *Annals of the American Academy* 259 (September 1948): 136–143; Hamilton Armstrong, "Foreign Policy and Party Politics," *Atlantic Monthly* 179 (April 1947): 56–63; James M. Burns, "Bipartisanship and the Weakness of the Party System" *American Perspectives* 4 (Spring 1950): 164–174; and George H. E. Smith, "Bipartisan Foreign Policy in Partisan Politics," *American Perspective* 4 (Spring 1950): 157–169.
2. Richard A. Watson, "The Tariff Revolution: A Study of Shifting Party Attitudes," *Journal of Politics* 18 (November 1956): 687–701.
3. Malcolm Jewell, in "The Senate Republican Policy Committee and Foreign Policy," *Western Political Quarterly* 12 (1959): 966–980, examined the congressional party machinery and concluded that policy positions are seldom decided by it.
4. George Belknap and Angus Campbell, "Political Party Identification and Attitudes Toward Foreign Policy," *Public Opinion Quarterly* 15 (Winter 1951): 601–623. See also Warren E. Miller, "Party Preferences and Attitudes on Political Issues: 1948–1951," *American Political Science Review* 47 (1953): 45–60. George L. Grassmuck, *Sectional Biases in Congress on Foreign Policy* (Baltimore: Johns Hopkins Press, 1951), found that party identification was a more dominant influence on foreign policy than sectional identification.

SECTION 4

Foreign Policymaking and Implementation

This section focuses on the transformation of American foreign policy brought on by four revolutions in post-World War II international politics and the advent of the United States as a superpower. The revolutions in weaponry, economics, statecraft, and the emergence of the Third World were discussed in chapter 2. Each revolution has presented new challenges and problems to the foreign policy of the United States.

The first effect of these revolutions was to bring more considerations into the decision-making process, a development discussed in chapter 9. Technology, the military, the intelligence community, and, to a lesser degree, the economic agencies, were all factors largely ignored or nonexistent prior to World War II; they are now an integral part of the foreign policymaking process.

The patterns of policy implementation and information input are the focus of chapter 10. It should be reemphasized that policy is not truly policy until it has been implemented in the field. The agencies that implement policy are usually the same ones that supply information to the decision maker.

Chapter 11 examines presidential responses to these changes, using four models as analytical tools. The major problem facing the President is control or management of the many agencies involved in the policymaking process.

The legislative response to contemporary political

changes is described in chapter 12. Within the legislative sphere many of the important and basic issues of policymaking are raised. The growth of executive power and congressional, especially Senate, restiveness have evoked important constitutional issues.

9

New Voices in Foreign Policy Formulation: The Problem of Coordination

Before World War II, American foreign policy formulation involved relatively few government agencies; the main actors were the Department of State and several economic agencies, primarily the departments of Commerce, Agriculture, and the Treasury. During times of war, the military departments joined diplomatic endeavors; occasionally, presidents would choose to circumvent everyone by appointing personal emissaries. Woodrow Wilson and Franklin Roosevelt, for example, asked trusted advisers to undertake international duties that they believed should not be left to cabinet officers.

After World War II, an erosion of the State Department's position as "first among equals" began as new voices infiltrated the foreign policymaking process. The revolutions in economics, weaponry, nationalism, and statecraft stimulated and accelerated the introduction of these new voices into administrative procedures used to formulate American diplomatic initiatives.

THE OLDEST VOICES: THE STATE DEPARTMENT AND ECONOMIC AGENCIES

The Department of State

The Department's Rigidity. Although showing occasional flashes of innovative policymaking during the post-war period, the Department of State was generally rigid and unable to adapt to revolutionary changes in the international system.[1] However, in the early post-war years, the Department of State's diplomatic record was impressive: creative thinking was displayed in the Marshall Plan, the North Atlantic Treaty, and containment theory. The Liberals and the Right-Wing and Left-Wing Revisionists would disagree with this evaluation because their images were not reflected in these decisions.

There were sufficient instances of rigidity in the State Department's thinking that served as portents of its sluggishness in meeting the challenges of the next twenty years. Department personnel refused to accept the intelligence and propaganda functions that grew out of World War II, and department officials expressed serious misgivings about the entrance of the military establishments into the policymaking process.

In short, State Department career personnel failed to perceive that the impact of the four revolutions in world politics had widened the spectrum of traditional diplomacy. The military, intelligence, economics, propaganda, and science did not merely represent an addition to international politics; they had become *integral parts* of the world arena. The department continued to think of diplomacy as a pastime of elite gentlemen, when in fact foreign policy had been popularized and new events and forces had placed it within the purview of new agencies, new nations, and new international organizations.

The Secretary of State. In the post-war world of complex international relations, no President has assumed all the functions of the Secretary of State.[2] The bureaucracy has grown too large and diplomatic problems have become too complex for the President to supervise personally the solution to even major problems imbedded in the international system. The President's relationship to his Secretary of State is a senior–junior partnership. Each secretary has brought to the position his own strengths, as well as weaknesses, and his own concept of how the secretaryship should operate. While post-World War II presidents have maintained control over the direction of foreign policy (some chief executives have done more than others), they have given their secretaries of state wide areas of latitude in formulating policy.

No clear-cut patterns have developed since 1945 for the office of Secretary of State. Early in the history of the United States, the office was viewed as a stepping stone to the White House, and future presidents served their apprenticeship as the Secretary of State. In the post-war period, however, this has not been a major consideration. Each of the secretaries appointed since 1945 has represented a combination of political needs and an acceptable mix of personalities on the part of both President and secretary. Harry S. Truman appointed James F. Byrnes (1945–47) to be Secretary of State because the vice-presidency was vacant, and the order of succession at that time placed the Secretary of State one step away from the White House. Truman replaced Edward Stettenus, who had no political experience in an elective office, with Byrnes, who did and who also had a large political following in the Democratic party. George C. Marshall (1947–49) was a non-political secretary who enjoyed support from both

Democrats and Republicans during the post-war bipartisan era of American foreign policy.

Most of the other post-World War II secretaries of state had a background in diplomatic service: Dean Acheson (1949–53), John Foster Dulles (1953–59), Christian Herter (1959–61), and Dean Rusk (1961–69). William P. Rogers (1969–73) and Henry Kissinger had had no previous stint with the State Department. Kissinger's unusual position as both Secretary of State and National Security Adviser will be discussed later in the chapter.

The Economic Voice

Economics speaks with an old, as well as a new, voice in the foreign policy-making process. Foreign trade is an old and perennial foreign policy issue, while international monetary management and foreign economic assistance are new. The needs and concerns of all three voices are considered as policy is formulated.

Foreign Trade. For a nation that is the world's largest trader, the United States possesses surprisingly little organizational structure to manipulate exports and imports. This situation is part of the national value system: Americans tend to believe in a free-market economy in which American businessmen can operate on their own initiative. Administrative agencies that operationalize these values are subjected to pressures from special-interest groups and businesses that lobby to maintain the government's "hands off" attitude toward the economy. At times this neutral stance shades over into a positive attitude toward helping American businesses solve their trade problems.

Policy decisions to implement congressional laws and presidential decisions on foreign trade are made within the administrative units of the bureaucracy. For example, the United States Tariff Commission established in 1916 conducts investigations on problems posed by tariff enforcements, such as whether a company is being hurt economically by the importation of foreign goods or whether a foreign company has "dumped" a large quantity of goods at lower than normal prices on the American market. Normally, the Commission will hold hearings and issue reports on the results of its findings. Also, the Bureau of International Commerce within the Department of Commerce is active in encouraging American businessmen and in aiding them in finding suitable foreign markets.

The U.S. Tariff Commission and the Bureau of International Commerce illustrate the decree-issuing and support-giving units of the bureaucracy that few Americans know exist. Businessmen dealing with international trade or overseas subsidiaries, of course, are well aware of their functions. Other better-known agencies (e.g., Export-Import Bank) will be discussed in chapter 18.

Overseas Economic Representatives. Some bureaucratic units have their own personnel overseas to assist the American businessman and to prosecute U.S. economic interests. The Department of Agriculture, another source of economic influence in the bureaucracy, has its own Foreign Agricultural Service (FAS), which boasts almost 100 agricultural attachés and officers in 60 foreign posts. The Agricultural Attaché is active in implementing the Food for Peace program and in pushing the sale of American agricultural produce abroad through trade fairs, centers, and missions. The FAS is becoming increasingly important in representing the United States government in formal trade negotiations on agricultural products. In discussions between the United States and the European Economic Community, agricultural tariffs and quotas have been a subject of intense negotiation.

Foreign Economic Assistance. International trade has spawned a long list of agencies to assist the American businessman because exports and imports have been a part of the national economy since 1789. Foreign economic assistance is of a more recent date. The Agency for International Development is the best known organization handling foreign economic assistance, but other bureaucratic units occasionally become involved.

The Department of Labor, an agency normally not connected with foreign affairs, sometimes is involved in foreign economic development. Labor cooperates with the Department of State in providing labor attachés who are concerned with helping developing nations solve the problems of unskilled laborers, trained labor being needed to move from an agricultural to an industrial society. The labor attachés also have been active in implementing programs that permit low-wage laborers to migrate from Mexico to help harvest crops on farms in the United States. Most of these programs have been phased out because of opposition from American labor unions.

American "Colonies." Another type of economic development is occurring in dependencies controlled by the United States: Guam, Samoa, the Virgin Islands, and the United Nations Trust Territories in the Pacific.[3] These developing areas are administered by the Interior Department, an agency usually not thought of as part of the foreign policymaking process, and the Panama Canal Zone is administered by the Navy. One reason for these unusual arrangements is the American disinclination to admit that the United States is, after all, a colonial power. Rather than have a colonial department or office (as do the British, who do not share the negative American reaction to possessing colonies), the United States has scattered its administration of overseas possessions among several departments.

Again, policy patterns in foreign aid and economic development are being formulated through channels other than the Agency for International Development. These patterns will be analyzed in chapter 18.

THE MILITARY VOICE

The Effect of the Revolution in Warfare

New genres of weapons, especially nuclear and thermonuclear devices, and a rebirth of guerrilla techniques have contributed to making the military voice a part of the decision-making process. Prior to 1945, the general feeling was that the military voice should be silent except in times of war. When to declare war and what goals to achieve from the fighting were political decisions; military expertise was called upon to implement the goals after the politicians had declared war. Since World War II, however, the military establishment has substantially transformed its traditional role as an implementor to that of a formulator of policy as well. As a result, the military has become an important voice in the decision-making machinery of government.

One reason for the change in the military's role is the advent of nuclear weapon technology and missile delivery systems, which reduce the time between the decision to declare war and the orders to operationalize this decision in the field. In the 19th century, when the United States was protected by two oceans, the decision to go to war was made, and then the military was called in to implement that decision. Today, because the time differential between the decision to go to war and actual fighting has been reduced to a matter of minutes, the professional military must be located close to the centers of decision making at all times.

The increasing occurrences of guerrilla conflicts also have left an imprint on the military's new role. Counter-insurgency warfare, as guerrilla conflicts are sometimes called, mesh civilian and military concerns together. For example, the pacification program in Vietnam during the late 1960s was a concerted effort to reclaim former Viet Cong guerrilla-controlled areas, establish security, and set up self-help projects to put the villages on a self-sustaining basis. While the pacification program included many aspects normally associated with economic development, it remained under the direction of the military in Vietnam.

Evolution of the Post-War Military Establishment

The Need for a New Organizational Framework. The creation of a Department of Defense in 1947–49 was the culmination of extensive debates over reorganization of the armed services.[4] The need for a more unified approach to problems of defense was underscored by the tendency on the part of the departments of War and Navy to act independently in World War II. The evolution of a third branch, the Air Force, added pressure for a new organizational framework for the military voice. The revolution in warfare, with its nuclear emphasis, dictated that the Air Force would be the most expensive component of military strategy.

The result of the debates over reorganization was the National Security Act of 1947 (and its amendments in 1949) which created the Department of Defense, presided over by a civilian secretary with a Joint Chief of Staff established to advise the President and Secretary of Defense. The three armed service departments were headed by civilian secretaries who were relatively independent of the Secretary of Defense.

Expansion of the Roles of the Secretary of Defense and J.C.S. Since the creation of the Department of Defense, the role and authority of both the Secretary of Defense and Joint Chiefs of Staff (J.C.S.) have grown, while the role and authority of the three service secretaries have diminished. By the late 1950s, the line of authority on matters of national security policy was clearly drawn: it extended from the President through the Secretary of Defense and the J.C.S. to the military command in the field. In 1959, the Secretary of Defense began to attend regularly J.C.S. meetings, a practice that has continued to the present day.

Robert McNamara. The Secretary of Defense has become the second most important cabinet position in the policy formulation process. In general, presidents have recruited able persons for the position.[5] Robert McNamara, especially, serving under Kennedy and Johnson, brought new ideas to the post and attempted to exert his sense of direction over the department. His innovations in military strategy will be discussed in chapter 13.

As the military voice increasingly became involved in the foreign policymaking process in the executive branch, McNamara developed organizational units to assist him in making decisions. One organization was the Bureau of International Security Affairs (ISA), which became the Defense Department's "little state department," since it was organized into regional directorates and functional divisions similar to those of the State Department. ISA furnishes the Secretary of Defense with information that enables the defense establishment to contribute to the decision-making process. McNamara also established the Defense Intelligence Agency, discussed later in this chapter.

Mobilization of Opinion. Not only does the Defense Department employ the largest number of bureaucrats and spend the most tax money, it also mounts the most extensive program to mobilize public opinion.

The department attempts to mobilize the influential public through a series of "VIP" tours for community elites. Business, religious, communication, political, and labor leaders are invited to visit military installations, escorted by generals and admirals. During these visits, they are introduced to the problems of maintaining a military readiness and the strategy and tactics used in employing various weapon systems. The purpose of the

chapter 9   New Voices in Foreign Policy Formulation   147

tour is to convince them that the political and economic rationale for a large military establishment is sound. These leaders, the Pentagon hopes, will return to their communities and influence others.

The knowledgeable public is reached through speakers from the Defense Department who appear before special interest, civic, religious, and social groups to explain the department's orientation on current issues. The speakers vary in rank, depending on the prestige and size of the group. For the mass public, there is an extensive repertoire of films, shopping-center displays, and public demonstrations held on military bases on special occasions, such as Armed Forces Day.

THE INTELLIGENCE COMMUNITY

Development of the American Intelligence Community

The American intelligence community is a stepchild of the Cold War.[6] While its inception predates 1945, it has grown larger and has developed more varied activities as the East–West conflict has waxed hotter. In part, then, the community has matured and has been nurtured by a superpower's need for accurate information in an international system populated by another superpower, the Soviet Union.

Pre-World War II Intelligence. Until World War II, the American intelligence community was largely oriented to the military. The War and Navy departments possessed small intelligence units that focused on their particular needs; the State Department at times established offices with limited intelligence functions; and the Federal Bureau of Investigation functioned as the primary counter-intelligence agency. This haphazardly organized community was jolted by the Japanese attack on Pearl Harbor.[7] In 1941, although the Japanese codes had been "broken," the Japanese navy launched a successful surprise attack. The American government had agencies to evaluate combat intelligence and to counteract foreign nations' attempts to gain secret information, but it had no agency responsible for gathering information of strategic value.

The Intelligence Community. The intelligence community is composed of nine agencies brought together in a loose confederation under the supervision of the Director of Central Intelligence (DCI). The DCI occupies two positions, serving as director of the Central Intelligence Agency (CIA) and as head of the United States Intelligence Board. The other eight members of the intelligence community are the three service agencies, the State Department's Bureau of Intelligence and Research, the Defense Department's Intelligence Agency, the National Security Agency, the FBI, and the Atomic Energy Commission. Other departments carry on intelligence activities in one form or another: Bureau of Agricultural Economics in the Department of Agriculture; Bureau of Foreign and Domestic Commerce in the Department of Commerce; Civil Service Commission (which conducts investigations for security clearances for other departments); postal inspectors; "T" (Treasury) men; and the Secret Service. The United States Information Agency, the various foreign-aid agencies, Department of Interior, and the Federal Communication Commission could be included also.

All these groups are engaged in the process of intelligence gathering and evaluation, but they are not formal members of the American intelligence community. The community may be pictured as a series of circles with the core composed of nine agencies which are members of the United States Intelligence Board (USIB). Other government agencies with intelligence functions that comprise a smaller percentage of their overall activities are located in concentric circles surrounding the community. For example, USIA and the Department of Health, Education, and Welfare are located in one of the circles more distant from the core.

The United States Intelligence Board. The USIB functions as a coordinating committee on jurisdictional problems that may arise among its members, and as a consensus board for submitting intelligence reports to the President through the National Security Council. It ensures that the intelligence community speaks with a single voice, although dissent is permitted, often in the form of a footnote to the USIB's final report. Several standing committees work under the direction of USIB, the most important and most famous being the Watch Committee. The Watch Committee consists of representatives from the intelligence agencies who man the Indications Center located in the Pentagon. Its function is to observe events in all parts of the world and to inform the appropriate decision makers of events considered vital to the national interest.

The Central Intelligence Agency

Among the functions assigned to the Central Intelligence Agency by the National Security Act is the responsibility for coordinating intelligence activities for the American government. The aim of this assignment is to synchronize the gathering and interpreting of intelligence so that the community would speak with one, clear voice to the President. The framers of the 1947 National Security Act wanted to avoid another Pearl Harbor and the CIA appeared to be the answer.

At the time of its establishment, the Central Intelligence Agency was made one of the most secretive bureaucratic units. The agency was prohibited from releasing employee's names or the total number employed (the most common estimate is 12,000). In addition, the agency was not required to give a public account of its funds (estimated at over 500 million dollars a year). The National Security Agency, however, has become more furtive than the CIA.

Atomic Energy Commission

The Atomic Energy Commission's Division of Intelligence plays an important role in estimating the nuclear strength of other nations. It is also responsible for monitoring nuclear blasts detonated by foreign countries and for determining the type of weapon and its yield.

Bureau for Intelligence and Research

State Department Antipathy to Intelligence. The original plan after World War II was for the State Department to serve as coordinator of all intelligence activities in the federal government; however, the department balked. For philosophical and internal reasons, it did not wish to assume the coordinating function for intelligence. The internal reasons referred to the geographical intelligence bureaus of the department in existence at that time, which were the locus of policy action in the department. These bureaus viewed a single, intact intelligence agency in the State Department as a threat to their traditional position. The philosophical reason was the department's view that intelligence activities represented the seamy side of diplomacy, and therefore, they had no place in the gentleman's world of diplomacy.

Secretary Marshall and INR. The State Department functioned without a separate intelligence unit until 1947 when George C. Marshall assumed the secretaryship. Marshall, because of his military background, was accustomed to making decisions on the basis of information gathered and interpreted by an intelligence unit. He overrode departmental inhibitions and established an intelligence bureau, which today is called the Bureau for Intelligence and Research or INR.

The Military Agencies

The two military departments of intelligence (War and Navy) that emerged from World War II eventually were joined by three more: Air Force, the National Security Agency, and the Defense Intelligence Agency. More than half of the nine-member intelligence community is connected to the military.

The Defense Intelligence Agency (DIA). The DIA became operational in 1961, over strong opposition from the three service agencies. Its purpose was to eliminate waste created in the intelligence activities of three separate agencies performing similar functions. The DIA also hoped to reduce the propensity of the three agencies to interpret intelligence information according to departmental biases, such as the Air Force's tendency to overestimate the number of Soviet missiles in order to justify increased appropriations.

Since DIA was established, the Secretary of Defense has had an organization to furnish him with coordinated strategic intelligence. Hence, DIA has contributed to the secretary's enlarged role in making foreign policy and to his capability in making judgments that heretofore have been left to the Central Intelligence Agency. DIA personnel number approximately one-third that of the CIA, yet the Defense Intelligence Agency is the CIA's competitor and perhaps will become its rival.

National Security Agency. The NSA is the largest, wealthiest, and most secretive of the intelligence agencies. Its size is estimated at 15,000 employees and its budget at over $1 billion, or approximately twice as large as the CIA's. The NSA's primary mission is cryptology, or the study of codes. It was established in 1952 to coordinate cryptological activities of all U. S. intelligence agencies. The agency "breaks" other nations' codes and protects American communications from enemy cryptanalysis and surveillance. A secondary mission is electronic intelligence (or ELINT) which employs sophisticated electronic surveillance equipment to listen in on conversations or record electronic emanations (e.g., radar). There are thousands of ELINT intercept stations located on land, sea, and in the air. ELINT airplanes penetrate Russian and Chinese territory, and communication ships eavesdrop on message exchanges.

Federal Bureau of Investigation

The FBI is assigned major responsibility for domestic counter-intelligence, including ferreting out individuals engaged in espionage, sabotage, and treason. Approximately 20 percent of the cases investigated by the FBI are counter-intelligence cases and are processed through the bureau's Domestic Intelligence Division. The primary FBI concern is the foreign spy (called an "illegal") brought into the U.S., or spies recruited from the American citizenry. The FBI keeps the Communist party apparatus under surveillance, but the party rarely is used for espionage purposes. Communist party members may recruit American citizens as spies, but an agent, once committed, usually severs all ties with the overt Communist organization in order not to draw suspicion to himself. Since the American Communist Party normally is not an intelligence agency for the Soviet Union, investigatory units such as the House Un-American Activities Committee and the Subversive Activities Control Board, who concern themselves with the Communist party in the U.S., are not considered *bona fide* counter-intelligence organizations.

The Intelligence Community's Problems

The Cold War stimulated the growth of the intelligence community. Until the Korean conflict, the community grew slowly. After June 1950, however, the White House and Congress rapidly increased budgets for agencies in existence and approved the establishment of new units.

Intelligence mistakes in the 1960s began to cool the ardor heaped on the community in the 1950s. The abortive attempt of the CIA to invade Cuba in 1961 was the first major embarrassment. In 1966, the public learned that CIA funds had been used to support non-governmental activities, such as the National Student Association. In the midst of the Vietnamese conflict, the Johnson and Nixon administrations used the intelligence community to spy on leaders of the peace movement.

The continued existence of the intelligence community forces a pertinent question: Can institutions wedded to the Cold War mentally transform their thinking, now that the Cold War is ended? The intelligence community possesses an image of world politics that was forged during the 1950s—an image outdated by events in the 1960s and 1970s. Consequently, policy recommendations emerging from the community may be influenced by a worldview that no longer corresponds to reality. The Nixon administration's detente with the Soviet Union and new relationship with the People's Republic of China signaled the end of the Cold War, a development that the intelligence community will have to adjust to in the 1970s and 1980s.

THE PROPAGANDA VOICE

One of the aspects of the revolution in statecraft is the emergence of new levels of communication among states. Traditionally, diplomacy focused on official exchanges between recognized representatives of government. The growth of intelligence, economics, military, science, and propaganda has expanded the activities of traditional diplomacy.

After World War II, the Truman administration attempted to integrate officials from the Office of War Information and other agencies into the Department of State. The State Department refused, arguing that mixing propaganda with diplomacy would be fatal to the latter. (The issues involved, as well as the debates that preceded the establishment of the United States Information Agency in 1953, are discussed in chapter 17). The State Department's response was a behavioral pattern similar to the one encountered with the intelligence community: opposition to new post-war diplomatic forces in American foreign policy.

THE VOICE OF SCIENCE

Science and the Four Revolutions

Science and technology are the most recent voices to be added to the foreign policy decision-making process.[8] Science has entered the process through a complex of channels, some institutionalized, such as the Atomic Energy Commission, National Aeronautics and Space Administration, and the Office of Science and Technology in the White House. Most agencies, including the Department of State, have in-house scientists functioning as policy advisers.

In part, the scientific voice has become louder in foreign policy because the scientists themselves have demanded a say in the way that their contributions to national power are used toward achieving the goals of American foreign policy. The laboratory is no longer separated from the policy-making room because the scientist has become vocal on how and when his contributions to national power are used.

All of the four revolutions in the post-war international system have contributed to making science and technology a necessary ingredient in U.S. diplomatic patterns. The developments in warfare have been the most important impetus to science, in conjunction with the decisions to pursue disarmament goals. The emergence of the Third World and the revolution in economics have brought requests to the agricultural scientist to perfect new insecticides, fertilizers, and "miracle" plants. The need for improved means of communication has dictated a scientific presence in the revolution in statecraft.

Principal Areas of Scientific Activity

The scientist is active principally in four areas that often involve him in the foreign policymaking process.

Development of Weapon Systems. "Weapon systems" refers to a new type of post-World War II fighting equipment; it is distinct from existing weapons that can be revised and updated.

The stimulus for searching for new families of weapons can come from either the military or the science community. In most cases, the military, with an eye toward the type of war that might be fought in the future, requests that the scientist develop new weapon systems that will enable the soldier to fight effectively. On the other hand, the scientist, at his drawing board or in the laboratory, may develop an entirely new instrument of death with such awesome power that it would force the military establishment to reevaluate its strategic doctrine.

Science and Intelligence. A second area of contribution for science has been intelligence gathering. The trend in gathering intelligence data is toward the use of ELINT, a trend noted in the discussion of the National Security Agency.

Science and Space Exploration. The Russian achievement in launching the first Sputnik in 1957 led to a rash of activity to bring the science community into the foreign policymaking process.[9] Prior to this time, the voice of the science community was largely ignored in the foreign policy process. The National Science Foundation, established in 1950, was assigned the primary function of developing and coordinating national science policies and, secondarily, of encouraging scientific research. It failed in performing its primary function, and therefore, concentrated on its alternative mandate. The effect of Sputnik was to stimulate the federal government to find a new structure to house attempts at developing national science policies. Thus, in 1957, two new groups were established: the Office of Special Assistant to the President for Science and Technology and the President's Science Advisory Committee. The President's Science Advisor (as the Special Assistant came to be called) was chairman of the committee, composed of distinguished representatives from the American scientific community.

The presence of the Science Advisor and the Science Advisory Committee offered to the President an access to advice from the American scientific community. The presence of this channel did not mean that the President would listen to the scientists. During the 1973 "energy crisis," members of the scientific community complained that their views were largely ignored by President Nixon. Decisions were made on technical problems on the basis of political considerations, not expertise.

Arms Control and Science. A fourth major activity that has required scientific expertise is arms-control and disarmament negotiations.[10] Some of the disarmament problems have revolved around devices to detect "cheating" on an arms-control agreement. The lack of technologically sophisticated detection equipment to distinguish between small earthquakes and underground nuclear explosions dictated that only above-ground, above-water, and atmospheric tests were outlawed in the 1963 Test Ban Agreement. The scientific capability of both the United States and the Soviet Union to detect radioactive fallout from above-ground tests means that violation of the agreement readily can be detected.

Science and the "Military-Industrial Complex." Because of the scientist's indispensable contributions to weapon development, intelligence, disarmament, and space negotiations, the scientific voice has become identified with the "military-industrial complex." The "complex" consists of special-interest groups, primarily composed of businesses and industries providing goods and services under contract to the Pentagon, and including the bureaucracy of the military establishment. The scientist, conducting research in a laboratory owned by one of these industries or by a local university, contributes to the "complex."

The "military-industrial complex" has thereby encouraged the development of a scientific elite that vies for Defense Department contracts. Before the Vietnam War began to drain the Pentagon's budget for research and development in the late 1960s, large amounts of defense funds were available to natural and social scientists for projects.

Cross-National Communications. Not all scientists were active in building the military strength of the United States. Individual men of science in different nations have attempted to establish lines of communication apart from government channels to find areas of common concern. Bertrand Russell, with the support of Albert Einstein, started the Pugwash movement in 1955. Moreover, multinational cooperation on scientific endeavors has occurred between states with political and ideological differences, such as during the International Geophysical Year in which the United States and the Soviet Union sponsored a series of joint space explorations.

The Social Sciences

Social scientists appear within an institutionalized framework in three forms: on advisory commissions, as consultants on specialized problems, and through research funded by the government.

Consultantships. The consultant is usually called in to evaluate a topic of immediate concern to the policymaker. His expertise is specialized, and therefore, he is able to provide a more detailed analysis than the bureaucrat, who of necessity is a generalist handling many multifaceted problems.

Consultantships occasionally raise ethical problems for the social scientist involved. Ideally, he is selected because the bureaucracy needs a viewpoint generated from a wealth of knowledge and experience accumulated by the specialist. But the consultant may be screened to ensure that views widely divergent from the bureaucratic consensus do not appear. Criticism of the government's policy in speeches or publications by consultants sometimes results in a consultantship not being renewed. Criticism of United States policy in Vietnam in the late 1960s resulted in the removal of social scientists from the Department of Defense's roster of consultants.

The "Think Tanks." Another source of social science input is the privately founded research organization that contracts with the government to provide in-depth evaluations of long-range problems.[11] The justification for this type of research contract is built around the bureaucracy's lack of personnel with either the expertise or the time to undertake extensive research projects. The research organizations, or "think tanks" as they are called, can draw in social scientists with specialized training for a project and then release them after the study is completed. Federal agencies, subject to the rigidities of civil service requirements, are not quite so flexible.

The history of the think tank–bureaucracy relationship has evolved its own set of ethical problems. Some government agencies have established their own research organizations; the Rand Corporation, for example, was founded with a special relationship to the Air Force. The temptation exists for these organizations to consciously, or unconsciously, reflect the bureaucratic biases of their parent. Research organizations also serve as conduits for the Central Intelligence Agency, thereby raising further ethical implications.

The think tank–bureaucracy relationship also has been the object of public controversy. Some studies, based on hypothetical situations in which the researcher examines possible—but not too probable—scenarios, occasionally have irritated the public and Congress. One study by the Rand Corporation on the possible conditions under which the United States might surrender to an opponent provoked criticism from some congressmen.

Another problem area has been security laxities in the think tanks. Although the researcher may be "cleared" to use classified information in his research, he has opportunities to duplicate classified material, remove it from the premises, and release it to mass media. Research organizations, as a rule, have been lax in their security precautions. In this way, in 1972, at least two researchers working on a history of the Vietnam War, made available to the press reams of documents which became known as the "Pentagon Papers." While their efforts were generally applauded in non-government circles, their successes pointed up the security laxities that exist in think tanks.

Another problem area is the occasional tendency on the part of think tanks to undertake research projects in the field that become embroiled in U.S. relations with foreign nations. Sometimes these problems are ill-conceived, or ill-executed, but the results are the same. In the mid-1960s, "Operation Camelot," a research effort funded by the Department of Defense, investigated the conditions under which revolutions might occur in Latin America. Researchers in Latin American nations quickly found themselves under suspicion, much to the embarrassment of the U.S. government.

THE PROBLEM OF COORDINATION

The Need for Coordination

Lack of bureaucratic synchronization is characteristic of many institutions. In government, one section of the bureaucracy may enforce policy that is opposed by another sector, or one decision maker may enunciate policy statements that are at variance with another's declaration. These scenarios have been repeated often to the embarrassment of the government in power.

In formulating and executing the affairs of diplomacy, a disjointed bureaucracy charging off in different directions may have a comic air to it at times, but during periods of crisis when the very survival of a nation is at stake, bureaucratic blunders are more serious.

Executive Machinery for Coordination

The President and the State Department. It is much too simplistic to say that the President is the bureaucratic coordinator. Although this role is one that the President and his staff attempt, coordination occurs much further down the decisional structure. In theory, only the most difficult decisions are brought to the President for resolution—decisions that involve the most serious problems of national survival. While in practice this may not be the situation all the time, it can be assumed that the President cannot coordinate all policy.

When the State Department enjoyed primacy in the foreign policy process, coordination was not as great a problem. However, the need for it still existed, especially *within* the department among regional and functional bureaus. While the essence of the problem of coordination remains the same, the magnitude has certainly increased. The State Department's voice is now only one of many that must be harmonized to assure that policy intention matches policy outcome.

The National Security Council (NSC). The problem of coordination was attacked by erecting a structure to serve as an arena within which the various voices allow their messages to be heard. The need for such a structure was recognized early in the post-war period; in 1947, the National Security Council was established by the National Security Act.[12] This act was a far-sighted effort to revise the organizational approach to American foreign policy that traditionally had characterized the executive branch. It essentially occurred before the Cold War was underway; thus, it was more of a response to internal demands for revision than to external pressure from a perceived threat. It recognized that foreign policy was no longer the exclusive purview of the State Department and that there were more voices that had to be heard by the President in order for him to make appropriate decisions.

Originally, the council was composed of the President, Vice-President, secretaries of State, Defense, Army, Navy, and Air Force, and the directors of the Office of Emergency Planning and Central Intelligence Agency. The National Security Act divided these individuals into "members" and "advisers," a distinction that has become largely meaningless. As the role of the service secretaries was reduced, they were omitted from the council, and the Chairman of the Joint Chiefs of Staff was added. Other individuals were invited as temporary visitors but remained on a quasi-permanent basis. President Eisenhower brought in the Secretary of the Treasury and the Director of the Bureau of the Budget. While this move was widely interpreted as an indication of the Eisenhower administration's concern for economy, it also brought the economic voice into the council. The science community is still omitted from the council.

Presidential Style and the NSC. Every post-war President has adapted the National Security Council to his idiosyncratic style of behavior. At first, Truman neglected the Council and made major decisions (e.g., the recognition of Israel) without consulting it. He often did not attend NSC meetings, ostensibly to encourage freer discussion of policy alternatives. Perhaps Truman viewed the council as an interloper in decisional areas that he felt should be reserved for the President; if so, he misread the coordinating role of the council as a decision-making function. He may have believed that the council gave too much representation to the military sector in the foreign policy process. Toward the end of his term, however, he made greater use of the council.

During the Eisenhower tenure (1953–1961), the National Security Council's role was expanded. It met weekly, with discussion centering around drafts of policy proposals prepared by the Planning Board, chaired by the President's Special Assistant for National Security Affairs. The Planning Board consisted of representatives of the NSC members, usually assistant secretaries concerned with the specific problem under discussion. For example, a draft on policy in the Congo would bring together the assistant secretaries (or their equivalent) for African Affairs in the various agencies. The policy proposal would be drafted for discussion at the NSC.

During the NSC discussion, the President's National Security Affairs Assistant served as executive secretary. He wrote a "record of action" which summarized the consensus of the council on the policy paper under discussion. After the President reviewed and approved the record of action (perhaps requesting changes), it would become at that point a *policy decision.* Implementing the decision was a function of the Operations Coordinating Board, presided over by the Undersecretary of State and composed of representatives from the Department of Defense, Central Intelligence Agency, United States Information Agency, and others.

The National Security Council under Eisenhower was a highly structured coordinator for American foreign policy. Not only was the council enlarged to include the economic voice, but the information-input function (i.e., the Planning Board) and the decision-implementing function (i.e., the Operations Coordinating Board) were also coordinated.

President Kennedy's idiosyncratic style of political decision-making was markedly different from Eisenhower's, and it was reflected in his use of the National Security Council. He dissolved the Operations Coordinating Board and transformed the council's role from coordination to policy initiation. The council was divided into small task forces, which were assigned a specific policy problem to solve within a limited period of time. In many cases, the President would assign his brother, Robert Kennedy, to the task force as well as individuals with opposing views on each issue. The minority members, dissenting from the task force report to the President, were assured that they could argue their case without endangering their status.

SIG/IRG. While Lyndon Johnson continued the Kennedy approach to the National Security Council, he also instituted a separate framework known as SIG/IRG to coordinate policy, since the council had fallen into disuse as a coordinator through the task force approach. SIG is an acronym for Senior Interdepartmental Group, chaired by the Undersecretary of State and composed of the Deputy Secretary of Defense, Chairman of the Joint Chiefs of Staff, the Director of the Central Intelligence Agency, and the President's Special Assistant for National Security Affairs. Interdepartmental Regional Groups (IRGs), composed of assistant secretaries from various departments concerned with foreign affairs, were established for each geographical area, such as Africa or the Americas. The Assistant Secretary of the Department of State presided over the meetings, also attended by regional directors from the CIA, Defense Department, AID, and USIA.

The intent of the SIG/IRG framework was to solve problems at the lowest possible level in the bureaucracy and to coordinate the solutions with the major agencies involved. If a regional issue could not be resolved in the IRG, it would then be the subject of discussion and negotiation by the SIG. Hopefully, a consensus on the policy would be arrived at and the problem therefore "solved." If disagreement continued, however, the issue would then be brought to the attention of the President with the secretaries of State and Defense and other individuals brought in as the President desired. Only the thorniest and most controversial problems would make their way up the SIG/IRG framework and eventually reach the President; there would be adequate consultation and coordination at lower levels within the SIG/IRG arrangement on the less controversial issues.

SIG/IRG, despite its promise and attractive logic, was never given an adequate trial during the Johnson years, but it was made part of the Nixon–Kissinger revival of the NSC. The Vietnamese conflict arrested almost all of the Johnson administration's attention to the neglect of other areas of the world. Coordination and decision making became more a function of the "Tuesday luncheon" group, composed of the President, secretaries of State and Defense, and the President's Special Assistant for National Security Affairs; they would discuss foreign affairs problems, most of which centered around Southeast Asia. No agenda was distributed before the meeting and no minutes were taken. With no official record of consensus and decisions, each participant was guided only by his memory of the discussion and he acted accordingly.

Nixon's Revival of NSC. President Nixon revived the National Security Council, which had been dormant since the Eisenhower years. Under the direction of Nixon's National Security Affairs Assistant, Henry Kissinger, the NSC structure was revised. The Nixon administration's use of the council placed more power and more responsibility on the President's staff for coordinating foreign policy and especially upon his Assistant for National Security Affairs. The Department of State was lowered yet another notch and assumed less of a role in formulating policy initiatives.

In 1973, two dramatic events changed State Department's relationship to the NSC. First, Kissinger, putting on another hat, was appointed Secretary of State while retaining his position as National Security Advisor. With this move the Department of State was catapulted into a position in the policymaking process that approximated its pre-World War II position. In 1973 the Nixon administration became mired in scandal, resignations, impeachment charges, and dismissals of key personnel. As a result, President Nixon began to leave foreign affairs initiatives in Kissinger's hands. The President's attention was riveted to his domestic problems while his Secretary of State–National Security Adviser was left largely alone to meet international crises, such as renewed fighting in the Middle East in 1973.

Other Levels and Areas of Coordination. Coordination occurs at different levels and with varying degrees of formality. The State Department's Country Director, for example, may meet with his counterpart in the CIA or the Pentagon's Defense Intelligence Agency to hammer out differences over a current proposal. Highly structured interagency committees abound since the various voices, each representing an organizational interest, have common problems and jurisdictional disputes.[13] The National Aeronautics and Space Council advises the President on space programs while the Committee of Principals brings together agencies with an interest in disarmament.

Some interagency coordinators are not quite so well-known. The Berlin Task Force, for instance, attempts to mold a united approach to issues that arise out of negotiations with the Soviet Union and the crises that occur when the East Germans undertake policies considered threatening to American interests. Other groups, such as the Interagency Committee on Oceanography and the Interdepartmental Radio Advisory Committee, seldom make headlines, but often their discussions involve international problems.

The Office of Management and Budget. Not to be overlooked as a coordinating unit within the executive offices of the White House is the Office of Management and Budget (OMB), entrusted with the function of translating political priorities into economic figures. One of its units handles budgetary allocations for international affairs. Since interdepartmental friction usually centers around scarce resources, OMB plays a coordinating role by working out compromises among competing bureaucratic voices.

COORDINATING THE VOICES: IS NEW MACHINERY NEEDED?

The record of coordinating these new voices in the foreign policy process has not been impressive. The National Security Council machinery established in the late 1940s has been transformed, ignored, and used according to the idiosyncratic style of successive presidents. At NSC's nadir Johnson's "Tuesday lunch" group of three subordinates held unstructured meetings with no agenda and with no official minutes. At NSC's apex was Henry Kissinger's tenure as National Security Advisor during Nixon's first term. Does this erratic use of the NSC imply a need for new systems for coordination?

Two suggestions for coordination to help the President have never progressed far despite the persistence of the problem that they attempt to solve. One suggestion is to create a position of First Secretary, presiding over a foreign policy cabinet composed of officials mainly concerned with diplomacy. The First Secretary would be similar to the British Prime Minister, and he or she would have power to act for the President.

It has also been suggested that a position of "Vice-President for Foreign Affairs" be created. Two vice presidents would be elected every four years, one charged with foreign, and the other with domestic affairs. The Vice-President for Foreign Affairs would head the various offices of the White House dealing with diplomacy, rather than a cabinet as envisioned by the former proposal. Neither idea has caught on.

The solution to the problem of coordination lies in exercising control over the voices and their massive bureaucracies. A President who acts decisively, who can recruit talented subordinates, who permits criticism of proposals, who protects individuals holding minority positions, and who establishes safeguards against unilateral actions by bureaucratic units is able to control the voices. The desirable outcome of coordination is the orchestration of the many bureaucratic voices.

Coordination is not natural to bureaucracy. It is an art that must be practiced in order to be mastered. The coordinating decision maker needs organizational skills, a huge reservoir of patience, and a large amount of time to devote to the task.

NOTES

1. Literature on the Department of State abounds, and the reader will see more of it referenced in chapter 10. For a general analysis, *see* H. Field Haviland, *The Formation and Administration of United States Foreign Policy* (Washington, D.C.: Brookings Institution, 1960); Robert E. Elder, *The Policy Machine: The Department of State and American Foreign Policy* (Syracuse, N.Y.: Syracuse University Press, 1960); John P. Leacacos, *Fires in the In-Basket: The ABC's of the State Department* (New York: World Publishing Co., 1968); Arthur W. MacMahon, *Administration in Foreign Affairs* (University, Ala.: University of Alabama Press, 1953); John U. Terrell, *The U.S. Department of State: Story of Diplomats, Embassies, and Foreign Policy* (New York: Meredith Press, 1968); Graham H. Stuart, *The Department of State: A History of Its Organization, Procedure, and Personnel* (New York: Macmillan, 1949); James L. McCamy, *Conduct of*

the New Diplomacy (New York: Harper & Row, 1964) and *The Administration of American Foreign Affairs* (New York: Alfred A. Knopf, 1950); Richard A. Johnson, *The Administration of United States Foreign Policy* (Austin: University of Texas, 1971); and Dean G. Pruitt, *Problem Solving in the Department of State* (Denver, Colo.: University of Denver Press, 1964).

2. Works on the Secretary of State include: Norman A. Graebner, *An Uncertain Tradition: American Secretaries of State in the Twentieth Century* (New York: McGraw-Hill, 1961); Don K. Price, *The Secretary of State* (Englewood Cliffs, N.J.: Prentice-Hall, 1960); Alexander De Conde, *The American Secretary of State: An Interpretation* (New York: Praeger, 1962); and Samuel Flagg Bemis, *The American Secretaries of State and Their Diplomacy* (New York: Cooper Square Publishers, 1963).

3. Stanley A. de Smith, *Microstates and Micronesia: Problems of America's Pacific Islands and Other Minute Territories* (New York: New York University Center for International Studies, 1970); and Eugenie Anderson and William R. Norwood, "The Trust Territory of the Pacific Islands," *Department of State Bulletin* 55 (Sept. 13, 1966): 387–400.

4. William R. Kintner, *Forging a New Sword: A Study of the Department of Defense* (New York: Harper & Row, 1958); Patrick W. Powers, *A Guide to National Defense: The Organization of the U.S. Military Establishment* (New York: Praeger, 1964); John C. Ries, *The Management of Defense: Organization and Control of the U.S. Armed Forces* (Baltimore: Johns Hopkins Press, 1964); Harry B. Yoshpe and Theodore W. Bauer, *Defense Organization and Management* (Washington, D.C.: Industrial College of the Armed Forces, 1967); Clark R. Mollenhoff, *The Pentagon: Politics, Profits and Plunder* (New York: G.P. Putnam's Sons, 1967); J. W. Fulbright, *The Pentagon Propaganda Machine* (New York: Liveright, 1970); Paul Y. Hammond, *Organizing for Defense: The American Military Establishment in the 20th Century* (Princeton, N.J.: Princeton University Press, 1961); C. W. Borklund, *The Department of Defense* (New York: Praeger, 1968); and Charles J. Hitch, *Decision-Making for Defense* (Berkeley: University of California Press, 1965).

5. Carl W. Borklund, *Men of the Pentagon: From Forrestal to McNamara* (New York: Praeger, 1966).

6. For general discussion of the intelligence community, see Harry Howe Ransom, *The Intelligence Establishment* (Cambridge: Harvard University Press, 1970); Monro MacCloskey, *The American Intelligence Community* (New York: Rosen, 1967); Michael Elliot-Bateman (ed.), *The Fourth Dimension of Warfare: Intelligence, Subversion, Resistance*, vol. I (New York: Praeger, 1970); Sir Kenneth Strong, *Men of Intelligence: A Study of the Roles and Decisions of Chiefs of Intelligence from World War I to the Present Day* (New York: St. Martin's, 1972); Roger Hilsman, *Strategic Intelligence and National Decisions*

(Glencoe, Ill.: Free Press, 1956); and Sherman Kent, *Strategic Intelligence for American World Policy* (Princeton, N.J.: Princeton University Press, 1949).

7. The problems of intelligence gathering and evaluation prior to Pearl Harbor are discussed by Roberta Wholstetter, *Pearl Harbor: Warning and Decision* (Stanford, Calif.: Stanford University Press, 1962); Paul Burtness and Warren U. Ober, "Research Methodology: Problem of Pearl Harbor Intelligence Reports," *Military Affairs* 25 (Fall 1961): 132–146. For a discussion of "breaking" codes, see David Kahn, *The Codebreakers: The Story of Secret Writing* (New York: Macmillan, 1967).

8. The general literature on this subject includes Eugene B. Skolnikoff, *Science, Technology, and American Foreign Policy* (Cambridge: MIT Press, 1967); Dean Schooler, Jr., *Science, Scientists, and Public Policy* (Glencoe, Ill.: Free Press, 1971); Donald A. Strickland, *Scientists in Politics: The Atomic Scientists Movement, 1945–46* (Lafayette, Ind.: Purdue University Studies, 1971); Lee A. DuBridge, "Policy and the Scientists," *Foreign Affairs* 41 (April 1963): 571–588; and Robert Gilpin, *American Scientists and Nuclear Weapons Policy* (Princeton, N.J.: Princeton University Press, 1962).

9. Don Kash, *The Politics of Space Cooperation* (Lafayette, Ind.: Purdue University Studies, 1971).

10. Harold K. Jacobson and Eric Stein, *Diplomats, Scientists and Politicians: The United States and the Nuclear Test Ban Negotiations* (Ann Arbor: University of Michigan Press, 1966); Donald A. Strickland, "Scientists as Negotiators: The 1958 Geneva Conference of Experts," *Midwest Journal of Political Science* 8 (November 1964): 372–384.

11. For additional information, see Roy E. Licklider, *The Private Nuclear Strategists* (Columbus: Ohio State University Press, 1971); Gene M. Lyons and Louis Morton, *Schools for Strategy: Education and Research in National Security Affairs* (New York: Praeger, 1965); and Arthur Herzog, *The War-Peace Establishment* (New York: Harper & Row, 1965).

12. Stanley L. Falk, *The National Security Council under Truman, Eisenhower and Kennedy* (Beverly Hills, Calif.: Glencoe Press, 1968); Robert Cutler, "The Development of the National Security Council," *Foreign Affairs* 34 (April 1956): 441–458; Paul Y. Hammond, "The National Security Council as a Device for Interdepartmental Coordination," *American Political Science Review* 54 (December 1960): 899–910; Henry Jackson (ed.), *The National Security Council* (New York: Praeger, 1965); Hans J. Morgenthau, "Can We Entrust Defense to a Committee?" *New York Times Magazine*, June 7, 1959, pp. 62–66; George A. Wyeth, "The National Security Council," *Journal of International Affairs* 8 (1954): 185–195; Keith Clark and L. J. Legere (eds.), *The President and the Management of National Security* (New York: Praeger, 1969); Edward A. Kolodziej, "The National Security Coun-

cil: Innovations and Implications," *Public Administration Review* 29 Nov.–Dec. 1969): 573–585; Robert H. Johnson, "The National Security Council: The Relevance of Its Past to Its Future," *Orbis* 13 (Fall 1969): 709–735.

13. *See also* Randall B. Ripley, "Interagency Committee and Incrementalism: The Case of Aid to India," *Midwest Journal of Political Science* 8 (May 1964): 143–165; Mary T. Reynolds, *Interdepartmental Committees in the National Administration, 1932–1936* (1939), reprinted by AMS Press of New York; David Howard Davis, *How the Bureaucracy Makes Foreign Policy: An Exchange Analysis* (Lexington, Mass.: D. C. Heath, 1972).

10

Functions of Bureaucracy: Information and Implementation

Providing information and implementing policy are the two primary functions of the foreign policy bureaucracy. Information input and implementation of policy are usually performed by the same agency, a point that raises questions of propriety as well as of efficiency.

Accurate information and faithful execution are vital ingredients to a successful foreign policy. A government must have adequate sources of information to describe its international environment and trained analysts to evaluate that information. The nation with sensitive antennae to receive data and with a bureaucracy respected for its ability to distill masses of factual information into manageable, meaningful, and useable facts obviously has an edge on an opponent less talented in information reception and analysis.

Decisions by constitutionally recognized officials may be based on the most accurate information but they can be distorted, modified, or pigeonholed before they get to the field. Policy decisions made by the President become policy at the time of implementation, not at the point of verbalization of the decision. The implementors, therefore, are the true policy-makers because they interpret and enact the President's directives. In this chapter, the process of information and implementation and the problems that this process presents are examined. In the next chapter, the President's options in managing the bureaucracy will be explored.

Before this discussion is begun, three basic assumptions of the nature of bureaucracy should be enunciated. First, bureaucracy is not a "necessary evil," but an essential actor in the drama of politics. Thus, "bureaucracy" and "bureaucratic" are not used here as pejorative terms to describe undesirable aspects of the policy formulation process.

Second, the problems attributed to the American bureaucracy are not unique but are ubiquitous, infecting all bureaucracies in the world. Because the Washington bureaucracy is one of the largest in the world, these problems may appear more often. Moreover, American democracy may introduce control and management difficulties not found in less open forms of government.

And finally, except for an occasional plea from the Realists for upgrading the Foreign Service, the imageholders have largely neglected the role of bureaucracy in formulating foreign policy. This fact alone should make one cautious in accepting one of the four images as a guide to studying American foreign policy.

INFORMATION INPUT

The Cuban Missile Crisis: An Illustration

In the opening chapter of his book, *Thirteen Days*, Robert Kennedy describes the following scene:

> At 11:45 that same morning (October 28, 1962), in the Cabinet Room, a formal presentation was made by the Central Intelligence Agency to a number of high officials of the government. Photographs were shown to us. Experts arrived with their charts and their pointers and told us that if we looked carefully, we could see there was a missile base being constructed in a field near San Cristobal, Cuba. I, for one, had to take their word for it. I examined the picture carefully, and what I saw appeared to be no more than the clearing of a field for a farm or the basement of a house. I was relieved to hear later that this was the same reaction of virtually everyone at the meeting, including President Kennedy. Even a few days later, when more work had taken place on the site, he remarked that it looked like a football field.[1]

This vignette illustrates the difficulties encountered by decision makers, including the President, in evaluating incoming information. The President must work with incomplete, and sometimes suspect, data that are interpreted for him by technicians whose personal or bureaucratic motivations are not beyond question. He must evaluate technical information, which he has no expertise to analyze, or data obtained through sources that are too technologically sophisticated for him to comprehend. In October 1962, President Kennedy accepted the belief of his intelligence community that the photo that he was examining was of a missile site and not of a football field. On the basis of this information, he chose a series of policy options that brought the world close to nuclear conflict.

Information Input: The Gatekeeper

"Information is Power." Perhaps this simple statement appears trite, but it is the essence of the analysis presented here: the individual (or group) that controls the spigot to turn on or to regulate the flow of information can

influence the formulation of policy. Moreover, this power is pervasive, because control over information collection, evaluation, and dissemination is a characteristic of almost every bureaucrat who occupies a niche in the decisional pyramid. Since information is power and one of the functions of bureaucracy is to supply information, then bureaucracy possesses power to influence the direction of American foreign policy. The power over information is the power to pass along bits and pieces of data, to file them, to scramble their content, or to discard them. Each bureaucrat, then, is a "gatekeeper."

The Gatekeeper Effect. Each day, verbiage by the ton flows into the executive bureaucracy. Obviously, not all of the messages reach the very top echelon; this means decision makers at each level must decide between the more important and the less important, and then pass the former up to the next level and file away the latter. Figure 10–1 illustrates this process of transmitting selected information up through the bureaucratic ranks. As the information moves up the structure, more parts of it are omitted, summarized in broad statements, or placed in appendices. Finally, the document that reaches the President's desk is a brief distillation of the myriad messages received by the bureaucracy. Since all data cannot be proposed for review at the top, the bureaucrat must trust his own sense of values as to what are the most important aspects of the situation. To say that the President alone makes policy is to overlook the countless policy decisions already made by faceless government employees at all levels of

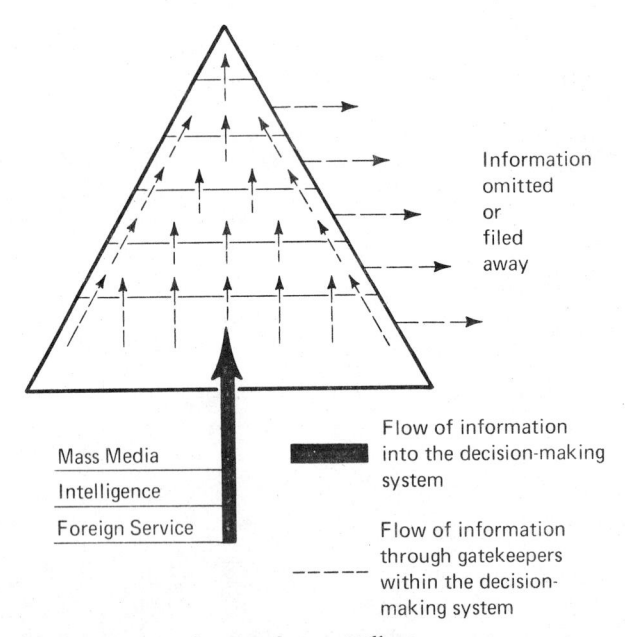

Figure 10–1. The Gatekeeper Effect.

the bureaucracy. Because each bureaucrat is a gatekeeper, he is a decision maker.

Facts do not have an independent existence; their existence and importance are a function of the policymaker. The bureaucrat, as a gatekeeper, places a value on the assortment of facts before him. If he is a decision maker in the Department of the Navy, he will be prone to pass information to higher levels on those events in the world that confirm his and his department's position. For example, if he discovers that the Soviet Union is building a modern navy, he might perceive that as a threat to American national security. Facts that confirm the opposite hypothesis might not be passed along, but probably would be filed away quietly.

Of the many voices contributing to formulating foreign policy, the most active in providing information and in implementing policy are the intelligence community, the military establishment, and the State Department, with its traditional links to the economic departments.

INTELLIGENCE: OVERT AND COVERT OPERATIONS

Intelligence and Information Input

The intelligence community draws upon mass media as sources of information, as well as on analysts and agents overseas. In fact, the bulk of information tapped by intelligence analysts—perhaps as much as 80 percent—is within the public domain. Examples of overt, or open, sources are newspapers, magazines, tourist reports, and public broadcasts. Little difficulty is involved in collecting this type of material, but much work is required in processing it. Since publications in the public domain are by far the largest suppliers of data, the typical intelligence officer is a researcher rather than a spy.

The intelligence community is the government's storehouse of knowledge on all foreign issues. Diplomats preparing for an international conference need biographical data on the individuals with whom they will negotiate. Military tacticians planning an amphibious assault require information on harbor depth, time and height of tides, and slope and type of beach terrain. The President may request a report on the present location of Soviet nuclear submarines in the world's oceans and seas. Not all requests are dramatic: the name of the Polish Minister of Education, the population of Peking, and last year's Bulgarian steel production are examples of the type of information that the community provides. The political decision maker needs accurate and detailed data to formulate policy, and the intelligence units usually supply that data.

The intelligence community's many and varied classified publications further contribute to the informational input. They range from the daily *Intelligence Checklist* (for the President to read each morning) to periodic journals that circulate both within and without the community. Each member of the community has its own publication focusing on the agency's special interests.

The document that best illustrates the informational input function is the National Intelligence Survey (NIS), which presents the community's encyclopedia of knowledge on an individual nation. The NIS document is compiled by many sources in the intelligence community; for example, the Bureau for Intelligence and Research writes the biographical sections. National Intelligence Surveys are comprehensive and represent the community's consensus of information about a country. They are updated periodically.

Functions of Intelligence. Accurate and readily available information reduces some of the risk involved in decision making. Because wartime intelligence agencies lacked information on landing beaches of Japanese-held islands, the American government had to issue a call for photographs taken by tourists who had visited the islands. The risk of failure was increased because of inadequate information. An intelligence community can contribute to national power through its information-input function.

Intelligence also can contribute to international stability by providing the decision maker with reliable information on the enemy's military capabilities and state of readiness. It does very little good for the U. S. government to inform the Soviet Union that no surprise attack is planned. The diplomatic channels of communication can carry faithfully this message, but little credibility would be attached to it by the other side. Only with verification from the Russian intelligence community would the Soviet decision makers believe that no surprise attack was planned. Aerial photographs taken by Russian "spy in the sky" satellites showing no mass movement of troops or redeploying aircraft would serve as "tangible evidence."

Both the U.S. and U.S.S.R. have built extensive intelligence operations to maintain surveillance of each other's military strength and activities. Unwritten rules of data gathering have been respected by both sides and both nations have tolerated a measure of the other's intelligence activities. Russian "fishing vessels" that violate American territorial waters or accompany American naval maneuvers are tolerated, as well as American violations of the Soviet domain. Smaller states, who may consider themselves above the rules, have acted differently, as did North Korea in seizing the spy ship, *Pueblo,* in February 1968. The North Korean government's action would make sense (in terms of the norms of international behavior) only if it had no spy ships carrying secret codes and gear that could be confiscated by the United States.

The American and Russian intelligence communities have not purposely given each other valuable information, but occasionally they have relaxed their guard sufficiently to permit surveillance. With a reliable assessment of the opponent's strength, and with verification that military forces were not being mobilized for a surprise attack, the intelligence community contributed to international stability in the Cold War.

Covert Sources of Information. "Black," "covert," and "clandestine" are words used to describe the personnel who furnish information as well as carry out policy directives. In general, covert sources are illegal sources of information within the jurisdiction of other nations. "Illegal" is defined in terms of the domestic laws of the foreign country involved; however, most states have prohibitions on espionage and treason. Because the sources are under foreign jurisdiction, a considerable risk is involved in obtaining the information desired and in getting it out of the country. The covert supplier may be either a machine or a person. Examples of machine-suppliers are manned and unmanned airplanes penetrating a foreign government's airspace, intelligence vessels violating territorial waters, and electronic listening devices.

Spys may operate as "legal" or "illegal" agents. As legal agents, they are protected by diplomatic "cover" and occupy positions in their government's embassy, ostensibly performing a diplomatic function, such as representing their government on a trade mission. Their true function normally is an open secret to the host government. While the legal agents are a nuisance to be watched, "illegal" ones can be more of a threat. Illegal agents are often highly-trained foreign nationals "dropped into place" with personal histories and supporting documents permitting them to assume a normal existence in the host country. The illegal may be recruited from citizens sympathetic to the employing government's position or ideology, or he may be bribed or blackmailed into providing classified information.

Although information from covert sources furnishes a small percentage of total intelligence, does its importance outweigh information from overt sources? The answer, surprisingly, is negative. Nor is it true that covert sources are necessarily more reliable than open or public suppliers.[2] Information from secret agents perhaps is more important as confirmation (or disconfirmation) of data obtained from open sources.

The Uses of Information

Information is not collected in a vacuum, nor is it gathered to be filed away and forgotten. The intelligence community collects information to form estimates of the enemy's probable behavior and to warn leaders of threatening actions. Estimates (or forecasts) are the most probable level of capability or the most probable course of action that the leaders of friendly or enemy states may choose.[3] The intelligence officer is not clairvoyant, but through his evaluation of incoming information he gathers data and puts together an intelligence "picture." If his picture, as assembled or projected into the future, depicts a threat to American national security, then it is his obligation to warn the decision maker. For example, during the autumn of 1962, Cuban refugees reported construction of unusual structures. Consequently, aircraft were ordered to fly over Cuba on photo reconnaissance flights. Interpretation of the photographs revealed that intermediate-range ballistic missile sites were being constructed. The intelligence picture was complete; an estimate was given of the most probable time that the missiles would be operational, and the decision maker was warned of the threat to American national security.

Estimating is most often a community-wide activity that results in the

National Intelligence Estimate (NIE). NIE drafts are written for the community by the Board of National Estimates located within the CIA. The board consists of approximately a dozen senior analysts with established reputations in the community.

Accuracy of Intelligence Estimates. Instances of incorrect estimates have been met with the "batting average" argument. The intelligence community purports to have more hits than strikes, but since the hits cannot be publicized, the score will never be known. Most criticism of estimates has focused on surprises which the intelligence community did not anticipate or consider probable. One can distinguish between "technical surprises," when an act is unanticipated but is nevertheless compatible with the past behavioral pattern of the actor, and "behavioral surprises," when the act is contradictory to the actor's past behavioral pattern. The Japanese attack on Pearl Harbor and Russia's missile armament in Cuba were behavioral surprises; both states acted in a way inconsistent with past behavioral patterns as perceived by American decision makers. It is difficult, if not impossible, to anticipate behavioral surprises. While the decision maker should prepare for all possible contingencies, he must estimate each contingency's probability of occurrence. He can always be surprised by an act that is considered least probable. Despite difficulties in forecasting behavioral surprises, the intelligence community continues to be held responsible for failures to give adequate warning.

Although incorrect estimates plague the intelligence community, instances where accurate estimates go unheeded by decision makers have also occurred. In his memoirs, President Johnson referred to many sources of information which influenced his thinking on Vietnam; none was an intelligence source. The "Pentagon Papers" further showed that the intelligence community was supplying reliable information about the North Vietnamese and Viet Cong capabilities and the success (or lack of it) of military operations undertaken against the enemy. These estimates, however, went unheeded.[4] During the Korean War, the Central Intelligence Agency reportedly warned General Douglas MacArthur about the massing of troops in Manchuria by the People's Republic of China and the possibility of Chinese intervention. These warnings also went unheeded.

Intelligence Doctrine. "Intelligence doctrine" is a term given to the community's traditional approach to interpreting data. It is taught to each intelligence analyst who undergoes an apprenticeship to learn his profession. The recruit is supervised by older and more experienced officers until he masters the art of intelligence evaluation. Because in-service apprenticeship is the primary road to becoming an efficient intelligence officer, the five military organizations (Army, Navy, Air Force, DIA, and NSA) and the State Department's Bureau of Intelligence and Research face a special problem caused by frequent rotation of personnel. It is difficult to teach intelligence skills during a two- or three-year tour of duty that a military or foreign service officer will spend with his agency. These organizations, however, have sizable components of civil service personnel who furnish a measure of continuity.

The basic premise of the intelligence doctrine is that all data should be evaluated independently of current policy in order to ensure objectivity. The intelligence officer should not be concerned with policy positions taken by the various decision makers. His function is to collect all the information that he can, sift through it, put the relevant pieces together into a picture, and finally, draw conclusions from the picture as assembled. To be effective, the analyst must be isolated from political infighting over pet policies advocated by the decision makers. The intelligence analyst views himself as a researcher whose occupation is secure even if he argues for an unpopular policy. He tends to think of himself as independent and realistic, and he feels the politician sometimes must yield to domestic and foreign pressures that he as an analyst can ignore.

Because the data available to an analyst are voluminous, the intelligence doctrine tends to create an expert who focuses on one specific, substantive area of foreign political activity. The analyst in the CIA's Bureau of Latin American Affairs who specializes in the Cuban economy or the analyst in the Air Force's Targets Division who specializes in railroad and highway bridges in China are examples of the narrow focus that characterizes the American intelligence community. The analyst receives daily stories clipped from American and foreign newspapers, reports from tourists, dispatches from Foreign Service officers, aerial photographs annotated by photo interpreters (another example of a specialized intelligence function), reports from covert agents, transcripts from foreign radio broadcasts, and a host of other material to be read and evaluated. Because the data are diverse, specialization is necessary to permit the analyst to adequately cover his subject area. The intelligence system is composed of cells of specialists who carve out a small segment of foreign political behavior, master its history, and remain aware of current developments.

The Intelligence Community and Policy Implementation

Policy implementation, the most controversial function of the intelligence community, is often meshed together with the information-input function. Policy implementation implies that the community processes an elaborate overseas mechanism to carry out executive directives. Overseas implementation of policy decisions is primarily the prerogative of the CIA, for it alone has overseas agents, also serving as sources of information. The agency is the "eyes and ears" of the National Security Council. On occasions, it has also served as its "arms," carrying out assigned clandestine activities.

CIA and Military Operations. The most controversial implementation operations of the Central Intelligence Agency concerns its use of military force to achieve goals. Aside from the constitutional problems evoked by these operations, there is serious doubt as to their efficiency.

Although the 1961 Bay of Pigs invasion was a CIA failure, other "failures" or "successes" have not been quite so dramatic or open to analysis. The CIA-inspired revolution in Iran in 1953 to reestablish the Shah's rule and the overthrow in 1954 of a government in Guatemala that was described as "Communist" are two incidents about which the facts are in question. The CIA has never claimed credit for these incidents; it is possible that they would have occurred without the agency's participation.

During the Vietnamese War, the CIA was involved in clandestine operations in Southeast Asia. The Senate Foreign Relations Committee reported in August 1971 that the agency spent over $100 million in Laos to halt what the CIA perceived to be North Vietnamese aggression in that nation. Some of the findings for CIA operations have been masked as part of the activities of the Agency for International Development.[5]

Assassinations. One of the more storied activities of the intelligence community is the murder of heads of state and other key individuals in foreign governments. Since this type of operation cannot be verified, it merits only a passing notice. The CIA was reportedly linked with the assassination of President Diem of South Vietnam in 1963. Obviously, no one in the agency would claim responsibility for the act or would even countenance it. The CIA is hypothesized as the culprit in many unexplained events in the world, for some of which the agency is indeed responsible.

The Intelligence Community in a Democracy. The policy-implementing function, while a small part of the community's overall duties, presents a twofold problem to an open, democratic society. First, the community might influence policymaking through a monopoly on certain types of information whose content or sources cannot be revealed to a democratic public. The temptation is to classify, as "secret," information that embarrasses the government because it reveals a foreign policy blunder.

Second, officials hidden in the CIA's bureaucracy may initiate small, and seemingly minor, activities which suddenly take on major significance. At the moment, it is doubtful that the CIA could undertake any major operation without executive approval. "Major" may be taken to include the assassination of a foreign leader or a Bay-of-Pigs type of operation. But does the far-flung intelligence bureaucracy permit an enterprising agent to initiate "minor" activities which have not been approved by upper-level decision makers? While the risk of this happening appears to be no greater —or no less—than those risks populating the bureaucracies of other agencies, both the State and Defense departments, for example, have an established framework for pre- and post-audit control. The intelligence community does not.

An illustration of a "minor" activity that caused momentary embarrassment to the American government occurred in Thailand in late 1973 and early 1974. A CIA agent, one of 50 in Thailand, sent a letter to the Thai government in the name of a leader of one of the country's insurgent groups. The idea was to divide the groups at war with the Thai government by making it appear that the unity of the guerrillas had collapsed. The move, of course, attempted to delude the Thai government as well, a point overlooked by the CIA agent. The letter went astray and was published by a Bangkok newspaper, which traced it to the agent. As a result, U.S.-Thai relations became strained, the agent was sent home, and the American ambassador felt compelled to apologize over and over again for the CIA's indiscretion.

Not all of the possible relationships between the intelligence community and a democracy focus on the CIA as the culprit. In the late 1960s, the Johnson administration used the facilities and personnel of army intelligence to maintain surveillance on civil rights meetings and public protests against the Vietnam War. Before his resignation, President Nixon revealed that he had used the CIA in an attempt to obstruct the FBI's investigation of the Watergate scandal. While the intelligence community presents a possible danger to a democracy, the misuse of an intelligence organization by elected leaders also presents a major threat to a citizen's rights.

Beyond the potential, and sometimes the actual, threat to a democracy, and beyond the abuses of power, the intelligence community engages in activities that at best are of questionable value to the policymaker. The elaborate lengths to which a CIA agent went to obtain a sample of Egyptian King Farouk's urine to check his health makes a good plot for a comedy.[6] This episode also indicates that the CIA is a bureaucracy with resources to waste on inconsequential activities.

THE FOREIGN SERVICE: THE GENERALIST ELITE

Characteristics of the Foreign Service Officer

Differences between Intelligence and Foreign Service. The intelligence community is larger and supplies more information to the executive establishment than does the Foreign Service.[7] Besides differences in the amount of information that each supplies, the intelligence community and the foreign service differ in their approach to personnel skills. The intelligence community emphasizes the specialist who has mastered a small area of knowledge; he then focuses on one aspect of the intelligence picture. The Foreign Service Officer, on the other hand, is a generalist: his tour of duty is rotated usually every few years, partly to ensure that he develops no personal attachment to the foreign country to which he is assigned. Organization of the foreign service is similar to that of the armed services where the army captain, for example, is trained to lead a unit in the field as well as fill an administrative slot in the Pentagon. The Foreign Service Officer is similarly versatile, able to occupy a country desk in the State Department or hold various positions in embassies and consulates abroad.

Composition of the Foreign Service. The total number of personnel employed by the Department of State is almost 25,000. Not all are American citizens; in fact, 40 percent are foreign nationals employed abroad, most of whom perform manual labor, such as serving as gardeners or domestics; others occupy translating and interpreting positions. Since the foreign nationals are not paid according to an American wage scale, substantial savings, as well as problems, accrue from this practice. Among the problems is the possibility of security leaks caused by foreign nationals who pass information to host governments.

The Americans on the State Department payroll work under either civil service (20 percent) or Foreign Service (40 percent) auspices. Civil service workers before 1954 comprised a much larger number of State Department employees. In 1954, Secretary of State John Foster Dulles directed that a large portion of civil service workers in the department be brought into Foreign Service. Dulles' move was based on the assumption that a healthier Foreign Service would result if most of the career workers in Washington were integrated into the service and their positions filled by personnel rotating between Washington and the field. Prior to that time, most of the major bureaucratic positions were filled by civil servants, while Foreign Service officers manned the embassies and consulates abroad. At times, friction developed between civil service headquarters and the Foreign Service field. The Foreign Service officers were accused of thinking of themselves as a snobbish elite, an exaggerated criticism, but with some basis.

The Foreign Service continues to be dominated by males; approximately 30 percent are women, hired mainly as secretaries, clerks, couriers, and receptionists in the Foreign Service Staff Corps. Another segment of the service is the Foreign Service Reserve Officers Corps (FSRO) comprised of specialists brought in for technical duties. For example, the embassy in Saudi Arabia may have a petroleum engineer assigned to it as a FSRO, since the Foreign Service Officer, a generalist, could not be expected to supply this type of expertise.

The Foreign Service Officers occupy one of the most coveted and highly competitive positions in American government. Each year, of the 6,000 applicants who sit for the written examination, approximately one-fourth pass. A high attrition rate exists among candidates who successfully pass the written exam and the oral exam because many candidates decide on other careers or choose to attend graduate school. Of the 800 to 900 applicants who appear before a board of examiners, 400 to 500 pass. From this number, 125 to 200 Foreign Service officers are chosen and certified for appointment, depending primarily on the number of resignations from the service. Consequently, of the 6,000 young men and women who aspire to careers in the Foreign Service, 3 to 4 percent eventually enter.

The background of the successful Foreign Service applicant includes a good knowledge of American history and culture. The examination process is based on the assumption that the officer should know his own nation in order to represent it effectively to other people. He usually is an individual with a wide range of interests and a broad acquaintance with the many aspects of American life—art, music, and literature, as well as politics and economics. The successful candidate does equally well on multiple-choice examinations and in oral interviews. He has a bachelor's degree, and many times, a post-graduate degree.

Throughout his service, the FSO is faced with the process of "promotion up-selection out." If the FSO is not promoted within a length of time (from 10 to 15 years, depending on the grade), or is ranked in the lowest 10 percent of his class for two consecutive years, he is dismissed from the service. Each year, the FSO's in each class are compared with one another by selection boards.

The Foreign Service Officer as a Gatekeeper

The Amount of Information. Since the amount of reporting generated by the United States diplomatic corps amounts to between 400,000 and 500,000 words each day, the upper-echelon decision makers do not have enough time to read all the incoming and outgoing pieces of correspondence. In 1964, Secretary of State Dean Rusk estimated that he saw only 6 of the 1,000 cables sent by the State Department each day, while the President, or one of his assistants, saw only 1 or 2. Of the 1,300 incoming cables, the Secretary stated that he read between 20 to 30 that involved the most urgent crises of the day.[8] This situation is far removed from 18th- and 19th-century diplomacy when Secretary of State Thomas Jefferson read all of the reports from American embassies abroad, making marginal notations. Today the Secretary of State sees less than 1 percent of the cable business transacted by his department. This means that a multitude of decisions on policy are made by Department of State gatekeepers in the lower echelons of the decision-making pyramid.

Most of the incoming pieces of information are not cables, making these statistics even more astonishing. Diplomatic couriers shuttling between embassies in the field and between the embassies and Washington carry briefcases filled with reports and correspondence. Material is also sent by airpouch, and that of less priority, by surface pouch. The last category accounts for the largest supply of incoming information. Cables are but a small part of the iceberg of information that the upper-echelon policy-maker sees.

The locus of the State Department's attempt to handle rapidly unfolding events of crisis proportions is the Operations Center, established after the Bay of Pigs failure in April 1961.[9] The Operations Center is part of the department's Executive Secretariat; it receives urgent messages, either telephone calls or telegrams, 24 hours a day. Crises abroad that erupt at all hours of the night are reported by embassy personnel to the Operations Center, which then informs the proper departmental officials. News of a coup d'etat in an African state, war between two Asian nations, or a natural disaster, such as an earthquake, would be flashed to the Operations Center. Similar organizations exist in other areas of the government. In the Pentagon, the Department of Defense mans the National Military Command

Center while the Central Intelligence Agency operates its Situation Room for the intelligence community. In the White House, there is another situation room which supplies the President with information on crises.

The Country Director. The man sitting at the bottom of the State Department bureaucracy in the geographical bureaus is the Country Director. In some cases, where nations are small and relatively unimportant to American foreign policy, the director may handle two or three countries. The Country Director is normally a Foreign Service Officer in the middle range of his career who is an expert in the country or countries under his purview. He spends the largest amount of his time reading reports and communications from the U.S. Embassy, written material from other sources in the executive branch, such as the intelligence communities, and from the press services (again illustrating the role of mass media as part of the information input), and in drafting and coordinating communications to the field. An ambassador or other embassy personnel may request information or may request permission to undertake a policy initiative; the director is responsible for supplying the information requested and for obtaining the requested permission. He must also coordinate all communications written by other segments within the department bureaucracy.

Another important and challenging duty of the director is to participate in drafting position papers and other studies on current issues involving the country for which he is responsible. A position paper, as the title implies, summarizes the background of a foreign policy problem and recommends one of several alternatives to be implemented in American foreign policy. The director for Brazil, for example, might develop a position paper on the Brazilian government's decision to nationalize American-owned companies. Moreover, there are many ad hoc conferences in which the Country Director contributes his expertise to a discussion of problems in American foreign policy.

A very important function of the director is to brief individuals and groups on American policy toward the nation for which he is responsible and to prepare briefing papers for department and White House personnel. Included in his briefing meetings are U.S. ambassadors assigned to the country, subcommittees of the Senate Foreign Relations and House Foreign Affairs committees that focus on the region within which his country is found, and important American visitors on official business traveling to that nation. In this capacity, the director can push for his own or the department's position on contemporary problems. For instance, the Country Director for Japan will have opportunities to furnish suggestions for policy when he briefs upper-echelon government officials on U.S.–Japanese relations. If he or the Bureau for East Asian Affairs believes that Japan should remain disarmed, he can propose this course of action when briefing congressmen, ambassadors, or the Secretary of State.

The Country Director's position is a coveted rank among Foreign Service Officers. He is usually the resource person on an individual country. Under normal circumstances, it is the director who serves as a very important gatekeeper in the flow of information to the top.

Overseas Sources of Information

The Embassy. The United States government maintains over 120 embassies abroad to collect and report information, to represent American interests, and to carry on negotiations with foreign governments. Some of the embassies in countries that Washington considers important employ large staffs. In the mid-1960s, the embassy in London was staffed by over 700 people employed by 32 agencies, again raising the problem of coordination. Not only must policy be coordinated in Washington, but in the field as well, where the ambassador has primary responsibility.

The Ambassador. Contrary to the popular stereotype, the "typical" (from a statistical point of view) American ambassador is not a political hack whose position is the result of past favors done for the party in power.[10] Seventy percent of the ambassadorial posts are held by career Foreign Service officers; typically, the officer is in his fifties, can speak at least one language other than English, and spends almost three years at his post. Admittedly, the bulk of these positions are assignments to small nations whose weight on the international scales is not very great. While there are political reasons for this arrangement, one factor often overlooked is that ambassadorships to large nations, such as Great Britain, France, and Japan, entail a significant amount of entertaining: "significant" in that the cost is usually greater than the expense account alotted by Congress. Unless an ambassador possesses a source of wealth independent from the limited sums available to him through government funds, he will find posts in the larger states to be an unbearable financial burden.

While most of the ambassadors are Foreign Service officers (with the rank of Career Minister or Career Ambassador), the non-career ambassadors can bring certain advantages to their posts. Since he (or she) is appointed by the President for personal as well as political reasons, the ambassador may have direct lines of communication to the White House; this can be advantageous in the event of a dispute over policy with the State Department. A political appointee can threaten to resign and tell all to the President, if the State Department does not change its mind. A career ambassador does not possess this type of weapon; but perhaps he does not need it because his judgment may be more respected by headquarters in the debate over "Washington clearance."

"Washington clearance" is a post-World War II development in foreign policy implementation. In the days before rapid communications, ambassadors were left to their own devices to implement the general instructions issued to them as they assumed their posts. Today the American ambassador abroad is in constant, day-by-day communication with the State Department. All too often, "Washington clearance" means that a Country Director passes judgment on and sometimes overrules policy suggestions from the field. The ambassador is usually in a position to know what policy initiatives and alternatives are most practical. On the other hand, Washington can see the overall implications of any policy decision—its effects on other nations, especially neighbors, and on other areas of policy with which the ambassador will not be acquainted.

The ambassador is head of the "country team," composed of the personnel of all the federal agencies in the foreign capital, with the exception of commanders of armed service units that may be stationed in the country. The practical question involved is: How can the ambassador *control* or at least *oversee* the personnel under his embassy's roof when their primary loyalty is to their individual departments in Washington? The ambassador cannot regulate the quality of personnel sent to work at his mission, nor can he dismiss an individual with whose policy recommendations he disagrees. Disputes between the ambassador and the CIA officer, for example, normally must be resolved in Washington at the department, rather than the embassy, level. However, in theory, the country team concept dictates that all policy initiatives are coordinated through the ambassador's office. Consequently, the problems of coordination in the executive branch in Washington are duplicated in the field.

Criticisms of the Foreign Service

Most strictures are not aimed at the officers themselves (who obviously represent a talented group of men and women), but at the structure or system of foreign services.

Criticisms of the Foreign Service's Internal Structure. The "promotion up–selection out" process is the focus of many criticisms of the internal structure of the Foreign Service. It is argued that this procedure tends to reward caution and conservatism among FSOs, who are forced to avoid "black marks" on their record in order to escape a supervisor's adverse evaluation. A FSO who advocates an unpopular policy, who disagrees with the ambassador's decision, or who attempts to anticipate political events —but fails—endangers his position. Risk-taking and behavior deemed uncooperative are frowned upon. This situation has led to a tendency to overstaff, on the assumption that there is safety in numbers. An officer, as part of a committee recommending an unsuccessful proposal, is not held personally responsible for a recommendation that turns sour.[11]

Criticisms of the State Department Bureaucracy. The organization of the State Department is one of the most neglected of all the agencies in Washington. Few secretaries have shown an inclination to reorganize the department's bureaucracy; for those who have, even fewer secretaries have experienced tranquil periods in American diplomacy that would permit restructuring the decisional channels of the department. George C. Marshall stands apart because of his interest in updating the antiquated bureaucracy of the State Department. He was understandably appalled at the lack of long-range planning in American diplomacy. The policymakers' time was given over to current crises with little attention reserved for the long-range effects of today's decisions on future events. Consequently, he established the Policy Planning Staff, a group of "thinkers" freed from the demands of daily moving papers between an inbox and an outbox. He also reorganized the Executive Secretariat and established the Foreign Service Institute to furnish in-service training for department personnel.

Criticisms of the Field. The Foreign Service in the field pours forth mountains of verbiage, but the Department of State headquarters is still not well informed. The reason for this is the tendency of the field to submit too many reports on issues of secondary importance. Since the FSO is judged more on the quantity, rather than the quality, of his reports, the system encourages overreporting.

THE MILITARY ESTABLISHMENT: POLICY IMPLEMENTER AND INFORMATION GATHERER

The military establishment is the largest implementer of policy decisions because of its worldwide network of forces, bases, fleets, and advisory units. As a superpower, the United States possesses military capabilities that are truly international. Various strategies that have developed since World War II to deploy and employ these capabilities will be discussed in chapter 13.

Since five of the nine agencies that compose the intelligence community are part of the military establishment, the Pentagon is also the largest gatherer and supplier of information for the foreign policy formulation process. In most of the crises of the post-war period, the White House and Congress have had to act on the basis of initial information from military channels: the 1950 North Korean attack, the 1962 Cuban Missile Crisis, and the 1964 Gulf of Tonkin incident. The inaccuracies reported in the last case should not overshadow the excellent execution found in the Cuban Missile Crisis and the North Korean attack. At the same time, the Gulf of Tonkin incident is one of two case studies that illustrate the problems and dangers inherent in the military establishment's rather exclusive reporting of events and implementing of orders.

Gulf of Tonkin Incident. On August 2, 1964, during a presidential campaign in the United States, the American military command in Saigon reported to the Pentagon, and then to the President, that three small North Vietnamese naval craft attacked a U.S. destroyer in international waters some 30 miles from shore in the Gulf of Tonkin. Two days later, the Johnson administration alleged that two destroyers were attacked again in international waters, this time 65 miles from shore. On the same day, August 4, President Johnson ordered a limited, retaliatory bombing attack on specific targets in North Vietnam.

On August 7, both houses of Congress passed a resolution which stated that the U.S. "is prepared, as the President determines, to take all necessary steps, including the use of armed force, to assist any member or protocol state of the Southeast Asia Collective Defense Treaty requesting assistance in defense of its freedom." This resolution, based on military reporting, became one of the legal justifications for the growing involvement of the U.S. in Vietnam.

Years later, a fuller account of the Gulf of Tonkin incident was pieced together from bits of information either conveniently omitted from the initial story or originally reported in distorted form. A background of hit-and-run raids against North Vietnam targets by South Vietnamese troops under American naval protection originally was omitted. The North Vietnamese Navy, smarting from these attacks, had taken on the American destroyers either in reprisal or in the belief that the U.S. ships were carrying more South Vietnamese commando raiders.

Other facts were dubious, especially the number of North Vietnamese vessels involved in the attacks. Overlooked, or at least played down in the reports, was the lack of damage to American vessels inflicted by the North Vietnamese attacks. This incident underscores two points: facts do not speak for themselves but are given meaning through the reporter's interpretation; and a bureaucrat serves as a gatekeeper, choosing which facts to report and which to omit.

Unauthorized Policymaking. In early 1972, Air Force Lieut. Gen. John D. Lavelle ordered more than 200 pilots to attack targets in North Vietnam over a three-month period without orders from Washington and in violation of a presidentially proclaimed bombing halt.[13] Reports of the bombings were falsified to appear as "protective reaction strikes," the Air Force term for occasions when U.S. aircraft attack a hostile enemy plane or missile site that intends to interfere with normal operations. General Lavelle's attacks, however, were clearcut initiatives, not in any way "protective reaction" raids triggered by North Vietnamese interference or aggression.

General Lavelle felt that his orders were broad enough to permit such actions. He believed that the build-up of enemy strength should not be allowed to continue without appropriate action. The Pentagon and President Nixon believed differently and retired Lavelle with a demotion in rank.

The Lavelle case illustrates how an implementor in the field can pursue a policy unauthorized by Washington. This instance is unusual only in its scope: it is rather unique for such bombing to be carried out for three months without Gen. Lavelle's superiors in Saigon and Washington being aware of it.

The Role of the Military in American Society

The Gulf of Tonkin and Lavelle cases are not restricted to the military establishment, but can be reproduced in the intelligence community and the Foreign Service. Because of its size, these incidents are more common in the military establishment. Another dimension of the military establishment gives the Pentagon's bureaucratic sabotage a more sinister meaning: the alleged difference in values held by the military establishment as compared to the civilian agencies.[14]

At the heart of concern expressed over the large military presence in the foreign policy formulation process is the cluster of values ascribed to the man in uniform. One tends to stereotype the military mind as placing a higher priority on obedience than on dissent, as desiring to use force to resolve conflicts rather than techniques of peaceful settlement, and as being more interested in order than freedom. One result of this stereotype has been the traditional 19th-century policy of isolating the man in uniform from the rest of American society. Periodically the nation summons him to protect the nation's security. After performing his assigned task, the military professional of the pre-World War II era returned to forts or bases to await the next crisis.

The Cold War changed this pattern of American military life and dissolved many of the traditional stereotypes about the man in uniform. The military establishment is no longer a skeletal force but a large, complex, fighting machine, pervading every aspect of American life. The citizen soldier has given way to the professional soldier; in 1973, conscription was replaced by an all-volunteer army.

Advocates in favor of military participation in the policymaking process argue that the values of the professional soldier do not constitute any more of a threat to American democracy than FBI agents or policemen.[15] The military should not be isolated from American society but integrated into it. If a soldier is to defend a democratic society, he should be a part of that society's structure and values.

The military man is a professional who knows how to perform an assigned task. He is expertly trained to do his job and to do it well. Since the United States Constitution provides for civilian control over the military, political considerations sometimes may impede the performance of military duty. In the Cold War, political restraints were placed on the professional military man, especially during the limited wars of Korea and Vietnam. The disputes that arose between President Truman and General Douglas MacArthur illustrate the conflict that grows out of political restraints on military expertise.

BUREAUCRATIC RIGIDITY AND IMAGES

Bureaucratic behavior encourages the development of patterns in foreign policy. The position of primacy that the intelligence community, foreign service, and military establishment have gained in the policy formulation process—and the alliances that they have developed among themselves, with special-interest groups, and with members of Congress—all contribute to bureaucratic rigidity. The implementing information-input agencies have carved out domains of policy and established accompanying budgetary expenditures. One reason that the voices of science and propaganda will never achieve much more than a toehold in the formulation process is the resistance from the intelligence community, the Pentagon, and the Foreign Service career officers who feel threats to their established positions.

Bureaucracy and the Realist Image

The spectacular growth of the intelligence community and the Pentagon since 1945 occurred because the elected officials possessed an image of international politics conducive to the expansion of covert and military activities. The Realist perception framed the world in terms of political and military balances and of revisionist and status quo states. Since diplomacy was the vehicle for solving disputes, an efficient foreign service was important. Knowledge of the enemy's capabilities and the military's might to match, if not surpass, those capabilities was equally important. However, the Realists were blind to other voices: they really never saw the economic thrust of American expansionism, nor did they think very highly of propaganda as a useful diplomatic tool.

Real and Imagined Dangers

It appears that the popular military hero is no longer a threat to civilian control because American wars of the post-1945 era have not been overly conducive to the development of heroes. The Vietnam War is a case in point; many military reputations were made on infamous, rather than famous, grounds.

However, the danger of investing too much power in a military officer must be guarded against, as well as the conditions that feed it, such as frustrating and confusing wars that solve no problems but increase the call for quick, easy solutions to complicated and complex issues. The military establishment must not be isolated from the traditional values of American democracy. If this is a goal, then the all-volunteer army should be reexamined: Would not a citizen's army, despite all of its inconveniences, ensure that traditional values are absorbed by the military establishment?

The real and immediate danger of the bureaucracy is its rigidity. The elected officials' image of the world has changed in the 1960s and 1970s, but the bureaucracy seems to continue to operate through its accustomed channels of policy. Organizational interests appear to supercede national interests.

What can the elected officials do to control the bureaucracy and to introduce new patterns of behavior into American foreign policy? This question is the focus of the next chapter.

NOTES

1. Robert Kennedy, *Thirteen Days: A Memoir of the Cuban Missile Crisis* (New York: W. W. Norton, 1968), pp. 23–24.
2. Paul W. Blackstock, *The Strategy of Subversion: Manipulating the Politics of Other Nations* (Chicago: Quadrangle Books, 1964), p. 304. Blackstock observes that the "effectiveness of covert operations as a means of control or conquest has been overrated . . ." See also Harold Nicholson, "Intelligence Sources: Their Use and Misuse," *Harper's* 215 (November 1957): 12–20, and William M. McGovern, *Strategic Intelligence and the Shape of Tomorrow* (Chicago: Henry Regnery, 1961), pp. 12–14. For an account of a legal agent, see Pawel Monet, *Spy in the U.S.* (New York: Harper & Row, 1961).
3. For more information on this topic, consult: Klaus Knorr, "Failures in National Intelligence Estimates," *World Politics* 16 (April 1964): 455–467; Benno Wasserman, "The Failure of Intelligence Prediction," *Political Studies* 8 (June 1960): 156–169; and Riley Suderland, "Strategic Estimates or Strategic Studies?" *Army* 11 (January 1961): 50–54.
4. C. L. Cooper, "The CIA and Decision-Making," *Foreign Affairs* 50 (January 1972): 223–236.
5. *New York Times* (March 19, 1972): sec. 7, p. 1.
6. Patrick J. McGarvey, *CIA: The Myth and the Madness* (Baltimore: Penguin Books, 1972), p. 53.
7. The literature on the Foreign Service is voluminous: W. Wendell Blanke, *The Foreign Service of the United States* (New York: Praeger, 1969); H. Bradford Westerfield, *The Instruments of America's Foreign Policy* (New York: Crowell, 1963); Henry Wriston, *Diplomacy in a Democracy* (New York: Harper & Row, 1956); H. Waldo Heinrichs, Jr., "Bureaucracy and Professionalism in the Development of American Career Diplomacy," in John Braeman, R. H. Bremner, and David Brody (eds.), *Twentieth-Century American Foreign Policy* (Columbus: Ohio State University Press, 1971); James R. Childs, *American Foreign Service* (New York: Macmillan, 1958); Vincent Barnett (ed.), *The Representation of the United States Abroad,* rev. ed. (New York: Praeger, 1965); Chadwick F. Alger, "The External Bureaucracy in United States Foreign Affairs," *Administrative Science Quarterly* 7 (June 1962): 50–78; William Barnes and John H. Morgan, *The Foreign Service of the United States: Origins, Development, and Functions* (Washington, D.C.: Government Printing Office, 1961); Charles W. Thayer, *Diplomat* (New York: Harper & Row, 1959); Robert D. Murphy, *Diplomat Among Warriors* (Garden City, N.Y.: Doubleday, 1964); John E. Harr, *The Professional Diplomat* (Princeton, N.J.: Princeton University Press, 1969); Robert E. Elder, *Overseas Repre-*

sentation and Services for Federal Domestic Agencies (New York: Carnegie Endowment for International Peace, 1965); Arthur G. Jones, *The Evolution of Personnel Systems for U.S. Foreign Affairs: A History of Reform Efforts* (New York: Carnegie Endowment for International Peace, 1962); James L. McCamy, "Rebuilding the Foreign Service," *Harper's* 219 (November 1959): 80–84.

8. *Department of State Newsletter* (February 1964): 2.
9. William B. Connett, Jr., "Operations Center: Locus of 'Crisis Management'," *Department of State Newsletter* (August 1964): 16–18.
10. Henry M. Jackson (ed.), *The Secretary of State and the Ambassador* (New York: Praeger, 1964); Subcommittee on National Security and Operation, *The Ambassador and the Problem of Coordination* (Washington, D.C.: Government Printing Office, 1963); and Waldo H. Heinrichs, Jr., *American Ambassador: Joseph C. Grew and the Development of the United States Diplomatic Tradition* (Boston: Little, Brown and Co., 1966).
11. Chris Argyris, *Some Causes of Organizational Ineffectiveness within the Department of State* (Washington, D.C.: Department of State Center for International System Research, 1967). Argyris studied FSO attitudes and found that most officers were reluctant to offer suggestions or criticisms that would "rock the boat." Junior FSOs felt that their positions were more secure if they always accepted a senior FSO's suggestion. Since the senior FSO writes an evaluation of subordinates, junior FSOs avoided expressing their own opinions. See also Bernard Mennis, *American Foreign Policy Officials: Who They Are and What They Believe* (Columbus: Ohio State University Press, 1971); John E. Harr, *The Development of Careers in the Foreign Service* (New York: Carnegie Endowment for International Peace, 1965); Zara S. Steiner, *Present Problems of the Foreign Service* (Princeton, N.J.: Center for International Studies, 1961); Regis Walther, *Orientations and Behavioral Styles of Foreign Service Officers* (New York: Carnegie Endowment for International Peace, 1965).
12. *New York Times,* March 19, 1972, sec. 2, p. 1.
13. See *The New York Times,* June 11, 1972, sec. 1, p. 1, and Sept. 17, 1972, sec. 4, p. 1.
14. Several authors address this subject: Adam Yarmolinsky, *The Military Establishment: Its Impact on American Society* (New York: Harper & Row, 1971); Edward B. Glick, *Soldiers, Scholars, and Society: The Social Impact of the American Military* (Pacific Palisades, Calif.: Goodyear, 1971); James Clotfelter, *The Military in American Politics* (New York: Harper & Row, 1973); J. K. Galbraith, "How to Control the Military," *Harper's* 238 (June 1969): 31–49; William T. R. Fox, "Representativeness and Efficiency: Dual Problem of Civil-Military Relations," *Political Science Quarterly* 76: (September 1961): 354–366; Walter Millis, *Individual Freedom and the Common Defense* (New York: Fund for the Republic, 1957) and *The Constitution and The*

Common Defense (New York: Fund for the Republic, 1959); Col. Robert N. Ginsburgh, "The Challenge to Military Professionalism," *Foreign Affairs* 42 (January 1964): 255–268; Roger Hilsman, *The Politics of Policy Making in Defense and Foreign Affairs* (New York: Harper & Row, 1971); Donald F. Bletz, *The Role of the Military Professional in U.S. Foreign Policy* (New York: Praeger, 1972); William L. Hauser, *America's Army in Crisis: A Study in Civil Military Relations* (Baltimore: Johns Hopkins Press, 1973).

15. Samuel P. Huntington, for example, argues that the "image of military dominance is false and dangerous." *See* his "Power, Expertise, and the Military Profession," *Daedelus* 92 (Fall 1963): 793–801.

11

The President and the Bureaucracy: Patterns of Control

The executive bureaucracy should be viewed as a power to be managed, not as an evil to be destroyed. Despite the dangers that a complex bureaucracy presents to a democracy, American foreign policy cannot be carried on without it. The challenge that the President faces is to harness the power of the bureaucracy and to direct it toward the goals that serve the American national interest.

In this chapter, models of presidential behavior in relationship to the bureaucracy and the management techniques for controlling bureaucratic excesses are examined. The President's relationship to his bureaucracy is stressed because this relationship is the genesis of most of the patterns found in American foreign policy.

MODELS OF PRESIDENTIAL BEHAVIOR

Categories of Presidential Behavior

Presidential behavior depends on a variety of stimuli, such as the nature of the issue, the personality of the man in the White House, the pressures that he is receiving from Congress and public elites, and the bureaucratic interests involved.[1] The amount of time allotted to decision making by the nature of an issue is also important. If the problem is a crisis, the President must telescope into a reduced time frame (or even eliminate) many of the considerations and much of the consultation that he could do more leisurely during placid times.

The President also faces in two directions: inward as well as outward, domestic as well as foreign. Although foreign policy problems have always been considered more vital because they sometimes involve issues of national survival, domestic difficulties may impinge on the President's schedule to the point that he spends more time looking inward than outward. During most of 1973 and 1974, President Nixon's attention was focused primarily on the Watergate scandals that grew out of his election victory in 1972. During this period, the American foreign policy formulation process did not cease. The bureaucracy continued to carry on the business of diplomacy under the general direction of the secretaries of State, Defense, and the Treasury.

In order to facilitate the study of the many factors that intrude on presidential behavior, this chapter will focus on three areas: his office, his roles, and his personal preferences. From these areas, one can build models to use in analyzing the President's relationship to the bureaucracy.

The Office. The office of the President combines many of the factors that enter into the foreign policymaking process. The President has access to every political, economic, scientific, propaganda, and military skill available to make and to implement decisions. The instruments of policy at his disposal are more varied and more powerful than those possessed by any other world leader since the beginning of the nation-state system. The amount of power and talent at the disposal of the President is enormous.

However, this power is restrained. Past commitments negotiated with foreign governments by previous administrations restrict the number of options that an incumbent can consider. No American President, for example, would ignore his nation's obligations under the North Atlantic Treaty. Historical and constitutional precedents also restrain presidential actions. The presidency is rooted in two centuries of traditions that have become building blocks for executive action. Many of the precedents are outgrowths of presidential interpretation of the Constitution's broad provisions. Precedents and previous commitments can encourage action as well as restrain it. This point will be developed in more detail in the next chapter when the President's relationship with Congress is discussed.

Roles. Another cluster of variables that affect presidential behavior are the various roles that the President plays. Some of these roles are derived from the Constitution, but not all. The President, first of all, assumes the role of Head of State. It is to him alone that representatives of foreign leaders are accredited; and U.S. diplomatic personnel sent abroad officially represent him as Head of State.

The President is also Commander in Chief of a military force whose strength is matched only by the Soviet Union. As Commander in Chief, he can issue orders to military units that can precipitate conflict between the United States and foreign countries without the direct approval of Congress.

As head of his party, the President performs a role that the Founding Fathers never envisioned. If the President's party also controls Congress, his attempts to enact legislation usually are facilitated. As head of the party, the President normally has the support of citizens who identify with his party.

Idiosyncratic Behavior. The President is also an individual who brings to his position idiosyncratic behavior; i.e., his personal whims, values, peeves, image, and ways of doing things. One President may be described as possessing "charisma," and another as appearing "bland." Another President, such as Eisenhower, may prefer to receive decisions after a consensus has been arrived at by his staff. Another, such as Kennedy, may want all options identified by subordinates, with the ultimate choice left to him.

Models for Analyzing Presidential Behavior

Any model constructed to analyze the patterns of presidential behavior in the foreign policymaking process must combine the President's office, roles, and personality—all of which are related to the bureaucracy that he presides over. Models are ideal types and no President will conform perfectly to any of them. Indeed, the post-1945 presidents have tended to be a melange of the four models to be discussed in this chapter. Since these models are not mutually exclusive, several of them may be exercised by the same President as he responds to different issues.

These models should help to comprehend the relationship of the President to his bureaucracy. Pertinent questions should include: Why did a President receive the policy recommendations that he did? Why does a President appear indecisive on some issues, while acting decisively on others? Why are some presidential directives not implemented? Why does the President fail to give personal direction to all the important issues of American foreign policy? Advisers with whom the President surrounds himself must also be evaluated. And the strategies employed by the President to maintain control over the bureaucracy are important to the analysis.

The Strong Man Model

The Realists and Crises. The most popular approach to a crisis is the Strong Man Model (*see* Figure 11–1), which assumes that the President should be a decisive leader in the foreign policy process, willing to make unpopular decisions, act in the best interests of the nation, and marshal public opinion to support his policies. The Strong Man Model sounds suspiciously prescriptive, rather than analytical, especially when its most ardent advocates tend to be the Realists. Presidents who seem to fit the model's assumptions, such as Harry S. Truman and John F. Kennedy, are generally admired, while Dwight D. Eisenhower is not.

Since the Realists tend to assume that the most common decision-making context is a crisis, their predilection toward the Strong Man Model is understandable. The President, under the pressure of time, must make

```
              ┌─────────────┐
        ┌─────│  President  │
        │     └─────────────┘
        │       ╱ │ │ │ ╲
        │      ↙  ↓ ↓ ↓  ↘
   Review│    o  o  o  o  o ←── Options
        │          │
        │       Selection
        │          ↓
        │    ┌──────────────┐
        └───▶│Implementation│
             └──────────────┘
                    │
                    ↓
                  Policy
```

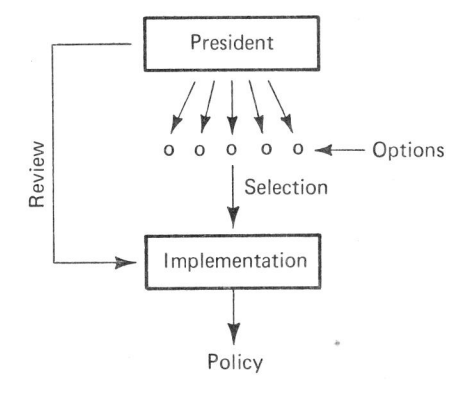

Figure 11-1. The Strong Man Model.

rapid decisions on the basis of confidential information that he cannot reveal to the public. He should have the strength of will to apply force to the problem, if its solution demands it.

Truman's reaction to the North Korean invasion in 1950 and Kennedy's behavior during the 1962 Cuban missile crisis are examples of presidents taking decisive actions in the midst of major turning points in history. The Strong Man Model also applies to various stages of the Vietnam War; in 1972, President Nixon took decisive action in mining North Vietnamese harbors and in unleashing an all-out bombing attack on North Vietnam.

Personal Issues. The crisis is not the only decision-making environment in which the Strong Man President functions. Two other types of issues are conducive to decisive action: those of very personal concern to the President and summit diplomacy.

On issues of intense, personal interest, the President is actively a part of each of the four stages in the decision-making process: he defines the problem as he sees it, evaluates the alternatives, selects the option most attractive to him, and then is vigilant throughout the implementation process to ensure that his intentions are not mutated or sabotaged.

Presidents have special interests and favored projects in foreign policy which may be opposed in varying degrees by bureaucratic agencies. Examples abound: Franklin Roosevelt's decision to recognize the Soviet Union in 1933 was opposed by the State Department; Harry Truman's support for a newly independent Israel in 1948 found both the State and Defense departments less than enthusiastic; and the State Department disapproved of Kennedy's Peace Corps proposal.

To protect his favored policies, the President usually brings a project under the shelter of his own administrative roof by making it part of the Executive Offices of the White House. Kennedy placed both the Peace Corps and the Trade Expansion Act Negotiations (known as the "Kennedy round") within the Executive Offices of the White House. He let the Peace Corps grow and gain both acceptance and strength before permitting it to have an organizational existence of its own. Mr. Kennedy's personal interest in the Trade Expansion Act and his fear that special-interest groups might interfere with its implementation, prompted him to place the Office of the Special Representative for Trade Negotiations in the Executive Offices.

In fact, very few foreign policy ideas are initiated by the President. Because of the pressure of time, the President conjures up only a limited number of proposals. Moreover, the space limits of the Executive Offices of the White House dictate that the President cannot house every foreign policymaking body nearby. Consequently, the Strong Man Model serves as a useful evaluative tool for only a small number of presidential behavioral patterns; but it does furnish us with a rationale for behavior that otherwise would go unexplained—the way the President acts when he has a personal interest in a specific aspect of American foreign policy.

Summit Diplomacy. The Strong Man Model is also useful to analyze instances of personal diplomacy. By using personal representatives on diplomatic missions, the President can maintain personal control over diplomatic initiatives that he does not trust to the bureaucracy. Frequent trips abroad by Colonel Edward M. House for Woodrow Wilson and by Harry Hopkins for Franklin Roosevelt illustrate this point. Both presidents did not have sufficient confidence in the traditional channels of diplomacy to report faithfully foreign views or to deliver important messages. On the other hand, Secretary of State Kissinger's success in negotiating truce agreements between Arab and Israeli armies in 1974 was based on activities of a subordinate with a wide latitude of policymaking powers. Kissinger was absent from Washington for over a month while he negotiated the truce. Although he maintained contact with the President, he made major decisions on his own initiative.

Summit diplomacy, the periodic meetings of heads of state, and trips abroad by the President also serve as foci for the Strong Man Model. But the number of instances in which summitry is practiced in American foreign policy, especially when compared to the frequency of more traditional patterns of diplomacy, suggests that the model is only occasionally useful as a framework for analysis. Summit diplomacy has proven to be unproductive as far as concrete accomplishments are concerned; and at times, such as during the 1960 Paris Summit following the U–2 incident in which Soviet Premier Khrushchev personally and openly berated President Eisenhower, it has been counterproductive. The unfortunate results of the wartime conferences (especially Yalta) have appeared to leave the American government reluctant to engage in summitry. The buildup of expectations that accompanies the pageantry of a summit meeting, only to be followed by rather vague and sometimes meaningless pronouncements, has discouraged its extensive use.

President Nixon's extensive use of summitry in 1972 (meeting with the chiefs of state of the Soviet Union, People's Republic of China, Japan, Great Britain, France, and Canada) illustrates the use of personal diplomacy, exposing both its good and bad profiles. Occurring before the November presidential election, this extensive summitry smacked of political maneuvering on the part of a President up for reelection and trying to keep his image before the American people. Presidential esteem, as reflected in the public opinion polls, usually increases after a trip abroad. The reception of the U.S. chief executive characterized by the accolades of foreigners evidently increases national pride. In 1974 Mr. Nixon's summit excursions to the Middle East, Europe, and the U.S.S.R. again coincided with his domestic political needs. The House of Representatives at the time was considering whether or not to hold an impeachment trial.

On the positive side, the President's trip to the People's Republic of China was a potent beginning to a new era of diplomatic relations between two previously avowed enemies. And at the Moscow summit, several important agreements were signed as a capstone to hard negotiations that had preceded the meeting. Whatever the long-range effects of Nixon's summit meetings, the series represents a well-organized orchestration of personal diplomacy on the part of a President. The summit conference represents an opportunity to use the Strong Man Model to analyze executive behavior because the President is portrayed as a world leader, proposing, negotiating, and creating good will.

In conclusion, the Strong Man Model does have application on a limited number of issues. It should not be neglected, however, because the central concept of the President's role is personal power. He can command and he can attempt to persuade; his success at both or either depends on his personal charisma, skills, and good fortune. The Strong Man Model views the bureaucracy as a servant of the President, willing to faithfully carry out his foreign policy initiatives.

The Muddling Through Model

Assumptions of the Model. The Muddling Through Model begins with the assumption that the President, or any other decision maker, can only know a small part of the decision-making processes, usually the intentions and capabilities of his opponent and his own capabilities to achieve his projected goals. As a result, the President formulates policy with incomplete information and with a high degree of risk.

It thus appears that American foreign policymaking is often more akin to stumbling around in the dark. The term, "muddling through," which has been used to describe British foreign policy behavior, can also be applied to the manner in which American—or Russian or French—diplomacy is formulated and conducted. The President can see only a short distance down the policy road, for he has no assurances that the outcome of his policy will be as he has intended. He only can estimate the impact that his decision will have on friends and foes alike.

Advantages of Muddling Through. A Muddling Through approach to foreign policy, strange as it may seem, can work to the advantage of a President. A President with a "grand design," who appears to know all the variables involved, could lead the United States into an even greater disaster than a President who improvises as he sees events unfolding. Muddling Through permits a decision maker to take advantage of his targets of opportunity. Concern with the task of building domestic consensus may be reduced by the Muddling Through approach, but the President's indecisiveness may heighten public anxieties. Because the President has not chosen alternatives, he has no policy option to sell to the American people. The price that he may pay for his flexibility in choosing alternatives is growing public concern and criticism.

Undoubtedly, no President will claim to muddle through a foreign policy crisis. He desires to appear before the American people as a decisive leader who knows where his policy initiatives are heading. Grand designs always produce a better press than does the portrayal of a President uncertain about the outcome of his major policy decisions.

Muddling Through and International Economics. The Muddling Through approach can be applied to the problems of international economics. The search for a solution to the American balance-of-payments problems in the 1960s and 1970s was characterized more by trial-and-error than by an overall plan. Many of the proposed solutions divided the academic community as well as government decision makers. Devaluation of the dollar, seen as a last resort to correcting the imbalance, was attempted in 1972 and 1973 with little more initial success than the many other previous attempts at finding a solution. Chapter 19 will discuss these attempts in more detail.

Vietnam and Muddling Through. The Vietnam War, as it unfolded in the mid-1960s, illustrated some of the points of the Muddling Through approach.[2] The nature of the enemy involved—the Viet Cong in the South and the Hanoi government in the North—was virtually unknown to American decision makers. Information on the enemy's capabilities was also a blank page in the policymaker's intelligence manuals: How much bombing would they absorb? How long would their morale sustain them in combat? How effective are guerrilla tactics against superior conventional firepower? In addition, questions of American capabilities were unanswered: Could the preponderance of American forces bring victory in the field? How decisive is bombing a peasant or underdeveloped society in a guerrilla war? What are the specific objectives that American foreign policy intends to achieve in Vietnam?

The history of American commitment of power in Vietnam from early 1965 followed the Muddling Through model. Military action was followed by unanticipated reaction from the enemy. Various strategic and tactical approaches were used in the war and then abandoned when they failed to produce a defeated enemy. Military commanders were reduced to a "trial-and-error" approach in finding successful methods in the field.

Observations on Muddling Through. The Muddling Through approach questions the confidence and certainty that the citizenry has in the President's actions. However, there are times when the President may project an image of hesitancy and indecision, stumbling from decision point to decision point with no clearcut vision of where the nation is heading. The Muddling Through Model would posit that these times occur more often than one would like to think.

Two models may apply to the same event in American diplomacy. Although one study of the 1962 Cuban missile crisis emphasizes the Strong Man Model, another approach impresses us with the idea that President Kennedy was never really sure of the outcome of his decisions. Soviet intentions and reactions were unknown and unpredictable, and World War III could have been ignited by any one of the several policy decisions made during the thirteen-day period.

The Competing Bureaucracies Model

Percolation and Policy. The Competing Bureaucracies Model (*see* Figure 11-2) assumes that policy proposals are born within the bureaucracy and percolate upward to the President for acceptance, rejection, or modification. As proposals percolate up through the bureaucratic framework, they are examined by agencies who have their own vested interests to look after. Since policy proposals involve priority decisions, and priority decisions ultimately involve budgeting, each bureaucratic center of power will fight for its own interests, as well as subject a proposal to a thorough analysis of its strengths and weaknesses. Often, alternative proposals will be submitted by dissidents within the bureaucracy who disagree with the original suggestion.

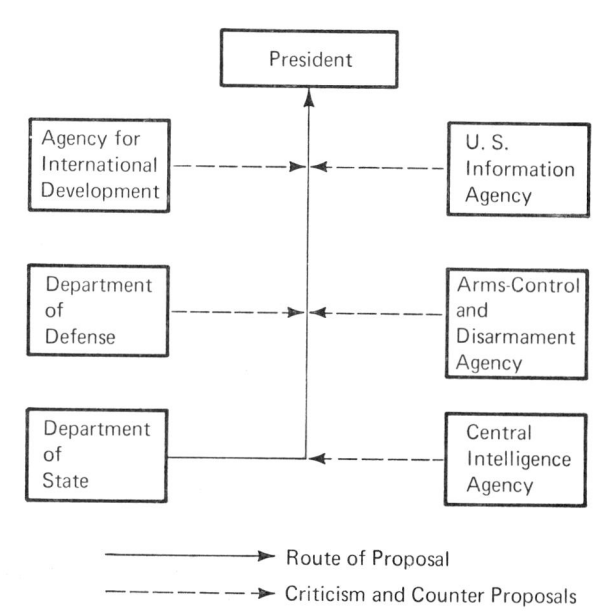

Figure 11-2. The Competing Bureaucracies Model.

The President is then free to accept the new proposal, realizing its strengths and weaknesses, or to accept an alternative initiative that emerged from the bureaucratic infighting.

Bureaucratic Espionage. While competition among government bureaucratic units has always existed in some form, the extent to which it is present is difficult to document. Occasionally, shocking evidence of the existence of a competitive atmosphere surfaces. In early 1974, Pentagon attempts to procure information from the National Security Council came to light. Defense Department personnel assigned to the NSC admitted that they lifted copies of reports for the Joint Chiefs of Staff.

Because bureaucratic espionage is always a threat, agency leaders must take security precautions. When Henry Kissinger, then only National Security Adviser, carried on negotiations with the Chinese in 1972, he refused to use State Department translators because he did not want the Secretary of State and his staff to know the content, progress, and direction of Sino-American talks. He used, instead, translators supplied by the People's Republic of China.

When agencies are competing for scarce budgetary resources or for the President's blessing on a pet project, bureaucratic espionage is felt necessary to remain abreast of the competing agencies' proposals and strategies. To the citizen, bureaucratic espionage is a waste of time and tax money.

"Common Denominator" Policy. One danger inherent in the Competing Bureaucracies approach is that the result may be watered-down policy. Fresh, innovative proposals that run the gamut on the way to the President may finally reach him as bland recommendations to continue in the same policy vein followed in the past. Although the Competing Bureaucracies approach may build consensus among government agencies interested in the policy, it often results in recommendations to the President that are divested of new approaches to diplomatic problems. Compromises negotiated between bureaucratic centers of power foster this sort of policy recommendation.

The Problem of the Omitted Agency. One possible source of friction within the Competing Bureaucracies Model is the decision to bypass or omit an agency when a specific policy is being discussed. The decision to omit an agency is a purposeful one and is made usually because the agency's position is known to be rigid and at variance with what the President intends to do. Only the President can make and enforce the decision to omit an agency.

In times of crisis, the number of bureaucratic agents brought into the policy coordinating process is reduced because of the time element. During non-crisis situations, when the President has already settled on a course of action, he may exclude the opinion of the bureaucracy because he anticipates opposition.

The Competing Bureaucracies approach to foreign policymaking does not always stifle opposition to policy proposals in the executive branch.

The dissident department or agency can file a minority report with the President, stating its reasons for disapproval and proposing an alternative. The President, then, must decide among the alternatives. The dissident agency may fight for its lost proposal by leaking its side of the conflict to the mass media in an attempt to build public support. Or the agency may carry its case to Congress.

The Problem of Bureaucratic Indecisiveness. The bureaucracy's inability to act is often the result of effective counterbalancing of powerful agencies. One unit's initiative, proposed out of its own self-interest, will be blocked by another unit. The indecisive Muddling Through decision-maker is sometimes complemented by the indecisiveness of bureaucratic competition.

The much-publicized incident of the State Department's reply to a letter from Soviet Prime Minister Nikita Khrushchev in 1961 illustrates bureaucratic indecisiveness. President Kennedy forwarded Khrushchev's letter to the State Department and was appalled when the department took months to frame a reply. The letter evidently touched off heated debates within the department over the diplomatic posture that the United States should assume toward the Soviet Union. The result of the bureaucratic infighting clearly was indecisiveness.

Because of indecisiveness, the Competing Bureaucracies Model can take on some of the marks of the Muddling Through Model. Whereas Muddling Through is primarily the result of incomplete information and improvisation, the indecisiveness of competing bureaucracies is the consequence of countervailing forces among agencies who effectively destroy each other's positions until positive action is all but discouraged.

The Bay of Pigs Invasion (1961). Policy that flows through the Competing Bureaucracies Model should have its strong and weak points clearly outlined for the President because each agency presents its own critical analysis of the proposal. If he chooses to go ahead with the initiative, at least he can be prepared for criticisms that may arise over it. On the other hand, the price that the President may pay for unexamined and undisciplined policy is too high.

The abortive Bay of Pigs invasion attempted during April 1961 by the new Kennedy administration illustrates policy enacted without bureaucratic cross-examination.[3] The idea for an invasion attempt to overthrow the Cuban government of Fidel Castro arose within the Central Intelligence Agency. Once hammered out internally within that agency, the policy was approved as first proposed with a few changes. The Central Intelligence Agency was the only major foreign affairs agency that did not undergo a change in leadership as the Eisenhower administration left office and the Kennedy people came in. President Kennedy's administrators, new to government bureaucracy, did not question the weaknesses of the CIA plan. As a result, the plan was never closely scrutinized by other agencies and was an embarrassing failure of American diplomacy.

The Corporate Leader Model

The President: A Corporation Executive. The Corporate Leader Model views the President in a role with powers similar to those of a board chairman of a major corporation, such as General Electric or International Business Machines. The President can give general direction to the bureaucracy, but he has very little personal control over the specifics of policy execution. Just as the President of General Motors can establish guidelines and goals for selling Chevrolets, but has little power over the individual salesman in the showroom, the President can broadly outline American foreign policy, but cannot control the Central Intelligence Agent or Foreign Service Officer in the field. Figure 11-3 illustrates the Corporate Leader Model.

A Captive of the Bureaucracy? The Corporate Leader Model verges on making the President a captive, rather than an executor, of the government's policy-implementing machinery because he can exercise only broad control over the direction of the massive federal bureaucracy. His edicts can be manipulated, reinterpreted, or in some cases, completely ignored. Truman's observation that President Eisenhower, accustomed to the chain-of-command

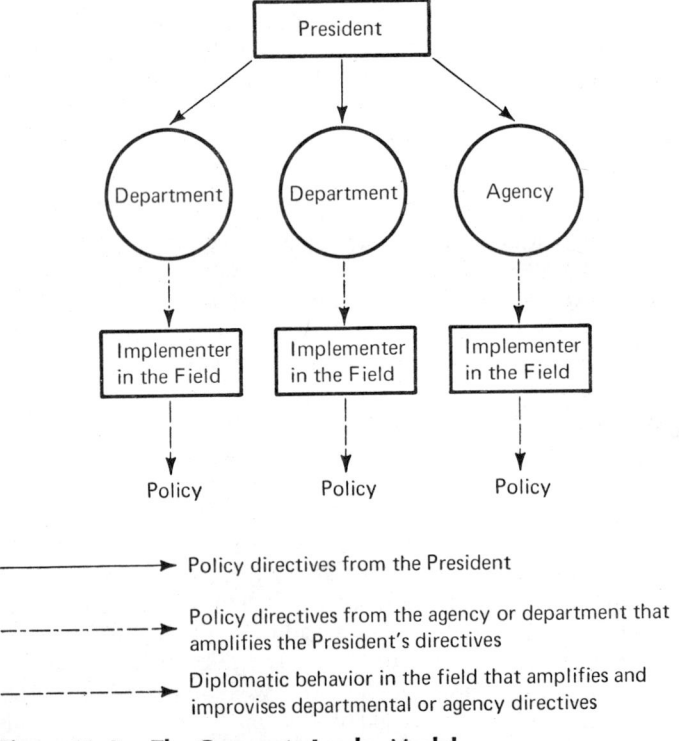

⟶ Policy directives from the President

⟶ Policy directives from the agency or department that amplifies the President's directives

⟶ Diplomatic behavior in the field that amplifies and improvises departmental or agency directives

Figure 11-3. The Corporate Leader Model.

structure of the Army, would feel helpless in the White House because his order may not be carried out illustrates the Corporate Leader's dilemma. The chain-of-command from the President to the American representative in a foreign country is not well-defined and has "dead ends" where policy directives can be lost. The intricacies of bureaucratic organization do not permit an accounting of who is responsible for failing to implement policy decisions of the President.

However, the modern President can realize that his foreign policy role on some issues is that of a Corporate Leader, and thus, adjust his behavioral patterns accordingly. What is essential in these instances is the development of an efficient bureaucracy that can be policed by presidential assistants. This model points up the importance of the White House staff and judges the effectiveness of the President on his ability to manipulate and direct a large and diverse administrative structure through delegating authority to subordinates.

Conflicting Policies. This model aids the reader in explaining several curious phenomena in American foreign policy: how one segment of the bureaucracy (e.g., the Central Intelligence Agency) can work toward toppling a government that another segment (e.g., the Agency for International Development) is supporting; how one president can order a policy followed only to find out that his orders have been ignored; how two high-level administrators can discuss the same issue and enunciate two divergent policy positions.

The Four Models: A Comparison

Each of the four models can be used to analyze presidential patterns of behavior in the policy process; indeed, all models should be employed to analyze executive behavior. A President may tend to prefer one or more patterns embodied in the models for reasons of personality, but one can assume that the decision-making style of each President will at one point or another permit the use of all the models. The President will emphasize his personal projects, muddle through problems, choose among proposals that have emerged from the bureaucracy, or act as a corporate leader sitting atop a massive bureaucracy and dispensing edicts that he hopes will be implemented.

While all the models may be applied to behavioral patterns in any single administration, some of them are mutually exclusive and others are compatible. The Strong Man Model is obviously incompatible with the assumptions that a decision maker knows only a small portion of diplomatic information, is only the recipient of proposals from the bureaucracy, or, especially, plays the role of giving only general direction to foreign policy.

On the other hand, the Corporate Leader, Competing Bureaucracy, and Muddling Through approaches are both complementary and supplementary. Any decision maker—whether he is the President or a Country Director in the State Department percolating up proposals for the President's approval—

is subjected to the gaps in information that the muddlers argue exist. The Corporate Leader's policy directives filtering down through the bureaucracy will be subjected to intensive competition from bureaucratic agents who either will support or drag their policy-implementing feet.

All the models, except the Strong Man approach, point up some aspect of the limitations placed on a President: lack of information, pressure of time, and insufficient capabilities to accomplish stated goals. To this listing, one can add constitutional bounds, lack of public support (however the "public" is defined), and the limitations placed on the present occupant of the White House by previous presidents. The President of the United States may occupy the most powerful position in the world, but he is bound by forces that do not permit unfettered activity.

While these models emphasize the President's relationship to the executive bureaucracy and tend to dwell on the office and roles of the presidency, the idiosyncratic aspects of presidential behavior should not be neglected. Differences between presidents exist, and at key decisional points, they are important. President Nixon's tendency to seclude himself and face a major crisis alone meant that he cut himself off from opinions of bureaucratic and non-bureaucratic experts. To decide, as he did in December 1972, to resume bombing of North Vietnam without consulting his own Joint Chiefs of Staff illustrates an aspect of presidential style that a model cannot capture. A President's style may favor one of the models, but it is doubtful that one model would dominate the decision-making process.

THE PRESIDENT'S MANAGEMENT OF THE BUREAUCRACY

The multiplication of new voices in the bureaucracy, the danger of sabotage, the presence of espionage, and the possibility that implementors will initiate unauthorized policy combine to raise the problem of control. "Control" does not necessarily mean that the two elected officials of the executive branch, the President and Vice-President, oversee every information-input and policy-implementing activity. It does mean, however, that the President avails himself of techniques to *manage* all the voices of the bureaucracy. Management techniques should ensure that the President receives accurate and unbiased information and that his most important directives are being carried out faithfully.

The President as a Generalist. Coupled with the problem of possible distortion of information inputs by the bureaucracy are the innate problems of the complex and technical substance of information. A President, after all, is a generalist. He must rely on scientists in the Atomic Energy Commission for evaluation of Soviet nuclear capability, on military advisers in the Pentagon for a judgment as to whether an amphibious landing will succeed or fail, and on economists in the Treasury and Commerce departments for an analysis and solution to the balance-of-payments dilemma. The

President, as a political animal, ordinarily does not possess the background to speak the languages of science, the military, or economics and to question the technical advice that he receives from the bureaucracy. What is his defense against receiving and following poor advice masked by technical verbiage?

The President's Staff. One line of defense has been the President's staff, composed of individuals who can advise him on technical and complex proposals made by the bureaucracy.[4] The President's assistants are not intended to be small-scale departments. The Special Assistant to the President for National Security Affairs and his few subordinates are not wiser than the Secretary of Defense and his several thousand employees, nor is the President's Military Advisor more able than the combined talents of the Joint Chiefs of Staff. Through these men and their expertise, however, the President can understand the esoteric concepts under discussion. The assistant can ensure that dissidents within the bureaucracy who have not been heard, or perhaps stifled, will have their alternative proposals considered by the President. The White House staff guards against the bureaucratic centers of power deciding on one policy outcome and presenting it to the President as a fait accompli.

The White House staff was instituted in 1939 by Franklin Roosevelt; it has grown in prestige and functions as the cabinet has declined. Today, the influence on the President of the cabinet, as an institution, is relatively minor. Individual cabinet members may be influential with the President because they have personal access to the Chief Executive and he values their advice. Thus, personal relationships rather than institutional channels are more important in evaluating the effectiveness of cabinet influence in foreign policymaking.

The White House staff is not the total solution since it, too, can assume characteristics of a bureaucracy. During the Nixon administration, key presidential subordinates became gatekeepers and often edited information flowing to the President. Rather than becoming part of a solution to bureaucratic excesses, Nixon's staff became part of the problem.

Reorganization. A second line of defense that the President can erect is periodic reorganization of the bureaucracy. The bureaucracy tends to propose policy that continues the traditional approach to solving problems defined by bureaucratic leaders. Bureaucracy has its own built-in momentum: as long as there are no radical breaks in the cadence or any major failures or massive changes in the international system, the bureaucracy will resist attempts to move its policy from channels carved out over a period of time. A President, then, wishing to make a fresh start in foreign policy often must break up bureaucratic centers of power by reorganizing administrative units.[5]

Bureaucracy has a tendency to become routinized, cautious, and sluggish in making foreign policy. It is conscious of other centers of power that must be coordinated in making a policy proposal. These characteristics also persist in times of crisis, when the bureaucracy must move quickly within a short time span. As long as foreign policy is free from trauma, the bureaucracy will function smoothly, smug in its assurances that it will outlast all elected and appointed decision makers. Bureaucracy is a machine that perpetually hums along, dealing with a myriad of foreign policy problems that face the American nation. Massive studies of the federal bureaucracy, such as the one headed by Herbert Hoover after World War II, must be conducted periodically to guide meaningful reorganization efforts.

In addition to reorganization, the President can also rotate personnel to break up bureaucratic centers of power. New personnel may bring in fresh ideas and different perspectives. Two problems arise with this approach: first, personnel rotation usually applies only to the upper-level decision makers, since the middle- and lower-range individuals are locked into well-established career patterns; and second, the difficulty with policymaking has not been too little rotation, but rather too much. An appointed Secretary or Assistant Secretary barely learns the bureaucratic ropes before he is ready to return to private life.

The cost involved in reorganization and personnel rotation can be prohibitive. Not only is the cost measured in terms of training new people to perform new (or old) tasks, but the disruption of policy patterns during the adjustment period also must be taken into account.

Recruitment of Personnel. To improve the quality of personnel in the middle and lower decision-making positions, the President can undertake recruiting programs that bring in more qualified and better-educated administrators and can institute personnel policies that encourage experienced personnel to stay in the Foreign Service rather than leave it for more attractive jobs elsewhere. The President may not have more control over the foreign policy bureaucracy, but he can be assured of a better bureaucrat to run it.

The recruitment process may inject new blood into a bureaucracy, but the process itself may harbor biases. There is a tendency for personnel officers to reflect the dominant image of the organization and to favor applicants with the values of that image. If the realist image is held by a majority of Foreign Service officers, for example, new selections into the diplomatic corps probably will reflect the values of Realism.

Appointments to Subcabinet Positions. The President can also use his power to appoint personnel to subcabinet positions, such as assistant secretaries of State and of Defense, to maintain a check on the bureaucracy. President Kennedy appointed individuals from outside the bureaucracy to these positions, while President Eisenhower tended to promote personnel already within the department.[6] The outside specialist, with no commitments to past patterns or values, would be more likely to question procedures and goals than would individuals associated with former decisions in the department.

Budgeting Procedures. The increased use of program budgeting should work to increase the President's control over the foreign policy bureaucracy. Program budgeting slices the economic pie available according to functions rather than departments.[7] Money is earmarked, for example, for "strategic offensive forces," which includes the Air Forces' strategic Air Command, the Navy's Polaris submarines, and the Army's Strike Command. Instead of appropriating funds for the departments of Air Force, Navy, and Army, program budgeting focuses on functions that cut across department lines. Program budgeting began with the Department of Defense under Secretary Robert McNamara in the early 1960s and since then has spread to other executive departments.

Control Over Policy Implementation

Management of the policy-implementation phase is more difficult than control over the information-input functions. The President can have his advisers question the validity of incoming information and search for data that will confirm or contradict a department's or an agency's proposals. Following the policy decision through the bureaucratic labyrinth from the Oval Office to the field is more taxing and time-consuming than gatekeeping functions.

Control of the intelligence community provides a case study of the problems that a President faces in managing policy-implementers. "Control," in this context, is not interpreted to mean public scrutiny of intelligence activities; rather, it connotes pre- and post-audit responsibilities by elected or appointed officials in whom the public has confidence.[8]

Task Forces. Since the 1947 National Security Act, several investigations of the intelligence community have been undertaken by groups that have varied in size and composition and have been constituted in response to different stimuli. In 1954, a task force was appointed to forestall a congressional investigation by Senator Joseph McCarthy, who had accused the CIA of Communist infiltration. In 1961, President Kennedy appointed a committee to investigate the CIA's failure in invading Cuba. The committee's report contained two major recommendations: (1) that the Director of Central Intelligence be separated from the CIA Director and that he be appointed as a presidential assistant to supervise all intelligence activities, and (2) that the CIA not be permitted to undertake clandestine activities that involve large-scale military operations. The CIA lacked the expertise to plan and execute military operations of the size of the Bay of Pigs invasion attempt, the group stated. Kennedy accepted the second recommendation, but not the first. Except for losing the capability of conducting major military operations, CIA powers were not diminished. In 1967, President Johnson asked for an investigation of the CIA's activities in financing private organizations, such as the National Student Association. The committee's report concluded that CIA activities were in accordance with National Security policies established in the early 1950s.

In general, the intelligence community has fared well in task-force investigations. The task-force group has kept the intelligence community alert to criticisms, although the committee recommendations have seldom resulted in major changes.

Executive Surveillance. The most effective control over the intelligence community has been exercised through the President's office. In addition to appointing periodic task forces, the President has maintained surveillance through two committees and a bureau.

The purpose of the NSC's Forty Committee is to review in detail proposed operations of the intelligence community. The community, composed of the National Security Adviser, the Director of Central Intelligence, and representatives from the State and Defense departments, meets weekly to discuss intelligence activities. A predecessor organization that performed a similar function was the 54–12 Group established by Eisenhower in 1954.

The Forty Committee does not post-audit intelligence operations, but limits itself to reviewing proposals for intelligence operations. It does not concern itself with whether the intelligence unit performs the approved operation or with how well it is performed.

The second group is the Foreign Intelligence Advisory Board, established in 1955 after the Hoover Commission called for an executive "watchdog" committee. It usually meets each month for one or two days to agree on recommendations for the President. A third control agent is the Office of Management and Budget, which increased its surveillance of the intelligence community's expenditures after the Bay of Pigs invasion.

Most of the official approval of intelligence activities comes from the Forty Committee because the Foreign Intelligence Advisory Board meets too infrequently to supervise intelligence operations. Whether or not the pre-audit activities of the Forty Committee are a sufficient control remains an open question because of insufficient data. But it seems obvious that post-audit control is needed to evaluate completed covert operations in order to ascertain whether they complied with committee recommendations and whether orders were efficiently carried out.

Control of the Foreign Service. The Department of State has been guilty of bureaucratic sabotage, a criticism that can be leveled at the intelligence community and the military establishment as well. There are occasions in which the department does not approve of a policy and will either ignore it or change its emphasis while attempting to carry it out.

President Kennedy's attempts to remove obsolete missiles from Turkey before the Cuban missile crisis in 1962 is a story of bureaucratic sabotage. In 1961 and 1962, during the first days of the Kennedy administration, the President ordered the State Department to begin negotiations with Turkey to withdraw the obsolete Jupiter missiles there. The Turkish government objected and Secretary Rusk was reluctant to pursue the matter. Robert Kennedy recorded that the President "was told by the State Department that they felt it unwise to press the matter with Turkey. But the President disagreed. He wanted the missiles removed even if it would cause political problems for our government. The State Department representatives discussed it again with the Turks and, finding that they still objected, did not pursue the matter."

At this point, Robert Kennedy observed, the President "dismissed the matter from his mind" because "the President believed that he was President and that, his wishes having been made clear, they would be followed and the missiles removed." But President Kennedy was mistaken. During the Cuban missile crisis in October 1962, some eighteen months after the President had initiated action on the Jupiter missiles, he found them still in Turkey. The President's reaction: "He was angry."[9]

Several possibilities can be suggested to explain the State Department's behavior. The most plausible explanation is that the State Department was reluctant to carry out a presidential wish that would cause some abrasion with a foreign government. One can only assume that the American ambassador to Turkey and the Country Director for Turkey—both information-input personnel—recommended a "go slow" policy. The motivations involved range from outright sabotage of the President's wishes, because they ran counter to the bureaucratic will, to a policy of foot dragging, in hopes that the President would either forget about the issue or that he might be replaced by another individual in agreement with the department's point of view.

Control of the Military. In 1951 President Truman relieved MacArthur of his command in the Korean conflict, thus providing students of American foreign policy with a case study of the issues involved in the civilian control of the military.[10] The issue involved was not the danger of a "man on horseback," or a charismatic military leader assuming control of the American government; rather, the issue was the liberal interpretation of orders to the point that the policy implemented in the field was at variance with the original intent of the President.

The Truman–MacArthur controversy, then, is rooted in the divergent images held by the President and his commander. Each viewed the international system from different vantage points, with distinct assumptions producing different results. Truman assumed that the major thrust of Soviet aggression would occur in Europe; Korea, therefore, was only a feint to draw off American strength to the Far East. The prosecution of the war should not antagonize the Soviet Union needlessly, since the possibility existed that World War III could be triggered by a minor conflict in a secondary region of the world. Korea was the wrong war at the wrong time in the wrong area of the world.

MacArthur's image was based on a different set of assumptions. The immediate enemy was the People's Republic of China, not the Soviet Union. Korea was a good excuse either to reclaim China for the "free world" or to deal it a blow that would cripple Chinese war-making potential for years. The Soviet Union would not intervene because of American superiority in nuclear weapons. Korea, therefore, was the right war at the right time and in the right region of the world.

These different images were the basis for the Truman–MacArthur conflict. The President, as Commander in Chief, issued orders to his commander in the field, orders that were, admittedly, broad and allowed MacArthur leeway in interpretation. Had the commander shared the President's image, no difficulty would have arisen in interpreting the orders. Since the orders were not specific in their wording, it was important for the commander to be in tune with the strategy of the administration. The alternative would be to spell out detailed orders to the commander; traditionally, however, the President has given his field commanders a margin for interpretation of orders. (Although in the Vietnam War, presidents Johnson and Nixon engaged in detailed military decisions, including the choosing of actual targets to bomb in North Vietnam.)

The Truman–MacArthur controversy is a case study of conflicting and different images attempting to implement policy; it does not represent the threat of a military takeover. It illustrates the administrative problems when the world image possessed by the President is at odds with a powerful military commander in the field. In the end, civilian authority was asserted and the commander was replaced.

The military establishment, while the potential source of bureaucratic sabotage and unilateral decision making, has not been subjected to extensive review as has the intelligence community. One explanation for this state of affairs is that military excesses tend to occur during times of war, and consequently, are shrugged off as an unfortunate, but necessary, part of military operations. The excesses must be brazen and on a large scale in order to attract attention, such as the My Lai atrocities during the Vietnam War.

Another explanation is that the military establishment has sufficient points of contact within and without the federal government to be protected from the task force and administrative surveillance imposed on the intelligence community. Task forces to investigate the Pentagon run a gauntlet of special-interest groups and key congressional leaders who protect the interests of the military establishment. The intelligence community can marshall the support of members of Congress, but it can appeal to only a handful of domestic interest groups for support.

EVALUATION OF MODELS

Which model is more effective in controlling bureaucratic mistakes and excesses? The Strong Man executive obviously manages his bureaucracy with a tighter rein than any of the other models, but the occasions on which the President can approach omnipotence are rare. In the Competing Bureaucracies Model, the agencies, departments, and bureaus are more likely to assume the initiative in the policymaking process, the President remaining more passive. The Muddling Through Model depicts both President and bureaucracy as captives of events who tend to make policy by instinctive reaction rather than by forethought.

The Corporate Decision Maker Model offers the best compromise between the Strong Man and Competing Bureaucracies approaches. The President supplies the general leadership to the complex system below him and expects his subordinates to carry out his directives. A President who acts as a corporate decision maker and employs techniques from other models has gone as far as an executive can go in managing the bureaucracy. Excesses can still occur under the Corporate Decision Maker Model, such as sabotage and unauthorized policymaking. For disclosure of these breaches of faith, the President must rely on the instruments of mass media. At the same time, the President permits the multiple voices of the bureaucracy, as well as his staff, to propose initiatives to him.[11]

The student of American foreign policy must be aware of the problems that exist with the decision maker's relationship to the bureaucracy. Perhaps one explanation for Henry Kissinger's successes as National Security Adviser and Secretary of State is his comprehension of the bureaucracy's role. In 1966 he wrote that the "vast bureaucratic mechanisms . . . develop a momentum and a vested interest of their own."[12] He pointed out that the purpose of bureaucracy is to cope with the routine problems of policymaking. The point at which bureaucracy becomes an "obstacle" is when it "defines as routine" those issues that are highly significant, or when it follows a "prescribed mode of action" that is irrelevant to the problem.[13]

To overcome this obstacle, Kissinger advised decision makers to assemble efficient staffs and to rely on them, a management technique mentioned in this chapter. Although staffs can develop "a momentum of their own,"[14] the decision maker would be reluctant to overrule his staff too frequently, fearing decline of its morale and efficiency. However, the defense erected to control bureaucracy—the staff assistants—begins to take on many of the characteristics of the bureaucracy itself.

In the final analysis, the President first must be aware of the power of the bureaucracy and then be conversant with the techniques available to him to manage this power. Foreign policymaking in a democracy depends on the elected official's skills in managing the bureaucracy. Under normal conditions, this task is difficult. The second Nixon administration certainly cannot be classified as "normal," due to Watergate. As Nixon became more encumbered with his domestic problems, it was his foreign policy bureaucracy led by Secretary Kissinger that saved U.S. foreign policy from paralysis.[15] How long Kissinger could have singlehandedly continued to overcome the Watergate paralysis became a moot point when Nixon became the first U.S. President to resign from office.

NOTES

1. Surprisingly, the number of books on the President's role in foreign affairs is limited. Recommended literature includes: Edgar E. Robinson, *Powers of the President in Foreign Affairs, 1945–1965* (San Francisco: Commonwealth Club of California, 1966); Norman L. Hill,

The New Democracy in Foreign Policy Making (Omaha: University of Nebraska Press, 1970); Sidney Warren, *The President as World Leader* (Philadelphia: J. B. Lippincott, 1964); Edward S. Corwin, *The President's Control of Foreign Relations* (Princeton, N.J.: Princeton University Press, 1917); Mark Kosselman, "Presidential Leadership in Congress on Foreign Policy: A Replication of a Hypothesis," *Midwest Journal of Political Science* 9 (1965): 401–406; and Graham H. Stuart, "Presidential Control of Foreign Policy," *Current History* 22 (April 1952): 207–210.

2. Townsend Hoopes, *The Limits of Intervention: An Inside Account of How the Johnson Policy of Escalation in Vietnam Was Reversed* (New York: David Mckay, 1969).

3. Haynes Johnson, et al., *The Bay of Pigs: The Leader's Story of Brigade 2506* (New York: W. W. Norton, 1964); Karl E. Meyer and Tad Szulc, *The Cuban Invasion: The Chronicle of a Disaster* (New York: Praeger, 1962).

4. Thomas E. Cronin and S. D. Greenberg, *The Presidential Advisory System* (New York: Harper & Row, 1969).

5. The difficulty encountered in reforming the bureaucracy is discussed in Benjamin Wells, "Katzenbach Finds State Department Bureaucracy an Impediment to Reform," *New York Times,* Nov. 12, 1967, p. 78; Charles Frankel, *High on Foggy Bottom; An Outsider's Inside View of the Government* (New York: Harper & Row, 1969); I. M. Destler, *Presidents, Bureaucrats, and Foreign Policy: The Politics of Organizational Reform* (Princeton, N. J.: Princeton University Press, 1972); Graham Allison and Morton H. Halperin, *Bureaucratic Politics in Foreign Policy* (Washington, D.C.: Brookings Institution, 1974).

6. Dean E. Mann with Jameson W. Doig, *The Assistant Secretaries: Problems and Processes of Appointment* (Washington, D.C.: Brookings Institution, 1965), pp. 87–123; 191–231.

7. Frederick C. Mosher and John E. Harr, *Programming Systems and Foreign Affairs Leadership* (New York: Oxford University Press, 1970).

8. Literature on the possible dangers to a democracy of the intelligence community includes David Wise and Thomas B. Ross, *Invisible Government* (New York: Bantam Books, 1964); Harry Rowe Ransom, *Can American Democracy Survive Cold War?* (Garden City, N.J.: Doubleday, 1964); Young Hum Kin, *The Central Intelligence Agency: Secrecy versus Democracy* (Lexington, Mass.: D. C. Heath, 1968); Hanson W. Baldwin, "The Growing Risks of Bureaucratic Intelligence," *The Reporter* 29 (Aug. 12, 1963): 48–52.

9. Robert Kennedy, *Thirteen Days: A Memoir of the Cuban Missile Crisis* (New York: W. W. Norton, 1968), pp. 94–95.

10. John Spanier, *The Truman-MacArthur Controversy and the Korean War* (Cambridge, Mass.: Belknap Press, 1959); Charles A. Willoughby

and John Chamberlain, *MacArthur, 1949–1951* (New York: McGraw-Hill, 1954).
11. Alexander L. George, "The Case for Multiple Advocacy in Making Foreign Policy," *American Political Science Review* 66 (September 1972): 751–785.
12. Henry A. Kissinger, "Domestic Structures and Foreign Policy," *Daedalus* 95 (Spring 1966), reprinted in Kissinger's *American Foreign Policy* (New York: W. W. Norton, 1969), p. 17.
13. *Ibid*, p. 18.
14. *Ibid*, p. 20.
15. Chalmers M. Roberts, "Foreign Policy under a Paralyzed Presidency," *Foreign Affairs* 52 (July 1974): 675–689. *See also* Raymond Aron, "Richard Nixon and the Future of American Foreign Policy," *Daedalus* 101 (Fall 1972): 1–24; and Arthur M. Schlesinger, Jr., *The Imperial Presidency* (Boston: Houghton Mifflin, 1973).

12

Congress, the Supreme Court, and the President: Partners in Policy Formulation

On one level, American foreign policy may be conceived of as a product of a partnership comprised of the three branches of U.S. government. Congress serves as the junior partner to the President, and the Supreme Court remains a silent partner whose occasional interventions have helped the President more than the legislative branch. The relationships within this triad have been dynamic and have had an impact on the patterns of U.S. diplomatic behavior.

THE GROWTH OF PRESIDENTIAL POWER

Presidential Power in Ascendancy

Unilateral Activities. After World War II, and extending into the early 1970s, the powers that the American presidency often assumed were awesome. It was not until 1973, when funds for bombing in Cambodia were terminated and a law was passed limiting executive war powers, that Congress began to reverse the trend toward presidential paramountcy in foreign policy. The catalog of uses of presidential power is impressive: commitment of troops to Korea before the United Nations, under whose auspices Truman justified his actions, had decided to act; Kennedy's decision to go to the brink of nuclear war over Soviet missiles in Cuba without consulting Congress and before the regional alliance system—the Organization of American States—acted; and the decision in 1965 to attack another nation, North Vietnam, without a declaration of war.

Reasons for Growth of Power. For three decades, the American presidency accrued power, sometimes requesting it from a compliant Congress, but most often boldly asserting the executive's self-interpreted "rights" and moving into policy frontiers without any challenges from the legislative branch.

Beyond the junior-partner relationship with the President that the Congress assumed, what are the reasons for the growth of executive power? From a chronological perspective, presidential ascendancy dates back to the 1930s and the crisis of depression and to the 1940s and World War II. The Cold War was but the third in a series of major crises that were interpreted to entail an enlarged federal bureaucracy and the delegation of increased power to the President. The habit of unilateral presidential behavior has its roots in the 1930s, not the 1950s.

The four revolutions in the international system — weapons, economics, statecraft, and nationalism—also encouraged the growth of presidential power. Each one enlarged the bureaucracy, complicated the concepts and procedures of international politics, and often necessitated rapid decision making. The tendency was to ignore Congress. Congressmen began to hear jargon previously never employed in hearings, such as "megatons," "positive neutralism," "skywar," and "take-off point." Not all the confusing parlance came from the bureaucracy: the biological, physical, and social science academic communities contributed their own nomenclature.

In addition, the image of international politics held by American leaders permitted the expansion of power of the executive branch. Realism furnished justification, as well as encouragement, for the President's unilateral decision making. However, one cannot be too harsh in judging Realism in this situation. Two other images, Liberalism and Right-Wing Revisionism, would have the same effect. Of the four images, only Left-Wing Revisionism could provide the rationale for a presidency with less power.

Finally, the Cold War itself mesmerized the American public. Because the Soviet Union was portrayed as revisionist and aggressive by the Realists, the elite and knowledgeable publics were willing to permit the President to take decisive action to halt Russian expansion. The Realists chose to allow the development of an executive office with awesome powers rather than consider the possibility (a false one, according to the Left-Wing Revisionists) of Communist domination of the international community.

Growth Not Predetermined. The growth of presidential power was not predetermined by constitutional provisions. The U.S. Constitution, through its separation-of-powers principle and its distribution of foreign policy functions between the legislative and executive branches, did not clearly delegate to either the President or Congress command of American diplomacy. Congress is empowered to declare war, to raise and support armies, navies, and militia, to regulate foreign commerce, and to provide for the common defense. The President, on the other hand, is commander-in-chief; by including this provision, the Founding Fathers were as much motivated by a desire for civilian control over the military as they were by the desire to invest the power of decisive action in one individual. Much of the increase in presidential authority has been justified by powers *implied* as head-of-state functions. Presidents in the post-World War II era have made full use of these implications, which has had the effect of elevating executive authority and of making Congress a junior partner in the foreign policymaking process.

CONGRESS: THE JUNIOR PARTNER

Congress' junior position in executive–legislative relations has been fostered by its lack of independent sources of information and by its internal divisions.[1] Neither problem is easily solved.

Congress and Information Input

Congress generally must rely on information released at the pleasure of the executive branch. Compared with the tens of thousands of Foreign Service officers, intelligence agents, and military personnel who supply data to the President, the information resources of Congress are indeed meager.

The Individual Congressman as a Source. The individual congressman can, and quite often does, develop foreign policy expertise. Through his personal study, trips abroad, and participation in committee investigations and hearings, a congressman builds up a reservoir of personal knowledge to use in evaluating international events. At times, he can request intelligence reports and participate in briefings by executive personnel.

The congressman is largely a domestic political animal. Rarely can he devote a majority of his time to foreign affairs, although senators and representatives from one-party districts with a safe political base may show more concern for international issues without fear of criticism by constituents that they are neglecting the people's needs. Most congressmen must attend to problems pertinent to their constituency; this means that foreign issues are usually secondary to domestic problems.

Most congressional expertise is found in the Senate Foreign Relations and House Foreign Affairs committees and in other committees that spend a large segment of their time on foreign affairs, such as the Armed Services committees of both houses.[2] These committees have further divided into subcommittees that focus on specific areas or topics (e.g., African affairs or disarmament). Within subcommittee groupings, the individual congressman develops a high degree of personal knowledge and proficiency.

Research Staffs and Information Input. The research staffs of House and Senate committees, especially the House Foreign Affairs and Senate Foreign Relations committees, are the most important sources of information and expertise on foreign policy in the Congress.[3] The staffs are not large—between 10 and 20 researchers, depending on the committee and the chamber—but traditionally they have been well-qualified and highly trained in their subject areas. Ideally, the staffs do not make policy. Their function is to outline the consequences of the executive policy proposal under discussion; on occasion, they may suggest alternative proposals. But their primary purpose is to help congressmen on the committees by supplying expert advice and factual background. Once the committee has arrived at a decision, a staff member is directed to draft a report, whether or not the committee's position corresponds to his or her personal values.

When Congress is not in session, the committee staff serves as a conduit for information by receiving and distributing to committee members communications from executive departments. The staffs maintain continuous contact with personnel in executive departments concerned with the committees' subject matter, as well as with research staffs in their own and the other chamber. Often the committee will request and receive Foreign Service and intelligence reports from the executive branch. In effect, the staff becomes a gatekeeper in the information-input process, appraising data and sometimes withholding information considered to be of secondary importance.

The Legislative Reference Service of the Library of Congress is another source of data for the legislative branch. The Foreign Affairs Section of the library, which employs approximately 15 researchers, is often called upon to do background studies on contemporary issues. Their studies are usually nonpartisan and they seldom suggest alternatives to the President's proposals.

Number of Experts. The number of individuals who give full- or part-time energy to gathering and evaluating foreign policy data is liberally estimated as 1,000 people. When this figure is compared with the personnel available to collect and evaluate information in the executive branch—an estimated 12,000 in the Central Intelligence Agency alone—it underscores the problem faced by the legislature in making valid judgments on foreign policy issues. Clearly, Congress is largely dependent on the executive for information about the world environment.

Congressional Disunity and Discontinuity

House and Senate Disunity. The lack of an independent source for world affairs data and of personnel to evaluate the data are not the only reasons for Congress' role as legitimator of executive policy initiatives. The legislative branch is disunited; divided into two branches, each branch is further split into many centers of power. The House especially lacks continuity, for it must reorganize itself every two years. Since only one-third of the Senate faces reelection biannually, the upper house does not have as much of a continuity problem.

Disunity and discontinuity contribute to Congress' dependence on the executive branch for leadership and information. In effect, executive–legislative relations are executive–committee relations. The committees are the centers of power in the legislative process; therefore, the administration woos them, assiduously supplying requested information and performing required favors. Each department in the executive branch has an office of congressional liaison responsive to the needs of individual congressmen.

The executive consults with some congressmen on almost every policy initiative. If the initiative is controversial and will come under attack from various interests within the body politic, the President will widen the circle of consultation to build a winning coalition of supporters. The President must build support for his policies within both houses of Congress.

In 1919, President Wilson ignored numerous warnings that his ideas would receive a hostile reception in the Senate. He refused to take a bona fide Republican leader to Versailles during the negotiations to end World War I. President Roosevelt, twenty-five years later, avoided a similar mistake and made certain that recognized Republican leaders were present at San Francisco when the United Nations Charter was finalized.

Sectionalism and Ideology. The disunity of Congress is exacerbated by the regional and ideological diversities that characterize the American political system.[4] Regional attitudes can be identified, although they are shifting. The Midwest traditionally produced congressmen who opposed increased American involvement in the international system, while southern legislators favored freer trade and a larger role for the United States in the world arena. Congressmen from the East and West coastal areas were identified with a broadened international outlook. In recent years, while the coastal states have remained true to their traditional viewpoint, the Midwest and South have tended to shift positions. The South has become more isolationist while the Midwest has turned more toward internationalism. The southern shift is explained in part by the growth of industrial areas. Southern congressmen now advocate higher tariffs to protect the growing industrial complexes in their region.

Ideological differences among congressmen also contribute to the legislature's diverse approaches to world problems. Classifying congressmen as "conservative" or "liberal" is not an easy task, however, because of the variety of motivations behind political decisions.[5]

Congressional Coordination. Can sensible foreign policy decisions result from this process, characterized by disunity and discontinuity? Although the committees are independent centers of power, they can be coordinated by House and Senate leadership to produce effective legislation. As long as the committees do not directly confront each other over highly important pieces of legislation, the process works smoothly. But when jurisdictional disputes arise, the coordination process breaks down. On several occasions, for example, the Senate Armed Services Committee and Foreign Relations Committee have claimed conflicting jurisdiction over legislative proposals involving matters of national security policy, especially budgetary requests. In 1969 when the administration requested funds to build an antiballistic missile system, both the Foreign Relations Committee, which was hostile to the proposal, and the Armed Services Committee, which was favorable, held hearings.

THE SUPREME COURT AND AMERICAN DIPLOMACY

The Court's View of the Presidency

The Supreme Court has seldom interfered with the exercise of presidential leadership in foreign policy. The President is, in the words of the Supreme Court, the "sole organ of the federal government in the field of international relations."[6]

The Supreme Court has been more of a restraint in domestic affairs than it has in foreign relations. In the Curtiss–Wright case, the Court declared that the President had "a degree of discretion and freedom from statutory restriction which would not be admissible were domestic affairs alone involved." At no time has the Court checkmated presidential authority in foreign policy as it did in declaring President Truman's decision to seize steel mills in 1952 unconstitutional.[7]

The judiciary has failed to curb executive authority in part because most of the cases come before the Court after the danger that stimulated them has past. Lincoln's excessive use of presidential power during the Civil War was struck down by the Court long after the fighting stopped. Consequently, the Court's curbs have produced more theoretical than practical effects.

The Court, therefore, has permitted the growth of presidential power. The judicial branch has rarely challenged executive authority in foreign affairs and has broadly expanded the parameters within which the President may act in the world arena.

The Court and Individual Liberties

While the Court has allowed presidential authority to expand at the international level, it has been less generous with domestic executive powers, particularly in cases involving civil rights. But an important distinction should be made: in most of these cases, the litigation involved *agencies* of the executive branch, and not the President. The restraints imposed grew out of judicial interpretations of powers given to subordinates of the President and the implementation of these delegated powers.

For example, at the beginning of the Cold War, Truman issued the President's Loyalty Order in 1947, which established an elaborate procedure to dismiss disloyal federal employees. A board was established to review cases and to draw up a list of subversive organizations. The Court immediately began to hear cases involving individuals who were dismissed on the basis of charges by unidentified informants and involving organizations complaining that they were unjustly listed as subversive. The Eisenhower security program continued the hazards of his predecessor's 1947 Loyalty Order.[8] While reorganizing the power of an executive agency to conduct such investigations, the Court attempted to guarantee that traditional rights of citizens were protected.

The Court's concern for civil liberty problems evoked by internal security programs and laws has covered a wide field of endeavors. State loyalty oaths, individuals denied admission to the bar because of state loyalty requirements, the deportation of aliens and denaturalization of citizens, and anti-sedition legislation were the legal battlefields throughout the Cold War of the 1940s and 1950s. Many times the Court took on the unpopular task of protecting the rights of Communist Party members and of judging whether executive procedures as implemented could discern the difference between a real and a suspected offender.

The Court's civil rights decisions attracted criticism from the Revisionists. A major theme of Right-Wing Revisionism is that domestic conditions, and especially a liberal ideology, work together to bring about an internal collapse of the American system.[9] The more radical Revisionists believe that the Court has "protected" Communists and made the government's task more difficult, thereby encouraging the inevitable collapse. In the 1960s and 1970s, the Left-Wing Revisionists contended that the Court was doing too little to protect the rights of individuals, especially of young men who refused for reasons of conscience to fight in Vietnam.[10]

The Court and Mass Media

Another domestic arena with foreign policy implications, within which the Court has countermanded executive authority, has been the right of mass media to publish information. In 1971, the Court voted 6 to 3 to sanction the publication of the Pentagon Papers by the *Washington Post* and *New York Times*. The Nixon administration had asked that both newspapers be enjoined from publishing the papers on the ground that it would cause "irreparable injury to the defense of the United States." Thus, the Court protected the right of mass media to publish foreign policy documents that may be embarrassing to the government.[11]

THE MIX: EXECUTIVE–CONGRESSIONAL–LEGISLATIVE RELATIONSHIPS

The separation-of-powers principle has imposed on the American system of government the need to mix the functions and authority of each branch in the foreign policy formulation process. Each branch has its role, but each role has two roots: the role as envisioned in the Constitution and the role as it is played according to the realities of today's politics. Four powers—declaring war, negotiating treaties, appointing presidential assistants, and formulating the budget—have a constitutional basis as well as a background of political traditions.

The Power to Declare War

An Anachronism? In modern times, the power given to both houses of Congress sitting jointly to declare war on the enemies of the United States is anachronistic.[12] The Constitution was conceived at a time when mobilization could be delayed until after the decision to declare war was made and when the United States had no far-flung military establishment abroad. Congressional approval was written into the Constitution as a safeguard against a selfish and enterprising President who might plunge this nation into war for insufficient and whimsical reasons. Even before the days of nuclear weaponry, however, President Polk could embark on questionable policy paths leading to a confrontation with Mexico in 1848.

Congress, with the power to declare war, is granted only the official duty to recognize that war already exists as a state of affairs between the United States and another nation. In *The Prize Cases,* decided in 1863, the Supreme Court defined war as "a state of things, and not an act of legislative will."[13] This act of recognition is important for legal reasons: to determine the starting time for expropriation of a belligerent's property; to order the expulsion of the enemy's embassy; and to give guidance to businessmen who may be in the process of trading with the enemy state.

Korea and Vietnam. In the two post-1945 conflicts, the President did not seek an official declaration that a state of war existed between the United States and an enemy nation. In Korea, President Truman asked for no congressional authorization to use force, justifying the American involvement under the United Nations Charter to which the Senate had given its consent. As the war dragged on, criticisms mounted from a Congress controlled by an opposition party, the Republicans. In 1964, President Johnson learned from Truman's experiences and obtained an official sanction from Congress for the use of force through the Gulf of Tonkin resolution.

In these cases, the President committed American power to two wars, one (Vietnam) the longest and costliest in U.S. history, without a constitutionally based declaration of war. These conflicts gave rise to the term "presidential wars," i.e., wars that were begun without consulting Congress. While the UN Charter was the justification for American involvement in Korea, the Southeast Asia Treaty, signed in 1954, was the basis for U. S. intervention into Vietnam.

Does a prior commitment by Congress obviate the need for the President to ask for a declaration of war? Admittedly, a defensive alliance with a provision defining the cause of war as an attack on any signatory to the agreement is not a debatable point when the attack occurs. There would still seem to be a need to honor the process: Congress should be asked to recognize that the action constituted a breach of the peace, unless the President has some doubts as to whether or not the treaty has been violated. The constitutional problem that Vietnam posed was whether or not the actions defined by the President as a breach of the agreement were, in fact, in violation of the treaty. Suspicion of the President's case for a treaty violation is one of the facts of political life in the Vietnam War. While the United States government used the Southeast Asia Treaty as justification for its actions in Vietnam, at no time did the signatories meet and declare that the circumstances in Vietnam constituted a breach of the peace as defined by the agreement.

The Effect of the Standing Army. Modern warfare, with its requirements for rapid decision making, has necessitated that Congress finance a constant state of military readiness; previously, national security relied on reserves. The first peacetime draft, enacted immediately prior to World War II, was continued until the early 1970s; at that point, the nation moved toward a volunteer army. With a large army in being, and with the power to draft more men, the President was free to initiate actions without having to approach Congress for its approval. The act of declaring war prior to World War II was the anchor point for other actions, such as authority to conscript an army. With the army already constituted and ready, the declaration of war became unnecessary, or easier to ignore.

Undeclare a War? Congressional responsibility after a war begins is ill-defined, except, of course, for the responsibility to provide money to fight it. Neither provision nor precedent exists that permits Congress to "undeclare" a war. The power to wage war, once declared, is an executive monopoly. And while wars begin through the action of both houses, they are terminated through the action of only one chamber, the Senate, through its treaty-ratifying responsibility which it holds jointly with the President. Wars can end without a treaty of peace, as did the conflict with North Korea in 1953.

Treaty Making

Article II, Section 2 of the Constitution states that the Senate is primarily responsible for giving its "advice and consent" on treaties with foreign nations and on the President's nominations of individuals for foreign policy positions.[14] This provision of the Constitution has spawned a small storm of controversy: When should the Senate give "advice"? At the early stages of negotiation or when the finished treaty is presented? Traditionally, advice has been solicited at the same time as consent. This situation has not been happily accepted by some senators, one of whom is J. William Fulbright, then Chairman of the Foreign Relations Committee. He observed that the post-war period has been characterized by a "shattering series of crises which have necessitated efforts by the executive branch to provide leadership." The legislative branch, on the other hand, "inspired by patriotism, importuned by Presidents, and deterred by lack of information," has tended to fall in line behind the executive. The result, according to Fulbright, has been that "the Senate's constitutional powers of advice and consent have atrophied into what is widely regarded as, though never asserted to be, a duty to give prompt consent with a minimum of advice."[15]

Stages in the Treaty Process. The treaty-making process involves five clearly defined, but sometimes misunderstood, formal stages. The *negotiation stage* consists of discussions between designated agents over the contents of the treaty, and, if agreement is reached, affixing a signature to the document. The signature by the President's diplomatic agent only binds the government; in international law, it does not bind the state. It signifies that the head of state approves the treaty, but that other centers of power in the decision-making process must also give their approval. In the American experience, the negotiation stage has remained almost entirely under the President's control. If consultations with the Senate are undertaken, they normally involve a handful of key senators. The draft of the treaty is not submitted to the Senate before the President's agent signs it.

The *advise and consent stage* obviously involves the Senate, which must approve all treaties by a two-thirds majority if they are to become the "law of the land." Several alternatives are open to the Senate at this stage: to approve or disapprove the draft as written; to approve with amendments or reservations (in which case, the draft must be resubmitted to the other parties to ascertain whether or not they will accept the proposed revisions); or to "smother" the draft by not acting on it in the committees. The Senate has considered approximately 25 treaties in each yearly session since the end of World War II. Approximately 75 percent of the treaties were approved by the Senate; the remaining 25 percent were either withdrawn by the President from the Foreign Relations Committee's consideration or "smothered" by inactivity. If the large percentage of approved treaties is considered, Fulbright's contention that the Senate is always asked to give "prompt consent with a minimum of advice" seems justified. But treaties are political instruments, and the enemy of all political instruments is time. Time makes political instruments outdated and useless because conditions, which formerly evoked their existence, change. The "smothering" process, therefore, is an effective way to force the President to change his mind.

The third stage is *ratification,* assuming the Senate has approved the treaty without amendments or reservations. In international law, "ratification" is a technical term that refers to the commitment by the head of state to adhere to the treaty by signing the formal document. Only the President, as head of state, can ratify a treaty; quite often, the Senate's "advise and consent" function is erroneously identified as the ratification stage. The Senate's approval, however, is necessary before ratification can occur.

The ratifications are then exchanged by the contracting parties. In most instances, the ratification process (stage three) and the *exchange of the signed treaty* (stage four) occur at the same time. At this point, the treaty is binding on the state as well as the government. And finally, the treaty is *promulgated,* or declared to be domestic law. This function belongs solely to the President.

Role of Treaties. Most of the treaties that the Senate approves concern economic or commercial agreements. As a rule, these treaties are noncontroversial and of mutual benefit to both the United States and the other contracting party. Treaties that commit American power to an alliance or treaties with specialized agencies of the United Nations have been the most controversial.

To focus on treaties per se is to underscore the relative importance of the Senate vis-à-vis the House in the foreign policymaking process. In reality, foreign policies are usually embellished in programs, not treaties, although a treaty may be an important aspect of a foreign policy program. Since *program,* and not *treaty,* is usually the focal point in American foreign policy, the House of Representatives has been very much a part of the decision-making process. While the House may never attain to the prestige and stature of the Senate in the diplomatic process, the lower chamber cannot be neglected because programs must be funded from year to year.

Executive Agreements. Executive agreements are formal accords which have been prominent in the conduct of American diplomacy. Executive agreements are compacts negotiated with other nations and ratified by the President; they are binding on the United States as long as the administration that negotiated the agreement is in power. The differences between treaties and executive agreements are: (1) Senate approval is not required for executive agreements as it is for treaties, and (2) treaties are binding on the United States *government,* until abrogated, while executive agreements are binding only on the presidential *administration* that negotiated them.

The first distinction is an important consideration only with *simple executive agreements.* The simple agreement is negotiated solely on the initiative of the President by the authority of his position as head of state or commander in chief. Compacts on commercial, copyright, and postal topics are usually simple executive agreements, as well as armistice agreements stipulating conditions under which armed hostilities will cease. Compacts to end wars, on the other hand, are usually treaties. Another type, the *delegated executive agreement,* is negotiated by the President as a result of powers delegated by a treaty (approved by the Senate) or by Congress. By far, the most controversial of the two types is the simple executive agreement. The second distinction is significant in theory, but not very important in practice, since an incoming administration usually reaffirms its commitment to all previous executive agreements. The foreign government, however, has no guarantee that the incoming President will honor executive agreements negotiated by the outgoing administration.

Thus, the legal status of executive agreements is a rank lower than treaties because agreements are not the "supreme law of the land." They are, however, a rank higher than state laws. Executive agreements have obviated laws passed by states, or have permitted the federal government to act in areas that the Supreme Court originally declared as unconstitutional. In *Missouri* v. *Holland,* the Court allowed the government to make laws based on an executive agreement with Canada that would protect migrating birds.[16] An earlier attempt to protect the birds by federal law was struck down by the Court as unconstitutional. Consequently, an executive agreement, approved by only the President, permitted the government to apply its power to an area that a law, passed by the Congress and signed by the President, did not.

Presidential Appointments

The Senate's power of "advice and consent" in appointments to executive posts involves many more decisions than its role in making treaties and declaring war; but it has raised fewer problems in executive–legislative relations.[17] In a normal year, the President will send approximately 700 nominations to the Senate Foreign Relations Committee for action. Most of the nominations are new officers appointed to the Foreign Service and promotions for Foreign Service officers already on duty. Fewer in number, but more often in the public's eye, are the nominations for ambassadorships to head American embassies abroad and nominations for the Secretary of State and his subcabinet members (the Under Secretary, deputy under secretaries, and assistant secretaries or their equivalent).

Only on rare occasions has the Senate refused to give the President his choice of subordinates in the foreign policy process. However, the "smothering" phenomena also can be employed when nominations are submitted. The Senate's reluctance to approve diplomatic relations with the Vatican, for example, in 1954 led to "smothering" the nomination of the ambassador-designate and to the eventual withdrawal of his name by the Eisenhower administration.

Appropriations and Foreign Policy

The fourth function that involves the legislative branch in foreign policy-making is control over the budget-making process.[18] Congress must approve appropriations; it also often attempts to audit expenditures through the General Services Administration. Of the four functional areas delegated to the Congress—declaration of war, confirmation of treaties and nominations, and control over appropriations—the last offers the most effective means to influence foreign policy.

Attempts to control appropriations underscore the problems of congressional participation in the foreign policy process. The executive branch controls the content of the budget; consequently, the President controls the input of information, as he does on most foreign policy issues. Congress is left to tinker with the budget's contents, which are too detailed and too complicated for any congressman to master. The congressman is cast in the role of nitpicking, inquiring into whether a proposed project could be funded at a reduced appropriation, striking a budgetary item, or adding one that the administration does not want. In the latter case, of course, the administration may not choose to spend the appropriated money. Nevertheless, the lamentable image of Congress as a branch concerned with minutiae, rather than the broadly gauged questions of foreign policy, and as a group of responsible leaders concerned with the insignificant rather than the consequential, is further reinforced. Congress again comes across as focusing on means and not ends of policy decisions.

However, the fact that Congress does review means (and sometimes ends) dictates to the executive branch the need to formulate foreign policies with the realities of congressional support in mind. Policies must be tailored to meet objections voiced by congressional leaders, who, once convinced to support the administration's position, will influence many of their colleagues. There are occasions, however, when the President may proceed with a policy position despite warning from congressional leadership that the legislature will not readily accept it; presidential foreign-aid requests of recent years have followed this pattern.

Because of the appropriation process, the House of Representatives has been brought more and more into foreign policy, even into areas normally reserved for the Senate. While the Senate's approval is necessary for treaties, many international compacts (including executive agreements) require enabling legislation to implement them. The House, therefore, becomes involved in enacting enabling legislation for treaties, although these treaties are passed without its consent in the constitutional process. Only on self-executing treaties—those that require no enabling legislation—can the wishes of the House of Representatives be safely ignored. Sooner or later, almost every facet of foreign policy must be translated into dollars and cents and written into the budget. Whenever this happens, the views of the House become extremely important to the executive branch.

CONGRESS:
A NEED TO CORRECT
THE BALANCE

In each of the four foreign policy arenas, the role of Congress in the legislative–executive relationship was that of a junior partner; the role of the Supreme Court was to legitimize the President's expansion of power or to stand aside. The legislative–executive balance by the early 1970s had tipped far in the direction of the executive, highlighting a need to introduce equilibrium into the relationship.

The need to right the balance was underscored by disastrous presidential policymaking in the 1960s. The decade began with the Bay of Pigs invasion failure in 1961 and ended with an American military build-up and growing commitment in Vietnam that eventually involved 500,000 men. This dismal record raised an important question: What contributions could Congress make to American foreign policy in spite of its lack of information and organizational disunity?

First Role: Keeping the Executive Honest

If one of the President's responsibilities is to control the executive bureaucracy, one of Congress' responsibilities is to control the President. In addition, the legislative branch must be assured that the President is fulfilling his responsibility toward the bureaucracy. Congress exercises these responsibilities through its investigatory powers.

Committee Hearings and Administration Failures. One function of committee hearings is to focus public opinion on policy failures in American diplomacy. These investigations serve as an instrument to discipline the executive branch, to make the bureaucracy aware of its mistakes, and, perhaps, to make it more cautious about future actions. Investigations have a shock effect on the bureaucracy, and they inform the public of the government's foibles, but they seldom have an impact on the course of American diplomacy. Congress may be an effective "watch dog" (a debatable point), but the watch dog function places congressmen in a negative role, rather than one providing positive leadership.

During investigations into executive failures, the instruments of mass media supply indispensable information. Facts about failures obviously will not be forthcoming from the agency or department involved. Where a policy mistake is made, the temptation is present to cover it up with a "secret" or "top secret" stamp. Mass media will bring the event to the attention of Congress and the public by publishing bureaucratic leaks or by interviewing the people involved. While failures make headlines, they are soon forgotten unless they engender a congressional investigation.

Congress and the Intelligence Community. Congressmen have not shown a strong inclination to control bureaucratic excesses of the intelligence community.[19] The Foreign Service officers and the military establishment largely have been left alone. However, congressional reluctance to examine the intelligence community throughout the Cold War era has begun to reverse itself in the 1970s.

The 1955 Hoover Commission recommendation for a Joint Congressional Committee on Central Intelligence was debated in the 84th Congress. It failed to pass the Senate and was never considered by the House of Representatives. Between 1949 and 1966, approximately 150 resolutions calling for more supervision of the community were introduced in Congress, but they never were reported to the floor of either house. The Senate did establish the Oversight Committee, composed of members of the Armed Services and Foreign Relations committees. The Oversight Committee's function was to review the Central Intelligence Agency's activities. In general, the Committee has been impotent; it failed to hold any meetings in 1971. Congressional supervision of the intelligence community also has been exercised through subcommittees of the House and Senate Appropriations and Armed Services committees.

The first effective congressional constraints on the CIA were imposed in 1972. Congress removed the provisions of the 1947 National Security Act that exempted the CIA from controls over obtaining funds, personnel, and material from other agencies without accounting for them. This congressional action was a far cry from a "watch dog" one, but it did represent the first time in 25 years that Congress sought to restrain the Central Intelligence Agency. As a result of a military takeover in Chile, which the CIA was active in promoting, President Ford in 1974 directed the NSC Forty Committee to meet periodically with congressional leaders.

Why has Congress been reluctant to exercise control over the intelligence community? Part of the answer lies in the enormity of the community: all the agencies spend approximately 3 billion dollars a year and constitute a large portion of the federal bureaucracy. Congressmen themselves lack the time and the staff personnel to keep track of the community's activities. Also, no congressman wants to appear as an obstacle to gathering information about Communist states.

The Court and Investigations. The Supreme Court, in a number of cases, has circumscribed the limits of congressional investigations.[20] Investigations cannot be conducted for the sake of exposure alone, but must have a valid legislative function. The rights of individuals appearing before committees must be protected. As the Court has expressed opinions on presidential foreign policy activities, it has also intervened in the congressional process when civil rights and liberties were involved.

Second Role: Making Laws

Another congressional foreign policy function is to enact laws that serve the national interest. Since the initiative in diplomacy has rested with the President, Congress' role has tended to be that of a legitimizer of executive proposals. This position must be qualified: Congress has shown flashes of initiative in making foreign policy, such as in the decision to establish a new instrument for economic development.[21] The executive branch has access to more personnel, but it does not have a monopoly on foreign policy ideas.

Limiting Presidential War Powers. In November 1973, Congress passed, over the President's veto, a law limiting executive war powers. This law is one of the most important pieces of foreign policy legislation defining executive–legislative relations since World War II.

The law, debated in Congress in various forms before a consensus was reached, requires the President to report to both Houses within 48 hours of either committing U.S. troops abroad or increasing "substantially" U.S. troops abroad. If this commitment or increase were not approved by Congress within 60 days, the President would be required to cease hostilities. The deadline might be extended another 30 days if additional time were needed to safely withdraw American soldiers. If Congress chooses, both houses could pass a concurrent resolution within the 60-to-90 day period calling for immediate withdrawal; this resolution would not be subject to a presidential veto.

It remains to be seen whether or not this piece of legislation lives up to its promises. Most wars are popular during their early stages, making it difficult for Congress to cancel a military initiative undertaken by the President during this period of time. Some of the congressional opponents of this law argued that it gave the President the unilateral power to start wars. They contended that the President should be required to ask for legislative approval for troop commitments of any size and for any length of time.

The Role of the Committee Chairman. The instrument for the executive's will in foreign policy is the committee chairman. He cannot be dictated to, nor should he ever be taken for granted. In general, however, he is a supporter of the President's wishes (especially if they are members of the same party). His position on any piece of legislation relating to foreign affairs is crucial.

On most foreign policy issues, the individual congressman will follow the lead of the committee chairman. Members of Congress receive fewer behavioral cues on foreign policy from their publics than they do on domestic policy. Thus, congressmen turn more often to the Senate or House leadership for guidance on matters of diplomacy than to their constituents.

Third Role: Defining Goals for American Foreign Policy

Cold War Goals. The President in the Cold War era has shouldered ultimate responsibility for formulating intermediate objectives and long-range goals for American foreign policy. Especially on issues that were more encompassing and more controversial, such as alliances, trade, and disarmament policy, the executive branch was given a wide latitude in defining the problems to be solved and the goals to be achieved.

Congress, on the other hand, seldom engaged in defining goals for American diplomacy, except on issues that were highly specialized and somewhat removed from the public eye. Maritime policy, immigration, tariffs and quotas on specific goods, and policy on stockpiling and importing natural resources are examples of particular areas of diplomacy in which Congress traditionally enacted laws without, and sometimes in contradiction to, executive leadership.

Accepting the President's definition of most problems because the executive possesses a quasi-monopoly over information input, Congress has usually contented itself with arguing over strategy and tactics. For example, Congress accepted Truman's image of the U.S.S.R. as the enemy and the goal of containment (rather than annihilation of the Soviet Union or surrender to the Russians); however, the legislative branch has argued for alternative methods to reach this goal. Sometimes the disagreements over strategy and tactics have become volatile: bombers not requested by the President have been written into the budget and foreign-aid funds requested for a specific nation have been refused.

Congress' Revolt. In the midst of the Vietnam War, the Senate began to suggest alternative goals for American foreign policy in the Far East. The "revolt" centered in the Senate Foreign Relations Committee, chaired by Senator J. William Fulbright. Prior to 1965, Fulbright dutifully performed the functions of a committee chairman, i.e., shepherding presidential legislation through hearings and floor debates. On most issues, the Senate Foreign Relations Committee continued to perform this function; but on questions of the Vietnamese conflict, the Committee began to question the President's definition of the policy context, and especially, began to propose alternative goals. Debate, therefore, shifted from a focus on strategy and tactics to a more substantive discussion. It is significant that those who initiated the critique of policy were of the same majority party as the President (until 1968 and the election of Richard Nixon).

By the 1970s, the revolt was in full swing. The Gulf of Tonkin resolution was retracted. In 1973, Congress halted all funding for bombing strikes in Cambodia, which was experiencing a revolution against a government recognized by the United States, and the war powers limitation law was passed. The disarray of the Nixon administration resulting from the Watergate scandals encouraged Congress to assume more initiative in the policy-making process.

THE THREE BRANCHES: RECEDING, RESURGING, AND REASSESSING

The President and Congress. Until the war in Vietnam, Congress chose not to concern itself with the closed politics of the Cold War. It dutifully accepted executive-prescribed goals and assumptions and contented itself with evaluating proposed means in the light of accepted objectives. The vast amount of executive information used in making decisions was not called forth by the legislative branch. Moreover, Congress seldom sought out dissenting voices within the executive departments who had disagreed with the proposed policy. However the executive branch arrived at its decisions was not the concern of Congress. The issue of Vietnam brought the contradictory voices within the executive into the open; the mountains of data not shared with Congress were then requested and portions of it revealed. Before Vietnam, crises were handled by the President, with Congress accepting executive decisions without much debate. Congressional criticism was muted by the call for unity in the midst of another crisis. Vietnam was an elongated crisis, drawn out over agonizing years; its duration permitted Congress to deliberate on events as they unfolded. One cannot conclude from the Vietnamese experience, however, that Congress is no longer a reactive, but an initiatory, body.

The resurgence of congressional influence may have been stimulated by Vietnam, but it also was fueled by Watergate. The internal problems of the White House transformed Nixon into an invisible President, rarely holding news conferences, leaving major foreign policy decisions to Secretary of State Kissinger, and exercising little leadership over the Republican party in Congress. Nixon retreated from the position of a President exercising enormous decision-making powers; he was aided in this retreat substantially by untrustworthy assistants, a Vice-President who accepted bribes, and a White House intelligence unit with little regard for traditional American liberties.

Because Congress constitutionally controls the tax spigots, it will always be asked to provide the means for achieving presidential goals. Congressmen have grown accustomed to questioning executive goals and may substitute new ones in the decision-making process. If the executive goals are accepted, Congress will continue to resist attempts by the President to gain blanket grants of power to use any means "as he sees fit" to implement goals. In such cases, Congress loses its only effective contribution to the foreign policy process, i.e., scrutiny and discipline of the means to carry out objectives determined by the executive to be in the national interest. In past crises, presidents have asked Congress for "blank checks" with broad authority to employ executive power as they saw fit. In 1957, President Eisenhower asked for and received the authorization to employ U.S. armed forces in the Middle East "against overt armed aggression from any nation controlled by International Communism." American marines landed in Lebanon in 1958 for a brief stay under the provisions of this "blank check." American troops in Vietnam were beefed up under another broad grant—the 1964 Gulf of Tonkin resolution—and their stay was much longer.

If Congress is to continue its resurgence, means of providing more information to congressmen must be established. Without an independent source of intelligence, congressmen must rely on the bits and pieces of information doled out by the executive. More radical reforms include roving task forces that can be sent to trouble spots to report back to Congress, or even a separate, congressional intelligence organization overseas to collect and evaluate information independently of the executive's intelligence community. Less radical reforms include increasing the research capacity of Congress, furnishing individual congressmen with larger staffs, and enlarging the evaluation staffs of the Library of Congress.

Questioning goals, of course, requires accurate intelligence; but it also requires the willingness to kick a few sacred foreign policy cows. To doubt foreign dangers conceived by the executive branch, to question whether a proposal will achieve a prescribed end, or to assume that a nation's actions are friendly when the executive has labeled them hostile are examples of questions previously considered too "sacred" to broach.

The Court. Throughout this process of resurgence and recession, the Supreme Court continues to reassess. Law is not a static social instrument; it changes, although its transformation pace is much slower than other political instruments. The Court will continue to beat back the executive and legislative attempts to impinge on individual freedoms. It is doubtful, however, that the Court will diminish the primacy of the President in making foreign policy. Congress may approach equal partnership with the executive branch in formulating diplomacy, but the Court will be reluctant to change its dictum in the Curtiss–Wright case that the President is the "sole organ of federal government in the field of international relations."

The November 1973 act limiting the President's war-making powers is the type of legislation that can right the imbalance between Congress and the executive branch. Supreme Court decisions can be based on this legislation, but the Court cannot contribute greatly to a realignment of functions among the three branches.

NOTES

1. Among the general works on the role of Congress in making foreign policy are: Francis O. Wilcox, *Congress, the Executive, and Foreign Policy* (New York: Harper & Row, 1971); Robert Dahl, *Congress and Foreign Policy* (New York: W. W. Norton, 1950); James A. Robinson, *Congress and Foreign Policy-Making*, rev. ed. (Homewood, Ill.: Dorsey Press, 1967); Dean Acheson, *A Citizen Looks at Congress* (New York: Harper & Row, 1956); Kenneth W. Colegrove, "The Role of Congress and Public Opinion in Formulating Foreign Policy," *American Political Science Review* 38 (October 1944): 956–969; Benjamin V. Cohen, "The Evolving Role of Congress in Foreign Affairs," *Proceedings of the American Philosophical Society* (Oct. 25, 1948); Roger Hilsman, "Congressional-Executive Relations and the Foreign Policy Consensus, *American Political Science Review* 52 (1958): 725–744; John Hickey, "The Role of Congress in Foreign Policy. Case: The Cuban Disaster," *Journal of Inter-American Economic Affairs* 14 (Spring 1961): 67–89; and Nelson W. Polsby, "Foreign Policy and Congressional Activity," *World Politics* 15 (January 1963): 354–359.
2. See D. N. Farnsworth, *Senate Committee on Foreign Relations* (Urbana: University of Illinois Press, 1961) for a discussion of the Foreign Relations Committee and Holbert N. Carroll, *The House of Representatives and Foreign Affairs*, rev. ed. (Boston: Little, Brown and Co., 1966) for a discussion of the Committee on Foreign Affairs.
3. Kenneth Kofmehl, *Professional Staffs of Congress* (Lafayette, Ind.: Purdue University Studies, 1971); William L. Morrow, *Congressional Committees* (New York: Scribner's, 1969); Randall B. Ripley, "Congressional Government and Committee Management," in John D.

Montgomery and Arthur Smithies (eds.), *Public Policy* (Cambridge: Harvard University Press, 1965), vol. 14, pp. 28–48; and Samuel C. Patterson, "The Professional Staffs of Congressional Committees," *Administrative Science Quarterly* 15 (1970): 22–37.

4. On the subject of sectionalism, consult: George Grassmuck, *Sectional Biases in Congress on Foreign Policy* (Baltimore: Johns Hopkins University Press, 1951); Leroy N. Rieselbach, "The Demography of the Congressional Vote on Foreign Aid, 1939–1958," *American Political Science Review* 58 (1964): 577–578; Murray C. Havens, "Metropolitan Areas and Congress: Foreign Policy and National Security," *Journal of Politics* 26 (1964): 758–774; Malcolm E. Jewell, "Evaluating the Decline of Southern Internationalism Through Senatorial Role Call Votes," *Journal of Politics* 21 (1959): 624–646; and Charles O. Lerche, Jr., *The Uncertain South: Its Changing Patterns of Politics in Foreign Policy* (Chicago: Quadrangle Books, 1964).

5. Leroy N. Rieselbach, "Congressional Ideology, the Vote on Foreign Policy, and the Prospects for Party Reform," in John D. Montgomery and Arthur Smithies (eds.), *Public Policy* (Cambridge: Harvard University Press, 1965), vol. 14, pp. 49–70.

6. *United States* v. *Curtiss-Wright Exporting Company*, 229 U.S. 304 (1936). For a general discussion of the Constitution and U.S. diplomacy, *see* Louis Henkin, *Foreign Affairs and the Constitution* (Mineola, N.Y.: Foundation Press, 1972).

7. *Youngstown Sheet and Tube Company* v. *Sawyer*, 343 U.S. 579 (1952).

8. Some of these cases were *Bailey* v. *Richardson*, 341 U.S. 918 (1951); *Joint Anti-Fascist Refugees Committee* v. *McGrath*, 341 U.S. 123 (1951). For a discussion of these cases, *see* George W. Spicer, *The Supreme Court and Fundamental Freedoms* (New York: Appleton-Century-Crofts, 1959), pp. 206–244.

9. Rosalie M. Gordon, *Nine Men Against America* (New York: Devin-Adair, 1958), pp. 142–147.

10. Fred Cohn, "Soldiers Say No," in Robert Lefcourt (ed.), *Law Against the People* (New York: Random House, 1971), pp. 300–309; Fred Gardner, *The Unlawful Concert: An Account of the Presidio Mutiny Case* (New York: Viking Press, 1970); Robert Sherrill, *Military Justice is to Justice as Military Music is to Music* (New York: Harper & Row, 1970); Anthony A. D'Amato and Robert O'Neal, *The Judiciary and Vietnam* (New York: St. Martin's Press, 1972); and Lawrence R. Velvel, *Undeclared War and Civil Disobedience* (New York: Dunellen, 1970).

11. William A. Hachten, *The Supreme Court on Freedom of the Press* (Ames, Iowa: Iowa State University Press, 1968).

12. Edward S. Corwin, *Total War and the Constitution* (New York: Alfred A. Knopf, 1947); John M. Wells (ed.), *The People vs. Presidential War* (New York: Dunellen, 1970); and Jacob K. Javits with Don Kellerman, *Who Makes War* (New York: William Morrow, 1973).

13. 2 Black 635 (1863).
14. For a general discussion of the Senate's treaty-making responsibilities, see Malcolm E. Jewell, *Senatorial Politics and Foreign Policy* (Lexington: University of Kentucky Press, 1962); Randal H. Nelson, "Legislative Participation in the Treaty and Agreement Making Process," *Western Political Quarterly* 13 (March 1960): 154–172; W. Stull Holt, *Treaties Defeated by the Senate* (Baltimore: Johns Hopkins Press, 1933); Joseph P. Harris, *The Advice and Consent of the Senate* (Berkeley: University of California Press, 1953); D. F. Fleming, *The Treaty Veto of the American Senate* (New York: Putnam, 1930); Royden J. Dangerfield, *In Defense of the Senate: A Study in Treaty Making* (Norman: University of Oklahoma Press, 1933); F. E. Allen, *The Treaty as an Instrument of Legislation* (New York: Macmillan, 1952); Julian P. Boyd, "The Expanding Treaty Power," in Maurice H. Merrill (ed.), *Selected Essays on Constitutional Law*, vol. 3, (Chicago: The Foundation Press, 1938), pp. 410–435; Quincy Wright, "Treaties and the Constitutional Separation of Powers," *American Journal of International Law* 12 (1918): 64–95; and Edward S. Corwin, *National Supremacy: Treaty Power vs. State Power* (New York: Henry Holt, 1913). Supreme Court cases that focus on the treaty provision include: *Chinese Exclusion Case* 130 U.S. 581, 604, 606 (1798); *Fong Yue Ting* v. *U.S.* 130 U.S. 581 (1889); *Hauenstein* v. *Lynham* 100 U.S. 483, 25 L. Ed. 628 (1880); *Ware* v. *Hylton* 3 Dall. 199, 242–3 (1797); *U.S.* v. *Fox* 94 U.S. 315, 320 (1898); *Lattimer* v. *Poteet* 14 Pet. 4 (1840); *Hopkirk* v. *Bell* 3 Cr 454 (1806); *Foster* v. *Neilson* 2 Pet. 253, 314 (1819); *Lelima* v. *Bidwell* 182 U.S. 1 (1901); and *Taylor* v. *Morton* 23 Fed. Cas. No. 13, 799 (1855).
15. J. William Fulbright, *The Arrogance of Power* (New York: Random House, 1967), p. 45.
16. *Missouri* v. *Holland* 252 U.S. 416 (1920). Other cases on the status of executive agreements include: *Field* v. *Clark* 143, U.S. 649 (1892); *Altman and Company* v. *U.S.* 244 U.S. 583, 596 (1912); *U.S.* v. *Belmont* 301 U.S. 324 (1937); and *U.S.* v. *Pink* 315 U.S. 203 (1942). See also Elbert M. Byrd, *Treaties and Executive Agreements in the U.S.: Their Separate Roles and Limitations* (The Hague: M. Nijhoff, 1960); Wallace McClure, *International Executive Agreements: Democratic Procedure Under the Constitution of the United States* (New York: Columbia University Press, 1941); Quincy Wright, "The United States and International Agreements," in L. H. Chamberlain and Richard C. Snyder (eds.), *American Foreign Policy* (New York: Holt, Rinehart, and Winston, 1948), pp. 57–87; Henry S. Fraser, "The Constitutional Scope of Treaties and Executive Agreements," in William B. Stubbs and Cullen B. Gosnell (eds.), *Select Readings in American Government* (New York: Scribner's Sons, 1948).
17. Felix Nigro, "Senate Confirmation and Foreign Policy," *Journal of Politics* 14 (May 1952): 281–299.
18. Richard Fenno, *The Power of the Purse* (Boston: Little, Brown, and

Co., 1966); and Elias Huzar, *The Purse and the Sword* (Ithaca, N.Y.: Cornell University Press, 1950).

19. H. Bradford Westerfield, "Congress and Closed Politics in National Security Affairs," *Orbis* 10 (Fall 1966): 737–753.
20. *Kilbourne* v. *Thompson* 103 U.S. 168 (1881); *McGrain* v. *Daughtery* 273 U.S. 135 (1927); and *Watkins* v. *United States* 354 U.S. 128 (1957). For a general analysis, *see* James A. Perkins, "Congressional Investigations of Matters of International Importance," *American Political Science Review* 34 (April 1940): 284–294.
21. James A. Robinson, *The Monroney Resolution: Congressional Initiative in Foreign Policy-making* (New York: Henry Holt, 1959); and David A. Baldwin, "Congressional Initiative in Foreign Policy," *Journal of Politics* 28 (November 1966): 754–773.

SECTION 5

Issues in American Foreign Policy

This section focuses on the pattern of policies generated by the decision-making process and the influences of the domestic sources. In analyzing policy outcomes, one should continue to keep in mind that decisions do not become policy until implemented in the field. Consequently, while concentrating on policy outcomes, the various implementers of American diplomacy will be drawn into the analysis.

Chapter 13 evaluates the impact of the revolution in warfare (described in chapter 2) on American foreign policy. The timing and substance of military power—when to use it and in what form—is a primary issue of foreign policy.

Simultaneous with the creation of the most powerful military machine in the history of the state system, a dialogue has occurred over how to dismantle it. Chapter 14 surveys the patterns of disarmament and arms-control policy. Negotiations over disarmament resulted in much rhetoric and little agreement until the 1962 Cuban missile crisis. The collective self-defense or alliance systems, other approaches to national survival, are examined in chapter 15. American decision makers have sought to augment their military strength with that of European, Latin American, Middle Eastern, and Asian nations. The United Nations is also viewed as an instrument to ensure American security, a point discussed in chapter 16. International law, on the other hand, is perceived as too abstract to contribute to U.S. survival.

"Public Diplomacy," the subject of chapter 17, explores policy areas often overlooked, such as educational and cultural affairs, tourism, and the many private contacts between Americans and foreign nationals. This chapter broadens the parameters of the study of American diplomacy to include activities traditionally not thought of as part of U.S. foreign policy.

The last two chapters in this section focus on the economic patterns in American foreign policy. Chapter 18 examines the foreign assistance programs that have developed in the post-World War II period in response to Europe's reconstruction problem and to the emergence of the Third World. Chapter 19 tackles one of the most complex problems in contemporary American diplomacy—international monetary and trade policy. The revolution in economics (also described in chapter 2) has spawned a wide variety of intractable problems.

It is important to remember that although these patterns are discussed under various rubrics and separate headings, they are interrelated. A national military strategy, for example, that calls for a substantial commitment of American troops to Europe or for fighting a limited war in Vietnam will have a profound impact on the U.S. balance of payments. Disarmament initiatives during the 1940s and 1950s were largely kept alive by Third World nations who used the United Nations as an instrument to prod the superpowers into talking about arms control, although they were not overly interested. Foreign policy issues are discussed in isolation in this section for convenience, but they are interrelated.

13

Patterns of American Military Strategy

The revolution in warfare encompasses not only the introduction of new and awesome weapons but, in some cases, a revival of old instruments of destructive means. Nuclear and thermonuclear devices, dropped from aircraft or carried by missiles, are only part of the revolution. Guerrilla warfare, witnessed in Vietnam in the 1960s, did not require modern, sophisticated weaponry. It was a revitalization of military tactics as old as the state system itself.

American Images and the Cold War

The Cold War Competition. Besides the revolution in warfare, the development of a competitive environment between two dynamic societies, the United States and the Soviet Union, also had an impact on military strategy. The divergence of national values that conditioned Soviet and American images contributed to the hostility of the post-World War II era.

Competition between two vigorous states, such as the U.S. and U.S.S.R., was inevitable; the attitude with which American leaders viewed this competition, however, was not. The Realist image, which dominated American thinking after World War II, perceived the Soviet-American rivalry as a threat to U.S. security, as did the Right-Wing Revisionist image. Only the Left-Wing Revisionists recognized Soviet weaknesses as a result of wartime losses, but the Left-Wing image did not gather support until the 1960s.

Both the Realists and Right-Wing Revisionists perceived the Soviet Union as aggressive. The Right-Wing image, however, attributed Russian aggressiveness to ideology and tended to advocate the total defeat or (in the case of the more Radical Right-Wing advocates) annihilation of the U.S.S.R. The Realists never went that far. The Soviet Union would "mellow" or undergo internal transformation when it learned that Western strength and the will to use it stood in the way of unreasonable Russian designs.

233

Changes in the American Attitude. President Nixon in the early 1970s undertook fresh initiatives to normalize American relations with the People's Republic of China and Cuba, and he continued the policy trend, begun under President Kennedy, to find ways to relax tensions in Soviet–American relations. The Cold War, in effect, was over. The obvious question, then, is: What effect does this change in the international system have on American military strategy and doctrine? While tentative answers are included in this chapter, a more detailed answer is offered in the concluding chapter of this book.

THE DEVELOPMENT OF AMERICAN MILITARY STRATEGY

"Military strategy" denotes the planned use of force to obtain political objectives; hence, military strategy encompasses the pattern of decisions to develop, to deploy, and to apply national power.[1] "Military doctrine" and "military strategy" conceptually are the same, although "doctrine" can refer to definitive strategic patterns that have developed over a period of time. In this chapter, "doctrine" and "strategy" will be used interchangeably.

Purpose of Military Strategy

Reality and Strategy. The primary purpose of American military strategy is to preserve the independence of the United States. To be effective, therefore, strategy must reflect the realities of the international system, realities that include an accurate assessment of American and allied strength, as well as the opponent's intentions and strength. No strategic framework can totally capture all the salient points of the real world, but there should be a high degree of correlation between American military strategy and the realities of international political life. If not, then the United States government could be devoting a lion's share of its budget to deter threats that exist only in the collective American psyche.

Unfortunately, military doctrine, no matter how carefully developed, possesses distortions that can result in misjudgments. The military prophets of the 1920s and 1930s predicted that the next war would be fought with poison gas, a prediction that led to intensive gas-defense training among civilians as well as military personnel. The possible consequences of miscalculation in planning military strategy in the nuclear era are even greater. The United States, as well as the Soviet Union, may be preparing for the next war as if it will begin where the last war left off.

In the best of circumstances, the military mind is operating with a set of assumptions that lag several years behind contemporary developments. For the more sophisticated weapon system, a five or seven-year period from the drawing board, through prototypes, testing, training, and finally to deployment in the field is not uncommon. If the military strategist has guessed correctly, he has an up-to-date weapon system to use to protect national security. If he has guessed incorrectly, he has not only wasted funds on an obsolete weapon, but he may have jeopardized the security of his country.

Doctrinal Shifts

Military doctrine must remain in perpetual motion. Continual reevaluation of the strategic implication of new technological developments and of the relative strengths of friends and foes is necessary. New weapon systems must be devised and old ones modified to fill gaps in the framework of military strategy. Former enemies can become allies and past allies can become enemies. As a consequence, troop deployment, battle plans, and targeting must be changed. Since World War II, American military strategy has undergone at least four major, and a host of minor, shifts. The major transformations are usually identified with presidential administrations, although not always with presidents.[2]

The Truman Administration and Containment. The first significant shift in doctrine was the Truman administration's attempt to integrate nuclear weapons into a military strategy built around conventional arms. The major source of aggression, as perceived during the Truman years, was the Soviet Union, and the most probable site for this aggression to manifest itself was Europe. The doctrine of *containment*, proposed by George Kennan in 1947, was adopted in mutated form by President Truman. Any conventional attack by the U.S.S.R. on Western Europe would be answered by an American nuclear strike on the Russian heartland. Since the United States army did not possess the conventional capability of the Russian army, nuclear weapons would be used in the event of any form of aggression. Soviet initiatives of less-than-armed-conflict intensity would be met at an equivalent level. Subconventional conflicts, such as the Berlin blockade, would be met with firmness, but not necessarily with force.

Eisenhower and Massive Retaliation. The second major doctrinal shift occurred during the Eisenhower administration in 1954, when the doctrine of *massive retaliation* was propounded by Secretary of State John Foster Dulles.[3] The doctrine was a response to significant changes that had occurred during the early 1950's: the People's Republic of China was a fact of international life (hence, a friend, mainland China, had become a foe) and the U.S.S.R. successfully detonated nuclear and thermonuclear devices. The massive retaliation doctrine reserved the option for American decision makers to use nuclear weapons for any provocation by the U.S.S.R. and Communist China, whether or not conventional aggression was involved. The Far East, therefore, was added to the American nuclear umbrella, and the two Communist opponents assumed larger risks in undertaking diplomatic initiatives frowned on by the United States.

"Flexible Response" or the McNamara Doctrine. With the Kennedy administration, the third significant shift in military doctrine occurred. Soviet or Chinese initiatives now would be met at the level of force chosen by the aggressor. If the Russian or Chinese employed guerrilla tactics, a conventional attack, or nuclear weapons, the American government would respond in kind. The United States, therefore, would avoid the dilemma of responding to guerrilla warfare with a nuclear attack or of not responding at all. The Kennedy strategy has been dubbed *flexible response* or the McNamara Doctrine, after Robert S. McNamara, Kennedy's Secretary of Defense.[4] It dictated a strengthening of American ability to engage in conflicts at the subnuclear level.

The Nixon Doctrine and "Nuclear Sufficiency." The fourth major shift in American military strategy coincided with the Nixon administration's reevaluation of American intervention in Vietnam (resulting in the Nixon Doctrine) and the reevaluation of Soviet nuclear strength (resulting in the concept of "nuclear sufficiency").[5] Basically, the Nixon Doctrine postulated that the United States would not aid governments engaged in civil conflict unless American assistance was requested and unless the government under siege showed some indication of strength to survive. The Nixon Doctrine then ruled out extensive interventions in conflicts of the scale of Vietnam, which at its height claimed more than 500,000 American troops and annual expenditures of more than 30 billion dollars.

Although the Nixon Doctrine clearly said "no more Vietnams," what it excluded is less explicit. Shortly after the Doctrine was announced, President Nixon ordered American troops into Cambodia in 1970, a move that illustrated the difficulties of interpreting broad guidelines of policy. Was the Cambodian government strong enough to qualify for American support? Was the Cambodian incursion, using American as well as South Vietnamese troops, the type of support envisioned by the Doctrine? Neither of these questions had simple answers.

The concept of "nuclear sufficiency," unlike the Nixon Doctrine, displays a more discernible pattern. The background of the problem includes the decision made during the "flexible response" days of the Kennedy administration that slightly more than 1,000 intercontinental ballistic missiles constituted an adequate deterrent to Soviet aggression. These land-based missiles were augmented by nuclear warheads carried aboard long-range bombers, missiles in nuclear-powered submarines, and navy short-range bombers on aircraft carriers. Since nuclear power possessed by the United States was far superior to that possessed by the Soviet Union, the U.S.S.R. began to increase their nuclear arsenal. By 1970, the Russians had surpassed the United States in land-based missiles.

While the American nuclear force measured in total deliverable weapons was still greater than the Soviet Union's, the Russian buildup evoked a debate within and without the Nixon administration on "how much is sufficient." President Nixon, who had campaigned in 1968 on a platform of nuclear superiority, now postulated a doctrine of nuclear sufficiency: the United States would maintain a nuclear capability that was *sufficient* to deter the Soviet Union, rather than attempting to race the Russians in building more nuclear devices for a *superior* position. Since the United States in the early 1970s possessed an "overkill" capability of four times, additional missiles seemed meaningless. "Overkill" of this magnitude meant that the United States could kill every Soviet citizen at least four times. The obvious question is: Would the ability to kill every Russian *five* times enhance U.S. security?

Compromises in Strategy. Each of the four major doctrines illustrates the compromises that the American government had to make between the realities of international politics (as decision makers perceived them) and the resources available. "Total security"—a preponderance of military strength to dissuade all and any aggressors—does not exist.

With a quarter-century of hindsight, the division of American strategic thinking into four significant eras may appear to be superficial. In reviewing this history, the differences among eras appear less pronounced and their similarities more salient. In the end, nuclear weaponry has remained the primary and credible threat. Containment and flexible-response doctrines were moderated to emphasize Russian nuclear strength; massive retaliation was enlarged to include non-nuclear responses (such as landing marines in Lebanon in 1958 and aid to anti-Communist forces in Guatemala in 1954); and nuclear superiority gave way to nuclear sufficiency. However, the differences between the four eras, subtle though they may be, are important to the student of American foreign policy.

President Ford and Military Strategy. Gerald Ford began his tenure as President by promising to a joint session of Congress in 1974 that "Just as America's will for peace is second to none, so will America's strength be second to none." Questions of military strategy and strength were quickly forgotten, however, as the Ford administration became burdened with problems of domestic inflation and economic instability. Because Ford did not replace either the Secretary of State or the Secretary of Defense, a major break with Nixon's defense policies did not occur.

Flexibility and Rigidity in Strategy

Rigidity in Strategy. One of the rigidities encountered in planning the American defensive posture is the budgetary process that has permitted the self-interests of the armed services to be the overriding consideration in allocating funds. Each service is a bureaucracy with its own peculiar objectives. Each service tends to lobby for weapon systems and strategies with the most appeal to the President, his cabinet officers, and the Congress. Thus, the Air Force throughout the 1950s developed an imbalance between aircraft needs for strategic air power and aircraft needs for tactical missions, for continental defense, and for troop transportation. It was much easier for the Air Force to "sell" the Strategic Air Command to Congress and the American public. Similarly, the Navy found its case for nuclear, missile-carrying submarines to have more appeal. Since the American purse is not bottomless, priorities must be assigned and allocations must be made on the basis of priority rankings. As a result, the armed services have engaged in intensive lobbying to compete for the limited funds available in the budget.

The budgetary process also permits congressional politics to play a role in determining strategy.[6] Individual congressmen advocate one service's point of view, serving as lobbyists for strategic alternatives that would further the interests of one service over the others. Moreover, Congress has proposed strategy that occasionally has differed from doctrine embraced by the executive branch. Money may be appropriated for weapon systems, for example, which was not requested by the President; this occurred during the 1960s when Congress appropriated money for manned bombers despite executive feeling that emphasis should be placed on missiles. The Air Force, losing the battle with the President, took its case to sympathetic congressmen.[7]

Rigidity is also fostered by the propensity of military leaders to stay with "proven" strategies and weapon systems. The military mind would rather go into battle with a weapon free from defects and with well-trained troops who thoroughly know the weapon's strengths and shortcomings. New weapons, with unknown capabilities and using untried strategies, may undermine self-confidence in the fighting man. Morale and confidence are intangible factors that also must be taken into account. The military generally feels that the capability of a weapon system must be tested to determine whether the strategy proposed in developing the weapon is feasible.

Flexibility in Strategy. Factors exist that counterbalance the forces of rigidity in strategic planning and weapons development. In the interest of survival, the American government has learned to shift emphasis in its defense planning, even if the rigidities listed above do not permit major changes. There have been shifts from containment to massive retaliation to flexible response, for example.

In addition, flexibility is most often the result of relatively minor decisions in the field. The fighting man in battle frequently must adjust to the enemy's new tactics, strengths, and weapons, and to the indigenous terrain. Weapons have also been modified slightly—as exemplified by the infantryman who makes his own dum-dum bullets and the flight mechanic who adds armament to an airplane to protect a pilot. However, shifts in strategy and battlefield adjustments indicate only a small degree of flexibility.

TYPES OF WARFARE: NUCLEAR CONFLICT

Three broad types of warfare commonly identified are nuclear, conventional, and unconventional. Within the first two classifications, the subcategories of "limited" and "unlimited" also can be applied: unconventional war is always limited, at least from the standpoint of one side.

Deterrence

Definition. The key to American military strategy in the post-World War II period has been the concept of deterrence.[8] Deterrence denotes a situation in which an enemy must be convinced that there are too many risks and too much cost involved in beginning a conflict. The American government has attempted to deter the Soviet Union from unleashing a nuclear attack on the U.S. heartland and from undertaking non-nuclear or conventional aggression. The concept of deterrence has not been interpreted to mean that the Soviet Union could be stopped from initiating *any* policy action disapproved by the United States. Throughout the post-World War II period, nuclear weapons deliverable by intercontinental ballistic missiles (ICBMs) and long-range bombers have been central to the concept of deterrence: these weapons would unleash unacceptable punishment on an aggressor. Since the United States and the Soviet Union are both vulnerable to nuclear strike forces, both are deterred from choosing policy alternatives that threaten the vital interests of each other.

The Floor and Ceiling of Deterrence. Deterrence in the Cold War has largely meant that a ceiling has been clamped on the potential intensity of Soviet–American hostility. Neither government has pushed its quarrel to the point of the nuclear brink, because neither has been willing to escalate beyond the nuclear ceiling. At the same time, a floor of tensions undergirded East–West relations; this floor gradually was lowered as the Cold War reduced its intensity. The ceiling, on the other hand, has continued to remain in place.

Does Deterrence Deter? An initial evaluation of the success of American deterrence might credit it with forestalling military expansion of Communism since 1945. This evaluation, however, is based on the questionable premise that the Soviet Union was bent on worldwide revolution in the immediate post-war era. If Soviet foreign policy were indeed following a status quo orientation, then American foreign policy was responding to a distorted view of the world's environment. If this were the case, then both the American and Russian decision makers built elaborate and resource-demanding war machines to deter each other from embarking on an aggressive policy which, in fact, was never the intention of either country.

Nuclear weapons are not a universal deterrence; in fact, they deter primarily only those nations that possess them. The threat of dropping a nuclear device on Cuba, North Vietnam, or North Korea would not be credible to any of the three nations because their military prowess and economic potential are not suitable targets for nuclear weapons. To use them against these nations would be analogous to killing flies with a high-powered rifle.

The sophisticated weaponry that a nuclear power possesses is hardly applicable to crises in which subnuclear conflict occurs. Deterrence not only depends on the presence of a superior force, but on the belief that the possessing nation will probably use the weapons in a given crisis. The *possibility* of using nuclear weapons always exists, but the *probability* is calculated by decision makers when formulating policy.

Based on the relative improbability that the United States would employ its nuclear weapons in a subnuclear conflict, the non-nuclear powers have enjoyed a freedom of action in pursuing their foreign policy objectives. If Fidel Castro were bent on exporting the Cuban revolution during the 1960s, the United States, with its nuclear weapons, could not do much about it. An ultimatum to cease revolutionary activities or face the destruction of Havana with a few well-placed nuclear weapons was not a credible threat to the Cubans.

General Nuclear War

General nuclear war is the most discussed and the most dreaded form of contemporary conflict.[9] Preventing a nuclear attack by the Soviet Union has been the primary objective of American deterrence strategy since the U.S.S.R. successfully detonated a nuclear device in 1949 and built adequate delivery vehicles by the mid-1950s.

Retaliation: First and Second Strike. In a significant departure from its traditional military behavior, American deterrence of Soviet strategic nuclear attack (and vice versa) has depended primarily on offensive weapons. Adequate defenses (sometimes in the form of natural boundaries) and offensive power, either in existence or readily mobilized, were traditionally the primary deterrents of aggression. But in the post-World War II era, offensive weaponry has remained ahead of the defense; hence, deterrence has rested on the realization that the attacked nation, while absorbing a nuclear attack, could retaliate with sufficient nuclear force to destroy its aggressor.

To be able to attack a nuclear opponent *without* retaliation from that opponent is known as a *first-strike capability*. Total surprise is almost impossible today because an incoming missile attack, the first strike, would be detected in sufficient time to retaliate. Both the Soviet Union and the United States have the capability to respond with a devastating nuclear counter attack on an aggressor; hence, the *second-strike capability* is the capacity to repay a nuclear aggressor in kind. Second-strike capability may also include the capacity to absorb a nuclear attack and still respond with punishment unacceptable to the enemy.

The warning time that a President or Soviet Prime Minister has before an attack is usually put at fifteen minutes. While this time frame would normally permit a retaliation, in recent years new developments have complicated the awesome decision to "press the button." As the People's Republic of China achieved an elementary level of nuclear capability in the early 1970s, leaders in the United States and the Soviet Union might be required to act without certain knowledge of the source of the attack. Several horrifying but possible scenarios can be imagined: The President is told that U.S. radar has picked up incoming missiles over the North Pole and the impact time is thirteen minutes away. Or the President is uncertain who fired the missiles and the intelligence process of discovering their origin takes ten of the precious thirteen minutes. Another highly disconcerting thought is the possibility of unidentified flying objects registering on American (or Soviet or Chinese) radar; it could mean that an attack is underway or only that meteorites have entered the earth's atmosphere. These scenarios illustrate the dilemmas faced by both Soviet and American leaders in a nuclear age.

Retaliation: Counter-Force versus Counter-City Strategy. The first generation nuclear and thermonuclear devices were bombs dropped from aircraft with cities as primary targets. As intercontinental ballistic missiles were deployed and perfected in later generation models, the American military establishment in the early 1960s began to discuss the feasibility of targeting military complexes rather than cities. The goal of *counter-force* strategy, as contrasted with *counter-city* strategy, is to destroy an enemy's capabilities to wage war—not his civilian population. Cities would then remain intact if the enemy surrendered; or they would be used as hostages for future nuclear exchanges if he did not. The advantage would be that the conquered nation would have its industrial complexes largely intact, presenting only a minor reconstruction problem. One disadvantage is the doubt, or lack of assurance, that the Soviet Union would reciprocate by leaving American cities untouched in an initial nuclear exchange and instead use its own counter-force strategy. Since the American population and industrial centers are not as widely dispersed (one fourth of the American population is located in the Washington–Boston–Chicago triangle) as Soviet cities and industries, it is doubtful that Russian military strategists could make the sharp distinctions demanded in a counter-force strategy. Moreover, Soviet leaders have emphasized larger, "super" warheads as payloads for their ICBMs, whereas the Americans have shown a preference for the smaller warheads of one to five megatons (or million tons of TNT). The Soviet missile is more of a sledge hammer; the American missile can perform the task of a scalpel that a counter-force strategy demands.

In the past, counter-city strategies have been more consonant with second-strike, than first-strike, capability. There would be no strategic benefit to hitting the opponent's military targets, especially his missile emplacements, for a retaliatory attack. Assuming that the opponent strikes first, aiming missiles at his empty ICBM emplacements would hardly be a deterrent. On the other hand, if either the U.S. or U.S.S.R. decides on a first-strike capability, a counter-force strategy would be adopted. Complete surprise in destroying the opponent's missiles before they have been fired would be the aim of a first-strike strategy.

The United States and the U.S.S.R., to a lesser extent, have tended to diversify offensive means of delivering nuclear warheads. Both have land-based ICBMs, nuclear-powered submarines equipped with intermediate-range missiles, and bombers. Therefore, a counter-force strategy may be impossible to implement because of the variety of delivery systems that both superpowers possess.

Limited Nuclear War

Definition of "Limited." The problems connected with limited nuclear conflict are not as well understood as the strategies of general nuclear warfare.[10] It is difficult to define the threshold dividing limited and unlimited nuclear war. Generally, only tactical nuclear devices are employed in a limited conflict—devices of 20 kilotons (20,000 tons of TNT) or less. Warheads of this size can be carried by tactical nuclear aircraft, short-range (e.g., 200 miles) missiles, or fired by artillery pieces.

The strategy to be followed in fighting a limited nuclear conflict remains in an embryonic state of development three decades after the first nuclear blast. Obviously, the emphasis would be on mobility of self-contained troop units because large gatherings of armies, ships, and supplies are inviting targets to enemy strategists possessing tactical nuclear weapons. Since no tactical nuclear conflict has occurred, the problems to be encountered are the object of speculation.

The Reality of a Limited Nuclear War. Two questions suggest that limited nuclear warfare exists only as a theoretical category, rather than a real option for military strategists. Would a nation losing a tactical nuclear war, yet possessing strategic nuclear weapons, be content to accept defeat on the battlefield and refrain from escalating the conflict by attacking the enemy with its largest nuclear weapons? The answer to this hypothetical question depends on the political objectives involved, of course, and whether or not states would be willing to endure the stigma of defeat while not committing a large portion of its military power. And secondly: What would happen if the mythical 20-kiloton limit were breached in the battlefield? In other words, what if a warhead yielding 30 or 40 kilotons were employed because it more adequately served the tactical mission at the time?

Each question raises serious doubts about the reality of limited nuclear war. Perhaps tactical nuclear weapons could be used in battlefield situations against nations who possessed no means of retaliation, as was suggested in the Korean and Vietnamese conflicts. The present deployment of tactical nuclear weapons reaches beyond these situations, however. At the moment, nuclear warheads are stored on German soil for NATO use in the event of a Soviet attack. These weapons are under a "double-key" system of security: they can be armed for firing only with the approval of both German leaders and the Supreme Allied Commander of NATO (an American, who, in turn, cannot give approval without the permission of the President of the United States). Whether this check system could function sufficiently fast enough to open the "double lock" in the midst of an armed conflict with the Soviet Union is, at best, an open question.

Perhaps limited nuclear war will remain limited because of the counter-city deterrent. The belligerents would be reluctant to expand the conflict to their opponent's heartland, although weapons above the 20-kiloton range might be employed on the battlefield. In the final analysis, the relative value that national policymakers place on a limited war—i.e., the policy goal that they hope to achieve, and how important the goals are to them—will determine whether or not the conflict is permitted to escalate.

In short, limited nuclear war may exist in theory, and might occur in fact, but the threshold distinguishing it from general nuclear conflict is blurred.

TYPES OF WARFARE: CONVENTIONAL CONFLICTS

Unlimited Conventional Conflict

Frequency of Unlimited Wars. The type of warfare experienced twice in the 20th century has occurred seldom in the history of the state system. Except for the Thirty Years War (1618–1648) and the Napoleonic wars (ending in 1815), and the two world wars of the 20th century, most altercations in the international system have been limited. They have also been "conventional"; the choice between nuclear and conventional warfare has been available only to the post-1945 world. It is significant that national leaders have more often opted for limiting conflicts, rather than escalating them to the level of total mobilization and all-out war.

Unlimited conventional war, typified by World Wars I and II, probably will never be fought again. A nation facing defeat in an all-out conventional war—losing on the battlefield and with its homeland under bombardment—would not long refrain from using every weapon in its arsenal, including large nuclear warheads, to stave off defeat and possible annihilation. For this reason, American military leaders have devoted little time to offensive and defensive strategy in an unlimited conventional war. In general, the American government would find unlimited conventional war highly unattractive because of the imbalance between the number of U.S. troops compared with Russian and Chinese troops.

Conditions for Unlimited Conventional Wars. Nevertheless, two conceivable conditions exist under which unlimited conventional conflict might occur. First, a partial disarmament agreement which dismantled nuclear strike forces but left conventional forces intact might be negotiated among the major nuclear powers. Thus, neither the U.S. nor the U.S.S.R. would possess nuclear weapons, if the agreement were rigidly adhered to. And secondly, both sides might refuse to use their nuclear strike forces because of the fear of retaliation. A parallel would be the nonuse of poison gas in World War II: the Axis countries did not use gas, in part, because the United States possessed a superior poisonous substance.

Limited Conventional War

Characteristics of Limited Conventional Wars. Limited conventional wars have been the most common type of conflict since 1945. The Pakistan–India, India–China, U.S.–North Vietnam, India–Portugal (over Goa) wars were of this type. The parameters of limited conventional warfare, unlike limited nuclear conflicts, are fairly well-established: limited objectives, limited geography, limited weapon system, limited time, and limited psychological impact on the contending parties.[11]

LIMITED OBJECTIVES. Limited conventional wars are fought for political goals requiring less than total victory and unconditional surrender. Both contending parties refuse to escalate the conflict to obtain objectives that impinge on the vital national interests of either. Should the political goals be too broad, the conflict would most likely move from a limited setting to total warfare of nuclear or conventional variety.

The history of the state system is dotted with a myriad of limited conflicts fought for limited objectives, which often seem too petty to merit the expenditure of men and materiel. Sebastopol, a relatively meaningless village far removed from the Russia heartland, was the military objective in the Crimean War of the 1850s. Restoring the 38° north latitude as the boundary of South Korea was the military objective of the United States (and United Nations) following intervention into the conflict by Communist Chinese forces in late 1950. Since objectives of limited conventional war are decided by political considerations, military leaders have questioned them from the standpoint of military expediency. Conflict over limited objectives in war can raise problems of civil–military relations.[12]

The combatants view objectives from different vantage points. For the United States, the Korean and Vietnamese conflicts were limited, fought for limited goals with less than total mobilization. For North Korea and North Vietnam, states with more limited economic and military resources, the conflicts were total.

LIMITED GEOGRAPHY. The limited conventional war, within the confines of a restricted geographical area that often is of little economic or military consequence, leaves the important heartland of each side inviolate. During the Korean War, the United States government refused to bombard Chinese staging areas, while the Chinese undertook no military action against Okinawa, a center of logistical support for the American effort. Vietnam, however, offered both a confirmation and a contradiction to this principle. North Vietnam was the object of American land, naval, and air bombardment from 1965 to 1968. The heartland of one belligerent was brought under attack without retaliation because North Vietnam was incapable of striking American military complexes in Thailand, Guam, or even the Gulf of Tonkin. After the decision to stop bombing in 1968 and until 1972 when it was resumed, the Vietnamese conflict took on more of the characteristics of a limited conventional war. Early in the conflict, the

United States government perceived Communist China and the Soviet Union as the principal initiators of the Vietnam War. Therefore, the American government did not consider attacks against North Vietnam as violating the limited nature of the conflict since Chinese and Russian targets were not involved.

Geographical restrictions in limited warfare are the result of political decisions with which military tacticians may disagree. Refusing to attack Viet Cong staging areas in Cambodia, Laos, and North Vietnam (or Chinese staging areas in the Korean War) was viewed as granting a sanctuary to enemy forces. Traditional military victory (i.e., the destruction of the enemy's capability to wage war) was impossible under these conditions. Often these restrictions lead to the feeling among military personnel that "we could have won had the politicians left us alone."

LIMITED WEAPON SYSTEMS. Conventional warfare perforce excludes the use of nuclear weapons. In the post-World War II era, nuclear devices have not been used, even though the other side in the Korean and Vietnamese conflicts did not possess nuclear devices to use in retaliation. Part of the reluctance may be traced to the moral dilemmas posed by the fact that the United States used nuclear weapons for the first (and only) time against an Asian nation. Consequently, American leaders, consciously or unconsciously, do not want to promote the idea that the human subjects for military experimentation with the world's most destructive weapon are the non-whites of Asia.

A more plausible explanation is the lack of military targets to employ nuclear weapons in Vietnam and Korea. Perhaps Korea was an exception because conventional attacks by massed infantry were inviting targets for tactical nuclear devices; however, tactical nuclear weaponry was not as sophisticated in the early 1950s as it was during the Vietnamese conflict. Vietnam was partly conventional and partly guerrilla warfare devoid of large-scale battles. The targets presented to American military strategists in Vietnam were easily handled by conventional ordnance.

LIMITED IN TIME. In theory, the limited conventional war is shorter in timespan than the unlimited conventional conflict. Since it involves objectives less than total, a circumscribed geographical area, and only conventional weapon systems, the assumption is that the conflict will be of shorter duration. For the most part, the practice of Cold War limited engagements has corresponded to this theory: conflicts over Goa, the Sino–Indian and Pakistani–Indian borders, and Arab–Israeli differences have been brief, flaring for only days or weeks and then subsiding into harsh, but nonviolent, verbal battles between the parties. The Korean conflict, on the other hand, was much longer; it actually represented two wars. The North Korean invasion in June 1950 was successfully defeated within six months, while Communist Chinese intervention in November–December 1950 created an entirely new conflict which took two-and-one-half years to settle.

The Vietnam War, as far as the Americans were concerned, presented several problems of analysis, the date of its beginning only one of them.

Guerrilla conflicts have a way of hanging on for many, many years. The irony of Vietnam was that the United States fought two wars there—one conventional war against the North Vietnamese regulars and one unconventional or guerrilla war against the Viet Cong. On the conventional level, U.S. military forces usually were victorious in engagements with the North Vietnamese army. On the guerrilla level, the story was different; the American forces, at best, were only able to hold their own.

LIMITED PSYCHOLOGICAL IMPACT. Finally, limited war can remain less than total because the body politic does not become totally concerned about the demands that the war makes on national resources. The psychological impact of the goals of the conflict on the societies of both belligerents is circumscribed. The political decision makers do not attempt to arouse mass passion (such as hatred of the enemy and patriotism) because these passions could easily lead to demands for total victory. This prerequisite for limited warfare is understandable: an enemy described in the most absolute terms of moral degradation does not engender in the public mind an opponent with which to compromise. Deals are not made with "evil." Only total extinction usually can satisfy the public's aroused passions.

Democracy and Limited Wars. The dilemma posed here to a democracy such as the United States is to prosecute a limited engagement with sufficient public support so as not to invite political disaster to individual decision makers; and at the same time, to restrain public attitudes so as not to demand commitments to total goals (e.g., to gain a "just" peace or to halt "international" Communism). Certainly the public must be rallied to the national colors, but not over-inspired to carry on a holy war against an enemy who has been engaged in limited combat. Should the public be led to expect too much for so little a commitment, a stabilizing settlement, whatever its advantages to the American nation and allies, would be branded as an "appeasement" and "sellout."

Both the Korean and Southeast Asian conflicts represent attempts to walk the political tightrope between sufficient involvement and over-involvement of the body politic. As both wars dragged on, the public's initial support began to wane. Throughout this process, a sizable community of public opinion continued to opt for an enlargement of each conflict, to go "all the way."

TYPES OF WARFARE: GUERRILLA CONFLICTS

The fifth type of warfare that has demanded immediate attention in American military thinking is guerrilla conflict, characterized by irregulars fighting in small groups.[13] "Irregulars" implies that the combatants are not wearing uniforms because they seldom are part of a full-time army structure. Most often they hold occupational positions within their society, in addition to their military roles. The guerrilla may be a peasant farmer by day and a warrior by night. The effective guerrilla force may be highly organized, but normally it operates within a limited geographical area. It is not a mobile force that shifts from one geographical region to another. The guerrilla is usually fighting for his home in terrain with which he is most familiar.

Roots of Guerrilla Wars

Local Economic and Political Conditions. A successful guerrilla uprising grows out of mass discontent with the economic and political distribution of values and benefits within society. A society in which 10 percent of the population owns 90 percent of the land, for example, may produce rebellion among the landless peasants. A guerrilla conflict is in the making when the local landless peasants revolt, murder the local officials appointed by the central government (whose soldiers are sent in to protect the landowners' holdings), and establish their own governmental infrastructure. The guerrilla government then distributes the land of the absentee landlords, collects taxes, and provides protection for the local citizens.

The weapon systems used by guerrillas, especially in the early stages of their revolution, are usually quite obsolete by modern standards. They tend to be conventional arms that are portable, can be moved from one battle area to another, and can be hidden with little effort. The arms often are manufactured in small factories using unsophisticated machinery, purchased from a friendly foreign nation, or stolen and confiscated from government troops defeated in battle. The friendly foreign nation may become a source of armaments, but again, the arms are usually the most practical weapons of the infantry and artillery variety. The more sophisticated weapon systems, which require extensive training to use and constant maintenance to keep in the field, are usually avoided in the early stages of a guerrilla revolt. Moreover, sophisticated weapon systems are the more costly, and usually the coffers of a young revolutionary guerrilla movement are not overflowing with funds.

The guerrilla movement, despite the fact that it may receive military support from abroad, is indigenous. Internal conflict is usually the result of uniquely local factors—disagreements evolving from political, economic, social, ethnic, or religious conditions. If a foreign nation's influence is found within the guerrilla movement, it is usually the result of an invitation from the movement's leaders. The foreign nation becomes a source of economic and military assistance, but seldom does it control the guerrilla movement itself.

Guerrilla Tactics

Retreat and Surprise. Guerrillas retreat in the face of superior force and fight battles that bring prestige and propaganda victories to the movement. The object of the early stages of guerrilla conflict is not to engage the main strength of the government's forces, but rather to choose carefully the enemy's weaknesses and attack at these points. By gaining victories in the field over government forces (although they do little to decrease the overall fighting ability of the government) the guerrilla leaders attach to the central government an image of a weak and floundering institution.

A factor that accounts for guerrilla successes in the field is the element of surprise. Guerrillas are not burdened with the usual necessities of modern armies to launch an offensive: no massing of forces, no elongated supply lines, and no storing up of foodstuff and materiel. The guerrilla force can choose its target and move into position for attack usually without being detected. This capability does not mean that guerrilla bands are not highly trained instruments of warfare. Indeed, they are, or at least the most successful guerrillas are. Intricate and detailed planning precedes the guerrilla attack.

Terror. Terror is another weapon used by the guerrilla movement to further the revolutionary cause. And it is one weapon for which the guerrilla is roundly condemned by the advanced Western countries, such as the United States. American condemnation of terror in Vietnam was an indication of the United States' popular misunderstanding of the nature of guerrilla warfare. The purpose of terror there was twofold: first, to eliminate village representatives of the central government who were attempting to exercise supervision of village political life according to the wishes of Saigon. The village chief, appointed to his position or "elected" in a ballot that effectively barred opposition candidates, attempted to collect taxes according to the central government's dictates and enforced the absentee landlord's control. The village chief, therefore, became a prime target for the Viet Cong execution squads. Many times his death was welcomed by the local people.

A second purpose of terror in Vietnam was to maintain discipline of the populous under the control of the guerrilla infrastructure. Citizens suspected of dissidence or of supplying information to the central government were executed. This use of terror is abhorrent to Westerners, but terror tactics usually occur within a social context far removed from Western standards. Moreover, guerrilla movements do not unilaterally introduce terror into the developing society. The central government, in most instances, has already made extensive use of it for the same reason as the guerrilla movement—to assert control over the population. Often the use of terror by the government and its allies in a guerrilla conflict is overlooked, while official horror is expressed at the enemy's use of it.

The U.S. and Guerrilla Conflicts. During the early days of the American Revolutionary War, the Americans used guerrilla tactics because they did not have the training to stand in disciplined ranks, maneuver in cadence, and fire in volley, as the British army did. In the face of a superior military machine, they resorted to guerrilla tactics, until they received the training and armaments to fight a successful conventional war. Almost two centuries later, the American army had to relearn the lessons of guerrilla warfare in Vietnam.

MILITARY STRATEGY: COSTS AND BENEFITS

The cost of maintaining a military establishment is the most expensive item in the national budget, comprising approximately 30 percent of the federal government's total expenditures. Although the United States is a wealthy nation spending more money for defense than any other nation in the world, American leaders must make choices among weapons. These choices will determine military strategy for the future and are determined by strategy already formulated for past crises.[14]

Cost and Effectiveness

A policymaker, attempting to build a national security force, selects the least expensive weapons that will perform the mission envisioned in the strategy; both the *cost* and *effectiveness* of possible weapon systems are primary considerations. Determining the dollar cost of an instrument of destruction involves more than simply comparing the price of one hydrogen bomb with one artillery shell of conventional explosives. Other factors must be included, such as the cost of the delivery mechanism (airplane, missile, or artillery piece); the expense of training crews to deliver the system; and the cost of maintaining the weapons, the delivery vehicle, and the crews (e.g., the cost of hangers for bombers and of port facilities for nuclear submarines).

The effectiveness of a weapon is judged on the basis of how well it performs its assigned function. "Function" may be defined in terms of military effectiveness or the "kill power" of the weapon, i.e., the productive capacity destroyed by the weapon. Even political and psychological standards of effectiveness can be devised: Does the weapon change political institutions, or does it help destroy the morale of the enemy's population? Normally, military and economic considerations are the primary standards for effectiveness.

Efficiency does not necessarily imply economy; a weapon's capability to perform its mission also depends on the enemy's defenses. One type of American bomber, for example, may be the least expensive to manufacture and deploy, but Soviet defense may effectively destroy 50 percent of its attacking force. Another type of bomber, more sophisticated and more expensive, may have an attrition rate of 30 percent. Efficiency must also take into consideration the capability to survive a surprise attack. Polaris submarines are much more expensive than airplanes and they cannot deliver as large an atomic punch; however, they are less vulnerable to a Russian preemptive attack on the United States.

Benefits of the Military Establishment

The American nation has maintained a massive military establishment since the Korean War. U.S. power is impressive; no other state approximates it except the Soviet Union. It may well be that current military strength is overestimated and Russian intentions misjudged. Whether or not they are, Russian strength and intentions have been used as justifications for continued mobilization of American military might.

The American military establishment is assumed by many to be a beneficial institution, protecting American national interests from Soviet military expansion. Whether or not one accepts this evaluation depends on the image of Soviet behavior. Since Soviet aggression was perceived as a reality in the decades of the 1940s and 1950s, a buildup of American military strength was viewed as the most logical and necessary response. With the development of alternative interpretations of Soviet behavior, American military strength can be considered disproportionate and the result of unreal perceptions.

Another benefit sometimes cited is that the American military strategy has permitted the U.S. government to protect friendly nations abroad. In playing its role of protector or "policeman," the United States has made its presence felt in every part of the world except the Soviet sphere of influence, Eastern Europe. Washington has negotiated alliances in every part of the world except Africa and South Asia. Of the major powers, the United States has been the most active militarily in the post-World War II era. Two large-scale and continuous wars have been fought (Korea and Vietnam); troop landings in Latin America and the Middle East have been made; and veiled and unveiled threats have been issued to go to war over Berlin, Israel, Quemoy and Matsu, Cambodia, Laos, Trieste, and other small and sometimes inconsequential areas of the world.

Military spending can result in negative benefits because resources spent for international security are diverted from domestic needs. Large military budgets have led attention away from domestic concerns, such as pollution, depletion of non-renewable energy sources, and urban blight. The assumption is, of course, that money not spent for weapons would automatically be budgeted for domestic needs. However, Congress might choose not to spend it at all.

Strategy and Image

The development of military strategy is tied closely to the image that American decision makers possess of the international system. Only when the American leaders perceive a world without threats to national security will they abandon the need for an extensive array of weapons and the accompanying strategies of when and how to use them. Since a world devoid of enemies is utopian, military strategy will remain a part of the patterns of American foreign policy.

Advocates of increased spending for armaments continue to see the Soviet Union and the People's Republic of China as militarily stronger than the United States.[15] Their sense of security dictates the need for more power in an effort to maintain the United States in a superior position. For other analysts, the search for security leads them to the conclusion that armaments must be reduced, not increased. The debate over security does not end with the topic of military strategy. It is also cast in terms of disarmament, arms control, international organizations, and alliances; these issues will be discussed in chapters 14, 15, and 16.

NOTES

1. The subject of national security policy has attracted the attention of many analysts. Some of their works include: Samuel P. Huntington, *The Common Defense: Strategic Problems in National Politics* (New York: Columbia University Press, 1961); Maxwell D. Taylor, *The Uncertain Trumpet* (New York: Harper & Row, 1960) and *Responsibility and Response* (New York: Harper & Row, 1967); Thomas C. Schelling, *Arms and Influence* (New Haven: Yale University Press, 1966); Bernard Brodie, *Strategy in the Missile Age* (Princeton, N.J.: Princeton University Press, 1959); Adam Yarmolinsky, *United States Military Power and Foreign Policy* (Chicago: The University of Chicago Center for Policy Study, 1967); Dale O. Smith, *U.S. Military Doctrine, A Study and Appraisal* (New York: Duell, Sloan and Pearce, 1955); J. David Singer, *Deterrence, Arms Control, and Disarmament: Toward a Synthesis in National Security Policy* (Columbus: Ohio State University Press, 1962); Urs Schwarz, *American Strategy: A New Perspective* (Garden City, N.Y.: Doubleday, 1966); George C. Reinhardt, *American Strategy in the Atomic Age* (Norman: University of Oklahoma Press, 1955); Oskar Morgenstern, *The Question of National Defense* (New York: Random House, 1959); Walter Millis, *American Military Thought* (Indianapolis: Bobbs–Merrill Co., 1966); Robert A. Levine, *The Arms Debate* (Cambridge: Harvard University Press, 1963); Louis J. Halle, *Choice for Survival* (New York: Harper & Row, 1958); Robert N. Ginsburgh, *U.S. Military Strategy in the Sixties* (New York: W. W. Norton, 1965); James N. Gavin, *War and Peace in the Space Age* (New York: Harper & Row, 1958); Thomas K. Finletter, *Power and Policy: U.S. Foreign Policy and Military Power in the Hydrogen Age* (New York: Harcourt, Brace, and World, 1954); Timothy W. Stanley, *American Defense and National Security* (Washington, D.C.: Public Affairs Press, 1956); David W. Tarr, *American Strategy in the Nuclear Age* (New York: Macmillan, 1966); Robert

W. Tucker, *The Just War: A Study in Contemporary American Doctrine* (Baltimore: The Johns Hopkins Press, 1960); Alfred Vagts, *Defense and Diplomacy* (New York: King's Crown Press, 1956); and David M. Abshire and Richard V. Allen (eds.), *National Security: Political, Military, and Economic Strategies in the Decade Ahead* (New York: Praeger, 1963).

2. For an analysis of military strategy prior to 1945, see C. Joseph Bernardo and Eugene H. Bacon, *American Military Policy, Its Development since 1775*, 2nd ed. (Harrisburg, Pa.: Military Service Publishing Co., 1961); and Raymond G. O'Connor (ed.), *American Defense Policy in Perspective from the Colonial Times to the Present* (New York: John Wiley, 1965).

3. See Paul Peeters, *Massive Retaliation: The Policy and Its Critics* (Chicago: H. Regnery, 1959).

4. William W. Kaufmann, *The McNamara Strategy* (New York: Harper & Row, 1964); James M. Roherty, *Robert S. McNamara: A Study of the Secretary of Defense* (Miami, Fla.: University of Miami Press, 1970); McGeorge Bundy, "The End of Either/Or," *Foreign Affairs* 45 (January 1967): 189–201; Charles H. Longley, "McNamara and Military Behavior," *American Journal of Political Science* 18 (February 1974): 1–22; Robert S. McNamara, *The Essence of Security: Reflections in Office* (New York: Harper & Row, 1968) and "Security in the Contemporary World," *Department of State Bulletin* 54 (June 6, 1961): 874–881. Henry A. Kissinger's *The Necessity for Choice* (Garden City, N.Y.: Doubleday, 1962), advocates a policy similar to the one eventually adopted by President Kennedy and Secretary of Defense McNamara.

5. Harland B. Moulton, *From Superiority to Parity: The United States and the Strategic Arms Race, 1961–1971* (Westport, Conn.: Greenwood Press, 1973).

6. Edward A. Kolodziej, *The Uncommon Defense and Congress, 1945–1963* (Columbus, Ohio: Ohio State University Press, 1966).

7. Vincent Davis, *Postwar Defense Policy and the U.S. Navy, 1943–1946* (Chapel Hill: University of North Carolina Press, 1966) and *The Admiral's Lobby* (Chapel Hill: University of North Carolina Press, 1967); Michael H. Armacost, *The Politics of Weapons Innovation: The Thor-Jupiter Controversy* (New York: Columbia University Press, 1969); and Harvey M. Sapolsky, *The Polaris System Development; Bureaucratic and Programmatic Success in Government* (Cambridge: Harvard University Press, 1972).

8. George E. Lowe, *The Age of Deterrence* (Boston: Little, Brown and Co., 1964).

9. Authors who discuss nuclear warfare are: K. S. Tripathi, *Evolution of Nuclear Strategy* (Delhi, India: Vikas, 1970); Philip Green, *Deadly Logic: The Theory of Nuclear Deterrence* (Columbus: Ohio State University Press, 1966); Arthur I. Waskow (ed.), *The Debate over Ther-*

chapter 13 American Military Strategy

monuclear Strategy (Lexington, Mass.: D. C. Heath, 1965); Henry A. Kissinger, *Nuclear Weapons and Foreign Policy* (New York: Harper & Row, 1957); Bernard Brodie, *Escalation and the Nuclear Option* (Princeton, N.J.: Princeton University Press, 1966); Herman Kahn, *On Thermonuclear War* (Princeton, N.J.: Princeton University Press, 1962); and Raymond Aron, *The Great Debate: Theories of Nuclear Strategy* (Garden City, N.Y.: Doubleday, 1965). Two books examine nuclear warfare from an ethical viewpoint: Justus George Lawler, *Nuclear War: The Ethic, the Rhetoric, the Reality: A Catholic Assessment* (Westminster, Md.: Newman Press, 1965) and Paul Ramsey, *The Limits of Nuclear War* (New York: Council on Religion and International Affairs, 1964).

10. Philip W. Dyer, "Will Tactical Nuclear Weapons Ever Be Used?" *Political Science Quarterly* 88 (June 1973): 214–230.

11. Seymour J. Deitchman, *Limited War and American Defense Policy* (Cambridge, Mass.: M.I.T. Press, 1964); Robert E. Osgood, *Limited War: The Challenge to American Strategy* (Chicago: University of Chicago Press, 1957); and Otto Heibrunn, *Conventional War in the Nuclear Age* (New York: Praeger, 1965).

12. Civil–military relations are examined in chapter 11. For a discussion of the Korean conflict, see Dean Acheson, *The Korean War* (New York: W. W. Norton, 1971) and Glenn D. Paige, *The Korean Decision* (New York: Free Press, 1968).

13. John S. Pustay, *Counterinsurgency Warfare* (New York: Free Press, 1965) and James E. Cross, *Conflict in the Shadows: Nature and Politics of Guerrilla War* (Garden City, N.Y.: Doubleday, 1963).

14. General references on the cost of weapons and their impact on the American economy are: Bruce M. Russett, *What Price Vigilance? The Burdens of National Defense* (New Haven, Conn.: Yale University Press, 1970); Charles J. Hitch and Roland N. McKean, *The Economics of Defense in the Nuclear Age* (Cambridge: Harvard University Press, 1960); Warner Schilling, Paul Y. Hammond, and Glenn Snyder, *Strategy, Politics and Defense Budgets* (New York: Columbia University Press, 1962); Max E. Fieser, *Economic Policy and War Potential* (Washington, D.C.: Public Affairs Press, 1964); James R. Schlesinger, *The Political Economy of National Security* (New York: Praeger, 1960); John J. Clark, *The New Economics of National Defense* (New York: Random House, 1966); Alain C. Enthoven and K. Wayne Smith, *How Much Is Enough? Shaping the Defense Program, 1961–1969* (New York: Harper & Row, 1972); and Daniel Lang, *An Inquiry into Enoughness: Of Bombs and Men and Staying Alive* (New York: McGraw-Hill, 1965).

15. Nathan F. Twining, *Neither Liberty nor Safety: A Hard Look at U.S. Military Policy and Strategy* (New York: Holt, Rinehart, and Winston, 1966); Thomas S. Powers, *Design for Survival* (New York: Coward–McCann, 1965); and William P. Kintner, *Peace and the Strategy Conflict* (New York: Praeger, 1967).

14

Patterns of Arms-Control and Disarmament Policies

Arms-control and disarmament negotiations can be viewed from two angles of vision, both of which are not necessarily exclusive. One perspective views them as a bridge to a more peaceful international system and as a countervailing force to the headlong rush towards building awesome military machines in the post-World War II period. Inhibitions placed on arms construction programs counteract the revolution in warfare. National leaders, therefore, propose disarmament and arms-control packages as a means of defusing the arms race and introducing less risk and more sanity into international relations.

Another viewpoint considers arms-control and disarmament policies as an extension of national security policy. These policies are proposed to ensure the survival of the state, the objective of national security programs. Arms-limitation proposals are submitted because a nation's sense of security does not increase as a result of spending more for weapons. Because national purses are not bottomless, decision makers are willing to halt their own spiraling arms programs, if they can be assured that their opponents will do the same. The relative position of both sides becomes important since neither side can gain an absolute advantage over the other.

Both of these views have been present in the debates over U.S. disarmament negotiating positions in the post-World War II period.

STIMULI FOR DISARMAMENT AND ARMS-CONTROL NEGOTIATIONS

"Arms control" and "disarmament" are concepts with different emphases. Arms control refers to proposals that limit, on a selective basis, the warmaking capabilities of states; "disarmament" designates those proposals

chapter 14   Arms-Control and Disarmament Policies   255

that reduce a nation's overall military establishment to a force-level of military capability not sufficient to begin or to engage in war. Under arms-control agreements, a reduction may not be required at all; the signatories may agree to limit a particular weapon system at its present level. If a reduction is negotiated, the arms-control agreement is selective in its impact, applying only to one or a limited number of weapon systems. The nation can still wage war under a series of arms-control agreements. Disarmament, however, allows a state none of the sophisticated weaponry to engage in international conflicts, but permits a sufficient conventional force to keep order within the confines of its national boundaries.

Both arms control and disarmament have been discussed extensively since 1946.[1] The United States and Soviet Union have been willing to negotiate on these two issues when neither has been willing to talk about much else. The amount of verbiage contrasted sharply with the paucity of agreements, at least until the 1960s. Why did the Soviet Union and the United States invest diplomatic efforts in obviously fruitless discussions? Six possible answers to this question exist, although some of the justifications developed later in the post-war period.

1. Disarmament and arms-control issues created effective arenas for propaganda exchanges. Each side wanted to prove that it was the world's most peace-loving nation.
2. Both sides proposed arrangements that, if accepted, would have trapped an opponent in an inferior position. Since the Russian and American leaders are not political novices, they never failed to read the disarmament proposal's fine print with its built-in disadvantages.
3. Disarmament and arms control were but two of the very few Cold War issues on which East and West could seriously negotiate. Both the Soviet Union and the United States took hard, non-negotiable stands on Berlin, Korea, and a host of other Cold War topics. East-West communication, though ladened with propaganda, was possible on disarmament and arms control.
4. The nuclear have-not nations, especially the non-Western neutrals, have prodded the two superstates into disarmament discussions. Because the neutrals believed that armed conflict between the U.S. and U.S.S.R. would not be limited to the destruction of the Soviet and American heartlands, but would spill over into other areas of the world, they repeatedly called for negotiations when the Soviet Union and United States were not overly interested in disarmament and arms control.
5. The arms race has not brought to either bloc of the East-West confrontation a feeling of security. Despite significant increases in military power, neither side has been able to amass sufficient strength to dictate political settlement to its opponent. New increments of power by one faction have been matched by the other; neither has achieved a technological breakthrough that would result in military superiority.
6. For the United States and Soviet Union, the arms race has si-

phoned off funds badly needed for internal development. Consequently, both sides, weary of the nonproductive competition, have come to the conference table to find areas of agreement that might reduce the intensity of the arms race and thereby release resources for domestic needs.

Of the six stimuli, the last two, which began to emerge in the 1960s, resulted in significant arms-control agreements. The first four conditions, unfortunately, led to more than fifteen years of fruitless negotiations in which the U.S. and U.S.S.R. appeared to be engaging in a diplomatic charade.

NEGOTIATIONS OF THE 1940s AND 1950s

The United States took the offensive at the beginning of the post-World War II period on disarmament and arms control. The early American initiatives gave way to Soviet initiatives in the mid-1950s. The record of accomplishments during the one-and-one-half decades after 1946 is one of impressive propaganda victories, but is barren of substantive agreements. The 1959 Antarctica Treaty stands as the sole accomplishment of the first fifteen years of negotiating.[2]

First Proposals

The Baruch Plan. Disarmament and arms-control proposals were placed in a United Nations setting from the beginning.[3] In January 1946, the General Assembly established the Atomic Energy Commission as the negotiating vehicle to work out agreements among the other major military powers. On June 14, Bernard Baruch, the U.S. permanent representative to the United Nations, proposed a program to bring nuclear weapons under international control.

The Baruch Plan called for a United Nations agency to control the production of all nuclear energy facilities. After the agency was established and in operation, all existing nuclear weapons would be destroyed. Eventually, the agency would own and manage all mines and plants producing atomic fuel and would be given the exclusive right to carry on atomic energy research and to license the results of its research to nations for peaceful purposes. The agency could inspect plants within national boundaries to ascertain if unlawful research and development facilities existed.

The Baruch Plan protected American nuclear superiority. Only when assured that no other nation was capable of producing nuclear weapons would the American government destroy its own stockpile. For the Soviet Union, the price demanded was unacceptable: they were asked to open their closed society to inspections by a UN agency and to forego development of atomic weapons in return for the promise that the United States would abandon its nuclear weapons at a future date. The Soviet Union was asked to assume the risk that the United States would indeed destroy all of its nuclear weapons. The Soviets were afraid that the U.S. would hide atomic devices the size of first-generation weapons dropped on Hiroshima and Nagasaki and later use them to threaten the U.S.S.R. in a crisis involving vital American national interests.

The Russian Plan. The Soviet delegate presented a plan before the UN Atomic Energy Commission a few days after Mr. Baruch's presentation. The Russian proposal called for the immediate destruction of all military atomic devices, an act to be supervised by a control unit established as an appendage of the UN Security Council. This unit would possess only limited powers of inspection because each state would police its own compliance to nuclear disarmament.

For the United States, the risks involved were too great. The American government would be forced to destroy its nuclear weapons and to cease their production without a guarantee that the Soviet Union would discontinue its search for an atomic bomb. Since the control commission was attached to the Security Council, a Soviet veto could effectively block any inspection of the Russian heartland.

Round One: An American Propaganda Victory. Both proposals set the pattern for Soviet–American negotiations for years to come. For the United States, it was inspection first and disarmament later; for the Russians, the order was reversed. When the discussions were broadened to include conventional weapons, both sides remained faithful to the pattern established in June 1946. After two years of fruitless discussions, the UN's Atomic Energy Commission reported that an agreement was stalled because of the Soviet refusal to accept controls and inspection. The first round, therefore, ended in an American propaganda victory; an attractive plan was put forth and blame for its failure was placed directly on the U.S.S.R.

The Soviet Search for Nuclear Parity: 1948–1952

Soviet Nuclear Weaknesses. It was clear to Soviet leaders that they must first obtain nuclear parity with the United States in order to protect Russian national interests. In September 1949, the U.S.S.R. successfully detonated a nuclear device; the Soviet Union solved the secret of the atom only four years after American scientists accomplished the same feat.

When the U.S.S.R. finally attained a measure of atomic parity, the United Nations again attempted to bring East and West together in disarmament talks. In January 1952, the UN's inept Atomic Energy Commission was dissolved and a new disarmament commission was established, but this attempt to get disarmament talks underway failed. The Korean conflict hardened negotiating positions in the Cold War. Moreover, the

United States was now a step ahead of the Soviet Union in the development of a hydrogen bomb. In November 1952, the U.S. exploded a hydrogen device, again placing the Soviet Union in a position of inferiority. It was a short-lived status, however, for the U.S.S.R. successfully tested its own hydrogen bomb in August 1953.

Soviet Proposals on Conventional Arms Limitation. During the Soviet search for nuclear parity with the United States, the Russian leaders assumed the initiative in limiting conventional arms. In 1948 the Soviet Union proposed to the UN General Assembly that East–West forces be reduced one-third within one year in addition to prohibitions on atomic weapons. Again, the Soviet proposal did not call for inspection. The West was slow in responding to this Soviet initiative on reduction of army, navy, and air force personnel. In May 1952, the United States, along with Great Britain and France, suggested that a ceiling be placed on men under arms, rather than a percentage reduction, as proposed by the U.S.S.R. The American, Russian, and Chinese armies, for example, could be no larger than 1.5 million men.

As was the case in nuclear disarmament proposals, a pattern emerged on reduction of conventional forces. For the U.S.S.R. with a much larger contingent of men under arms, annual reductions of 33 percent would continue Russian conventional superiority. The American response was to request that a lid be placed on force-levels; the United States would be given a figure equal to that of the Russians and Chinese, who had the two largest land armies in the world. It is interesting to speculate whether or not the American government was serious about a 1.5 million ceiling. During the Korean War, American troops numbered above 3 million. Either the State Department expected the Soviet Union to reject their proposal for a ceiling, or it felt that the end of the Korean conflict was in sight. Had the Soviet government accepted the Anglo-American-French plan, the Russian and American armed forces would have been of equal numerical strength; but the United States would have maintained nuclear superiority.

Conventional force-level reductions would have a different impact on the Russian and American armed forces. The United States military establishment, in pre-Korean War times, had a large strategic air force and navy, but a small army. The Soviet Union, on the other hand, possessed a large army with a small navy and strategic air force, although it did possess a sizable tactical air force to support the Soviet army. The main intent of American proposals was to limit the size of the huge Russian army. American force cuts would come, presumably, from branches of the service other than the Air Force; thus, the United States would continue to maintain its superiority in nuclear strike power.

Continued American Initiatives: 1953–1955

In July 1953, the Korean armistice was signed, and in August, the Soviet Union detonated a hydrogen bomb. New leadership came to both the

Russian and American governments following the death of Stalin and the election of President Eisenhower. With the Korean conflict disposed of, and the U.S.S.R. again achieving a measure of nuclear parity, disarmament negotiations also emerged from the doldrums. The American government assumed the initiative.

"Open Skies." Eisenhower spoke to the UN General Assembly in December 1953 and proposed the "Atoms for Peace" plan. He called for the creation of the International Atomic Energy Agency, which would serve as a depository for nuclear fuel contributed by the United States and Soviet Union. The agency, in turn, would establish nuclear reactors around the world for peaceful purposes. At first, the U.S.S.R. balked at contributing nuclear fuel to the agency. The American government, in a brilliant maneuver, honored its pledge to contribute despite Soviet intransigence. The Russians then repented and gave a very small amount of nuclear fuel. However, Soviet indecision again placed American disarmament policy in a good light for propaganda purposes.

American initiatives continued into 1955. In March, Eisenhower appointed a Special Assistant to the President for Disarmament with cabinet-level status. In July, at the Geneva summit conference, the President unveiled his "Open Skies" plan, in which he proposed that maps of military installations be exchanged and that aerial surveys be permitted of large areas of the United States and the Soviet Union. Premier Nikita Khrushchev, in a December speech before the Supreme Soviet, rejected the "Open Skies" proposal. The Soviet Union, a closed society, had more to lose through opening its heartland to surveillance. The United States again received a good press for its initiative in arms-control and disarmament policy.

The Soviet Reversal. Nineteen fifty-five marked the end of ten years of American propaganda victories. In May, two months before the Geneva Summit, the Soviet Union suddenly reversed its traditional stand on arms control and submitted a plan that accepted many of the provisions contained in previous Western plans. Instead of a percentage reduction in troops, the Soviet government proposed a ceiling, and it agreed to a reduction in conventional troops before disarming nuclear forces. Both points were departures from traditional Soviet positions.

What stimulated this diplomatic reversal? The answer is found in the West's decision to rearm West Germany and integrate the West German army into the North Atlantic Treaty Organization. The Soviets proposed that the ceiling on conventional forces be set as of December 31, 1954; this would preclude West German rearmament. The Russian plan also called for liquidating overseas bases by all signatories to the agreement. The Soviet government, in effect, was demanding the dissolution of NATO in exchange for accepting the ceiling concept on conventional armies.

The United States government was unprepared for this shift in Soviet diplomacy. Although the "Open Skies" proposal two months later helped to regain Western initiative, during the last half of the 1950s the United

States played a reactive role in negotiations over disarmament and arms control. The initiative now belonged to the Russians.

Nuclear Testing: 1956–1960

Trends of the Late 1950s. Two trends emerged in the last half of the 1950s. First, technological advances in nuclear weaponry outpaced the negotiators' attempts to reach agreement. The capability to mask underground nuclear explosions developed faster than the capability to detect them. Soviet missile capabilities also appeared to be ahead of those of the United States. The Russians were first in space with an earth satellite in 1957 and first to hit the surface of the moon with a rocket in 1959. A "missile gap" apparently developed between the United States and the Soviet Union, with the latter in the superior position. Soviet struggles to master the secrets of nuclear and thermonuclear power, to build an arsenal, and then to develop a delivery system, lifted the Russians from a position of inferiority in the 1940s, to a status of parity in the early 1950s, and eventually to a level of superiority in the late 1950s.

Second, along with their newly built nuclear strength, the Russians developed disarmament proposals that were effective in mobilizing support from the nonaligned nations. In the May 1955 Soviet Plan, the Russian government proposed a moratorium on testing nuclear weapons. When the American government did not accept the Russian offer, the Soviet Union announced in March 1958 a unilateral moratorium on testing. Moreover, the Russians accepted a limited version of Eisenhower's "Open Skies" plan, proposed that earth satellites and all pilotless missiles be placed under international control, and supported a Polish proposal for a nuclear-free zone to be created in central Europe, which would include both Germanies, Czechoslovakia, and Poland. Finally, Khrushchev called for a new, more comprehensive approach to East–West negotiations known as complete and general disarmament. This was to replace talks on arms-control proposals.

The American Response. The United States negotiators were unprepared for most of the new Russian proposals. The American government was especially unwilling to agree to a testing moratorium without the safeguards of inspection. The Soviet's unilateral moratorium was announced after the Russians had completed a series of tests of their Intercontinental Ballistic Missile (ICBM) armed with nuclear warheads. President Eisenhower, in April, refused to adhere to a moratorium, citing the need to develop smaller and "cleaner" tactical nuclear weapons. The Eisenhower administration eventually reversed itself and agreed to a one-year, uninspected moratorium.

American leadership was not altogether lacking during this period of Soviet initiatives and growing power. Eisenhower suggested that East and West scientists meet to discuss the technical difficulties connected with identifying nuclear bursts. The Eisenhower administration invited eleven nations to a Washington conference on the peaceful preservation of Antarctica, a meeting which resulted in the first arms-control agreement in the Cold War. The signatories of the treaty agreed in 1959 to keep the Antarctic free from the arms race. No agency was established to inspect the area, but any signatory was given the right of inspection.

Why did it take fifteen years of bargaining to produce a small and relatively insignificant agreement? Disarmament or arms control rarely occurs when one side perceives itself in an inferior position vis-à-vis its opponent. Consequently, the Soviet Union was in no mood to bargain as long as the United States maintained a lead in atomic weaponry. When, in the late 1950s, the U.S.S.R. apparently reached parity with, and perhaps superiority to, American nuclear power, the Russians felt secure enough to agree on minor restraints on their freedom of action. It was then that the American government hesitated to seriously negotiate until some measure of parity was restored.

THE FRUITFUL 1960s

Disarmament negotiations following the 1959 Antarctica Treaty had to wait until Soviet–American relations stabilized after a series of events. In 1960, Eisenhower announced that the United States would resume underground testing of nuclear devices, thus ending the moratorium in effect since 1958. In 1960, the U–2 episode and the abortive Paris Summit meeting further strained Soviet-American relations. The French became the fourth nuclear power in the world. And in 1961, the Kennedy administration sponsored a disastrous invasion attempt into Cuba.

Early Kennedy Initiatives

The Kennedy administration brought a renewed interest in disarmament and arms-control issues to American foreign policy. The new President spent the first three months of 1961 assessing disarmament proposals.

Kennedy's Five Proposals for Disarmament. In September 1961 Kennedy presented five proposals for disarmament agreements between East and West: (1) that a nuclear test-ban be negotiated; (2) that the production of nuclear materials for purposes of war be halted; (3) that an agreement be negotiated on the distribution of atomic weapons to countries who do not possess them; (4) that East and West agree to ban the presence of nuclear weapons in outer space; and (5) that existing nuclear weapons should be destroyed and fissionable materials should be converted to peaceful uses. Significantly, all but two of these proposals (2 and 5) were eventually translated into agreements within the decade after President Kennedy's statement.

ACDA. As part of the Kennedy reassessment, the Arms Control and Disarmament Agency (ACDA) was established in September 1961.[4] Previous to 1961, the major responsibility for formulating and executing arms-control and disarmament policy was vested in the Department of State. In 1955, President Eisenhower appointed Harold Stassen as Special Assistant for Disarmament, a position that carried both cabinet rank and representation on the National Security Council. While Stassen's appointment placed him within the Executive Office of the President, he was still under the general supervision of the Secretary of State, John Foster Dulles. Since Stassen was given only a small staff, he relied on task forces to produce ideas and studies for negotiations. He drew on the departments of State, Defense, Justice, as well as the Central Intelligence Agency, the Atomic Energy Commission, and the United States Information Agency. After three years, differences with Dulles forced Stassen's retirement, and arms control and disarmament reverted again to the Department of State. The Secretary of State was assigned a Special Assistant for Disarmament; and in 1960, the Disarmament Administration was created, a precursor to ACDA.

The Soviet Response. The Kennedy diplomatic offensive for disarmament and arms control during 1961 did not meet with an immediate favorable response from the U.S.S.R. On September 1, the U.S.S.R. resumed testing, detonating bursts in the 50-to-60 megaton range. It appeared that disarmament negotiations were set back. On September 20, however, the U.S. and U.S.S.R. submitted a statement of agreed principles for disarmament to the United Nations General Assembly. And in December, a joint U.S.–U.S.S.R. resolution to the United Nations called for new negotiations.

Soviet–American Differences

Verification and Inspection. Differences between the Kennedy and Khrushchev approaches to disarmament revealed conflict over several important points, the issue of inspection being the most crucial. The American government insisted on verification of each step, while the U.S.S.R. argued that inspection was a subterfuge for espionage. On the issue of nuclear testing, Soviet–American differences over inspection were especially apparent. The U.S.S.R. wanted an uninspected moratorium on testing, including underground bursts. The American government was afraid that the Soviet Union would continue testing nuclear devices underground, and thus push ahead of the United States in weapon development. Since it was difficult to distinguish between small underground bursts and earthquakes, the Kennedy administration insisted on the right to visit the area of the disturbance.

Size of Conventional Forces. The United States and Soviet Union further disagreed on the size of the armed forces. The Americans proposed that the ceiling be 2.1 million men under arms; the Russians held to a 1.7 million figure. The United States government believed that the Soviet proposal would render the American armed forces incapable of fulfilling commitments abroad. Moreover, the Kennedy administration proposed that an international police force be created under United Nations auspices, but the Russians were cool to any multinational armed force.

An Inferior Position? Kennedy entered the presidency at a time when doubts existed that the American military establishment was equal to that of the Soviet Union. While the much publicized "missile gap" in 1959–60 resulted from errors in intelligence analysis, American capacity to match Russian ability to deliver nuclear warheads was generally considered inferior. The Kennedy administration, consequently, set out to increase American military strength to equal, and perhaps surpass, that of the Soviet Union. As long as the Russian government was considered ahead in the arms race, the United States would not agree to any disarmament proposal that would permanently freeze its armed forces in a position of inferiority. The American motivations were similar to those of the U.S.S.R. during its period of nuclear inferiority in the late 1940s and early 1950s.

What was needed, then, was an incident that constituted a test of strength for both sides, which would show the Russians that American nuclear capability was a credible deterrent force, equal, if not superior, to theirs. The test would also prove to both sides the fruitlessness of ever-spiraling attempts to best each other in an arms race. As long as both the Russians and Americans held out hope for a technological breakthrough that would produce a position of superiority, disarmament and arms-control negotiations would continue to produce only a mountain of verbiage and a dearth of minor agreements that characterized the previous fifteen years. The United States and U.S.S.R., in short, would have to be shown that neither was ahead of the other militarily and that neither was likely to be in the near future. The situation which met all these requirements was the Cuban missile crisis of October 1962.

The Cuban Missile Crisis. Although this incident had many ramifications on world politics, it was also extremely important as a stimulus to arms-control and disarmament negotiations. As a facedown between the two superpowers, it underscored the approximate match of power as both nations stood near to war. The awesome power that each possessed was tangible proof that neither the Soviet Union nor the United States could dictate to the other the outcome of world political issues.

Progress After the Missile Crisis

The Cuban missile crisis ushered in a period of agreements that contrasted sharply with the limited progress of the previous fifteen years.

The Hot Line. In December 1962, President Kennedy proposed that a direct line of communication between the White House and Kremlin be built for instantaneous exchange of messages. During the missile crisis,

Kennedy and Premier Khrushchev were forced to rely on public broadcasts of their positions because the communication links of traditional diplomacy moved messages much too slowly for the fast pace of events. The "hot line" agreement, signed in June 1963, established a teletype system of communication. It was used for the first time during the June 1967 Middle-East conflict.

Limited Test Ban Agreement. The first major breakthrough in disarmament negotiations was the 1963 treaty to prohibit nuclear testing in the atmosphere, in outer space, and underwater. Bursts of nuclear devices underground were omitted from the agreement because of American insistence on inspection safeguards that the U.S.S.R. was unwilling to grant.

More Agreements. There followed in rapid succession several agreements, some of which can be considered minor. In October 1963, the U.S. and U.S.S.R. agreed to a United Nations resolution calling upon all nations to refrain from placing nuclear weapons in outer space. This resolution was written into treaty form in 1967; it banned testing or placing nuclear weapons on celestial bodies and orbiting space satellites that could be used as platforms to launch missiles with nuclear warheads. In April 1964, the United States, United Kingdom, and Soviet Union made simultaneous announcements to decrease production of fissionable material for weapons and to divert it to peaceful purposes. In 1967, 22 Latin American nations agreed to make their area of the world a nuclear-free zone in the Treaty for the Prohibition of Nuclear Weapons in Latin America.[5] In 1968, the treaty on non-proliferation of nuclear weapons was ratified; the nuclear states pledged not to transfer nuclear weapons to nations who did not possess them, and the non-nuclear states pledged not to manufacture or acquire nuclear weapons. In 1969, the United States and Soviet Union proposed a treaty that banned placing nuclear weapons and other devices of mass destruction, such as launching platforms, on the seabed and ocean floor beyond the 12-mile limit. This treaty was ratified in February 1971. And in 1970, the Strategic Arms Limitations Talks (referred to as SALT) began.

Arms Control and Stability. Despite obvious loopholes in these agreements (for example, the seabed treaty does not prohibit missiles fired from submarines within the 12-mile limit and the non-proliferation agreement does not exclude stationing missiles in countries that are alliance partners), they did contribute to the stability of the international system in two ways. In the first place, the arms-control accords reflected Soviet and American recognition that facets of the arms race were either too dangerous or too nonproductive in the Cold War. Removing Antarctica, outer space, the seabed, and nuclear sales to other nations from East–West competition contributed to international stability by eliminating areas of possible conflict.

Second, the Soviet and American governments realized the disequilibrating influence of the "Nth country" problem. Six nations have the bomb (U.S., U.S.S.R., Great Britain, France, China, and India), while more nations, perhaps as many as fifteen, possess the capability to build a nuclear device. The 1963 Test Ban Treaty, the 1967 treaty prohibiting nuclear weapons in Latin America, and the 1968 proliferation agreement were attempts by the Americans and Russians to keep other nations from building and perfecting nuclear arsenals.

Peaceful Uses of Nuclear Energy. The destructive aspects of nuclear energy are obvious, but it also can serve peaceful purposes. Nuclear science can be used for medical research or to produce domestic energy sources. Approximately 40 nations now have nuclear reactors for peaceful uses; the United States, Western European nations, and the U.S.S.R. are competing with each other to sell reactors to other developing nations for peaceful uses only. During his trip to the Middle East in 1974, President Nixon agreed to aid Egypt and Israel in constructing nuclear reactors. How can the seller be sure that the reactors will be used for peaceful purposes? Since the natural by-product of a reactor is plutonium, which can be used to build nuclear weapons, the non-proliferation treaty calls for inspections by an international control agency. If the reactor is used for weapon-building purposes, the treaty's signatories have agreed to cease sales of nuclear equipment and fissionable material to the guilty country. At the moment, the problem is finding a balance between proliferating nuclear knowledge for peaceful purposes and proliferating nuclear knowledge that might be used for destructive purposes.

THE 1970s: STRATEGIC, DEFENSIVE, AND BCW WEAPONS

Control of Strategic Weapons

The 1970s and SALT. The many agreements of the 1960s tended to prohibit weapon development in areas in which both the United States and Soviet Union had only marginal interests: Antarctica, celestial bodies, and the seabed. At the same time, both states slowed their pace in developing new systems as a result of the Limited Test Ban Agreement. This agreement, plus the Nuclear Proliferation Treaty, also slowed the progress of non-nuclear states toward developing their own nuclear strike force. China and France exempted themselves from these limitations by refusing to become a party to the Test Ban Treaty.

Both the American and Russian governments refused to discuss the essence of their superpower status—their nuclear arsenal. In the 1970s, however, the U.S. and U.S.S.R. began to explore areas of possible agreement on strategic weapons in the Strategic Arms Limitation Talks. Two major SALT agreements, which took two-and-a-half years to negotiate, were signed in 1972 when President Nixon visited the Soviet Union: The Interim Agreement on Offensive Missiles and the ABM Treaty.

The Interim Agreement on Offensive Missiles. The Interim Agreement is unique among the post-World War II disarmament documents. It freezes U.S. and U.S.S.R. nuclear development for a brief time while their negotiators work on a more detailed and comprehensive agreement. Since the Interim Agreement omits long-range bombers, fighter bombers, and Intermediate Range Ballistic Missiles (IRBM), the U.S. and U.S.S.R. needed more time to arrive at a mutually accepted formula to cover these weapon systems as well. Consequently, the Interim Agreement is a classic example of the two signatories agreeing to disagree for the moment, while continuing serious negotiations.

Both sides compromised to establish the Interim Agreement. The U.S. accepted Russian superiority in launch vehicles, but the Russians accepted American superiority in number of warheads. All facts considered, however, both sides accepted their nuclear *parity* and were willing to call a pause to the arms race in strategic weapons to ascertain if a permanent arrangement could be negotiated.

Limits placed on ICBMs, submarines, and submarine-launched ballistic missiles (SLBMs) by the Interim Agreement are given in Table 14-1. In total number of missiles, the U.S.S.R. is given the legal basis for building 2,568 launch vehicles (both ICBMs and SLBMs). The United States, on the other hand, can construct only 1,264 launch vehicles over the five-year period of the agreement.

Table 14-1. 1977 Nuclear Limits Set by Interim Agreement

	ICBMs	Nuclear submarines	SLBMs
United States	1,054	44	710
Soviet Union	1,618	62	950

Source: *Department of State News Release,* August 1, 1972, p. 7.

On the surface, the imbalance between American and Soviet launch vehicles hardly suggests that parity was the principle followed in negotiating the Interim Agreement. Two additional factors, however, must be considered: the agreement did not cover bombers and Multiple Independent Re-entry Vehicles (MIRV) deployment. In both of these areas, the United States is ahead of the Soviet Union. Figure 14-1 is a comparison of the two countries' bomber forces, showing the American lead and the even greater lead projected for 1977. The first assumption implicit in these figures, released by the Department of State, is that the United States will build and have operational a follow-up bomber to the aging B-52. The Pentagon has proposed the supersonic B-1 heavy bomber as the B-52 successor. A second assumption is that the U.S.S.R. will not develop a large heavy bomber force in the 1970s, but will continue to rely on ICBMs to deliver their nuclear warheads. And the third assumption is that aircraft will continue to be a viable offensive weapon.

At the signing of the Interim Agreement, the United States had outstripped the U.S.S.R. in developing and deploying the MIRV. Conse-

chapter 14   Arms-Control and Disarmament Policies

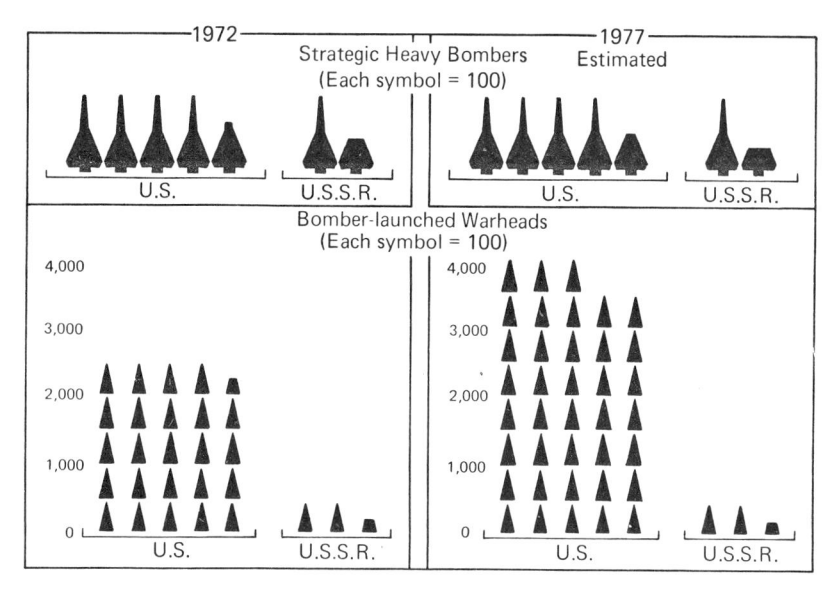

Figure 14-1.   A Comparison of U.S. and U.S.S.R. Bombers and Bomber-Launched Warheads (Not Limited by SALT). *(Source:* Department of State News Release, August 1, 1972, p. 7.)

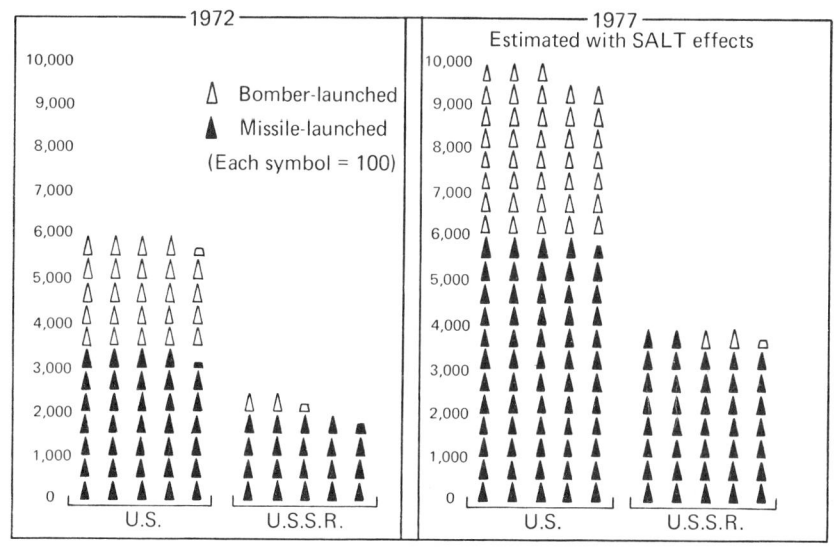

Figure 14-2.   A Comparison of U.S. and U.S.S.R. Strategic Nuclear Warheads. *(Source:* Department of State News Release, August 1, 1972, p. 8.)

quently, the U.S. government could feel confident in agreeing to an inferior position in launch vehicle numbers. The total number of warheads available to each nation is compared in Figure 14-2. The American lead is approximately 2.5 to 1. "Parity," then, was a compromise between American superiority in bombers and MIRVs and Soviet superiority in ICBMs and SLBMs. Although both sides were comparing dissimilar objects—warhead apples with missile oranges—the agreement does give an appearance of balance.

An additional American motivation for signing the agreement is suggested in Figure 14–3: the United States was interested in halting the Soviet missile build-up before it reached a level that would entail a major expenditure in the U.S. budget to keep apace. The alternative would have been to accept a position inferior to the Soviet Union. The U.S.S.R. had undertaken a massive missile-construction program after the Cuban missile crisis had shown the superior status of the United States. The Interim Agreement, therefore, placed an upper limit on Soviet missiles, short of a figure that was within reach of Russian resources. On the other hand, the limit that the United States accepted was a level that the Americans had already decided to stay within. The Interim Agreement acted as a leash to the Russians, but not to the Americans.

The ABM Agreement. The treaty to limit anti-ballistic missiles was also unique among the post-World War II pacts: it was the first agreement limiting a defensive weapon system. Prior to the agreement, the U.S.S.R. had built an ABM site around Moscow; the Nixon administration had initiated its Safeguard System that ultimately envisioned twelve sites primarily protecting ICBM launch sites. One site was already operational in North Dakota.

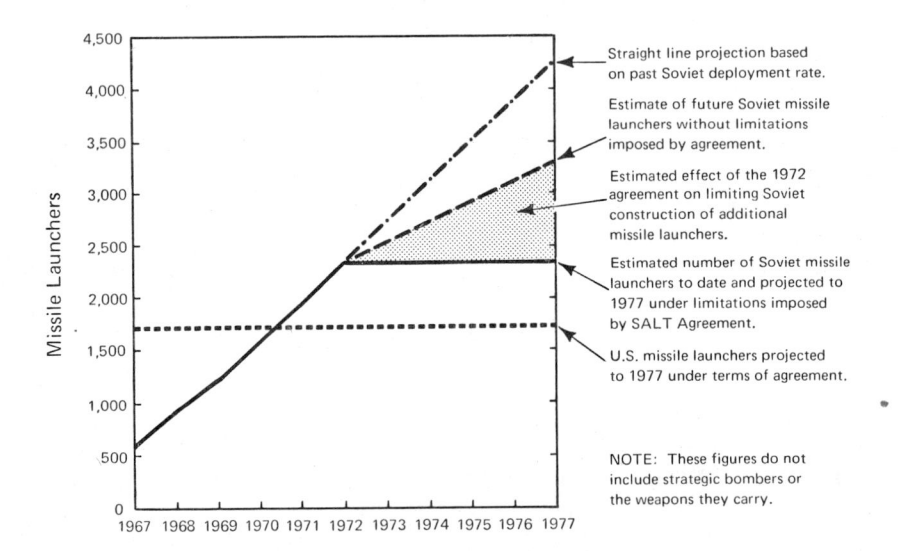

Figure 14–3. A Comparison of U.S. and U.S.S.R. ICBM/SLBM Missile Launchers. *(Source:* Department of State News Release, August 1, 1972, p. 8.)

The Moscow treaty limited both sides to two sites of not more than 200 missiles at each site. The 200 missiles could be equally divided between 100 ABMs and 100 interceptor missiles. Both nations also pledged to forego developments that would modify ABM missile launchers to make them into ICBMs or to develop a rapid-loading launcher that would increase the number of missiles above the limit of 200.

Evaluation of the 1972 SALT Agreements. The ABM agreement is significant because both nations pledged to leave most of their cities and military targets unprotected and vulnerable to a missile attack. In effect, each side purposely lowered its guard. Ironically, the Soviet Union and United States supposedly should feel more secure because they know that their missile attack cannot be deflected by their opponent's ABM system. The balance of terror continued as part of the international system because the Interim Agreement left both sides with a sufficient nuclear force to destroy an aggressor. The number of ICBMs and SLBMs (and bombers, in the case of the U.S.) permitted was sufficient to allow the attacked nation to absorb a nuclear strike and still retain the capability to destroy its opponent.

Verification of the agreements was left to national means, i.e., the sophisticated surveillance equipment developed by Russian and American scientists. Both sides had sufficient confidence in their electronic intelligence-gathering devices to sign the agreements.[6]

During Nixon's 1974 visit to Moscow, the 1972 agreements were modified. Because little progress had been made in SALT, both nations left open the possibility of extending the time frame for the Interim Agreement. The ABM accord was amended to reduce the number of sites to one. An amendment also was added to the 1963 Test Ban Treaty: certain sizes of underground detonations were outlawed, although no provisions were made for inspection. While progress continued to be made, agreements in the 1970s limiting strategic weapons were proving more difficult to negotiate than those signed in the 1960s.

In the early 1970s, the U.S. was spending approximately 10 percent of its gross national product on military programs. The U.S.S.R., a much poorer nation, was spending between 11 and 14 percent. Whether the 1972 and 1974 agreements will permit these percentages to decrease remains to be seen. Both sides will continue to appropriate large sums for research and development projects to create new families of weapons. The avoidance of more devastating weapons will depend on the success of future SALT meetings.[7]

Conventional Forces in Europe

As the two nuclear superpowers moved toward agreements on strategic weapons in the early 1970s, it was only a matter of time before discussions would begin over reducing conventional forces in Europe. The North Atlantic Treaty Organization (NATO) had never achieved its full military potential. And the diplomatic "openings to the East" first begun by French President De Gaulle and later practiced by most Western European nations, including the Federal Republic of Germany, reduced the level of tensions in the region.

Mutual and Balanced Force Reduction (MBFR). A comparison of the 1971 force levels of NATO and the Warsaw Pact (the formal defensive alliance of the Soviet bloc nations) is given in Table 14–2. In addition to the obvious superiority of the Warsaw Pact over NATO forces, the geographical proximity of the Soviet army means that even larger forces are available to the U.S.S.R.'s allies. Throughout the 1950s and early 1960s, the United States was unwilling to discuss troop reductions in Europe because it meant that American forces would be withdrawn across an ocean while Russian troops would simply have to step over a border.

Table 14–2. Comparison of Force Levels in Europe, 1974

	NATO	Warsaw Pact
Personnel	777,000	925,000
Tanks	6,000	15,500

Source: "Department of State, "Europe: Mutual and Balanced Force Reductions," *Foreign Policy Outlines* (May 1974), p. 1.

As the likelihood of a Soviet conventional attack decreased and as Soviet troops were called on primarily to quash national uprisings in East Europe, American and NATO policy began to change. In 1968, the NATO allies agreed to explore the possibility of a mutual and balanced force reduction, but Soviet intervention in Czechoslovakia during the summer led to a cooling in East–West relations. During the 1972 and 1974 Moscow summits, American and Soviet leaders agreed to explore the possibility of MBFR.

Biological and Chemical Weapons

The Arsenal of BCW Weapons. While not used extensively in past wars, weapons using chemical and biological agents have been manufactured in sufficient quantities by several nations to attract the concern of disarmament negotiators. Chemical agents include nonlethal gases (such as tear gas) used to force an opponent into the open for capture or for killing (in which case, the nonlethal gases can no longer be considered "nonlethal"). Poison gases have been developed that range from mustard gas from World War I fame to modern nerve gas, a tasteless, colorless substance capable of paralyzing an individual's nervous system and of killing within minutes. Nontoxic agents for plants *(herbicides)* and for trees *(defoliants)* were used extensively in the Vietnamese conflict as tactical weapons; their purpose was to deprive enemy guerrillas of protective cover over jungle trails, rest camps, and food supplies. Both lethal and nonlethal gases have been deployed overseas as well as the defoliants and herbicides. Psychochemicals have also been developed, one of which increases the emotion of fear in the enemy. These are all considered tactical weapons.

The biological agents, on the other hand, are considered strategic weapons and are not deployed overseas. As strategic weapons, they can be used to attack population areas of the enemy's heartland. The biologicals, as they are sometimes called, include disease-producing substances for animals as well as for humans.

The usual reaction to this description of the agents of biological and chemical warfare (BCW) is one of horror, primarily because our thinking is not geared to accept them as part of modern-day conflict.[8] Death by plague is no more horrifying than death by the fireball of a thermonuclear burst. Yet there are differences between BCW and nuclear warfare that cause a healthy amount of concern. In the first place, it is more difficult to control the biologicals once they are released (the same problem is encountered with the chemical agents, but not of the same magnitude). Some of the biologicals will remain alive for years. Secondly, once released, the ultimate extent of destruction by the biologicals cannot be controlled. It is not known whether the attacker can escape from the eventual affects of biological agents released in warfare; anthrax virus, for example, cannot be trained to stay within the confines of the Soviet Union. And finally, biological agents, unlike chemical and nuclear weapons, cannot be stockpiled. They must be manufactured constantly and kept in a state of readiness.

The 1971 Convention on Biological Weapons. The 1970s also witnessed a major agreement on biological weapons and an attempt by the United States to catch up with the rest of the world in regard to chemical weapons. In 1971, the U.S. began to destroy its biological weapon stockpiles; the American and Soviet representatives to the UN Committee on Disarmament simultaneously proposed parallel drafts of a convention prohibiting the use of biological weapons in warfare. In the following year, the UN General Assembly approved the convention, and it was opened for signatures in three capitals—Washington, London, and Moscow. Some of the signatories reserved the right to use biological weapons in retaliation, but the United States did not.

The Geneva Protocol Revisited. The United States and the Soviet Union could not reach an agreement on chemical agents to accompany the Convention on Biological Weapons. One of the major obstacles in the negotiations was American insistence that riot-control gases (such as tear gas), herbicides, and defoliates should not be prohibited by any treaty. All three of these chemical agents were employed in Vietnam. To restrict their use would make the American government appear to be in violation of international law.

In 1970, the Nixon administration resubmitted the 1925 Geneva Protocol, which prohibited the use in war of asphyxiating, poisonous, and other gases, as well as bacteriological methods of warfare. The U.S. government had proposed this treaty in 1925 in response to the horrifying experiences with mustard and other poisonous gases in World War I. When the Protocol was submitted to the Senate in 1926, it was effectively smothered for 20 years. The Senate finally returned it to the President in 1947 without taking action.

When President Nixon resubmitted the Protocol in 1970, he declared that the United States government interpreted its provisions as excluding riot-control gases, herbicides, and defoliates. The United Nations General Assembly, in an apparent slap at the President, quickly voted 80 to 3 that the Protocol include all three chemical agents. The United States also reserved the right to use chemicals in retaliation, a reservation not made in the Convention on Biological Weapons.

Obstacles to Future Agreements

Because of the slow, but continuous and encouraging, arms-control progress in the 1960s and 1970s, it is possible to overlook significant obstacles to future agreements.

The Continuing Revolution in Warfare. Military technology is dynamic, not static: the cyclical pattern of military technology is for new offensive weapons to be developed, put into the field, grow obsolete, and be replaced by a new generation of more effective weapons. The chief characteristic of the revolution in warfare since 1945 has been the superiority of offensive over defensive systems.

As the U.S. and U.S.S.R. reach agreements on the nuclear family of weapons spawned by technological breakthroughs in the 1940s, it appears that new systems based on different scientific principles, such as the laser, will soon be ready for deployment. Whether or not the Russians and Americans will be willing to compete over new and undeployed weapons in the hope of establishing a position of superiority is an open question. It could be that both states have learned that security is not a product of an arms race and that competition over more sophisticated and destructive instruments still on the drawing boards offers no security. Perhaps the superpowers have also come to realize the arms race's drain on resources needed elsewhere.

France and China. The game of tag that offensive nuclear weaponry has been playing with defensive weaponry—and continuously winning—has not been the only contributor to instability. Small or medium powers aspiring to become great powers are also a destabilizing force in the international system. Both France and the People's Republic of China have attempted throughout the 1960s and 1970s to acquire a respectable nuclear force, and with it, the status of a world power.

Neither France nor China has acceded to the major arms control agreements since 1962. To them, these treaties would have frozen their nuclear development into a permanent state of inferiority. Just as the United States and the Soviet Union refused to negotiate seriously on disarmament throughout the unfruitful 1940s and 1950s, the French and Chinese refused to consider any agreement that would hinder their own nuclear development. Both countries will continue their independent course until they attain the level of a nuclear power.

The Nth Country Problem. As the U.S. and U.S.S.R. move on to more awesome and sophisticated weapon systems, and as France and China gain great power status, the nuclear nations yet-to-be-born (the Nth Country problem) present their own obstacles to arms-reduction efforts.[9] Although the Nth Country problem is normally applied to small nations with neighborhood quarrels, the Federal Republic of Germany and Japan, both possessing the economic base to be superpowers in their own right, have yet to make the decision to add nuclear weapons to their arsenals. Both nations are confined by agreements growing out of World War II. As the memories of that conflict fade, as new circumstances in Europe and the Far East intrude, and as the national climate within each nation changes, the Germans and Japanese will probably face the decision of whether or not to build nuclear weapons.

The Nth Country's dilemma will be the same one presently faced by the French and Chinese: to agree to the compacts of the 1960s and 1970s worked out by two superpowers, and thus be frozen into an inferior position, or to add nuclear weapons to their foreign policy-implementing instruments.

India's detonation of a nuclear device in 1974 also underscores the realities of the Nth Country problem. The nuclear club is certain to grow as other nations follow India's example, making it more difficult to negotiate arms-control and disarmament agreements.

DISARMAMENT AND ARMS CONTROL: GAMES NATIONS PLAY

Dangerous Gamesmanship

Disarmament and arms-control policies often appear to be games that nations play rather than serious endeavors. In these games, each nation attempts to win propaganda victories by negotiating with an eye to the gallery and with the intent of embarrassing the opponent. Disarmament and arms-control negotiations have indeed involved an element of gamesmanship.

On the other hand, disarmament and arms-control policy must be viewed as part of a nation's strategy to maintain its own security. If the United States could convince the Soviet Union to lower its armament spending, to postpone current spending for military programs, or to accept limits lower than it originally envisioned, then American security would be enhanced. Security, after all, is a primary goal of state policy.

Neither superpower has behaved naively. Both American and Soviet leaders have resisted attempts to freeze their military powers into a position of permanent inferiority. This prime motivation behind national policy toward disarmament proposals is understandable and has characterized both U.S. and U.S.S.R. approaches.

Disarmament and the Images

The American attitude toward disarmament and arms control is conditioned by U.S. decision makers' images of their world. Viewing the U.S.S.R. as aggressive and untrustworthy, American leaders were suspicious of Russian claims that the Soviet government was serious about arms control and disarmament issues. Russian leaders mirrored a similar view of American intentions. The agreements of the 1960s were based on a mutual respect for each others' global power, demonstrated during the 1962 Cuban missile crisis. Most Right-Wing Revisionists continue to oppose negotiations with the Russians, believing that the Soviet Union is too untrustworthy to keep its word without a foolproof inspection system.[10] The danger of a Soviet breakthrough in the development of a new weapon system is too great. The American government, so the Right-Wing image-holders argue, must continue its own arms buildup to maintain its own security.

Congress and Arms Control

Although the executive bureaucracy has made significant proposals for disarmament and arms control, a few congressional leaders have suggested arrangements that are more extensive. During the 1972 presidential campaign, Senator McGovern argued for a large reduction in the Pentagon's budget.[11] The Senate also has indicated its willingness to reduce American troops in Europe without a reciprocal reduction of Soviet strength. Thus far, however, arms-control and disarmament leadership have rested with the President, not Congress.

Continuing Weapon Development

With the continuing development of weapon systems, disarmament and arms-control negotiations face new problems. It may well be that military technology will outrun the diplomatic attempts to work out complicated balances among the world's most powerful nations. For example, MaRV (Maneuverable Re-entry Vehicle), a nuclear warhead that can be controlled in flight, has been developed to surpass MIRV capability. It can evade defensive missiles as it approaches its target, a capability that an American MIRV does not possess. The development of MaRV again places the Soviet Union at a disadvantage.

When will it all stop? It is doubtful that an answer can be found in the immediate future unless SALT supplies it.[12] The search for security continues.

NOTES

1. The literature written on disarmament and arms control is voluminous, equaling the verbiage of negotiators. The Library of Congress publishes a bibliography of articles, books, and monographs under the title *Arms Control and Disarmament: A Quarterly Bibliography with Abstracts and Annotations* (Washington, D.C.: U.S. Government Printing Office). Standard works on arms control and disarmament include: Hedley Bull, *The Control of the Arms Race*, 2nd ed. (New York: Praeger, 1965); and J. David Singer, *Deterrence, Arms Control, and Disarmament* (Columbus: Ohio State University Press, 1962). In addition, there are compilations of articles and symposiums that compare many different viewpoints: Donald G. Brennan (ed.), *Arms Control, Disarmament, and National Security* (New York: Braziller, 1961); Ernest W. Lefever (ed.), *Arms and Arms Control: A Symposium* (New York: Praeger, 1962); Wayland H. Young (ed.), *Existing Mechanisms of Arms Control* (Elmsford, N.Y.: Pergamon Press, 1966); and James E. Dougherty and J. F. Lehman, Jr. (eds.), *Arms Control for the Late Sixties* (New York: Van Nostrand Reinhold Co., 1967).
2. Three histories of arms-control and disarmament negotiations are Bernard C. Beggiefer, *Postwar Negotiations for Arms Control* (Washington, D.C.: Brookings Institution, 1961); Henry W. Forbes, *The Strategy of Disarmament* (Washington, D.C.: Public Affairs Press, 1962); John W. Spanier and Joseph L. Nogee, *The Politics of Disarmament: A Study in Soviet-American Gamesmanship* (New York: Praeger, 1962).
3. The UN's role in disarmament and arms-control negotiations is summarized in a book published by the United Nations Secretariat, *The United Nations and Disarmament, 1946–1965* (New York: United Nations, 1967). A dated, though useful, supplement is Yves Collart, *Disarmament, A Study Guide and Bibliography on the Efforts of the United Nations* (The Hague: M. Nijhoff, 1958). See also Walter Goldstein, "Disarmament, The UN, and the Nuclear Club," *The Correspondent* 34 (Spring–Summer 1965): 43–44; 47–54.
4. For more information on ACDA, *see* the agency's annual reports. For a critical review, *see* Laurence W. Martin, "Disarmament: An Agency in Search of a Policy," *The Reporter* 29 (July 4, 1963): 22–26.
5. Latin America is one of several areas in which the regional effects of arms-control and disarmament proposals are discussed by Karl W.

Deutsch, *Arms Control and the Atlantic Alliance* (New York: John Wiley, 1967); Stanford University Arms Control Project, *Arms Control Arrangement for the Far East* (Stanford, Calif.: Hoover Institutions on War, Revolution, and Peace, Stanford University, 1967); Lincoln P. Bloomfield and Amelia C. Leiss, "Arms Control and the Developing Countries," *World Politics* 18 (October 1965): 1–20; and A. Buchan and Philip Windsor, *Arms and Stability in Europe* (New York: Praeger, 1963).

6. The problems of inspection and control have been discussed by James K. Batten, *Arms Control and the Problem of Evasion* (Princeton, N.J.: Center for International Studies, Princeton University, 1962); Paul Y. Hammond, "Some Difficulties of Self-Enforcing Arms Agreements," *Journal of Conflict Resolutions* 6 (June 1962): 603–615; Seymour Melman (ed.), *Inspection for Disarmament* (New York: Columbia University Press, 1958); Henry A. Kissinger, "Inspection and Surprise Attack," *Foreign Affairs* 38 (July 1960): 557–575; and Lewis C. Bohn, "Whose Nuclear Test: Non Physical Inspection and the Test Ban," *Journal of Conflict Resolution* 7 (1963): 379–393. The legal aspects of inspection and control have attracted the attention of scholars who have discussed the impact of inspection on domestic laws and the obstacles that domestic legal norms pose to inspection. See Louis Henkin, *Arms Control and Inspection in American Law* (New York: Columbia University Press, 1958); Dennis S. Aronowitz, *Legal Aspects of Arms Control Verification in the United States* (Dobbs Ferry, N.Y.: Oceana Publishers, 1965); and Harold J. Berman and Peter B. Maggs, *Disarmament Inspection under Soviet Law* (Dobbs Ferry, N.Y.: Oceana Publications, 1967).

7. The following writers are concerned with the question of the impact on disarmament of the United States and world economics: Battelle Memorial Institute, *The Implications of Reduced Defense Demand for the Electronics Industry* (Washington, D.C.: U.S. Government Printing Office, 1965); John J. Clark, *The New Economics of National Defense* (New York: Random House, 1966); Roger E. Bolton (ed.), *Defense and Disarmament: The Economics of Transition* (Englewood Cliffs, N.J.: Prentice-Hall, 1966); and Emile Benoit and Kenneth E. Boulding (eds.), *Disarmament and the Economy* (New York: Harper & Row, 1963).

8. Seymour M. Hersh, *Chemical and Biological Warfare: America's Hidden Arsenal* (Indianapolis: Bobbs-Merrill Co., 1969) and Steven Rose (ed.), *CBW: Chemical and Biological Warfare* (Boston: Beacon Press, 1969).

9. Nuclear proliferation and the "Nth Country" problem are analyzed by Ian Brownlie, "Nuclear Proliferation: Some Problems of Control," *International Affairs* 42 (October 1966): 600–608; E. L. M. Burns, "Can the Spread of Nuclear Weapons be Stopped?" *International Organization* 19 (Autumn 1965): 851–869; Kenneth Younger, "The Spectre of Nuclear Proliferation," *International Affairs* 42 (January

1966): 14–23; John A. Hall, "Atoms for Peace or War," *Foreign Affairs* 43 (July 1965): 602–615; Klaus Knorr, "Nuclear Weapons: 'Haves' and 'Have Nots'," *Ibid.* 36 (October 1957): 167–178; Mason Willrich, "Guarantees to Non-Nuclear Nations," *Ibid.* 45 (July 1967): 662–669; and William B. Bader, *The United States and the Spread of Nuclear Weapons* (Indianapolis: Pegasus, Bobbs-Merrill Co., 1968).

10. See Edward Teller, "Alterations for Security," *Foreign Affairs* 36 (January 1958): 201–208. The Radicals of the Right-Wing image have been adamant in their opposition to disarmament negotiations. See Kent and Phoebe Courtney, *Disarmament: A Blueprint for Surrender* (New Orleans: Conservative Society of America, 1963). A critical examination of the 1963 test ban treaty is James H. McBride, *The Test Ban Treaty: Military, Technological, and Political Implications* (Chicago: Regnery, 1967).

11. There is a sizable amount of literature on proposals for arms control and disarmament that tends to depart from the traditional tacks followed by Soviet and American diplomats: John Burton, *Peace Theory: Preconditions of Disarmament* (New York: Alfred A. Knopf, 1962); Walter Millis and James Real, *The Abolition of War* (New York: Macmillan, 1963); Walter Millis, *An End to Arms* (New York: Atheneum, 1965); Bertrand Russell, *Common Sense and Nuclear Warfare* (New York: Simon and Schuster, 1959); Jeremy J. Stone, *Containing the Arms Race* (Cambridge, Mass.: M.I.T. Press, 1966) and *Strategic Persuasion: Arms Limitations Through Dialogue* (New York: Columbia University Press, 1967); Richard J. Barnet and Richard A. Falk (eds.), *Security in Disarmament* (Princeton, N.J.: Princeton University Press, 1965); Philip Seed, *The Psychological Problem of Disarmament* (London: Housmans, 1966); and D. H. Frisch, *Arms Reduction: Program and Issues* (New York: Twentieth Century Fund, 1961).

12. For an analysis of SALT, *see* John Newhouse, *Cold Dawn: The Story of SALT* (New York: Holt, Rinehart, and Winston, 1973). As this book was going to press, a second SALT agreement was reached between the U.S. and U.S.S.R. at Vladivostok in November 1974. The two nations agreed to limit delivery vehicles (including bombers) to 2,400. Of these, only 1,320 could be outfitted with MIRVs. The Vladivostok agreement was to last ten years.

15

Alliances and Patterns of American Diplomacy

National survival has been pursued in different ways by the American government since World War II. The strategic use of military force and the many attempts to strike a bargain with the Soviet Union on mutual disarmament and arms-control issues are two avenues used to ensure this survival. Negotiating alliances with other nations is another.

Collective self-defense arrangements that the United States government has negotiated are defensive alliances established for the purpose of containing an aggressor.[1] The signatories share a mutual fear of the aggressor's power or a mutual suspicion of his intentions. Other motivations, however, are sometimes involved, a point illustrated by the Organization of American States, discussed later in this chapter.

THE AMERICAN IMAGE OF REGIONAL ALLIANCES

Reasons for Coalitions

The classical reason for building a coalition is to augment national military capability against a common enemy. Since the common opponent is viewed as aggressive, a joint declaration of peace-loving states, whose combined capability is greater, should discourage any imperialist tendencies. Conflict as a result of miscalculation may still occur, since the aggressor nation may not accept the coalition's strength as greater, or may believe that the alliance's declaration is a bluff. Or war by "accident" may result: one side may set in motion a series of automatic responses to its opponent's maneuvers that cannot be stopped at midpoint. During the 1967 Arab–Israeli conflict, U.S. carriers in the Mediterranean launched planes when an American spy vessel was attacked by Israel. To allay Russian fears that the "scramble" was aimed at Russian targets, President Johnson used the "hot line" to inform Soviet leaders of the circumstances. The incident illustrates the possibility of war by accident, caused when one nation undertakes moves that are misinterpreted by an opponent.

Three other lines of reasoning may also operate in place of, or in addition to, the classical reason for alliance making. First, as the Cold War became a part of the international political landscape after 1945, the American government tended to see the world as bipolar or split into two ideological camps. Each nation was required to take sides; the Americans did not entertain any doubts that most states, given the freedom to choose, would identify themselves with the Western camp. Within the bipolar world of the Cold War, neutrality did not exist. The American government then set about to organize its half of the world into regional alliances.

Regional organizations were justified, in the second place, on the basis of anticipated Soviet aggression into neighboring areas that possessed little or no military strength. By ringing the Soviet perimeter with strong defensive alliances, the Russians would be "contained" and discouraged from intervening in the affairs of smaller and weaker states who were considered targets for a future Communist revolution. Central to the American image, then, is a revisionist Soviet Union bent on world domination after World War II.

Finally, the Americans perceived world politics as a "zero-sum" game in which there is always a winner and a loser. If one side in the Cold War won, the other must lose, for the "zero-sum" game rules do not allow two winners or both sides to lose. The American strategy, then, was to persuade as many states as possible to join the Western camp and to bring them under the protection of the United States' nuclear umbrella. Any state signed up for the Western side was a loss to the Soviets in the "zero-sum" game of the Cold War.

Reasons for Regional Alliances

The American image of the world could have evolved a different response. The United States' nuclear monopoly could have permitted a unilateral policing of Soviet behavior, punishing wrong doing and rewarding the right patterns. This response would have been more in keeping with traditional American policy in the 19th century, but it would have been effective only until the Russians developed nuclear weapons. Or the United States, if it needed assistance from other states, could have built a series of bilateral alliances with states seemingly threatened by Soviet expansion. In the final reckoning, the regional approach was decided on for a number of reasons.

To begin with, regional organizations made it possible for the United States to express its worldwide interests through cooperative efforts. U.S. national interests extended into every region through a consensus of the regional states. American national interest was submerged in an organization of regional interests and, therefore, did not appear to be imperialist and self-serving. At least, Washington did not think that it appeared so.

Second, the American government believed that the Soviet leaders had to be convinced that the United States would support its alliance pledges. Bilateral arrangements with individual small countries could be broken or used as pawns in negotiating important agreements, but the public and pledged word of regional alliance would be much more meaningful to Soviet leaders. Washington believed that the Soviet government would be more convinced of the intensity of American commitment if the alliance agreement were made on a regional basis rather than on a bilateral one.

Third, the American government viewed itself as the military, political, and moral leader of the "free world." As a leader, the United States was obliged to protect its followers against the evils of Communist aggression. For the sake of convenience, American protection could be more effectively dispensed through a broad regional organization, rather than through arrangements with followers on a seriatim basis. In this way, the United States could not be accused of favoritism, a charge that might be leveled at American foreign policy if bilateral arrangements were negotiated.

The Mystique of Regionalism

As a result of the American image of the world in a bipolar context and the need (so the American leaders thought) of regional alliances to shore up the Western or "free world" part of the bipolar balance, a mystique developed about regionalism. Regionalism gradually became an *end* of policy rather than a *means*.

The mystique surrounding regionalism often caused U.S. policy to place more emphasis on the maintenance of the alliance than on the purpose the alliance was supposed to serve. Small nations, such as Portugal (a member of NATO), sometimes demanded a higher payoff to be "enticed" to stay with the alliance—much too high, in fact, in light of the paucity of military strength that they contributed. The small nations usually created a drain on the alliance's manpower commitments and contingency plans, rather than contributing to the coalition's strength. As long as the world was viewed from Cold War perspectives, however, the presence of small nations in the alliance was absolutely necessary. If they were not members of a Western bloc, the Soviet Union might attack, subvert, or lure them away. The result was a type of "blackmail" by small nations; they were able to extract commitments for increased economic and military aid from the U.S., along with support of colonial policies about which the American government would have serious doubts under other conditions.

The mystique of regionalism further demanded that alliance unity was the most important value of the regional relationship. The region should speak with one voice; a multiplicity of voices would give the illusion of disunity to the Soviets who then might be tempted to embark on aggressive policies. As long as the regional partners viewed Soviet aggression as a probable threat and as long as they needed American military presence to defend themselves, alliance members were willing to support American leadership to receive American aid. As the Soviet threat came to be viewed as less probable, alliance members began to demonstrate more independence and less reliance on the U.S. Tension within the alliances resulted because the American perception of the Soviet threat did not undergo a similar transformation. As a result, the United States government wanted to maintain the united voice of the alliance which its partners were questioning.

In NATO, for example, the central problem is one of the partners' differing world views. The American government's image of Soviet aggression remains essentially the same as it was in 1947 when the alliance was conceived. The European image has changed, although the 1968 Soviet invasion of Czechoslovakia tended to pull the alliance partners closer to the American image. In international politics, a nation's image is its reality; thus, American policy has been built on a "reality" that differs from the European perception of its environment.

The result of the mystique of regionalism in part was responsible for the United States building or joining four collective security alliances, shown in Figure 15–1. Not all regions are covered: Africa and South Asia (except for Pakistan) are surprisingly open to Soviet expansion; and South Asia, so near to Russia and so militarily weak, is especially vulnerable. In this region, major states—India and Burma primarily—have steered a middle course in the Cold War. Africa has done so as well; but further removed from the Soviet heartland, it has not presented as inviting a target as South Asia, if indeed the threat of Soviet expansion is a reality in contemporary international politics. Another region, the Far East, is also devoid of a regional alliance grouping, although the United States has bilateral defensive alliances with three nations (Japan, South Korea, and Taiwan).

THE ORGANIZATION OF AMERICAN STATES

Regional Community Building in Central and South America

Following World War II, one goal of the United States government was to build a strong inter-American community to withstand aggression from powers outside the region.[2] The Central and South American states cooperated in this venture for two reasons: (1) they wanted American support to develop their economies and (2) they did not desire to give to a nation outside their hemisphere, or even to a world organization, a major voice in inter-American affairs. Although the American government was interested in community building, the pressure for organizing the community into an effective regional body came from the Latin Americans them-

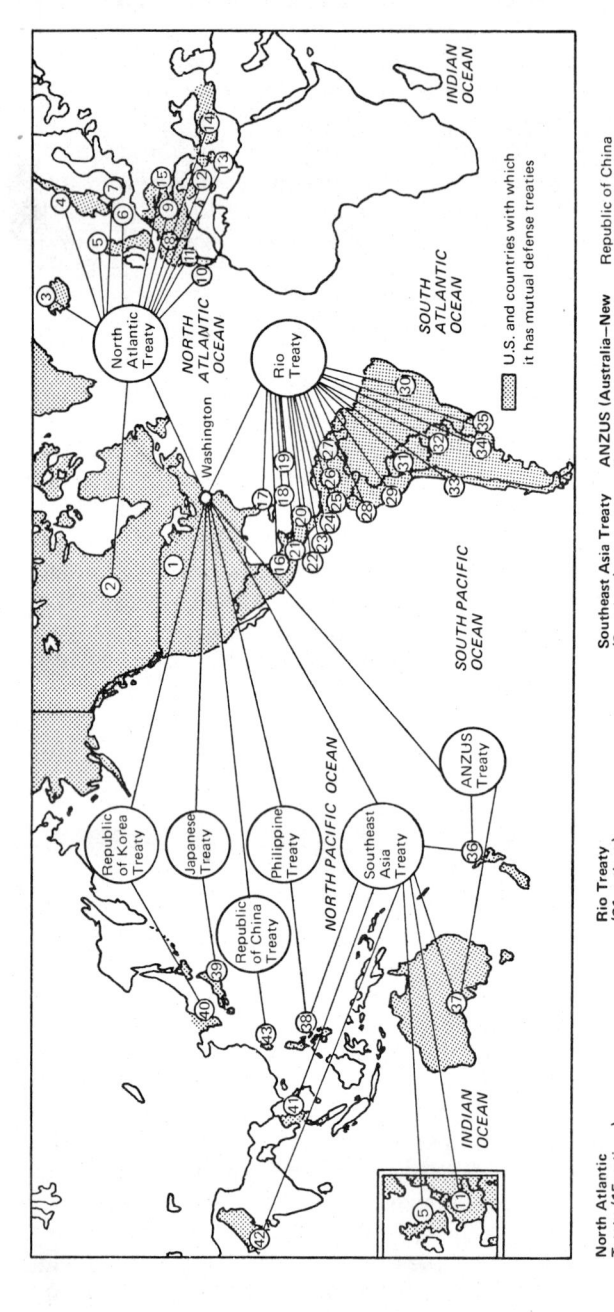

Figure 15-1. United States Collective Defense Arrangements. (Source: Adapted from Department of State Bulletin 57 [Oct. 9, 1967]: 460–461.)

North Atlantic Treaty (15 nations)
1 United States
2 Canada
3 Iceland
4 Norway
5 United Kingdom
6 Netherlands
7 Denmark
8 Belgium
9 Luxembourg
10 Portugal
11 France
12 Italy
13 Greece
14 Turkey
15 Federal Republic of Germany

Japanese Treaty (bilateral)
1 United States
39 Japan

Rio Treaty (21 nations)
1 United States
16 Mexico
17 Cuba
18 Haiti
19 Dominican Republic
20 Honduras
21 Guatemala
22 El Salvador
23 Nicaragua
24 Costa Rica
25 Panama
26 Colombia
27 Venezuela
28 Ecuador
29 Peru
30 Brazil
31 Bolivia
32 Paraguay
33 Chile
34 Argentina
35 Uruguay

Southeast Asia Treaty (8 nations)
1 United States
5 United Kingdom
11 France
36 New Zealand
37 Australia
38 Philippines
41 Thailand
42 Pakistan

ANZUS (Australia–New Zealand–United States) Treaty (3 nations)
1 United States
36 New Zealand
37 Australia

Philippine Treaty (bilateral)
1 United States
38 Philippines

Republic of China (Taiwan) (bilateral)
1 United States
43 Republic of China (Taiwan)

Republic of Korea (South Korea) Treaty (bilateral)
1 United States
40 Republic of Korea

282

selves. Their concern was motivated in part by the possibility that a strong United Nations organization might impose its collective will on smaller nations.

The American states to the south followed a two-pronged strategy in their quest for an inter-American community structure. The first thrust was to lobby for recognition of the fact that regional groupings should have first jurisdiction over regional problems. The results of their successful efforts were Articles 51 and 52 of the United Nations Charter which stated that disputes should first be remanded to the regional organization before the UN could consider them. The United States supported the Latin American governments because Articles 51 and 52 meant that regional problems could be handled without the threat of a veto by any of the other four permanent members of the Security Council, especially the U.S.S.R. These articles further denied to the Soviet Union the legal rights to bring embarrassing or potentially explosive problems in Central and South America to world attention.

The American nations to the South composed approximately one-third of the members of the United Nations when it was first established. Articles 51 and 52, therefore, were tailored to the needs of Latin America since no other region was readily identifiable within the United Nations structure. Europe was divided between East and West and the unborn Afro-Asian nations were under colonial rule.

The second prong of Latin American strategy was to build an identifiable regional structure once provisions were made for regional primacy within the UN Charter. This objective was achieved by three treaties: (1) the Act of Chapultepec, (2) the Organization of American States, and (3) the Rio Pact.

The Act of Chapultepec

The Act of Chapultepec, negotiated in March 1945 in Mexico City, declared that all nations in the Western Hemisphere juridically were equal and sovereign. The signatories agreed to respect the inviolability of each other's territory and to conisder an act of aggression against one as an attack on all. While the Central and South American states wanted to maintain their special relationship to the United States, they also wanted legal safeguards on their own sovereign equality within the inter-American system. The Act of Chapultepec guaranteed juridical equality at a time when the Latin American states were willing to accept American hegemony over the region and to prohibit political influence in the area from any state except the U.S.

The Pan American Union

However, the inter-American system lacked a political structure or a decision-making body that could qualify under Articles 51 and 52 of the

United Nations Charter. The Pan American Union existed, but its antecedents were primarily economic; the original "International Union of American Republics" was established in 1889 as a bureau for the collection and distribution of commercial information. Post-World War II events dictated needs for an enlarged organization with powers and duties beyond gathering and dispersing economic data. Two years following Chapultepec and two years preceding the North Atlantic Treaty, the United States and its southern neighbors framed a 1947 treaty of alliance and a regional security organization, the Organization of American States.

The Rio Treaty

The Rio Treaty, also signed in 1947, bound its signatories to come to the aid of each other in the event of an attack on any Latin American nation, as did Chapultepec. The differences between the Chapultepec and Rio agreements were two-fold. First, the Rio Treaty extended protection to certain non-Latin American areas in the Western hemisphere. Treaty members could respond to an attack on Iceland, for example. Second, the Rio agreement was coupled with a formalized structure, the Organization of American States (OAS).

Patterns of U.S.–Latin American Relations

Patterns of Neglect and Interest. Following the Chapultepec and Rio conferences, U.S. attitudes toward Latin America oscillated between long periods of neglect and brief periods of interest. During the first period of neglect (1948–1953), American attention was directed to other parts of the world—Europe, the Far East, and Middle East—where crises were considered much more important. In 1954, Communism's first threat in the hemisphere quickly brought back U.S. interest in inter-American problems.

The apparent drift toward Communism in Guatemala ended six years of U.S. neglect. The American response was to mobilize OAS support against Communism and to convince its members that intervention was the only answer to ridding the hemisphere of this political contagion. The first objective was achieved at Caracas when Secretary of State Dulles pushed for a resolution declaring that the presence of "International Communism" in the Inter-American community was an act of aggression under the terms of the Rio Pact. The OAS members were less than enthusiastic about Dulles' move, but eventually they supported it.

Implementing the Caracas Doctrine (as it came to be called) was a more difficult task. The OAS membership refused to brand Guatemala an agent of "International Communism"; the Latin American states were unwilling to unseat the government of Guatemala by force. In the face of OAS refusal to act on the Caracas Doctrine, the Eisenhower administration allowed the CIA to finance a coup. The Guatemalan government was overthrown, although the credit should be given to the regular Guatemalan army and not to the CIA invaders whose efforts were only minimally effective. Again the perceived threat of Communism generated American concern.

With Communism in retreat in the hemisphere, Washington slipped into another period of neglect (1955–1958). In 1958, Vice President Nixon toured Latin American countries and was greeted by stones, spittle, and anti-American sentiment. If Nixon's treatment jarred the sensitivities of the American government and people, the successful revolution of Fidel Castro early in 1959 confirmed their worst suspicions. Washington initially welcomed Castro, but began to cool toward him until diplomatic relations were broken in January 1961.

Much of what follows has already been discussed in earlier chapters of this book: the 1961 Bay of Pigs invasion attempt and the 1962 Cuban missile crisis. The OAS was largely ignored throughout these crises or was used to make American unilateral decisions appear to be legitimate regional decisions. The pattern that the Guatemala incident set was clearly ingrained in American policy; if the OAS dragged its feet on issues that Washington considered important, the United States would take unilateral action. OAS approval gave American policy a facade of multilateralism.

Patterns of Policy toward Revolutions. Another pattern that developed in U.S.–Latin American relations was the American tendency to consider any revolution to the Left to be Communist or Communist-inspired. The 1954 Guatemalan and the 1961 Cuban episodes illustrate this pattern, as does the 1965 intervention into the Dominican Republic.[3] Washington's inability to distinguish among gradations of leftist leaders in Latin America has led to a general lumping of all revolutionaries into the category of "Communist." This behavioral pattern, of course, is not limited to Latin America.

THE NORTH ATLANTIC TREATY ORGANIZATION

Steps toward NATO

When Winston Churchill suggested an Anglo-American alliance to James Byrnes in 1946, the American Secretary of State used unambiguous language to indicate that the United States was not interested. In the next two years, the European nations negotiated two smaller alliances that became building blocks of the 1949 North Atlantic Treaty.[4]

In 1947, France and Great Britain signed the Dunkirk Treaty, a defensive alliance aimed at Germany. A year later, the Dunkirk signatories joined with the Benelux nations (Belgium, The Netherlands, and Luxembourg) in the Brussels Treaty. While Article VII stated that the contracting parties would convene to discuss "the attitude to be adopted and the steps to be taken in case of a renewal by Germany of an aggressive policy," the signatories also had the Soviet Union in mind as a possible source of aggression. The Czechoslovakia coup d'etat occurred one month prior to the March 1948 signing of the Brussels Treaty, and the Berlin blockade began three months later.

The Vandenberg Resolution approved by the U.S. Senate in June 1948 indicated an American interest in participating with European nations in a regional alliance. Authored by Michigan Senator Arthur H. Vandenberg, the resolution recommended that the United States become associated with "such regional and other collective arrangements as are based on continuous and effective self-help and material aid." Negotiations on the North Atlantic Treaty were begun, and the document was finished and promulgated in March 1949 with 12 states signing it: the five Brussels Treaty nations (France, Great Britain, and the Benelux nations), Canada, the United States, Denmark, Iceland, Italy, Norway, and Portugal. Greece and Turkey acceded to the treaty in 1952 and the Federal Republic of Germany, in 1955.

Organizing the North Atlantic Treaty. While various steps were taken in 1949 and 1950 toward a common framework and policy among the North Atlantic Treaty signatories (e.g., Dwight Eisenhower was appointed Supreme Allied Commander in 1950), the organizational aspect was officially added at the Ottawa conference of September 1951 in an "Agreement on the Status of the North Atlantic Treaty Organization, National Representatives and International Staff." Thus, NATO, as a permanent organization, was established two years after the treaty was signed.

The organizational aspect made NATO a unique alliance: a joint command was established with an attempt to integrate weapons and battle plans. It gave the alliance an administrative structure, similar to an international organization such as the United Nations. It was this unique aspect to which the French objected a decade later.

Issues within the NATO Alliance

"Disarray" came to be the word to describe the North Atlantic Treaty Organization in the 1960s. The alliance developed internal dialogue which often reached the level of heated controversy over several issues.

The Soviet Threat. The major issue among NATO's members is the extent and nature of the Soviet threat. The image of Soviet aggression, born during the late 1940s, was reinforced by the Korean War—at least the Americans perceived Korea as a case of Soviet-supported and Soviet-instigated aggression. In the midst of the Far Eastern conflict, the United States also set about to build a credible presence in Europe. Korea, then, stimulated the Truman administration to shore up an area on the other side of the world. The Americans evidently felt that Korea was only a feint, with Europe the major Soviet target. So real was the threat of

Soviet aggression in Europe, that the decision was made to rearm Germany. In a classic example of reinforcement and counter-reinforcement, the Soviet Union built the Warsaw Pact in response to German rearmament and the threat of German aggression. The Warsaw Pact, in turn, reinforced American fears of Soviet conventional strength.

Is the Soviet threat to Western Europe a reality in the 1970s? The Soviet threat, essentially abstract and difficult to evaluate, has certainly changed from the 1940s. The 500,000 Russian troops in East Europe do not compare with the large Russian armies of World War II that occupied East European states. The East European states, now reconstructed after being devastated by countless battles between retreating Germans and the victorious Red armies, enjoy a measure of independence as seen in the foreign policies of Albania, Yugoslavia, and Rumania.

Rather than asking if the Soviet threat exists, American decision makers must ask: How large a risk is the United States willing to assume on the basis of a modified threat? "Risk" refers to the reduction of American commitments in Europe without corresponding Soviet reductions in Eastern Europe. If the United States qualifies its commitment, would the U.S.S.R. attempt a test of will and nerve that might bring the world to the brink of World War III? The American government has been reluctant to entertain any suggestions that unilaterally would weaken NATO. If American strength is reduced, it should be accomplished through mutual reductions of Soviet capabilities in the region.

The Issue of German Military Might. A second issue raised by NATO is German rearmament. The West German armed forces in the early 1970s numbered 450,000 men. While not the largest army of the alliance membership (the U.S., France, and Turkey have larger forces), it has the largest number of men committed to NATO defenses. Should NATO be dissolved, what would be done with the German army? Its creation was accompanied by promises to Europeans, who experienced two German-instigated wars in 25 years, that NATO's integrative command would guarantee that the new German armaments would be restricted to defensive functions. NATO is often supported, therefore, by decision makers who no longer see the alliance as relevant to Soviet foreign policy designs, but who have no viable alternative to house the modern German military might.

To what extent the German government itself is willing to invest all its security in NATO is an open question. In August 1970, the Bonn government signed a nonaggression pact with the U.S.S.R. While this step does not necessarily mean that the Germans have shifted the basis for their security from the alliance, it is one indication that their view of the Soviet threat has modified to the point that it can be met by a variety of different diplomatic instruments.

Conventional versus Nuclear Weaponry. A third issue within the alliance is the allocation of resources for conventional or nuclear weaponry. The United States spends almost 10 percent of its Gross National Product (GNP) on defense. No other alliance partner approaches this figure, except Portugal (at 8 percent), whose government until 1974 was a dictatorship that required rigid internal security. Most of the alliance partners spend less than 5 percent of their GNP on defense. To the American mind, the United States is bearing too heavy a burden as a free-world defender while the nations of Europe, especially the Common Market countries, are prospering under the aegis of American protection. As a result, the American government would like the European states to contribute more to the support of United States troops stationed in Europe. Moreover, the American government has consistently argued that Europeans should spend their money on conventional arms rather than undertaking expensive programs to develop nuclear weapons.

NATO Strategy: Sword, Shield, Pause

NATO's strategic planning divided allied military capability into *sword* and *shield* forces. The shield force was the conventional land army that the United States encouraged the West European states to build; the sword was the nuclear strike forces of the United States and Great Britain that remained outside the NATO command structure. The shield forces were an integral part of NATO and were commanded by an American general from the very beginning of the organization.

Assuming that a Soviet conventional thrust across central Europe had a very high probability factor, Western strategists hoped that NATO's shield could meet and hold Russian aggression as far to the east as possible. If successful, the Soviet leaders would then be saddled with the decision of escalating the conflict from a limited conventional to an unlimited nuclear level. Should the U.S.S.R. decide that national objectives warranted escalation, then the sword forces of the United States Strategic Air Command and the British Royal Air Force Bomber Command would attack the Soviet heartland.

These plans solidified in the early 1960s and were dubbed "forward strategy" and "pause theory." By meeting the Soviet thrust as far to the east as possible, NATO would respect the fears of Western Europeans (particularly West Germans) of having their homeland occupied by the Russian armies or churned up by a wide-ranging conflict in which the NATO armies would fight a series of rear guard actions. Shield forces of the forward strategy would be equipped with tactical nuclear weapons in the event that the conflict escalated from the conventional level.

According to the pause theory, the anticipated stalemate ensuing after NATO and Soviet bloc conventional forces had met in the field would be a critical period for both sides. The purpose of the pause is to afford Soviet leaders an opportunity to count the costs of aggression, especially the risks of escalating to the nuclear level. The Western nations would hope that the Russians would be dissuaded from continuing their aggression and persuaded not to use nuclear weapons to break the stalemate.

Although it may seem that the chief benefactor of forward strategy and the pause theory is the U.S.S.R., who could initiate a conventional attack without fear of immediate nuclear retaliation, the United States also accrues major advantages. First, Washington has argued that American taxpayers should not be required to pay for troops comprising the shield because the United States shoulders a much larger burden of the sword nuclear threat. And second, the forward strategy–pause plan gives the United States a credible non-nuclear option to a non-nuclear Soviet attack in Western Europe. Rather than facing a decision to unleash a nuclear attack in response to a Soviet conventional thrust, the American government has more flexibility. Previously, the only option open was to respond immediately with U.S. nuclear strike forces because conventional strength was not available. With a strong conventional force of its own, the Western powers could afford to meet the Russians at a subnuclear level of conflict.

French Criticisms of NATO

Criticisms of the forward strategy and pause theory have usually come from French military leaders, especially General Charles de Gaulle, French President during the 1958–1968 decade. The French point out that a Soviet attack on the West would not begin with a conventional thrust across Central Europe, but rather with an all-out missile attack on the United States with the objective of neutralizing the American nuclear strike force. The Russians would lead with a missile, not a tank, if they intended to start World War III.

American attempts to encourage, cajole, and badger large European commitments to the ranks of the conventional NATO shield became largely meaningless under the Gaullist argument.

The French strategists further contend that France should have the same right to build a nuclear strike force independent of the NATO command, as did the United States and Great Britain. The United States' argument that its financial resources were too heavily invested in nuclear hardware for additional commitments to land forces overlooks the fact that the Americans would have built nuclear credibility to deter Soviet actions even if NATO had never been organized. Because the Strategic Air Command primarily serves American, not European, interests, the French cannot be certain that the American nuclear capability will be committed to issues of supreme importance to France but only of peripheral importance to the national interests of the United States. American leaders, responsible as they are, would not risk unleashing a nuclear holocaust on their own heartland for policy objectives of little consequence to them.

The French argue that the Europeans must consider their long-term interests. While appreciating American intentions to defend Europe from Soviet aggression, the French believe that the New Europe must look to the time that the American military umbrella is removed. Can the Europeans be assured that American intentions to fight will be stated with as much fervor in the 1970s and 1980s as they were in the 1940s and 1950s? The long-term interests of European nations dictate an alternative to the American nuclear umbrella: either building their own nuclear forces or constructing a detente with the Soviet Union, or both.

DeGaulle's disenchantment with NATO eventually motivated him to withdraw French forces from the alliance's command structure. The French continued to adhere to the 1949 treaty provisions, but they took their leave of the organization that had been superimposed on the treaty in 1951. Another signatory, Greece, withdrew its forces in 1974 when Turkey invaded Cyprus.

THE CENTRAL TREATY ORGANIZATION

The Central Treaty Organization (CENTO) is unique among the West's regional organizations in that the United States is not legally a member, although in practice it operates as such.[5]

Alliances and Israel

The Americans early perceived the Middle East as a primary target for Soviet expansion. Indeed, the Cold War began in the Middle East long before disputes over Eastern Europe surfaced. The Russian attempt to assume a measure of control over the Turkish Straits, the Greek civil war, the presence of Soviet troops in Northern Iran, and the Russian request for a part in the trusteeship of Libya were all read in Washington as concrete indications of Soviet imperialist designs.

The emergence of an independent Israel in 1948 introduced into the Middle Eastern political picture a consideration which the United States believed had nothing to do with the threat of aggression. The Arab leaders strongly disagreed: to them, Israel was the primary source of imperialism in the region, not the Soviet Union. This picture was further complicated by Israel's rapidly assuming the posture of a client state of the United States. Foreign aid from the American government and private investment from the American Jewish community were vital to the continued existence of the new state. Israeli political life may have been won on the battlefield, but its economic life depended on American monetary support. The Truman administration earned a reputation for being pro-Israeli in its foreign policy.

The Tripartite Declaration of 1950

The Western powers—the U.S., United Kingdom, and France—attempted to stabilize the Arab–Israeli situation through the Tripartite Declaration of May 25, 1950. First, an arms balance was declared in effect in the Middle East. The Western powers refused to supply arms to Middle Eastern nations unless the purchasers promised not to use them against neighbors; by implication, the arms could be used only against the Russians. The beneficiary of this provision was Israel, who emerged from the 1948–1949 conflict with strong armies that more than matched any that the Arabs could put in the field, with the exception of Jordan's Arab Legion. The Arab states, especially Egypt, needed arms if they were to balance Israeli strength. Second, the three powers guaranteed the "frontiers or armistice lines" against violation by any state. This meant that an Arab attack on Israel to renew the armed conflict would be met by Anglo-American-French resistance. Few observers believed in 1950 that Israel would be willing to take on her Arab neighbors in the future, which she did in 1956, 1967, and 1973.

The Tripartite Declaration failed to bring stability to the region. The agreement had the effect, intended or not, of guaranteeing the territorial integrity of Israel at the boundaries drawn where the 1948–1949 fighting stopped. The Arab states refused to accept the armistice lines drawn by the cease fire as the legitimate boundaries of Israel because these lines granted Israel more territory than prescribed by the United Nations resolution on partition. Moreover, the Arab states refused to accept military weakness vis-à-vis Israel as a permanent characteristic of the Middle East scene. The tripartite agreement evidently envisioned an arms balance occurring when Israeli strength matched the *combined* might of her Arab neighbors. This meant that the strength of any single Arab state, such as Egypt, would always be inferior to that of Israel. Calculation of military strength between two nations is difficult; calculating *regional* strength is all but impossible.

The Baghdad Pact

The Truman administration attempted to construct an alliance system in the Middle East, but failed. Secretary of State Dulles interred the idea of a regional defense organization but did express an interest in the alliance of "northern tier" countries bordering the Soviet Union (Turkey, Iran, and Pakistan).

Dulles did little to put together the northern tier alliance. It remained for a bilateral arrangement between Turkey and a non-northern tier country, Iraq, to begin the process in February 1955. Later the British, Iranian, and Pakistani governments acceded to the agreement, but the United States resisted pressure to join. The Eisenhower administration was motivated by a desire to be more impartial in the Middle East than the Truman administration had been. Egypt's President Gamal Nasser might be antagonized, Washington believed, because he opposed the formation of the alliance. The State Department also feared that Israel might ask for a formal alliance relationship if the United States became a member of the Baghdad Pact.

The Baghdad Pact lost Baghdad when the Iraqi revolution of July 1958 brought into power a government whose views on the alliance were closer to Nasser's. The alliance was renamed CENTO.

U.S. policy toward CENTO was motivated by a desire to stay out of the area because the northern tier soon became one of over- not under-commitment. By 1958 Turkey was already a member of NATO; Pakistan, of SEATO; and Britain, of both. In addition, the United States negotiated bilateral alliances with all three northern tier nations. United States reluctance to become an official member of CENTO, largely due to its straddling diplomacy toward Egypt and Israel, is one of the most bizarre episodes in United States diplomacy.

Development of CENTO in the 1960s and 1970s

The Kennedy administration encouraged the evolution of the Central Treaty Organization from a military alliance to an economic instrument. Although the United States was not officially a member of CENTO, the American government did join its four major committees and continued to send an "observer" to the annual Council of Ministers meeting. It was quite clear to the Kennedy administration that CENTO forces were not formidable obstacles to Soviet aggression, if and when the Soviet army marched into the Middle East. Even the Turkish army lacked military balance (possessing a weak tactical air force and armor) to be a major threat to the Soviet Union. Therefore, CENTO gradually shifted from a military to an economic emphasis.

CENTO represents an alliance structure that has held together despite its major patron's official reluctance to become a member and despite its obvious military deficiencies. CENTO has survived by developing functions other than defense against Soviet aggression. Perhaps other alliances can learn the lesson of CENTO: that a military alliance should develop internal benefits for its members that are broader than defense and security. In this way, the alliance will continue to exist (at least in modified form) and perform vital services to the region.

SOUTHEAST ASIA TREATY ORGANIZATION

The Founding of SEATO

Unlike NATO, which grew logically from two smaller alliances in Europe, and CENTO, which developed at the instigation of nations in the region, the Southeast Asia Treaty Organization (SEATO) was an overnight offspring of a hastily arranged conference.[6] Its stimulus was the Geneva Conference of 1954, which ended the French presence in Indochina and created three new states: Laos, Cambodia, and Vietnam. Vietnam was "temporarily" divided; elections scheduled for 1956 were to unite the two halves and determine the government's leadership.

John Foster Dulles interpreted the Geneva accords as a Western setback and as one more indication of the People's Republic of China's aggressive designs. His response was two-fold: (1) to support right-wing, anti-Communist governments in Laos and South Vietnam and (2) to construct a regional alliance in the area. Consequently, only one-and-one-half months after the Geneva Conference disbanded, Dulles was able to persuade seven nations to meet with him in Manila to discuss a regional alliance for SoutheastAsia.

With little preparation, Australia, the Philippines, Great Britain, France, New Zealand, Thailand, Pakistan, and the United States engaged in the detailed negotiating required to form an alliance. The architect of the treaty was Dulles; his intense personal interest motivated him to handle much of the negotiating himself, and to hammer out a document acceptable to all parties. Dulles set forth his goal for the Manila conference in his opening statement: the contracting parties must band together so that "an attack upon the treaty area would occasion a reaction so united, so strong, and so well placed that the aggressor would lose more than it could hope to gain."

Unusual Characteristics of SEATO

The Southeast Asia Collective Defense Treaty is a political animal quite different from the other three regional groupings—the OAS, NATO, and CENTO. To begin with, SEATO spreads its alliance umbrella over non-signatories, i.e., the three Indochina nations, Cambodia, Laos, and Vietnam. According to the Protocol accompanying the treaty, any of the new Indochina states could request the intervention of the combined military might of the signatories. Since the Geneva Conference designated these three states as "neutral," SEATO, in effect, projected Western protection over an area that should have been kept out of the Cold War.

A second unusual characteristic of SEATO is its attempt to suppress internal subversion. SEATO is the only alliance with a provision against guerrilla activities written into its treaty. Alliances normally are aimed at halting overt aggression, in which case the attacking nation and its armed forces are readily identifiable. Unsuccessful French efforts against the Vietminh in Indochina demonstrated that the major threat in the region was not a conventional attack, but subversion and counter-insurgency warfare.

Problems in SEATO

The first problem that SEATO faced arose at the conference itself. Would SEATO establish a structure the same as that of NATO? Surprisingly, the United States, which pushed and cajoled for a common command structure in the North Atlantic, resisted all efforts to do likewise in Southeast Asia. The Thai government wanted member states to contribute troops and station them in Thailand; the Australian government, as a minimum concession, wanted a segment of U.S. power committed to the region. Dulles resisted both attempts.

The Manila conference also dealt with conflicts that a contracting party might have with a non-Communist nation; specifically, this referred to the friction between India and Pakistan. In an Understanding attached to the treaty, the U.S. delegation declared that it interpreted the treaty to offer protection to the three protocol nations and the signatories against attacks from Communist states only.

History of SEATO

The Laotian Crisis. The Southeast Asia Treaty Organization officially began functioning in February 1955; it faced its first challenge within months after its inception. The Communist forces in Laos, the Pathet Lao, began winning victories in the field against government armies. Thailand asked that SEATO intervene, a request made on the basis of three conditions: (1) that Laos was under the protection of the protocol; (2) that internal subversion was involved (although aggression by an external state was not); and (3) that the source of the subversion was Communism.

The immediate weakness of SEATO was quite evident. The request for the organization's intervention had not come from the protocol state itself. Also, opposition to the government was not entirely Communist, since the supporters of the neutralist prince, Souvanna Phouma, also opposed the group in power. The strategy for defeating an insurgency, a task the United States found difficult in the 1960s, had not been decided on by the SEATO powers. As a result, the crisis in Laos was met with inactivity.

The Quemoy–Matsu Crisis. The second crisis actually did not fall within a SEATO area of concern, but Secretary Dulles felt that the organization's united stand was needed. In 1958, it appeared that the People's Republic of China was ready to claim the two offshore islands, Quemoy and Matsu, that had remained in the hands of the Nationalist government of Taiwan since 1949. Here was a clear example—in Dulles' mind, at least —of Chinese Communist aggression involving the palpable expansion of the Chinese outside their borders. But stretching SEATO's umbrella to cover Quemoy and Matsu was too much for even the Thai government, the most avid supporter of the alliance.

SEATO's Demise. With the passing of Dulles in 1959, strong American backing of the alliance also died. Secretary of State Christian Herter rarely mentioned SEATO, even though the position of the Laotian government became less and less tenable as the strength of the Pathet Lao increased. The new Kennedy administration met the Pathet Lao threat by diplomatic, rather than military, initiatives. The United States dropped its support of the Laotian government, and instead backed the neutralist faction headed by Souvanna Phouma. In 1962, the Geneva Conference reconvened and by treaty recognized the neutrality of Laos and Souvanna Phouma as head of state.

By this time SEATO's demise was obvious. American diplomatic problems with France and Pakistan (over U.S. arms to India) meant that unanimity among the alliance nations was an impossibility on all issues except a direct Chinese or Soviet attack. To ease Thai fears, and as an admission that SEATO was not a viable alliance, the United States negotiated a bilateral treaty of defense with Thailand in 1962. Thus, the only member of the alliance not covered by another alliance arrangement was protected by Washington's umbrella.

SEATO and Vietnam

The dead SEATO alliance was resurrected, in spirit at least, in 1964 as American commitments to Vietnam were increased. During the Eisenhower and Kennedy years, increased military support for South Vietnam was justified by bilateral executive agreements. On October 23, 1954, President Eisenhower wrote Prime Minister Ngo Dinh Diem that the United States was willing to support the South Vietnamese government against "enemies without aided by their subversive collaborators within." This same theme was echoed in Kennedy's December 14, 1961, letter to Diem, at that time President of the Republic of Vietnam. The attacks on Diem's government, he wrote, were "supported and directed from the outside by the authorities at Hanoi."

The murders of Diem and Kennedy, occurring within weeks of each other in November 1963, brought to power new leaders in both the United States and South Vietnam. In the United States, the peaceful and orderly transition from Vice-President to President contrasted sharply with the procession of military juntas that followed each other in Saigon. U.S. military, economic, and political commitments to South Vietnam continued to mount gradually during the Johnson administration; after the Gulf of Tonkin incident in August 1964, it escalated rapidly.

The use of SEATO as a legal basis to justify American intervention into Indochina raised a major legal problem: no meeting was held in which the signatories unanimously agreed that South Vietnam, a protocol state, had been invaded by an outside Communist nation or that an outside Communist state had fomented revolution within South Vietnam. Washington interpreted the treaty's Article IV, which requires unanimity among all signatories, to mean that unanimous approval was necessary only of the interpretation of the *treaty*, not of the interpretation of the *threat*. If all members do not interpret an event as a threat, those signatories that do may act unilaterally. The Thai government supported the American position, while the French and British governments argued that unanimity was required for interpretation of both treaty provisions and threats. The question of legality did not hinder the American military buildup. The legal justification for U.S. intervention in the Vietnamese conflict, however, cannot be based on SEATO.

SEATO's Future

Of the four regional alliances with which the United States has direct or indirect affiliation, SEATO appears to have the bleakest future. Created hastily, impotent from the first, and interred by post-Dulles decision makers, it was ignored and put to questionable use by the United States as the Vietnamese conflict escalated.

After Vietnam, what? The alliance has not found a sufficient raison d'être as yet. It is doubtful that it will in the future.

DEFENSE ARRANGEMENTS IN EAST ASIA

In addition to these four major defense arrangements, the American government has negotiated one small regional alliance and several bilateral alliances in the East Asian region.[7] ANZUS brings together the U.S., Australia, and New Zealand. With the demise of British power in the post-war period, Australia and New Zealand, both Commonwealth nations, sought to be covered by the American nuclear umbrella.

Bilateral alliances were negotiated with Taiwan, South Korea, and Japan in the 1950s. All three states at the time were "high risk" areas because their military strength was minimal. These bilateral arrangements are evidence that diplomatic instruments other than regional alliances were available to American decision makers during the Cold War years.

CHANGE AND ALLIANCE POLITICS

In the 1940s and 1950s, the assumptions upon which U.S. policy toward regional alliances was based were consonant with the image that U.S. decision makers possessed of the world around them. The U.S.S.R. and the People's Republic of China were viewed as aggressive and the conflict between East and West was perceived as at hand.

American misperceptions go beyond Russian and Chinese behavior. Europe, too, has changed. A need to reexamine NATO is necessitated by new conditions among European allies. American decision makers in the 1960s erroneously diagnosed Gaullism and therefore failed to address themselves to the true nature of European problems. The French problem was not DeGaulle's irascibility or his lack of appreciation of the Soviet military threat; it was his perception of the United States as a nation that showed too few of the characteristics that he expected to find in a world leader. American naive stumbling presented as much of a threat to French security as did the Soviet army.

It may well be the judgment of political analysts of the 21st century (assuming that world civilization lasts that long) that the decision-making process that produced the greatest number of deleterious mistakes in the Cold War era was American alliance policy. U.S. activities in the Middle East—based on the failure to realize that Israel, and not the U.S.S.R., was the primary Arab concern—rapidly drained the reservoir of good will toward the American nation built up prior to 1948. SEATO thrust American power into a region that Washington's decision makers did not understand and that involved few vital U.S. national interests. The result was the longest and costliest, but unvictorious, war in American military history. Washington's use of the Organization of American States to legitimize U.S. policy in the Western Hemisphere has been resented by OAS members. Friends used as an instrument of policy or forced into taking positions that they dislike should not be expected to remain allies too long. The methods used by Dulles to push the British into SEATO illustrate this point.[8]

Traditionally, alliances are made for relatively short periods of time. They bring together states whose mutual interests happen to coincide for the moment. Since foreign policy is not static, alliances tend to break apart after the immediate danger has passed. For the Americans, new to international coalition building, alliances apparently were similar to marriage: made in heaven and meant to last eternally. Other states, especially in Europe, knew better; it remains for Washington to learn the same lesson.

NOTES

1. For a general discussion of alliances and U.S. foreign policy, consult: Arnold Wolfers, *Alliance Policy in the Cold War* (Baltimore: Johns Hopkins Press, 1959); Robert Rothstein, *Alliances and Small Powers* (New York: Columbia University Press, 1968); Robert E. Osgood, *Alliances and American Foreign Policy* (Baltimore: Johns Hopkins Press, 1968); and George Liska, *Alliances and the Third World* (Baltimore: Johns Hopkins Press, 1968).
2. For additional information on the OAS, consult: Ann Thomas, *The Organization of American States* (Dallas, Texas: Southern Methodist University Press, 1963); John C. Drier, *The Organization of American States and the Hemisphere Crisis* (New York: Harper & Row, 1962); Gordon Connell-Smith, *The Inter-American System* (New York: Oxford University Press, 1966); Norman A. Bailey (ed.), *Latin America: Politics, Economics, and Hemispheric Security* (New York: Praeger, 1965); Jerome Slater, *The OAS and United States Foreign Policy* (Columbus: Ohio State University Press, 1967); and Gene A. Sessions, "The Multilateralization of the Monroe Doctrine: The Rio Treaty, 1947," *World Affairs* 136 (Winter 1973–74): 259–274.
3. Abraham F. Lowenthal, *The Dominican Intervention* (Cambridge: Harvard University Press, 1972).

4. The following books offer additional analysis of NATO: Timothy W. Stanley, *NATO in Transition: Future of the Atlantic Alliance* (New York: Praeger, 1965); Massimo Salvadori, *NATO: A Twentieth Century Community of Nations* (New York: Van Nostrand, 1957); Robert E. Osgood, *NATO: The Entangling Alliance* (Chicago: University of Chicago Press, 1962); Klaus Knorr, *NATO and American Security* (Princeton: Princeton University Press, 1959); Henry A. Kissinger, *The Troubled Partnership: A Re-appraisal of the Atlantic Alliance* (New York: McGraw-Hill, 1965); Lawrence Kaplan, *NATO and the Policy of Containment* (Lexington, Mass.: D. C. Heath, 1968); William T. R. Fox and Annette B. Fox, *NATO and the Range of American Choice* (New York: Columbia University Press, 1967); Alastair Buchan, *NATO in the 1960's: The Implications of Interdependence* (New York: Praeger, 1965); Edwin H. Fedder, *NATO: The Dynamics of Alliance in the Postwar World* (New York: Dodd, Mead, and Co., 1972); Ben T. Moore, *NATO and the Future of Europe* (New York: Harper & Row, 1958); and David Calleo, *The Atlantic Fantasy: the U.S., NATO, and Europe* (Baltimore: Johns Hopkins Press, 1970).

5. For more information, consult Dankwort Rustow, "Defense of the Near East," *Foreign Affairs* 34 (1956): 271–286; John C. Campbell, *Defense of the Middle East: Problems of American Policy*, rev. ed. (New York: Praeger, 1960); M. Perlmann, "Facts Versus Pacts," *Middle Eastern Affairs* 7 (December 1955): 372–382; and Majid Khadduri, "The Problem of Regional Security in the Middle East," *Middle East Journal* 11 (Winter 1957): 12–22.

6. The following books discuss SEATO: Fred Greene, *U.S. Policy and the Security of Asia* (New York: McGraw-Hill, 1968); George Modelski (ed.), *SEATO: Six Studies* (Melbourne: F. W. Cheshire, 1962); W. Macmahon Ball, "A Political Re-examination of SEATO," *International Organization* 12 (Winter 1958): 17–25; August C. Miller, Jr., "SEATO: Segment of Collective Security," *Naval Institute Proceedings* 86 (February 1960): 50–62; Donald E. Nuechterlein, "Thailand and SEATO: A Ten-Year Appraisal," *Asian Survey* 4 (December 1964): 1174–1181; Nathaniel Peffer, "Regional Security in Southeast Asia," *International Organization* 8 (1954): 311–315; M. Ladd Thomas, "A Critical Appraisal of SEATO," *Western Political Quarterly* 10 (December 1957): 926–936; Guy J. Pauker, "Southeast Asia as a Problem Area in the Next Decade," *World Politics* 11 (April 1959): 325–345.

7. Perhaps "three-and-one-half" regional alliances would be a better quantitative expression, in light of the U.S.'s one-foot-in and one-foot-out relationship with CENTO.

8. *See* Charles O. Lerche, Jr., "The U.S., Great Britain and SEATO: A Case Study of Fait Accompli," *Journal of Politics* 18 (1956): 459–477.

16

Patterns of American Diplomacy in International Law and Organization

International organizations and alliances are separate entities based on separate concepts. The rationale for international organizations, such as the League of Nations and the United Nations, is collective security; for regional organizations, such as NATO and the OAS, it is collective self-defense. American leaders were drawn early in the post-World War II period to collective security as the concept around which to build a peaceful world. As it became obvious that collective security embodied in the United Nations would not adequately meet the perceived threat from the Soviet Union, Washington turned to building regional and bilateral self-defense arrangements.

THE UNITED STATES AND THE UNITED NATIONS

The UN and the Balance of Power

Initial American Reaction to the UN. After the 1945 Yalta Conference, President Franklin Roosevelt said of the United Nations: "It spells the end of the system of unilateral actions and exclusive alliances and spheres of influence and the balance of power, and all other expedients which have been tried for centuries—and failed."[1] Roosevelt's attitude summarizes the initial American response to the United Nations: it was a development counter to all the diplomatic patterns that had plunged the world into war.[2] The balance of power with its "exclusive alliances and spheres of influence" would be replaced by an international organization, including only "peace-loving" nations, and recognizing all regions of the world as equally independent of domination by large nations.[3]

The United States and the League of Nations. This initial response to the United Nations contrasted sharply with the American attitude toward the League of Nations.[4] The official view of the League is best summarized by Calvin Coolidge's remarks in 1923:

> The league exists as a foreign agency. We hope it will be helpful. But the United States sees no reason to limit its own freedom and independence of action by joining it. We will do well to recognize this basic fact of all national affairs and govern ourselves accordingly.[5]

Coolidge's words mirror the traditional pattern of unilateralism in American diplomacy, a pattern characterized by the United States seeking to maintain the widest possible latitude in pursuing its foreign policy goals. The League, then, "as a foreign agency," would restrict the freedom of action that the American government would otherwise enjoy.

UN or Alliance? The interpretation of the UN by American leaders tended to follow the same basic logic, but with a twist: the United Nations, rather than inhibiting American action, would tend to permit U.S. policy to be active in another, important arena of diplomacy. In part, this position evolved from the realization that the UN was populated by states that the U.S. saw as allies who would not pursue foreign policy lines too different from the U.S. Also, in part, the United States was protected by its early insistence on the veto in the Security Council. American leaders did not view the UN as a major restraint on the unilateralist foreign policy which had characterized traditional U.S. diplomacy.

Alternatives to building a strong international organization at the time were unacceptable to the United States. Winston Churchill's early attempts to convince Washington to form an alliance against the Soviet Union failed. Secretary of State James Byrnes in 1946 answered Churchill's invitation by declaring that the United States does not "seek security with the Soviet Union against Great Britain, or an alliance with Great Britain against the Soviet Union." Rather, he continued, an effort should be made through the UN "to secure equal justice for all nations and special privileges for no nation."[6] To practice the balance of power, playing off the British (who at that time appeared stronger militarily and economically than they actually were) against the Russians, was unthinkable to American leaders. To divide the world into spheres of influence was patently contrary to the moralism of American policy.

Contemporary View of the Balance of Power. Suspicion of the balance of power has not withered away in contemporary American diplomacy. John Kennedy in his 1961 Inaugural address invited the U.S.S.R. to join in "creating a new endeavor, not a new balance of power, but a new world of law, where the strong are just and the weak secure and the peace preserved." The traditional concept of the balance of power as a cause, rather than an inhibitor, of wars continued into the superpower era, despite the fact that the United States has constructed several coalitions since 1947.

To the American mind, the alliances that the United States joins are not part of the balance of power, while other nation's alliances may be construed as such.

The bipolar construct, or Cold War, that lasted from the late 1940s to the early 1960s encouraged a continuation of the unilateral approach to foreign policy that was characteristic of American diplomacy in the 19th and early 20th centuries. As British weaknesses became apparent in the early post-World War II period, American leaders viewed themselves as the sole bulwark against possible Soviet expansion. "The world is divided," President Truman declared in 1953, "not through our fault or failure, but by Soviet design."[7] In a 1959 address to the American nation, President Eisenhower attributed to the Soviet Union the power to create peace or disruptive incidents at will: "We have lived and will continue to live in a period where emergencies manufactured by the Soviets follow one another like beads on a string."[8]

The harshness of these statements, difficult to comprehend for Americans living this side of the Cold War, reflected the atmosphere of East–West hostility that existed. They also offered a justification for the American belief that the United States must provide leadership for all peace-loving nations in the UN.

Euphoria over the United Nations was quickly replaced by a realization that the UN was simply another arena for doing battle with the Soviet Union in the Cold War. The Soviet use of the veto was only a symptom of East–West differences that eventually hamstrung the UN. The United States government then turned to building a system of alliances to ensure its own security.

The UN and Aggression. The collective security approach, as expressed by the United Nations, depends on majority action. An act of aggression or breach of the peace is determined by a vote in the Security Council, a vote that assumes unanimity among the five permanent members: China, France, Great Britain, the U.S.S.R., and the United States. After the vote, all nations of the organization supposedly band together to form a solid and united phalanx against the aggressor. As the theory goes, the aggressor would then reevaluate his chances of success as he faced all other nations of the world.

Sanctions by the international organization against the aggressor nation are decided by voting. A crucial aspect of collective security is that the minority who voted against sanctions would willingly join the majority in punishing the outlaw state; there is no room for neutrals or for friends of the accused. It is on this point that collective security theory has floundered both in the League of Nations and in the United Nations.

U.S. Policy in the UN

In general, U.S.–UN relations can be divided into three periods during which American support has moved from an attitude of warm support to one of aloofness.

The UN as an Instrument of U.S. Policy: 1945–1955. During the first phase of U.S.–UN relations, the General Assembly was a "safe" place to bring up policy matters. Since the United States and its allies (primarily the Latin American and Western European states) constituted a majority in the UN, the American government usually could muster enough votes to support its proposals. In the Security Council, the Soviet veto effectively blocked most policy initiatives; thus, the U.S. encouraged a larger role for the General Assembly. The growth of the Secretary-General's power also was supported by the American government. From the American viewpoint, the UN was a reliable instrument of foreign policy. The actions of Communist states could be condemned and U.S. policy made "legitimate" by UN approval. In June 1950, for example, the UN approved the use of American force to halt North Korean aggression.

UN as an International Arena: 1955–1965. The end of the first phase of U.S.–UN relations may be dated from December 14, 1955, when 16 new members were admitted. Previously, U.S.–U.S.S.R. differences did not permit *en bloc* additions to the UN. The December 1955 decision broke the membership dikes and the Western complexion of the General Assembly gradually changed. No longer could the U.S. count on a favorable vote in the General Assembly. Issues that were embarrassing to American allies, such as colonial and disarmament questions, now were brought to the UN and debated. The U.S. could not put off debate and voting on the question of whether Peking or Taiwan was the representative of the Chinese people.

The UN became more of an international arena for debate on political issues of concern to the smaller states. Although the UN possesses little power to sanction actions by the large powers, it has encouraged the "give and take" of multilateral diplomacy. In addition, UN involvement in Middle Eastern and African problems provided an alternative to East–West intervention into areas of secondary importance to Soviet and American foreign policy.

The UN also contributed to world stability through non-political and less controversial activities which have brought about East–West cooperation when deep-seated ideological and strategic issues were divisive. The UN's functional commissions (e.g., on population, status of women) and specialized agencies (e.g., Universal Postal Union, World Health Organization) perform services to the international community without regard to political alignment.

UN and Disillusionment: 1965 to the Present. The contemporary troubles of the United Nations began with the peacekeeping operation in the Congo.[9] The Soviet Union, France, and several small nations objected to the General Assembly's decisions which became the legal basis for the UN's role in the Congo. The Russian and French governments argued that the Security Council alone could authorize peacekeeping activities, and that the Secretary General had assumed too much authority in carrying out the assembly's broad directives. The Russians and French refused to pay their assessments for the Congo operation.

Article 19 of the UN Charter states that a "member of the United Nations which is in arrears in the payment of its financial contributions to the organization shall have no vote in the General Assembly if the amount of its arrears equals or exceeds the amount of contributions due from it for the preceding two full years." The U.S.S.R. found itself in that position in December 1964 and the French in January 1965; the first major financial crisis faced the United Nations.

The French and Russian delegations contended that the UN Charter referred only to the regular budget and not to the peacekeeping operations. The U.S. delegates refused to accept this distinction and were supported by the International Court of Justice in an advisory opinion. Eventually, the American government retreated from its original position, and the UN permitted nations in arrears to keep their seats. Although the integrity of the United Nations was maintained (because two major powers were not expelled for failure to pay their bills), the UN was almost bankrupt. The UN survived only by floating a bond series, most of which was marketed in the United States.[10]

The increase in the Secretary General's power precipitated a constitutional crisis for the United Nations when the U.S.S.R. proposed a "troika" arrangement. The Secretariat would be divided into East, West, and Third World representatives, each with veto power. Not only would there be three secretary generals, but other key Secretariat decision-making positions would be split three ways. Whether the Russians were serious in proposing the "troika" arrangement is uncertain. The proposal may have been intended as a bargaining point for negotiations on the increased power of the Secretary General. It also could have been proposed for its shock effect, viz, to show the depth of Russian concern over the trends in the Secretariat. The American delegation joined with Third World nations in rejecting the "troika" proposal.

In the late 1960s the UN also proved to be an irritant to American policy in Vietnam. At first, the U.S. government made clear that it did not welcome the United Nations' concern over Vietnam. When the conflict began to drag on, the U.S. actively sought the UN's help in bringing the North Vietnamese to the conference table. However, the General Assembly was not willing to undertake a task that would prove as difficult as constructing a peaceful solution in the Middle East or the Congo. The American government occasionally showed its ire at UN Secretary General Kurt Waldheim's comments on U.S. diplomatic behavior. President Nixon publicly chastized Waldheim for his criticism of American bombing of North Vietnam in the early 1970s.

Since the UN mirrors the realities of the international system, it reflects a decline of American influence worldwide.[11] "Influence" is not easy to define and to operationalize, but the hypothesis here is that the economic, military, and political position of the United States eroded perceptibly in the 1960s. Incidents can be cited that give rise to this hypothesis: the chronic balance-of-payments problems; the inability to win, in a military sense, the guerrilla conflict in Vietnam; and the failure of the two-Chinas policy. Perhaps nothing so dramatically illustrates the American loss of political influence as the last example. The United States government attempted to persuade the UN membership to recognize the credentials of two competing Chinese governments, Peking and Taiwan, to represent the largest nation in the world. The vote in October 1971 rejecting the American proposal underscored the General Assembly's disinclination to follow the lead of the United States even on issues labeled as highly important by Washington.

Contemporary Issues of U.S.–UN Policy

As U.S. influence in the United Nations has diminished, American optimism about the UN's role has also decreased. This situation can be attributed to the general orientation of American foreign policy in the 1970s toward a reduced international commitment and to a general pique toward the UN over contemporary issues, unsuccessfully resolved from the American point-of-view.

Some of the issues appear to be quite small, but together they add up to a general disenchantment with the United Nations. In 1970, the United States abstained on the General Assembly vote for the UN budget. The American government was dissatisfied with the Third World's propensity to push the UN budget higher and higher in anticipation of the larger nations paying the bill. The 1971 budget was a 14 percent increase over the 1970 budget. The U.S.S.R. voted against the budget, and the U.S. and France abstained; together these three states accounted for over 50 percent of the total expenditures.

Following the October 1971 vote expelling the Republic of China and seating the People's Republic of China in its place, a reaction to the UN set in which eventually led to Congress voting in 1973 to reduce the American portion of the general budget from 30 to 25 percent. In 1970, Congress cut 3.7 million dollars from the 7.5 million dollars for the regular budget of the International Labor Organization. Congress was displeased with ILO's tendency to abandon its initial commitment to a tripartite representation of government, business, and labor.

The United States has been the largest contributor to UN peacekeeping operations, assuming almost one-half of the total cost. It has also been generous with the voluntary special programs, contributing on the average almost 40 percent of the total; some programs, such as the Children's Fund for Nigerian Relief, Vietnam programs, and the World Health Organization's activities, have been supported almost unilaterally by American funds.

U.S.–UN relations continued to deteriorate in the mid 1970s. With a delegate from the People's Republic of China on the Council and with France following a more independent course in world affairs, the United States found itself resorting to the veto power that it had insisted be written into the Charter. By 1974, the U.S. ambassador to the UN had cast several votes on issues supported by Russian, Chinese, and Third World nations. On these issues the French and British delegates either abstained (by choice or because they were a party to a dispute) or voted against the

American position. For example, the United States cast its first veto in the Security Council on a resolution that called for condemnation of the United Kingdom for failing to use force against Rhodesia.

Administration of U.S.–UN Policy

The American structure for implementing U.S. foreign policy through the UN is a twofold organization. One component is the State Department's Bureau of International Organization, which functions to give guidance to all U.S. diplomacy occurring through multilateral conferences. The U.S. attends over 600 conferences a year and belongs to 75 international and regional organizations. The bureau must prepare delegations for each conference and organization meeting; thus, its charge is much broader than providing policy guidance to the United States Mission to the United Nations, the second component of the structure.[12]

The U.S. Mission to the UN is the only American embassy on American soil and is headed by a permanent representative with the rank of an ambassador. The prestige of the U.S. ambassador to the United Nations is reflected in the presidential invitation to attend cabinet meetings.

The UN serves as a communication grid for states that have brought benefits to American foreign policy. The U.S. Mission to the UN serves as an important contact point with foreign nations and with other organizations associated with the United Nations (such as the Food and Agricultural Organization). One benefit, more important during the height of the Cold War, is that American and Soviet leaders can hold informal consultations during the October opening of the UN General Assembly session without publicity and fanfare; the American Secretary of State and Soviet Foreign Minister, in New York for the occasion, will usually meet. Heads of state from foreign nations often visit Washington to or from a trip to the General Assembly session.

For the United States, the UN serves as a meeting place for states with severed U.S. diplomatic ties. American relations with several small nations have been disrupted occasionally: Cuba, Egypt, Syria, and various Soviet bloc nations. When the People's Republic of China assumed the Chinese seat in October 1971, the UN began to serve as a formal meeting place for American and Chinese diplomats, since neither nation had recognized the legal existence of the other.

INTERNATIONAL LAW

International law evolves from several sources, one of which is international organization. The UN's International Court of Justice hands down decisions that become precedents for future cases (although they might not be followed by the disputants in later conflicts). The ICJ's decision on Soviet arrears was in the end ignored by Washington, where the request originated. Another source is the national court system of various nations. The U.S. Supreme Court's word on a variety of subjects has become part of the framework of international law.

Trends in International Law

As the United States matured to great-power status, the American concept of international law became more amorphous (*see* chapter 2). The pattern of legalism thus paralleled the pattern of foreign policy; goals shifted from specific to general ones as the U.S. moved from small- to great-power status. Several hypotheses are offered to explain this phenomenon. Perhaps a great power no longer needs to worry about the specifics of neighborhood and regional threats because of its expanded capabilities, while a small power with limited resources must be concerned about threatening problems closer to home. Or perhaps the acquisition of power deludes a strong nation to think in terms of grandeur and to ignore the mundane concerns of lesser states. Whatever the reason, the American view of world law became vague to the point of meaningless guidelines for policymakers.

The Rule of Law

American statements on international law made during the post-World War II period evolved from the concept of the "rule of law." Various American decision makers have contributed their views to the interpretation of this concept; by assembling these leaders' views, a collective picture of the rule of law can be drawn. President Truman, attempting to describe the need for a rule of law, referred to the frontier days when the gun prevailed as law until citizens banded together for self-protection.[13] He related this concept to collective action against international outlaws who attempted to unilaterally change the status quo. He also referred to the North Atlantic alliance as a contemporary example of the rule-of-law concept; the North Atlantic nations "are joined by a common heritage of democracy, and individual liberty, and rule of law."[14]

The rule of law assumes the absence of force in solving international problems. Secretary of State Christian Herter described the content of the rule of law as "a set of arrangements wherein states can settle their unresolved differences by peaceful means and without resort to force."[15] The rule of law provided the atmosphere within which changes in the international system could be made. American decision makers have not expressed opposition to change per se, but if changes do occur, they ought to be governed by the rule of law. As Secretary Dulles put it: "If change is to be peaceful and not destructive, then human conduct and national conduct must be based on principles of law and justice."[16] Changes brought on by nationalism, economic development, and technological expansion have been accepted in the post-World War II period because the status quo has not been, to use Secretary Byrnes' word, "sacrosanct."[17]

During the height of the Cold War, the first twenty years following World War II, the major threat to the rule of law was the Soviet Union. American spokesmen viewed the Russian code of conduct as based on the "rule of force" [18] or "rule of terror," [19] rather than the rule of law. At no other point in the history of American diplomacy have American leaders accused a nation of being a hazard to an international system based on law. During the Cold War, U.S. leaders perceived the Soviet Union as a threat to the rule of law, and they blamed the Russians for the concept's inability to influence international behavior.

U.S. Actions and International Law

Despite official statements, U.S. behavior as a superpower appeared to be rarely influenced by the content of international law. In 1962, President Kennedy declared that a "pacific blockade" had been imposed on Cuba and that all ships destined for Cuban ports would be searched for missile components. Since a blockade in international law is considered a belligerent act, to label it "pacific" represented, at best, an odd juxtaposition of two antipathetical concepts. Intervention in Korea was sanctioned by the United Nations, but intervention in other states (Lebanon in 1958 and Vietnam in 1964[20]) was justified on the basis of national interest, not by the legal sanction gained from an international organization. Since World War II, U.S. intervention in other areas was justified on the same basis (the Dominican Republic, Lebanon, and Cuba[21]).

Legalism, then, has not been a stable pattern in American foreign policy since 1945. While the rule of law was given a wide berth in official statements, American diplomacy has not achieved the high, almost utopian, level of behavior called for by the concept.

International Law in Disarray

The gap between American rhetoric and legal behavior, while lamentable, should not be blamed entirely on U.S. decision makers. International law has been in disarray during the post-World War II period because of three stimuli, all external to the United States. First, the Soviet Union, the system's other superpower, has brought its own views to international politics on the composition of international law. The Soviet approach to international legal norms is rooted in the Russian image of the world with its own cluster of values and assumptions. As a result, international law has been subjected to the same stresses that afflicted every other political subject in the Cold War.

Second, the Third World revolution has changed the European complexion of international law. European nations had dominated the international system since its inception. The rules of warfare, of boundaries, of diplomatic exchanges, and of a host of other topics are rooted in Western, Judeo-Christian, and European traditions. The Third World—non-Western, non-Hebrew, non-Christian, and non-European—has questioned international law as yet another vehicle to impose unacceptable cultural, political, and economic values on their societies.

Third, the revolution in warfare has created unforeseen obstacles to the development of international law. While the traditional distinction between combatants and non-combatants began to break down in the two unlimited wars of this century, the advent of nuclear weaponry and the reintroduction of guerrilla conflicts made the distinction all but impossible to respect. The use of nuclear weaponry (especially in counter-city strategies) and of guerrilla warfare tended to subject the entire population to the full force of military conflict. The nature of warfare has undergone revolutionary changes since the end of World War II; international law, traditionally slow to update itself, has not as yet reflected this transformation. International lawyers are giving dicta that apply to conflicts no longer raging and to distinctions no longer existing.

ABUSE OF INTERNATIONAL LAW AND ORGANIZATION

A case can be made for the position that the United States misused the United Nations during the organization's early years by attempting to annex it as an appendage to U.S. diplomacy. The United Nations survival of American domination is a tribute to the strength of the organization and to the faith in the UN possessed by many nations. American appropriation of the UN for its own national interest may be attributed to the naivete of a nation that suddenly found itself a world leader with little of the experience necessary to exercise that leadership.

American leaders in 1945 were also a captive of one of the last vestiges of Liberalism: a belief in international organization as a framework to encourage the development of a community of interests. As the Realist image took hold, and alliances received more emphasis, the UN began to recede into the background of American foreign policy.

International law, despite traditional reverence paid to it in American diplomatic history, has come to be viewed with suspicion in the post-World War II period. Although the U.S. has tended to use legal arguments to justify its policy decisions, the rule of law with its high-sounding phrases has had very little relevance to much of contemporary politics. To the occasional dismay of American decision makers, international lawyers have taken the U.S. to task as a violator of world legal norms. As yet, however, international law has not been a major restraint on American behavior.

Both the United Nations and international law have been appropriated to serve the goals of American foreign policy. However, the UN has matured to the point that Washington is no longer successfully manipulating it for its own ends. Little respect is given to the force of international law in the contemporary world. American policymakers have been free to abuse international law, and they have imposed their own interpretation of traditional legal norms on their own and other nations' behavior.

NOTES

1. Quoted in Ruth B. Russell, *A History of the United Nations Charter* (Washington, D.C.: Brookings Institution, 1958), p. 547.
2. The following books furnish a general discussion of the UN in American foreign policy: Richard N. Gardner, *In Pursuit of World Order: U.S. Foreign Policy and International Organization*, rev. ed. (New York: Praeger, 1966); Ernest B. Haas, *Tangle of Hopes: American Commitments and World Order* (Englewood Cliffs, N.J.: Prentice-Hall, 1969); Lincoln P. Bloomfield, *The UN and U.S. Foreign Policy: A New Look at the National Interest* (Boston: Little, Brown, and Co., 1967); John G. Stoessinger, *The United Nations and the Superpowers: United States–Soviet Interaction at the United Nations*, rev. ed. (New York: Random House, 1969); Franz B. Gross (ed.), *The United States and the United Nations* (Norman: University of Oklahoma Press, 1964); Francis O. Wilcox and H. Field Haviland (eds.), *The United States and the United Nations* (Baltimore: Johns Hopkins Press, 1961); Robert E. Riggs, *US/UN: Foreign Policy and International Organization* (New York: Appleton-Century-Crofts, 1971); B. J. Higgins, *The U.N. and U.S. Foreign Economic Policy* (Homewood, Ill.: Dorsey Press, 1962); Lawrence S. Finkelstein (ed.), *The United States and International Organization: The Changing Setting* (Cambridge, Mass.: MIT Press, 1969); Ruth B. Russell, *The United Nations and United States Security Policy* (Washington, D.C.: Brookings Institution, 1968); and Chadwick F. Alger, "The United States and the United Nations," *International Organization* 27, (1973): 1–23.
3. For an analysis of Roosevelt's views of the UN, consult Frank R. Donovan, *Mr. Roosevelt's Four Freedoms: The Story Behind the United Nations Charter* (New York: Dodd, Mead, 1966).
4. For a survey of U.S.–League of Nations relations, *see* Denna F. Flemming, *The United States and World Organization, 1920–1933* (New York: Columbia University Press, 1938).
5. Calvin Coolidge, State of the Union message, delivered Dec. 6, 1923.
6. James F. Byrnes, "United States Military Strength: Its Relation to the United Nations and World Peace," *Department of State Bulletin* 14 (March 24, 1946): 483.
7. Harry S. Truman, State of the Union message, delivered Jan. 7, 1953.
8. Dwight D. Eisenhower, "Security in the Free World," *Department of State Bulletin* 40 (April 6, 1959): 469.
9. Ernest W. Lefever, *Uncertain Mandate: Politics of the UN Congo Operation* (Baltimore: Johns Hopkins Press, 1967).
10. John G. Stoessinger, *Financing the United Nations System* (Washington: Brookings Institution, 1964).

11. Robert E. Riggs, *Politics in the United Nations: A Study of United States Influence in the General Assembly* (Urbana: University of Illinois Press, 1958).
12. John MacVane, *Embassy Extraordinary: The U.S. Mission to the United Nations* (New York: Public Affairs Committee, 1961) and Arnold Beichman, *The Other State Department: The U.S. Mission to the U.N. and Its Role in the Making of Foreign Policy* (New York: Basic Books, 1968).
13. *Department of State Bulletin* 24 (February 19, 1951): 283.
14. *Ibid.*, 20 (April 17, 1949): 482.
15. *Ibid.*, 42 (Feb. 15, 1960): 227.
16. *Ibid.*, 39 (Sept. 8, 1958): 37.
17. *Ibid.*, 14 (March 10, 1946): 357.
18. *Ibid.*, 26 (June 2, 1952): 848.
19. *Ibid.*, 40 (April 6, 1959): 469.
20. John N. Moore, "The Lawfulness of Military Assistance to the Republic of Vietnam," *American Journal of International Law* 61 (1967): 1–34 and Frank Browning and Dorothy Forman (eds.), *The Wasted Nations: Report of the International Commission of Enquiry into United States Crimes in Indochina* (New York: Harper & Row, 1972).
21. Quincy Wright, "United States Intervention in Lebanon," *American Journal of International Law* 53 (1959): 112–125; David S. Bogen, "The Law of Humanitarian Intervention: United States Policy in Cuba (1898) and the Dominican Republic (1965)," *Harvard International Law Club Journal* 7 (1966): 296–315; and Richard A. Falk, "American Intervention in Cuba and the Rule of Law," *Ohio State Law Journal* (Summer 1961): 546–585.

17

Patterns of Public Diplomacy

The revolution in statecraft has exposed societies in the international system to foreign ideas brought in by tourists, business enterprises, churches, and radio broadcasts. National boundaries, even those composed of natural barriers, are no longer obstacles to influences from foreign cultures that range from dress styles to political movements calling for overthrow of a government. The revolution in statecraft has spawned a number of activities that are grouped under the concept of *public diplomacy*.

Public diplomacy employs open communication between citizens of different countries or between the government of one and citizens of another. "Open communication" designates the exchange of information and ideas through various instruments of mass media, such as radio and books. "Citizens" are involved in communicative process as missionaries, tourists, and businessmen. Exchanges between citizens have become so common that one writer argues that the American public, as well as their leaders, must understand and appreciate foreign cultures to promote realistic responses to international events.[1]

Public diplomacy is as old as the state system itself. Spanish missionaries who accompanied the *conquistadores* to the Americas during the 16th century engaged in a public communication process through their evangelizing activities. Despite its ancient heritage, public diplomacy has been identified with the 20th century. The emergence of mass democracies after the American and the French revolutions, and later, of dictatorships founded on ideologies (particularly Communism and Fascism), stimulated extensive government participation in public diplomacy as an instrument to attain goals of national interest. Moreover, the development of more efficient instruments of the press, radio, and television, encouraged government participation.

Two other factors in the post-World War II period have contributed to the growing presence of public diplomacy: affluence and the Cold War.

Affluent Americans and foreigners traveling abroad have made tourism a significant contribution to public diplomacy. Competition between East and West also has stimulated propaganda programs. The Cold War was portrayed as a battle for men's minds; both the United States and Soviet Union invested heavily in public diplomacy techniques to ensure that their ideological side would "win." Although the Cold War has waned, the U.S. and U.S.S.R. continue propaganda activities; but the content of these activities exhibits less hostility toward each other.

The number of U.S. agencies engaged in public diplomacy is extensive: The Library of Congress purchases books published abroad; the Smithsonian Institution exchanges artifacts with similar national agencies in foreign countries; overseas branches of the Veterans Administration distribute information and benefits to ex-servicemen abroad; the American Battle Monuments Commission supervises cemeteries for Americans killed during wartime in foreign countries; the Interagency Committee on International Athletics coordinates policy on amateur participation in sports (such as the Olympic games); the Tennessee Valley Authority has overseas offices; and many other such bureaucratic units, most of which are rarely associated with foreign policy issues. In fact, almost 30 federal departments and agencies have a combined overseas employment of approximately 200,000; only one-tenth of this number represents the State Department.

Public diplomacy today generates more activity than any other aspect of American foreign policy, although it does not cost as much as other foreign policy-related programs. National defense generates enormous expenditures, while public diplomacy programs operate on shoe-string budgets. Public diplomacy expenditures by private institutions, however, are greater than the sums for propaganda and cultural exchanges listed in the federal budget.

Pre-World War II Activities

The first official attempt to enter the field of public diplomacy was the formation of the Creel Committee on Public Information, created by Woodrow Wilson to explain American wartime policy to both domestic and foreign audiences. The Creel Committee ended with World War I because Wilson became suspicious of propaganda, especially when carried out by a government agency and aimed at the American domestic audience. This suspicion is traditional in American diplomacy: presidents Roosevelt and Truman shared it during World War II.

World War II

During the Second World War, Roosevelt established three agencies, each of which was active in propaganda: the Foreign Informational Service, the Office of War Information, and the Office of Strategic Services. In part, this three-pronged approach to propaganda reflected Roosevelt's personal misgivings about the role that an information agency should play in a democratic society. He believed that the democratic process might be threatened by empowering government agencies with the function of interpreting world events for the public. He also reasoned that after the war it would be easier to disband three separate agencies than one large bureaucracy.

The post-war fate of these wartime agencies was similar to that of the Creel Committee in 1919, with two exceptions: the overseas activities of public diplomacy were continued (and later became the United States Information Service) and the Washington-based personnel, while reduced in number and bereft of their former organizational home, were assigned to the State Department. The State Department proved to be as unaccommodating to public diplomacy as it was to wartime intelligence.

Post-World War II

Early Post-War Problems. The government's public diplomacy activities were weak from 1945 to 1949. The difficulty was not altogether the Department of State's fault, although constant reorganization underscored the fact that public diplomacy had yet to find an organizational house that satisfied everyone. Congress could not make up its mind about the efficiency and prospects of public diplomacy, alternately increasing and then reducing appropriations.

The first step toward instituting public diplomatic activities was the result of congressional initiative. Congressmen who traveled to Europe during 1947 and 1948 were impressed by the lack of understanding of American policy positions among European statesmen and publics. They were equally impressed by the effectiveness and extent of Soviet informational activities. The result was the Smith-Mundt Act of January 1948, the first major law on cultural diplomacy.[2]

Official interest in public diplomacy continued to fluctuate throughout 1948 and 1949. The executive branch, and especially the State Department, remained largely apathetic to the need for public diplomacy to implement foreign policy objectives. Within Congress ran an undercurrent of thinking that the American instrument of public diplomacy should be independent of the State Department.

The "Campaign for Truth." Finally, in 1950 the Truman administration and Congress agreed on the need for a well-funded and active information program. Early in the year, Congress approved increased expenditures for the administration's grandiose propaganda program called the "Campaign for Truth."[3] The North Korean invasion in June 1950 helped to elicit congressional support. The new overseas information program with its enlarged resources immediately was crippled by Senator Joseph McCarthy's attacks; its propagandizing was contrary to the "truth" as he saw it. One of Senator McCarthy's investigations focused on "subversive" literature in United States Information Service libraries abroad and on personnel associated with "unAmerican" activities. Continued hostility toward propaganda within the State Department did not help matters. Career diplomats tended to believe that propaganda had no place in an organization responsible for negotiation and diplomatic communication. After a promising beginning in 1950 with the Campaign for Truth, public diplomacy was left demoralized and suspect.

Eisenhower's Contributions. The Eisenhower administration brought major changes to public diplomacy, most of them for the better. Although Secretary of State John Foster Dulles preferred to separate public diplomatic activities from his department, he permitted diplomatic exchanges to remain while information activities were placed in an independent agency. He believed that cultural exchanges would be downgraded if they were linked to propaganda. As a result, the United States Information Agency (USIA) was established in 1953. The USIS, established by Truman earlier, continued to administer both information and cultural exchange programs overseas.

Almost a decade passed after World War II before the American government decided that public diplomacy was sufficiently important as an instrument of foreign policy to be elevated to the level of an independent agency. This decision made public diplomacy the last of the foreign policy-implementing instruments to be established; the diplomatic, economic, military, intelligence, and organizational implementers had been functioning by this time.

INFORMATION AND PERSUASION

"Information" and "persuasion" are euphemisms for propaganda, which unfortunately, carries a pejorative connotation.[4] In this chapter, "information," "propaganda," and "persuasion" will be used interchangeably, all referring to the American government's attempts to convince other nations that they should endorse, or not oppose, foreign policy positions taken by the United States. A student of American foreign policy should not fall into the semantic trap of calling an opponent's attempts to persuade "propaganda," while labeling American attempts "information."

The American commitment to propaganda cannot be viewed as substantial when compared with other nations with smaller economic bases. The Soviet Union and the People's Republic of China spend more money; Egypt follows the U.S. in the amount spent on information and persuasion programs. The USIA budget is approximately 200 million dollars, a figure that does not include propaganda activities of the intelligence community.[5] Even if expenditures by the intelligence community and other privately financed information activities, such as Radio Free Europe,[6] are added to the published expenditures, it is still doubtful that the United States appropriates as much of its resources for propaganda as do the Russians and Chinese.

Growth of the USIA

Purposes of the USIA. President Eisenhower charged the new United States Information Agency to submit "evidence to peoples of other nations by means of communication techniques that the objectives and policies of the United States are in harmony with and will advance their legitimate aspirations for freedom, progress, and peace." The agency also was to counter the distortions of American foreign policy emanating from the information organs of unfriendly states and to project aspects of American life and culture that would enable other people to understand U.S. diplomacy.[7] These purposes underscored the fact that the USIA was an agent of the American government, and as such, would not travel a road independent from the State Department; it would be guided in foreign policy matters by the Secretary of State.

The USIA was not to be an objective voice in evaluating American diplomacy. In explaining American foreign policy to other peoples, the agency would attempt to supply information not transmitted through foreign mass media, to paint American policy decisions in the most flattering hues, and to correct misperceptions.

Eisenhower's reorganization of U.S. propaganda and cultural exchange programs resulted in a confusing division of labor. Overseas, the official arm of the United States' information program remained the United States Information Service, which administered *both* information persuasion and educational and cultural programs abroad. USIS personnel abroad who handle information programs report to the USIA, while those who administer cultural and educational exchange report to the State Department. The assignment of the U.S. Information Agency to Washington and the U.S. Information Service abroad has added to the confusion of this administrative tangle.

USIA–USIS Personnel. The number of information personnel has not grown precipitously, increasing from 9,300 workers in 1953 to approximately 12,000 today. Most employees are situated overseas and most are foreign nationals. Presently, five foreign nationals are employed for every American, including positions both overseas and at the Washington headquarters. The large percentage of foreign nationals raises a question of their effectiveness in explaining the rationale for American policy decisions. However, foreign nationals tend to be employed as technicians of mass media and as members of the press services and radio-relay stations; they also are employed extensively as native broadcasters for the Voice of America and as translators. The Voice of America should not be confused with Radio Free Europe and Radio Liberty, which are financed by contributions from private citizens.

Regional Distribution. Since 1953, the changing emphasis in U.S. programs has been reflected in regional shifts in overseas employment. During the early 1950s, most personnel were concentrated in Europe, the Far East, Near East/South Asia, and Latin America, in that order. The country with the largest contingent of overseas personnel was Germany. This distribution reflected the priorities of American foreign policy; most USIA-USIS informational activity was targeted for the Eastern European states of the Soviet bloc.

The present distribution of overseas personnel reflects a different ranking of priorities. East Asia and Near East/South Asia now command the most assignments. In third place is Latin America; Europe, first in 1953, is fourth today. Africa was made a separate bureau in the late 1950s when emerging African nations gained independence. In last place is a region completely missing in 1953, U.S.S.R. and Eastern Europe. The emphasis has shifted from cracking the Iron Curtain to persuading the nonaligned or neutral states to support American foreign policy.

The FSIO. In addition to the changes in the regional distribution of personnel since 1953, there have been continual attempts to upgrade the quality of American men and women working for the agency. This process finally culminated in 1968 with the creation of the Foreign Service Information Officers (FSIO) Corps, parallelling the Foreign Service Corps in almost every detail: entrance examinations, evaluation and selection-out procedure, and retirement benefits. Although the FSIO has not reached the stature of the Foreign Service Corps, it has become an attractive second choice for young Americans interested in overseas representation.

Propaganda and the USIA-USIS

Rules for Successful Propaganda. One of the cardinal rules of successful propaganda activities is to target a specific audience for propagandizing. Propaganda usually is ineffective if aimed at an audience that either does not exist or whose grievances are different from those played on by the propagandist. Scientists may be dissatisfied in Bulgaria, but contented in Poland; consequently, a propagandist cannot target the two groups of scientists in the same way. It is also unwise to ask impossible tasks of the targeted audience. Demands placed on audiences that cannot be met under existing conditions will inevitably lead to a loss of confidence in the propaganda machinery. To call on unarmed East German farmers to revolt against their Communist government, for example, is to ask them to commit suicide.

To be effective, the agency should have closer ties with the intelligence community, especially for information programs aimed at the Soviet Union, East European states, and the Communist nations of East Asia. Many of the decisions on which group in which country constitutes a potential target audience must be made on the basis of information available within the intelligence community itself.

Propaganda Targeting. Primary responsibility for targeting foreign audiences rests with the Public Affairs Officer, who prepares a country plan with the approval of the ambassador. The Public Affairs Officer heads the USIS mission in an American embassy abroad, and is assisted by the Information Officer. The country plan enumerates *psychological objectives,* or the attitudes that should be influenced in a direction that will advance American policy objectives. It also singles out *target audiences,* the people or groups whose attitudes should be influenced according to the psychological objectives. While the American information program may be aimed at the government decision makers, it also may be directed at specific groups, such as labor unions. The goals of propaganda will vary from group to group as will the content of the message and the instrument of mass media used to carry the message. The Public Affairs Officer then must carefully choose his target audience and put together an effective combination of propaganda instruments.

Evaluating Effectiveness. How effective are the propaganda or information and persuasion activities of the United States? The question is exceedingly difficult to answer because of the paucity of research on USIA activities. One of the few published studies found that information activities did not change Greek attitudes on human rights.[8] U.S. propaganda efforts attempted to convince Greeks to support the United Nations' human rights principles and to inform them that the Communists had no respect for these rights. Human rights proved too nebulous to be translated into an effective propaganda plan. This mistake has been repeated often in American foreign policy. Diplomatic objectives are framed in terms that are too general and idealistic; thus, USIA cannot be held responsible for its lack of success in operationalizing nebulous themes into the specifics of a country plan.

Another difficulty encountered in evaluating U.S. propaganda activities is the hazy relationship that the USIA has with other federal agencies. Eisenhower ordered the agency to be supervised by the Department of State vis-à-vis the content of its propaganda, but he did not involve the director of the agency in policymaking itself. The agency's expertise is not consulted until after the policy is determined. The USIA is essentially an implementor of American foreign policy decisions; it is largely neglected during the policymaking process itself.

The American Tradition of Empiricism. Perhaps the United States government is incapable of mounting an effective propaganda program because the American nation is steeped in a tradition of empiricism. Empiricism is dedicated to an assumption that facts speak for themselves; but propaganda is dedicated to the attitude that facts must be interpreted. Facts indeed do not possess "objective" meanings that all peoples will grasp with little difficulty.

Ironically, the United States, a nation whose economy is built around the concept that advertising creates markets for goods, is also a nation that has trouble "selling" its foreign politics to other peoples. Madison Avenue techniques, which succeed on the domestic level, have not been applied successfully at the international level.

JUSPAO Vietnam. Doubts about the effectiveness of American propaganda programs have raised questions about the organization (or lack of it) of American efforts. Since the USIA is divorced from intelligence, military, and Foreign Service operations, the question is raised: Would a joint effort be more successful than the disorganized activities that characterize U.S. propaganda programs? To attack this question, the Joint United States Public Affairs Office (JUSPAO) was created in Vietnam in 1965. JUSPAO's objective was to coordinate information programs for dissemination in the provinces of Vietnam and in the world community as well. JUSPAO worked directly with the South Vietnamese government to combine resources in propaganda activities. Personnel assigned to JUSPAO were drawn from the USIS, State Department, military organizations, and the Agency for International Development.

While the primary purpose of JUSPAO was to win the support of the Vietnamese people for the Saigon government, other target audiences were the Viet Cong, the North Vietnamese, and the world press. JUSPAO attempted to achieve objectives that appeared impossible: to generate support for the Saigon regime among the South Vietnamese citizens; to encourage defections from Viet Cong forces; to demoralize the North Vietnamese; and to convince the world that progress was being made in winning the war.

JUSPAO represented a radical departure from previous American propaganda activities. While the JUSPAO–host government relationship probably will never be repeated in other countries, the coordinated aspect of the Vietnamese propaganda operations offered organizational advantages that might be duplicated. It brought together bureaucratic groups concerned with information and persuasion; previously American information activities were fragmented and uncoordinated.

Although American psychological warfare capability has improved since the end of World War II, much remains to be done. As long as information programs remain uncoordinated and rigorous evaluations of these programs are not undertaken, U.S. propaganda activities will not be a major instrument to implement American foreign policy.

EDUCATIONAL AND CULTURAL DIPLOMACY

The State Department's education and cultural (E & C) exchanges are the second largest government activity in public diplomacy, with an official budget of 50 million dollars, or one-fourth of the amount spent for USIA–USIS propaganda programs.[9] Since E & C activities are also carried on by units of the executive bureaucracy other than the State Department, the total amount spent is unknown. The Fulbright Act of 1946 began E & C exchanges by using national currencies held by the U.S. government in foreign countries. These "counterpart funds," as they were called, were accumulated largely through the sale of surplus American farm products. Since most currencies, such as Indian rupees, received in payment for agricultural products are not in demand in the international money market, they are kept within the foreign country and used for limited purchases. They cannot be released for large purchases of goods; to do so might upset the internal equilibrium of the nation's domestic market. They can be used for projects such as financing Americans traveling or studying in the foreign nation under E & C auspices.

Administration of E & C Diplomacy

The major actor in administering E & C diplomacy abroad is the Cultural Affairs Officer (CAO), working under the direction of the embassy's Public Affairs Officer.[10] His work load is normally heavy and encompasses duties of immense diversity: he must be able to explain the daily events in American foreign policy to non-political people, such as artists, musicians, and educators; he also interprets areas of American cultural life, such as American jazz, art, and literature. His task, therefore, is a demanding one. The Cultural Affairs Officer, compared to the Information Officer, is generally better educated and older. Despite these differences, more Information Officers tended to be promoted to the top position of Public Affairs Officer than did the CAOs.[11]

The CAO usually follows a rigorous daily schedule that ranges from lecturing to a student group on Hemingway, to arranging exhibits on the United States at a local fair, to overseeing a translation of a book on American government into the native language. In larger embassies, the CAO may be assisted by a librarian, Women's Activities Officer, and Student Affairs Officer. Although only a handful of Women's Activities Officers have been appointed, a case for their existence can readily be made. In most underdeveloped countries, enfranchisement and social changes have elevated the position of women and have opened new political and economic opportunities to them. In some cases, such as Argentina, India, Ceylon, and Israel, women have risen to the highest political positions of decision making. The Student Affairs Officer, among other tasks, advises students preparing for studies in the United States.

Educational Exchange Programs

Since 1946, over 140,000 individuals have participated in E & C diplomacy. Approximately 30 percent of the participants were Americans going abroad and 70 percent were foreign nationals coming to the United States. During the Vietnamese conflict, a trend began to reduce "non-essential" spending. E & C diplomatic activities were cut drastically during the late 1960s and early 1970s. The best-known educational exchange is the study abroad program; however, study abroad is only one of seven such programs financed by the American government (*see* Figure 17-1).

Students, Scholars, and Teachers. The largest program for both American and foreign national recipients involves students. More than 120,000

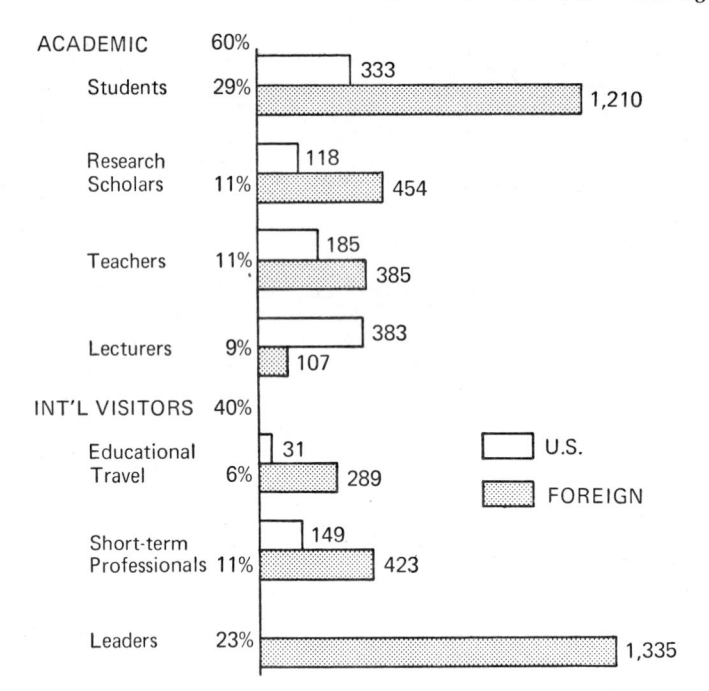

```
ACADEMIC          60%
                        ┌──────────┐ 333
    Students      29%
                        ├──────────────────────────────┐ 1,210

    Research            ┌───┐ 118
    Scholars      11%
                        ├──────────┐ 454

                        ┌─────┐ 185
    Teachers      11%
                        ├────────┐ 385

                        ┌─────────┐ 383
    Lecturers     9%
                        ├──┐ 107

INT'L VISITORS    40%
    Educational         ┌┐ 31                ☐ U.S.
    Travel        6%
                        ├──────┐ 289         ▨ FOREIGN

    Short-term          ┌───┐ 149
    Professionals 11%
                        ├──────────┐ 423

    Leaders       23%   ├──────────────────────────────────┐ 1,335
```

Figure 17-1. Types of Educational Exchange (Fiscal Year 1972). *(Source:* U.S. Department of State, *International Educational and Cultural Exchange* [Washington, D.C.: U.S. Government Printing Office, 1974], p. 22.)

foreign students annually come to the United States, but only 14 percent of them are supported by its federal budget, which reinforces the point that public diplomacy is much broader than government efforts. A second program for "research scholars" emphasizes post-doctoral grants. Foreign teachers are brought to the United States to observe school organization, teaching techniques, and curriculum development. American professors volunteer or are recruited for teaching positions in universities and colleges abroad.

International Visitors. The broad designation, "international visitors," harbors three programs, the largest of which introduces the foreign elites to American society. Leaders of religious groups, labor unions, and newspaper editors are brought to the United States to meet with and to confer with their American counterparts. The hope is that these foreign leaders will return to their countries with viewpoints that show an understanding of American foreign policy, or with the motivation to actively support U.S. policy positions. Because they are leaders in their own nation, their viewpoints are respected and may influence the opinions of others.[12]

chapter 17 Public Diplomacy

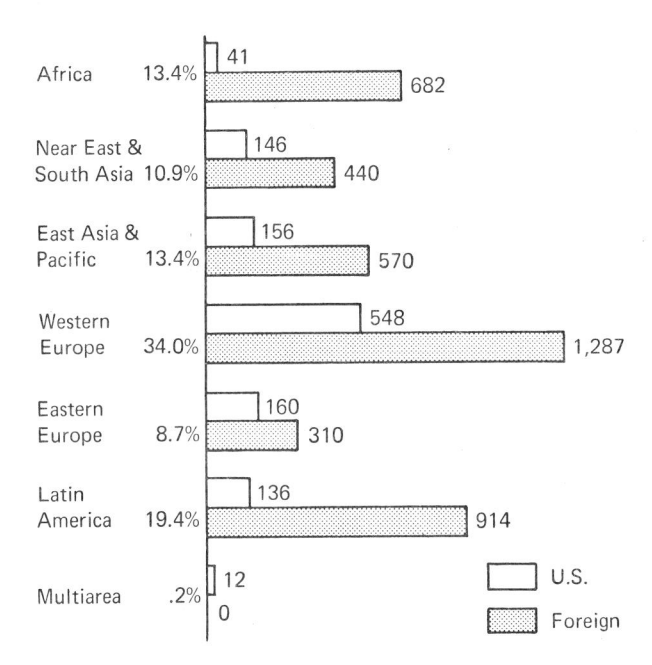

Region	%	U.S.	Foreign
Africa	13.4%	41	682
Near East & South Asia	10.9%	146	440
East Asia & Pacific	13.4%	156	570
Western Europe	34.0%	548	1,287
Eastern Europe	8.7%	160	310
Latin America	19.4%	136	914
Multiarea	.2%	12	0

Figure 17-2. Regional Selections of Grant Recipients (Fiscal Year 1972). *(Source:* U.S. Department of State, *International Educational and Cultural Exchange* [Washington, D.C.: U.S. Government Printing Office, 1974], p. 22.)

Regional Distribution of Educational Exchanges. The region of origin for foreign nationals who participate in educational exchanges and the region of destination of U.S. grantees are shown in Figure 17-2. Western Europe is the most popular area for Americans studying abroad and for foreign nationals receiving grants. While there has been a trend toward funding more non-Western recipients in recent years, the overwhelming choice for American grantees continues to be Western Europe. Educational exchanges with Eastern Europe were late in developing in this region until Cold War tensions were reduced. An exchange agreement was not signed with the Soviet Union until 1958.

Academic Fields of the Grantees. The academic fields represented by recipients of educational exchange awards (*see* Figure 17-3) offer some interesting comparisons. The largest field for foreign nationals is social science; most of the recipients study political science, government, international relations, and law. There is a persistent need in developing countries for public administrators who can operate government bureaucracy and who can represent their government as Foreign Service officers. Ironically, the

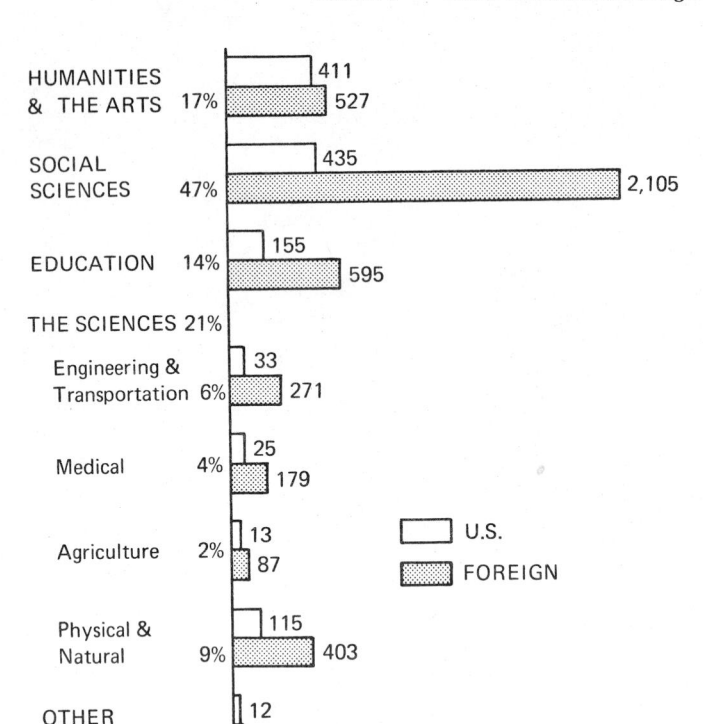

```
                              411
HUMANITIES
& THE ARTS   17%              527

SOCIAL                        435
SCIENCES     47%                                          2,105

                      155
EDUCATION    14%
                              595

THE SCIENCES 21%
                      33
  Engineering &
  Transportation 6%   271

                      25
  Medical    4%
                      179

                      13            U.S.
  Agriculture 2%
                      87            FOREIGN

                      115
  Physical &
  Natural    9%       403

OTHER                 12
(Sports, etc.)  1%    36
```

Figure 17–3. Fields of Study or Teaching of Recipients of Grants (Fiscal Year 1972). (Source: U.S. Department of State, International Educational and Cultural Exchange [Washington, D.C.: U.S. Government Printing Office, 1974], p. 22).

United States, a nation founded on the late 18th-century dictum "that government is best which governs least," has become a source of training to make government function well for emerging Third World nations in the 20th century. Science and education are popular fields for foreign nationals, another reflection of the needs of the developing world. The humanities rank last.

With the American recipients, humanities usually attract the most students, although in 1972 the social sciences nudged ahead. Interest in the humanities correlates with Western Europe's popularity as the place to study Western art, drama, music, or literature. Students of science and engineering also tend to choose universities in the more industrialized countries of Europe.

Cultural Exchanges

Of the three main components of public diplomacy—information, education, and culture—the latter is the most nebulous and the most pervasive. Everything that the American government does abroad can be considered as exporting or exhibiting the form and substance of American culture. In specific terms, however, cultural diplomacy is limited to exchanges in the arts, such as the extensive foreign tour by the Cincinnati Symphony Orchestra in 1967. In recent years, the State Department has moved from large ensembles to small performing groups because of budget cuts brought on by the Vietnamese conflict. In one year alone, 1967, the U.S. cultural exchange budget was reduced 40 percent.

Evaluating E & C Diplomacy

Evaluation of the results of educational and cultural diplomacy is extremely difficult. How many ties of friendship have been forged by a Voice of America jazz program? Have visits by the Russian basketball team increased American good will toward the U.S.S.R.? While there is no ready answer to these questions, E & C activities are not necessarily useless in international relations. Events that ordinarily would have little significance under normal conditions have been ascribed a measure of importance when placed in the context of world politics. For example, the visit of an American table tennis team to the People's Republic of China presaged a dramatic turn in Sino-American relations. The Olympic games are supposed to be apolitical, but Cold War rivalry between the U.S. and U.S.S.R. gave Olympic competition a political dimension.

The Brain Drain. One possible detrimental effect of E & C diplomatic activities is the brain drain, although the Department of State in the past has argued to the contrary.[13] The brain drain is normally applied to trained personnel, doctors and scientists especially, who migrate to the United States, attracted by higher wages for their services and more research opportunities for their specialties. A young medical doctor in Ghana, for example, interested in diseases of the heart and circulatory system would have little laboratory equipment and few human subjects in his country (because heart disease predominates in industrialized nations). His time would be given over to more common diseases which affect Ghanians but had been brought under control in the West. Migrating to the United States or one of the European countries with advanced medical technology would be a very tempting proposition.

For some of the young medical doctors, leaving their home country is more inviting because of internal conditions there. Autocratic governments may tend to view members of the intelligentsia (doctors, lawyers, teachers, and scientists) with suspicion. Since most of the intelligentsia have studied in Western nations and have experienced the measure of freedom that an open society creates, their return to a young nation, where all civil liberties and rights have not had time to take hold, often discourages them.

In some cases, the intelligentsia may be forced into political service in their own country. A young Gabonese, who earned his medical degree in France, may be taken out of the hospital, where his medical skills are needed, and assigned to the Gabon embassy in Paris because his knowledge of the country and his language skills are needed there by his government. This situation amounts to a self-imposed brain drain: governments of most of the emerging nations became independent without enough fully trained civil servants to assume the responsibilities that sovereignty bestows upon new countries.

Consequently, E & C diplomacy may have its own dark side. Rather than building good will by bringing foreign nationals to the United States, the American government (and other governments) may be contributing to the drain of the limited intellectual resources that Third World nations possess.

Library Burnings. During the 1950s and early 1960s, USIS libraries were frequently burned, indicating that American educational activities had a telling effect on forces that opposed U.S. foreign policy. Communists were presumed to be the culprits of the arsons by some analysts. Others reasoned that the USIS facilities were more vulnerable to mob action than the American embassy and thus were considered to be less of a risk in straining official relations with Washington. The State Department, in other words, would take a dimmer view of destroying an American embassy, protected by century-old traditions of international law, than it would of burning a USIS library. To be sure, State Department protests always followed library burnings, but diplomatic relations usually remained intact.

Eventually, the USIS library burnings decreased to the point of being a rare occurrence. This was due in part to the recognition that the libraries performed an important service to the host country—not to an increase in respect for American foreign policy. Evaluation of the diplomatic effects of the USIS libraries is largely speculation: it is possible that foreign students increase their appreciation of American culture through the use of the library facilities; or it is possible that students use them to confirm their original opinion that U.S. foreign policy is misdirected.

PUBLIC DIPLOMACY AND PRIVATE DIPLOMATS

Public diplomacy has its private diplomats, American citizens in a personal or corporate capacity communicating cultural values and a national image to foreign nationals. American industry maintains a payroll of approximately 500,000 employees to administer overseas branches or subsidiaries. Over 1 million American military personnel are stationed abroad and afloat. Points of contact between American citizens, too numerous to completely account for, include missionaries; labor unions that are members of international brotherhoods; foreign editions of American newspapers, such as *The New York Times;* American tourists abroad and foreign tourists visiting the United States; and movies.

Tourism

The exchange of short-term visitors involves the concern of several government agencies and many private organizations. The State Department supervises the issuance of passports and tourist visas. The United States Travel Service in the Department of Commerce in 1961 established overseas offices, as well as offices in each state capital in the U.S., that undertake campaigns to attract foreign tourists. The tourist industry in America touches the pocketbook of almost every citizen, involving not only the transport industries (air, rail, ship, auto, and bus), but hotels, motels, and restaurants as well. Tourist exchanges also have concerned the American government because of the gap between foreign nationals visiting the U.S. and American citizens going abroad. The travel deficit, over 1 billion dollars annually, has stimulated attempts to encourage more foreign tourists, as well as periodic efforts to discourage American tourists from going abroad. President Lyndon Johnson in 1968 proposed a tax on American tourists abroad, but the proposal was never enacted into law.

Motion Pictures

Foreign nationals glean information about the United States from commercial endeavors that American citizens seldom consider as image-building. American movies especially have been singled out as projecting an image of American life. King Hussein of Jordan wrote that he had hoped to visit the United States personally to verify or correct the impressions that he had gained through mass media. He wrote: "My impressions, . . . like those of everyone else who had never been there, were made up from books I had read, American magazines, and above all the movies. Of course, I did not expect to find cowboys and Indians stalking each other on the Western plains or gangsters shooting it out in the streets of Chicago. But I really had no idea what to expect. . . ."[14] Although American movies seldom focus on political issues, they do offer insights into the values in American culture.

Schools Abroad for American Dependents

Perhaps the best example of the private component of public diplomacy is the overseas school system run by the departments of Defense and State for dependents of American citizens. These schools also touch the lives of many foreign nationals as well as the children of individuals who are working abroad for American businesses. Overseas military personnel are usually assigned for short tours of duty, anticipating a return to the United States or assignment elsewhere in the world in two or three years. They desire an educational system closely patterned after curricula in the United States to minimize educational adjustment problems for children who periodically must change locations. The Defense Department operates over 300 schools with an enrollment of approximately 185,000 for dependents of military personnel overseas. This system does not engage in public diplomacy to any appreciable degree because children other than American dependents are excluded.

The State Department school system enrolls students from families of government employees (e.g., USIA, Foreign Service, AID), personnel from private industry and education, host-country families, and dependents from nations other than the U.S. and the host country. The international flavor of the schools is maintained by a policy of teacher recruitment that mixes instructors from the United States, the host country, and other nations.

In a very real sense, the State Department's overseas school system is a laboratory for American culture. In addition to providing education for children of government personnel, the schools bring together students of widely divergent backgrounds in a setting designed to increase their appreciation of each other's cultural values. They also serve as a display model of American educational techniques for educators of the host nation. They also encourage the study of English (the language used in instruction) and of American culture. Because the schools are operated by a locally elected board composed of the parents, they are a microcosm of self-government. Most of the cost of the program is borne by the parents.

Values Projected

Contacts between cultures are a two-way mirror, permitting citizens to view the values of each culture.[15] An American businessman, therefore, is the representative of his company and of his country as well. It may not be accurate for foreign observers to form conclusions about U.S. society from American missionaries, tourists, rock-and-roll performers, participants in international youth conferences, soldiers, and a host of other citizens who project the values of their nation. However, private emissaries of culture do have an impact on the relationship between the average Iranian and the average American.

THE PEACE CORPS

Economic Aid or Public Diplomacy?

The Peace Corps is more often related to foreign aid in the form of economic development than it is to public diplomacy.[16] Although the Peace Corps Volunteer (PCV) may contribute to the host nation's economic growth, his projects are more service oriented, on a much smaller scale, and normally found in places not necessarily chosen with an eye toward enlarging the nation's economic production. Another approach to the Peace Corps is to analyze it under the rubric of public diplomacy because it is essentially a people-to-people program. It brings small sections of the Third World nations into face-to-face contact with Americans, usually for the first time.

Origin of the Corps

The origins of the idea for a Peace Corps are uncertain, being variously ascribed to different congressmen in the late 1950s. Whatever its origin, the Peace Corps concept was adopted by John F. Kennedy during his campaign for the presidency in 1960. After his inauguration, Kennedy used the President's contingency funds as seed money to get the Corps underway. The pilot program, consisting of projects in three countries with 120 volunteers, was intended as a source of information and experience for formulating plans for a permanent organization. The pilot projects yielded encouraging results and a permanent Corps was established in August 1962, under authorization given by Congress. From this beginning, the Corps grew to 15,000 PCVs in 50 countries with a budget of over 100 million dollars. In recent years, Peace Corps budgets have been cut severely. In the early 1970s, funding leveled off at approximately 70 billion dollars annually.

Distribution of the Peace Corps

Most of the personnel in the Peace Corps organization are overseas, with the largest contingent of PCV's in Sub-Saharan Africa and Latin America. The Peace Corps, therefore, has enjoyed its warmest reception in, and given most of its attention to, regions largely neglected by other American foreign policy programs. In many countries, the Peace Corps works with private organizations in carrying out joint projects overseas. The Laubach Literacy Fund and the Young Men's Christian Association, for example, have coordinated activities in some host countries with Corps volunteers.

Recruitment and Training

The Volunteer: Ideology and Background. The Peace Corps appeals to the idealism in American youth, but it is doubtful that this trait is as widespread as expected. Most college and university graduates have firmly established career goals and tend to shun the Peace Corps because it does not contribute to, and in some cases may detract from, these goals. A small minority of American college youth rebel against the "establishment" and question dominant social, economic, and political values and institutions, including the Peace Corps. The group that supplies the majority of Peace Corps recruits is composed of young people who are service oriented and idealistic; they do not have cut-and-dried career goals in the traditional sense, and while they do not accept the predominant social values, they are not willing to use violence to destroy them.

The Service Period. The PCV's tour of duty is usually two years, during which time he is expected to live under conditions similar to those of the people with whom he works. He is denied access to air-conditioning, PX privileges, diplomatic immunity, extra pay for hardship posts, automobiles, residence in diplomatic compounds, and offices in American embassies. He receives an allowance commensurate with the living conditions of the people he serves, but an additional sum is deposited each month in the Volunteer's account in the United States and is given to him upon his severance from the Corps. Many host countries contribute to or pay all of his living allowance.

Evaluation of the Work of the Peace Corps

As a rule, participants in U.S. overseas programs tend to become part of the American compound in the host country and have most of their dealings with other Americans, with host government officials, or with citizens from the middle- and upper-classes. The Peace Corps does not follow this pattern. It is the only program that brings Americans into direct contact with the lower classes and other forgotten people of the host nations. The effectiveness of the Peace Corps must be evaluated as part of public diplomacy. In this respect, the Corps shares the ubiquitous problem of all phases of public diplomacy: relating its activities to American national interests.

As Peace Corps activities have contracted in the 1970s and regrouped with other service organizations that focus on U.S. domestic needs, the Corps has also undergone an internal transformation. More specialists and technicians are being recruited, such as nurses and agricultural specialists. The Corps is no longer an organization of young generalists because the well-trained specialist is now in demand in Third World nations. The reduction of Peace Corps activities in the 1970s is a political commentary on the Corps' effectiveness as an instrument of American foreign policy. The Nixon administration evidently thought that the Corps was expendable and that its activities should be replaced by programs designed to meet more pressing needs.

WAR AND THE MINDS OF MEN

The charter of the United Nations Economic, Social, and Cultural Organization declares that "wars begin in the minds of men," a statement most public diplomats would endorse. If conflict originates in the prejudices of race against race, in the greed of one group for the other group's possessions, and in the suspicion of one nation of the folkways of another nation, then public diplomacy can provide a solution to the problem of war. On the other hand, if conflict occurs over the clash of national interests (as the Realists contend) or over ideology (as the Right-Wing Revisionists argue), public diplomacy is an endeavor of marginal usefulness to American diplomacy.

Assuming public diplomacy to be relevant to the problems of war and peace, is there any indication that it changes attitudes from hate to love, from suspicion to respect, and from prejudice to acceptance? Advocates of public diplomacy assert that the more we know about the culture of another nation, the less we have to fear about that culture. But this assumption is not always true. A foreign student from Chad, for example, may return home with anti-American attitudes because of unfortunate experiences that he perceives as discrimination in U.S. society. Or a foreign student may naturally become more nationalistic toward his own country because he is constantly asked to contrast his society with American culture or because he is often challenged to defend his nation's foreign policy. However, Third World students were found to be (according to one study) more positive toward the United States than European students.[17] Third World students dislike some aspects of American society, but in general they have positive reactions to U.S. society.

The unanswered questions of public diplomacy should not lead to jettisoning it as an implementor of American foreign policy. Other implementors are equally clouded as to their effectiveness; foreign aid, discussed in the following chapter, is an expensive foreign policy program that also suffers from evaluation ills. Rigorous social science research is needed to answer questions of effectiveness which eventually will lead to more successful use of public diplomacy in American foreign policy.

NOTES

1. Glen H. Fisher, *Public Diplomacy and the Behavioral Sciences* (Bloomington: Indiana University Press, 1972).
2. J. Colligan, *The Fulbright Program: A History* (Chicago: University of Chicago Press, 1965).
3. See Edward W. Barrett, *Truth Is Our Weapon* (New York: Funk and Wagnalls, 1953).
4. For a general discussion of propaganda, consult: Terence H. Qualter, *Propaganda and Psychological Warfare* (New York: Random House, 1962); C. C. Havighurst (ed.), *International Control of Propaganda* (Dobbs Ferry, N.Y.: Oceana, 1968); and Murray Dyer, *The Weapon on the Wall: Rethinking Psychological Warfare* (Baltimore: Johns Hopkins Press, 1959).
5. For example, the intelligence community finances "black" and "white" radio broadcasts. "Black" radio broadcasts are aimed at the opponent's territory but are disguised as emanating from one of the opponent's radio stations. "White" radio broadcasts to the opponent's citizens, but identifies its point of origin.
6. For more information on Radio Free Europe, consult Robert T. Holt, *Radio Free Europe* (Minneapolis: University of Minnesota Press, 1958);

and George R. Urban (ed.), *Scaling the Wall: Talking to Eastern Europe: The Best of Radio Free Europe* (Detroit: Wayne State University Press, 1969).

7. For a discussion of USIA and other U.S. information activities, see R. W. Van de Velde, *Strategic Psychological Operations and American Foreign Policy* (Chicago: University of Chicago Press, 1960); Wilson P. Dizard, *The Strategy of Truth: The Story of the U.S. Information Service* (Washington, D.C.: Public Affairs Press, 1961); Robert E. Elder, *The Information Machine: The United States Information Agency and American Foreign Policy* (Syracuse, N.Y.: Syracuse University Press, 1968); Ronald I. Rubin, *The Objectives of the U.S. Information Agency: Controversies and Analysis* (New York: Praeger, 1968); Leo Bogart, "Operating Assumptions of the USIA," *Public Opinion Quarterly* 19 (1955–56): 369–379; John Sorenson, *The Word War* (New York: Harper & Row, 1968); Oren Stephens, *Facts to a Candid World: America's Overseas Information Program* (Stanford, Calif.: Stanford University Press, 1955); Charles A. H. Thomson, *Overseas Information Service of the U.S. Government* (Washington, D.C.: Brookings Institution, 1948); and George N. Gordon and Irving A. Falk, *The War of Ideas: America's Identity Crisis* (New York: Hastings House, 1973).

8. Leo Bogard, "Measuring the Effectiveness of an Overseas Information Campaign: A Case History," *Public Opinion Quarterly* 21 (1957–58): 475–498.

9. Charles Frankel, "The Era of Educational and Cultural Relations," *Department of State Bulletin* 56 (June 6, 1967): 889–897; Philip Coombs, *The Fourth Dimension of Foreign Policy: Educational and Cultural Affairs* (New York: Council on Foreign Relations, 1964); Charles A. Thompson and Walter H. C. Laves, *Cultural Relations and U.S. Foreign Policy* (Bloomington: Indiana University Press, 1963); The American Assembly, *Cultural Affairs and Foreign Relations,* rev. ed. (Englewood Cliffs, N.J.: Prentice-Hall, 1968); and Ruth E. McMurray and Muna Lee, *The Cultural Approach: Another Way in International Relations* (Chapel Hill: University of North Carolina Press, 1947).

10. Howard Lee Nostrand, *The Cultural Attaché: Field Organizer and Intellectual Leader in Six Areas of Cooperation Between Peoples* (New Haven, Conn.: Hazan Foundation, 1947).

11. Charles Frankel, *The Neglected Aspect of Foreign Affairs* (Washington, D.C.: Brookings Institution, 1965), pp. 20–22.

12. Robert E. Elder, *The Foreign Leader Program: Operations in the United States* (Washington, D.C.: Brookings Institution, 1961).

13. H. G. Grubel and A. D. Scott, "The Immigration of Scientists and Engineers to the United States, 1949–61," *Journal of Political Economy* 74 (1966): 368–378; and John R. Niland, *The Asian Engineering Brain Drain* (Lexington, Mass.: Lexington Books, 1970).

14. Hussein, *Uneasy Lies the Head* (New York: Bernard Geis Associates, 1962), p. 229.
15. Richard T. Morris, *The Two-Way Mirror* (Minneapolis: University of Minnesota Press, 1960).
16. Despite its brief existence, the Peace Corps has captured the attention of many writers: Charles E. Wingenbach, *Peace Corps: Who, How and Where,* rev. ed. (New York: McGraw-Hill, 1965); George Sullivan, *Story of the Peace Corps* (New York: Fleet Press Corp., 1964); Roy Hoopes, *The Peace Corps Experience* (New York: Clarkson N. Potter, 1968); Alan Weiss, *High Risk/High Gain: A Peace Corps Training Account of Free Wheeling* (New York: St. Martin's Press, 1968); Susan Whittlesey, *United States Peace Corps: The Challenge of Good Will* (New York: Coward-McCann, 1963); Glenn D. Kittler, *Peace Corps* (New York: Warner Paperback Library, 1963); Maurice L. Albertson, Andrew E. Rice, and Pauline E. Birky, *New Frontiers for American Youth: Perspective on the Peace Corps* (Washington, D.C.: Public Affairs Press, 1961); Pauline Madow, *Peace Corps* (New York: H. W. Wilson, 1964); Robert Textor (ed.), *Cultural Frontiers of the Peace Corps* (Cambridge: MIT Press, 1966); Robert A. Liston, *Sargent Shriver: A Candid Portrait* (New York: Farrar, Straus, and Giroux, 1964); and R. Sargent Shriver, *Point of the Lance* (New York: Harper & Row, 1964).
17. F. James Davis, "Cultural Perspectives of Middle Eastern Students in America," *Middle East Journal* 14 (Summer 1960): 256–264.

18

Patterns of U.S. Economic Assistance Policy

Of the approximately 3.5 billion people in the world, one-third are classified as "very poor" (with a per capita annual income of under 100 dollars and another one-third as "poor" (with a per capita annual income of between 100 and 250 dollars).[1] These statistics are disheartening in themselves, but even more alarming is the expectation that the rich (the one-third of the world's population with a per capita annual income of more than 250 dollars), who are primarily located in the Northern Hemisphere, will improve their already enviable position by the end of the 20th century at a much faster rate than the poor and very poor nations, located primarily in the Southern Hemisphere. The gulf between the rich and poor peoples and its projected widening presents to United States foreign policy one of the most challenging problems of the post-World War II period. As the Cold War has receded, the economic contrasts between the Northern and Southern Hemispheres have created new problems.

DEVELOPMENT OF U.S. FOREIGN-AID PROGRAMS

American foreign aid after World War II has exhibited several behavioral patterns in its attempts to close the gap between rich and poor nations. In order to analyze the contemporary role and problems of American aid activities, the historical trends in the development of U.S. economic assistance must first be reviewed.[2]

Lend-Lease and American Foreign Policy

The American government carried on extensive activities in economic and military assistance during World War II under the aegis of the Lend-Lease program, instituted before the U.S. entered the war to aid allies, or nations soon to become allies. Lend-Lease offered materiel to friendly nations to assist them in their war efforts against Germany, Japan, and Italy; eventually, all items (such as destroyers and trucks) were to be returned to the "lender" by the "borrower" or "leasee." Since military hardware has a tendency to become obsolete, the issue of the return of the equipment was academic (except in the case of the U.S.S.R., where the American government periodically demanded the return of Lend-Lease equipment as the Cold War developed).[3] Lend-Lease, in effect, was a euphemism for "gift" or "grant."

Almost 2 billion dollars in Lend-Lease programs were continued after World War II, but the American government believed that more effective agencies could be established to handle the problem of post-war reconstruction. Lend-Lease was phased out as two UN agencies became the focus for post-war rebuilding: the United Nations Relief and Rehabilitation Agency and the International Bank for Reconstruction and Development (IBRD), more often called the World Bank. The immensity of the rebuilding task as well as its complexity were far beyond the expectations of American decision makers in 1946–1947; neither agency, nor both together, possessed sufficient funds and functional powers to overcome obstacles to reconstruction.

Nor were the individual efforts of the United States sufficient to meet the challenge of reconstruction. Bilateral loans advanced by the United States to European nations were quickly depleted. The money was returned eventually to the American market to pay for importing tools and machinery needed to rebuild shattered European economies. Farm production had not recovered from the war, so the European governments used American loans to buy American food for their citizens. The combined shortcomings of United Nations and American efforts dictated a new approach: the Marshall Plan.

The Marshall Plan

In June 1947, Secretary of State George C. Marshall called for a united effort of the European nations to rebuild their economies.[4] The European states were called on to decide what they could do to help themselves, and then to determine how they could help each other. Marshall proposed that the deficit between self-help and realistic economic goals of recovery would be financed by the United States; it would provide the necessary funds after joint planning had revealed those areas of deficiency and need. The initial estimate of the Marshall Plan's cost ranged from 12 billion dollars to 17 billion dollars, a sum that staggered the collective imagination of the American body politic. The lower figure proved to be the more accurate, but even this amount represented two percent of the annual American gross national product.

The success of the 1948–1952 European Recovery Program (the official name for the Marshall Plan) in reaching or exceeding most goals injected a feeling of euphoria into other American foreign economic programs. Had the European experience proven less encouraging or had American decision makers realized that the European experience could not be replicated in other regions of the world, U.S. foreign economic policy might have continued on a more cautious note.

Trends in U.S. Foreign-Aid Policy Since the Marshall Plan

The outstanding success of the Marshall Plan was followed by several trends in American economic assistance programs as Washington searched for equally successful techniques to apply to the developing countries.

Trend toward Smaller Aid Appropriations. The American government's appropriations for foreign aid have followed a downward trend since the end of the Marshall Plan, as Figure 18–1 illustrates.[5] Appropriations for the Agency for International Development (AID) and its predecessor organizations remained fairly constant during the height of the Cold War. In the mid-1960s, disenchantment with the record of economic development since the Marshall Plan, coupled with continuing concern for the U.S. international trade position and the growing demands of the Vietnamese conflict, exerted an influence in favor of reduced AID appropriations. The AID budget is only one aspect of American foreign economic assistance, although it is the largest individual expenditure.

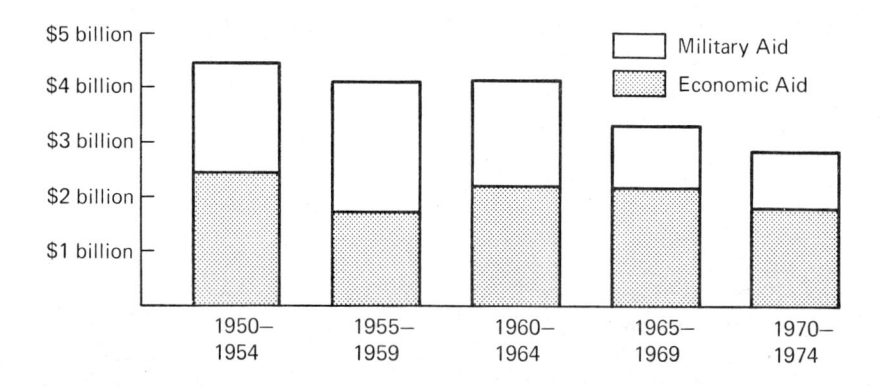

Figure 18–1. Agency for International Development: Military and Economic Assistance (Yearly Average). *(Source: Statistical Abstract of the United States.)*

chapter 18   U.S. Economic Assistance Policy

Trends in the Relationship of Economic to Military Aid. The United States began with an emphasis on economic aid in the early 1950s (*see* Figure 18–1), then moved to an emphasis on military assistance after the Korean War (during 1955–1959), then back to an emphasis on economic aid, and finally to a balance between military and economic assistance.[6] During the early 1970s, a renewed trend toward increased military aid was perceptible. The Nixon administration's "Vietnamization" program, initiated toward the end of the Indochina War, and increased military assistance to the Saigon government after American troops left Vietnam stimulated a rise in the military sector of the foreign-aid budget.

Trend toward Loans. According to Figure 18–2, economic assistance was largely in the form of grants or gifts; in the mid-1960s, loans became the major instrument for distributing assistance. Grants still account for over 50 percent of the AID budget. Grants have always been used extensively for military assistance, although some recipients began to purchase military equipment with long-term loans in the late 1950s.

The usual length of U.S. loans is 40 years and the interest rate is 2–3 percent, hardly covering the administrative costs of the loan. Forty years is an inordinately long period of time to tie up funds for most projects; projects with the lowest marginal utility should pay for themselves within four decades. Although the United States government has its money returned (and therefore cannot be accused of "giveaways"), the repayment period is protracted to the point that the usual diminution of purchasing power caused by inflation ensures that final payments are worth in dollars only a portion of their original value. Thus, the "giveaway" continues, but not as ostensibly as when grants outnumbered loans.

Aid for Developing Countries. Figure 18–3 contrasts the regional distribution of American foreign assistance during the three periods of the

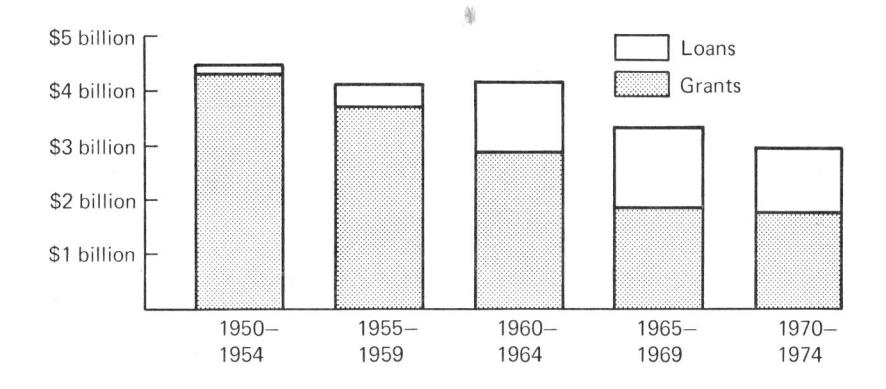

Figure 18–2. Foreign-Aid Grants and Loans (Yearly Average). *(Source: Statistical Abstract of the United States.)*

Figure 18-3. Regional Distribution of Foreign Aid (Yearly Average). *(Source: Statistical Abstract of the United States.)*

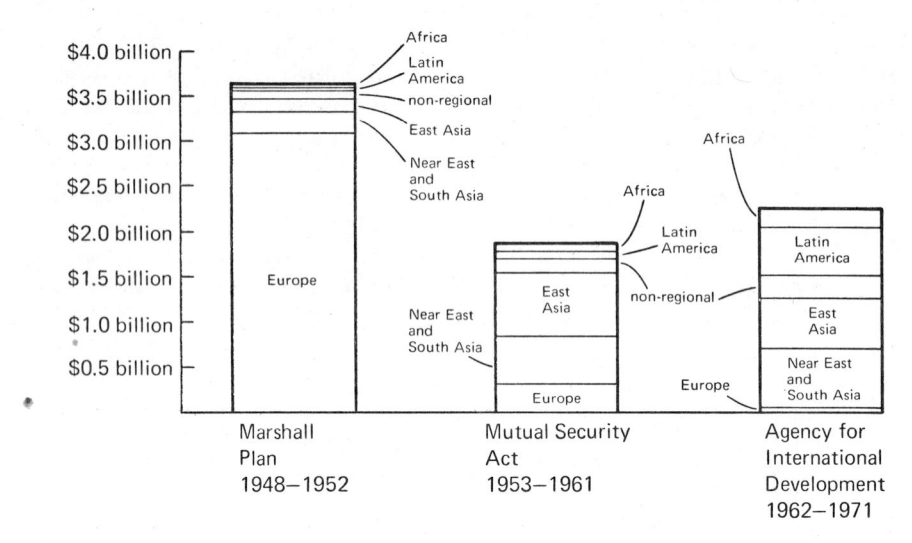

Marshall Plan, the Mutual Security Act (spanning the period of the Cold War), and the Agency for International Development. During the days of reconstruction from the devastation of World War II, European nations received 80 percent of American foreign-aid monies. The Near East/South Asian region was the second largest recipient because of sizable grants to Greece and Turkey, both of whom American decision makers perceived as prime targets for Soviet expansion. Within the East Asian region, the Republic of China (or Taiwan) received the most aid. Africa, which had few independent states at the time, and Latin America were the most neglected areas.

During the period of the Mutual Security Act, Washington's attention turned to Third World nations. The threat of Chinese Communist expansion in the Far East influenced the American government to spend most of its money there. Korea was the largest recipient, followed by Vietnam, where the French were bogged down in a guerrilla conflict. Aid to Africa and Latin America continued to be minimal.

During the 1960s, the Third World areas of East Asia, Latin America, and the Near East/South Asia received the largest shares of American economic assistance. Vietnam benefited the most, receiving more aid than all other nations in the East Asia area combined. Large appropriations to both India and Pakistan accounted for most of the rest of the money spent in the Near East/South Asian region. The Alliance for Progress prompted an increase in Latin American appropriations.

Trend toward Multilateral Aid. Figure 18-3 illustrates "non-regional" foreign aid that has been growing during the post-war period. This category encompasses grants to organizations, such as the United Nations and the

Inter-American Development Bank. The American government at first preferred to spend its money through direct negotiations with the recipient, rather than routing funds through an organization that would use its own criteria for disbursements. While "non-regional" appropriations are only 13 percent of the total aid budget, they are increasing and should be expected to do so throughout the 1970s.

Trends in Funding Projects. The early emphasis in American foreign-aid programs was on major, long-term, developmental programs, such as roads, dams, harbors, and irrigation projects. In recent years, the American government has shifted to projects that improve health, upgrade educational facilities, and increase agricultural production. These tend to be short term, with more immediate returns on the invested capital.

Trend toward Fewer Countries Receiving More Aid. Rather than attempting to support numerous projects in many countries, the U.S. government has begun to choose six or seven nations to receive larger amounts of money for development. States are chosen that are considered vital to the American national interest, that show promise of development, and that are important and powerful nations in the region. In the early 1970s, South Vietnam, South Korea, Indonesia, Brazil, Colombia, Chile, India, Pakistan, and Turkey received almost 85 percent of all foreign-aid funds.

SEARCH FOR A RATIONALE FOR ECONOMIC ASSISTANCE

Concomitant with the new trends in American economic assistance programs, a search has occurred for a rationale or justification for foreign aid itself. This search has led American decision makers through three phases.

The Justification for Early Programs

The brilliant successes of the Marshall Plan followed by the frustrations and disappointments of ensuing foreign-aid efforts have left many American decision makers and most of the American public disillusioned. The result has been a constant search for a credible justification for support of foreign-aid programs. American decision makers have followed one of several lines of argument to justify their early involvement in economic assistance activities. First, successive administrations perceived the less developed countries (LDCs) as politically unstable because of their lack of economic development. Instability generated chaos and dictatorship, especially dictatorship of the Communist Left. By strengthening the Third World economies, as they had the European economies, the United States would help remove destabilizing elements and thus discourage Communist revolutions. This rationale failed to take into account the disequilibrium that might be introduced by large injections of foreign aid. Economic assistance to LDCs overloaded their government bureaucracy and their communication and transportation systems. Aid was distributed unevenly throughout the economy; the lower classes received very little, and isolated pockets of middle and upper classes received a disproportionate share. The demand for skills created during the height of economic assistance tended to decrease so that workers were either unemployed or had to return to their previous jobs.

Only two states—Iran and Taiwan—have achieved economic growth without experiencing political and social instability and have requested that American technical assistance be terminated. Significantly, one state is governed by a strong monarchy (Iran) and the other by an equally strong military suzerainty (Taiwan). Both governments, judged at best as nondemocratic, guided their nations through the flux introduced by American economic aid. States without strong, authoritarian governments tend to experience the instability and chaos that American foreign aid is supposed to prevent.

American decision makers, in the second place, have justified military aid to LDCs with the argument that foreign armies could be developed with less cost and less risk than stationing American servicemen abroad. A West German, Turkish, Thai, or Pakistani soldier would entail from one-third to one-half the cost of an equivalent American soldier. This assumption also has been questioned by selected events in the post-war era. Pakistan's propensity to use its American-armed troops against India, rather than pointing them toward the Russian or Chinese "threat" to the north, has underscored the fact that the United States government has little control over these armies abroad. These armies may be a cheap means of defense, but American influence over their use is minimal.

Third, American foreign aid has served to ensure the support of governments friendly to the West in the Cold War. Jordan, for example, received significant amounts of American aid because the Jordanian monarchy showed promise of being more pro-West than any alternative ruling faction in contemporary Jordanian politics. This justification leaves American foreign policy open to the charge that the United States is more interested in buying allies than in developing economies. Perhaps this is part of the American "dollar psyche," a belief that money can stabilize tottering regimes and purchase inward allegiance as well as some outward manifestation of commitment. Normally, the influx of United States funds in these cases has propped up regimes that ordinarily would fall to pressures built up over unsolved domestic problems. When revolutions do come, they tend to topple American-supported rulers. The revolutionaries are portrayed as "anti-American" because they oppose an old regime openly supported by the United States.

Finally, humanitarian reasons for aid are often mentioned: eradication of disease, lowering of the infant mortality rate, increasing literacy, stimulating agricultural production, and raising the standard of living. Humanitarian motivations for foreign aid are difficult to assess. It is often asserted that they are platitudes serving as window dressing for politically motivated aid policies.

The Alliance for Progress: A New Rationale

With the traditional justification for foreign aid questioned, a new rationale was needed. In 1961, the Alliance for Progress, directed toward Latin America, offered a new approach based on different assumptions: a regional development with the recipients helping themselves and each other, after which the United States would assist in projects that the regional nations could not undertake alone or as a group.[7] The Alliance originally was scheduled for ten years, more than twice as long as the European Recovery Program, although the American investment was smaller (10 billion dollars as compared to the Marshall Plan's 13 billion dollars). The Alliance for Progress was based on the assumption that foreign aid should finance a *controlled* revolution in Latin America. Foreign aid previously had been used to bolster governments in power with either military or economic support in order to withstand an attempted coup d'etat from revolutionary groups. The Alliance, on the other hand, would finance revolutionary programs such as land reform; it would also encourage literacy and slum clearance programs. Assuming that violent revolution was inevitable in most Latin American countries, the Alliance attempted gradually and with minimum disruption to bring about change in a nonviolent way. The Alliance was revolutionary in goals but not in means.

The first decade of the Alliance for Progress expired in 1971 with a mixed record of success and failure. In part, the failure can be traced to forces within the Latin American states themselves—forces that opposed revolutionary means. The landed aristocracy, some clerics, and the military, sometimes in concert, sometimes alone, upheld the traditional way of life and the vested interests that they enjoyed under it. Communist parties, ordinarily revolutionary forces, refused to support a foreign-aid program that usurped their most popular aims and objectives.

A second major cause of failure was the shift in American policy. Gradually, the Johnson administration in the 1960s shifted from a regional approach to an individual-country approach. This shift was motivated by an understandable disenchantment with the performance, or lack of it, of the Latin American countries. And, as the Johnson administration became more involved in the Vietnam War after 1964, it began to neglect all other parts of the world, not only Latin America.

Finally, the basic defect of economic aid programs began to show itself in the Alliance for Progress as it has in other attempts to assist LDCs. Trade imbalances became so critical that economic aid constituted only a bailing-out endeavor, permitting the LDCs to remain afloat by constantly covering the difference between exports and imports. If the LDCs (and Latin America in particular) are to grow as fast as the developed nations, they must first solve the problems of a severely imbalanced trade position. In its second decade, the Alliance for Progress nations chose to work toward a regional trading association, a step discussed in chapter 19.

Political Development

Political Development and Vietnam. Political development, as an approach to and justification for the use of foreign-aid appropriations, refers to a policy of building a viable political system in a Third World nation. More than economic development is involved: the donor nation may take a direct interest in domestic matters, pacification activities, and construction of an efficient administrative structure. While economic development is a traditional focus for foreign-aid programs, political development is of more recent origin.

While the Alliance for Progress eventually led to financing regional trade arrangements as a justification for aid, a different set of assumptions resulted in a new rationale in Vietnam: political development. It remains to be seen whether political development will become a part of the patterns of American foreign policy. Political development, however, could signal a new shift in emphasis, in an attempt to make the Third World economic assistance programs more viable. For the United States, the Vietnamese conflict was the laboratory for applying and perfecting the concept of political development. In Vietnam, economic development was complicated by the absence of internal stability and by a central government whose hegemony extended to only a part of the territory ascribed to it on world maps. Consequently, the normal procedures for dispersing aid had to be modified and new objectives developed. Aid money for refugees, for veterans (especially the disabled), and for widows and orphans were a few examples of the demands that political development made on the traditional economic assistance program in Vietnam.[8]

Political development also entailed a much larger American involvement in the planning and implementation processes than had been the case in normal economic development. AID personnel assumed a greater role in domestic decision making to the point that the Vietnam situation became an example of an underdeveloped nation that was penetrated almost totally by the politics of a developed country.

Political development was a continuing, and highly frustrating, activity largely brought on by the interrelationship of problems in a country torn by civil war. For economic development to occur, for example, effective military control had to be established over the countryside dominated by the Viet Cong. Otherwise, funds for fertilizer to grow larger rice yields would only benefit the enemy. Saigon's control often extended to the daylight hours only, while the night belonged to the Viet Cong, a condition that made continuous economic development largely impossible. Since economic development had to wait until the fighting stopped in an area, political development demanded a pacification program as a prerequisite to growth.

Other Examples of Political Development. Besides Vietnam, only a handful of examples of political development can be studied. In Latin America, American foreign-aid funds have often been employed to finance civic action projects by the recipient's army.[9] These projects, which benefit the local population, include building roads, bridges, or schoolhouses. If political development becomes the rationale for foreign-aid programs, it will be as a result of the Latin American experience and not that of Vietnam.[10]

CONTEMPORARY PROBLEMS OF FOREIGN DOMESTIC ASSISTANCE

As American decision makers search for a rationale for present programs in economic assistance, fresh problems continue to arise that make their task more difficult. The new problems challenged many of the basic assumptions undergirding American foreign-aid programs. They also engendered criticism of the implementation of various programs in the field. The four most salient problems are: (1) the inability of the LDCs to significantly increase their agricultural production; (2) increases in population that all but wiped out economic growth in most Third World states; (3) the behavior of the American investor that has raised serious doubts in the non-Western leader's mind about private sources of funds; and (4) the fear that "modernization" also means "Westernization," a threat to the integrity and identity of Third World cultures.

The Problem of World Agricultural Production

The LDCs and Agricultural Production. While dire predictions of worldwide hunger have not proven true, the present-day picture of food supply and need is not encouraging. Starvation is a possibility in most developing nations, and malnutrition is a reality in most underdeveloped ones. The prospects for the future are not much brighter because the world's population is growing at a rate of 3 percent annually, while food production is increasing only 1 percent each year.

Public Law 480. United States foreign aid has gone increasingly into projects that stimulate agricultural production, not only because agricultural needs of the non-West are critical, but food-production activities are relatively inexpensive (except for irrigation projects) and yield rapid and tangible results to show both to the indigenous population and to the U.S. Congress. Another, more tenured aspect of U.S. economic assistance in the agricultural area is the Food for Peace program of Public Law 480. Passed in 1954, it represents an attempt to redistribute American agricultural surpluses among emerging nations. It is realized that the program cannot eliminate hunger, because American agricultural surpluses are not large enough to feed the populations of the Third World.

Public Law 480 programs are an outgrowth of an imbalance that characterized the American domestic agricultural market before the 1970s. Agricultural prices of selected products (such as rice and wheat) were supported by the U.S. government; whenever their market price fell, the government was committed to purchasing the products to maintain the specified level. As a result, the American government possessed large quantities of surplus products that had to be stored at significant costs. By the early 1950s, it was evident that storage was becoming a problem and that the Third World nations, which were becoming independent in large numbers after World War II, needed agricultural assistance. Consequently, Public Law 480 was developed to provide a means of disposing of stored food in a way that would not interfere with normal commercial sales overseas. American farmers supported the law because it helped eliminate an obvious problem that could eventually scuttle the entire farm subsidy program: large surpluses growing larger every year.[11] Public Law 480 is an example of a foreign policy outcome influenced by domestic politics. It also has a humanitarian motivation, captured in the title bestowed upon the program in 1961, "Food for Peace."

Food for Peace "Sales." The food shipped abroad under Public Law 480 is sold to recipient nations. Food for Peace shipments, however, bear a close resemblance to grants because the purchaser pays for the food in his own national currency, rather than gold or U.S. dollars. Consequently, "nondear" or "soft" currencies are used in the transactions. The currencies earned (called *counterpart funds*) are restricted by mutual agreement between the United States and the recipient nation. The currencies received for American agricultural products are subjected to rigorous restrictions of their use because of the weakened condition of most Third World economies. Counterpart funds cannot be taken out of the recipient nation, nor can they be spent on goods within the recipient country and those goods exported. The money can be spent, but only on highly circumscribed occasions, such as for travel expenses by Congressmen visiting the recipient nation. The funds may also be used to cover costs of operating the U. S. embassy, consulate, or USIS facilities in the country. Some of the collected counterpart funds represent large sums of money which, if released into the recipient nation's economy, might contribute to domestic inflation.

The worth of the counterpart funds is, in reality, dubious. Inflation in the emerging nations receiving Food for Peace has sapped the amassed counterpart funds of much of their purchasing power.

Amounts and Regional Distribution. The American government has distributed almost 20 billion dollars in agricultural surpluses since the end of World War II. While Public Law 480, passed in 1954, dates the major thrust of selling American agricultural surpluses abroad, this activity was carried out on an ad hoc basis in the late 1940s and early 1950s. The program reached its peak in the mid 1960s, as Figure 18–4 reveals. Rising agricultural prices in the 1970s meant that the U.S. government's farm price-support system was no longer needed. With a market to sell produce and with a limited amount in storage, Food for Peace activity receded. President Nixon's diplomatic initiatives toward the People's Republic of China and the Soviet Union also opened up new markets for American ag-

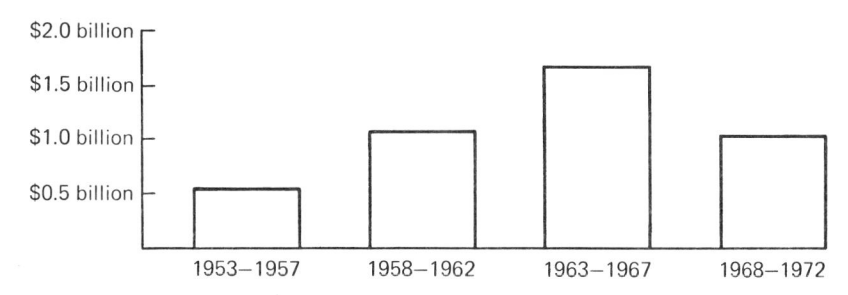

```
$2.0 billion ┐
$1.5 billion ┤
$1.0 billion ┤
$0.5 billion ┤
              1953–1957   1958–1962   1963–1967   1968–1972
```

Figure 18–4. Food for Peace Appropriations (Yearly Average). *(Source: U.S. Overseas Grants and Loans and the Statistical Abstract of the United States, 1972.)*

riculture. In 1972 the Soviet Union purchased 11 million tons of American wheat, one-fourth of the U.S. harvest for the year. The European and Japanese market for American soybeans continued to grow as well.

The region that has profited the most from Food for Peace is the Near East/South Asia, receiving almost 50 percent of the total cumulative and fiscal year funds. India, the second most populous state in the world, and the single largest recipient of Food for Peace shipments, is responsible for the high figure in this region. In the same region, Egypt has received large quantities of Public Law 480 food, ranking fourth in total receipts behind India, Yugoslavia, and Pakistan. The Egyptian Food for Peace purchases demonstrate that the program has been administered without an overly large amount of deference paid to ideology. The American government has kept Food for Peace shipments sailing to nations that have been critical of, and sometimes very hostile toward, American foreign policy.

Occasionally, Congress and the President have disagreed over the list of nations to receive Food for Peace shipments. Congress has attempted to use the program as a wedge against nations whose foreign policy objectives appear to contradict those embraced by American diplomacy. In 1966, for example, Congress tacked on a provision that would prohibit Public Law 480 sales to nations trading with the North Vietnamese. The ban covered more than the simple selling of strategic as well as non-strategic goods; it also encompassed transporting goods to Hanoi. A similar ban was imposed on nations doing business with Cuba, but in this case the President was given discretionary power to waive the sanctions if the goods shipped to Castro were medical supplies or agricultural products. These decisions tended to make the Food for Peace program an ideological instrument of American foreign policy, which in turn generated suspicions among Third World nations about the sincerity and motivations of the United States.

Problems of Food for Peace. The Public Law 480 program is not without its problems, political as well as economic. Foremost among the problems is the disequilibrium that the injection of American agricultural surpluses can cause within the LDC's economy. Since its population is in dire need of food, the disequilibrium is tolerated. In some cases, especially in India and other cultures subsisting on rice, the traditional eating habits of the people have had to be modified to accept surplus wheat from the United States.

Another set of problems is posed by the lack of internal processing and distribution techniques of most Third World nations. The incoming surplus products many times must go through an intermediate stage before they can be consumed. Distribution problems run the gamut from corruption within government circles, which permits Public Law 480 food to be siphoned off and sold on the black market for personal gain, to prejudice among the distributing officials against certain tribes or classes of people, and to the lack of adequate roads and vehicles to get the foodstuff into the hinterlands where malnutrition is sometimes worse than in the cities.

Problems internal to the Washington bureaucracy have beset the program.[12] Competition for administrative control over the Food for Peace program stimulated a decade of jockeying between the departments of State and Agriculture after Public Law 480 was passed in 1954. The outcome: the Department of Agriculture was empowered to administer the program while the Department of State would decide who should receive the food. Day-to-day problems encountered in coordinating the Food for Peace program are solved by an interagency staff committee composed of representatives of the departments of State, Agriculture, Treasury, Commerce, Defense, the Office of Management and Budgeting, and the Agency for International Development.

The Problem of Population and Economic Growth

The relationship of population increases to economic growth is the second problem facing contemporary American foreign-aid programs. A developing nation growing at a respectable 5 percent (of its GNP) each year will receive only limited benefits from its efforts if its annual population increase is 3 percent. An increase in food production may not significantly contribute to a more nourished population even though that population may have more income and consumer goods as a result of a greater industrial output.[13]

While the relationship between population growth and economic prosperity is obvious, it was ignored by the American government until the late 1960s. In part, United States policy was dictated by religious considerations. The Roman Catholic Church has traditionally opposed family planning for its converts, and it frowned on a public policy that would provide contraceptives to the Third World. Moreover, the puritanical strain in American Protestantism has had an undetermined influence on the issue of contraception.

In the post-war era, two developing nations, Taiwan and South Korea, have achieved a perceptible reduction in birth rates. By making inexpensive contraceptives available (such as intrauterine devices), by liberalizing abortion laws, by financially rewarding sterilization volunteers, and by providing information on family planning, the rate of population increase has been reduced. The United States has permitted foreign-aid funds to be used to support these programs.

Population control is all the more important as elementary health procedures are instituted in the Third World nations. Birth rates are always high in these states, but an equally high infant mortality rate has been the macabre means by which population growth has been restrained. Better-trained midwives, more sterile conditions for birth, and eradication of diseases such as malaria have contributed to lowering the infant mortality rate. The life span has been further lengthened by improvements in medical treatment in the emerging nations. Generally, health procedures introduced are quite inexpensive yet yield significant results. Eradicating fatal diseases, such as smallpox and cholera, and treating energy-sapping hookworms involve relatively simple and invariably effective procedures that have been common to industrialized societies for decades. Consequently, the life span, which in some LDCs was as low as 30 years, has been gradually increasing as advances in medical science are brought to the Third World peoples.

The lengthening of the life span and lowering of the infant mortality rate are additional reasons for urgency in defusing the population bomb. The present world population is expected to double by the year 2000 to over 7 billion people, with 80 percent living in Third World nations. These facts belatedly convinced the United States government to invest some of its foreign-aid funds in family-planning projects.

The Problem of Private Investment and Development

Rationale for Private Investment. American leadership emerged from World War II with a view that foreign aid would be needed only to supplement the private efforts of American businessmen in rebuilding war-devastated Europe and the small number of nations emerging from colonial rule. Under no conditions would governmental efforts displace or discourage those of the private investor who would develop the Third World economies. This idealism was founded on the optimistic expectation that American private investment would rapidly increase from the small 14.7 billion dollars committed abroad in 1945. Indeed, this expectation proved accurate; the increase has been sevenfold and is now above the 100-billion-dollar mark.[14]

Although the expectations of growth were realized, the expectations of results were not. The private investor neglected the Third World and concentrated his money in "safe" places, primarily Canada and Europe. If he ventured outside these safe havens of stable economies, he opted for the Republic of South Africa, Australia, or New Zealand, hardly non-Western nations. The private investor viewed as too risky those LDC governments who needed capital and who found that the quickest way to obtain it was to confiscate foreign holdings. Nor did the investors want to venture into a country rent by constant turmoil and revolution.

Moreover, the developing nations have learned through unfortunate experiences to distrust the private investor.[15] The investor's emphasis largely has been on extractive industries: raw materials that can be taken out of the nation and processed elsewhere, and natural resources. After decades of watching the private investor take his profits home at the expense of depleting national resources, the Third World's suspicion that the private investor is hardly interested in its economic development has been confirmed. Gradually, Third World leaders have moved to claim a larger share of the profits derived from private investments.

Characteristics of Private Investment. Private investment can be characterized according to type, location, industry, and returns.

TYPES OF PRIVATE INVESTMENT. Private investment is divided into direct and indirect categories. *Direct investments* are branches and subsidiaries of American companies established abroad; *indirect,* or *portfolio, investments* are purchases of securities (stocks and bonds) on foreign markets. Usually a combination of both types of investment is found in each country, although direct investment is greater and more important than indirect. Indirect investments amounted to 27 billion dollars in 1970; direct investments were almost 80 billion dollars.

LOCATION OF INVESTMENTS. American private investment is located overwhelmingly in Canada, Western Europe, and Latin America. These areas account for over 80 percent of the total direct investment (*see* Figure 18-5). In Latin America, the most popular places for investors are Vene-

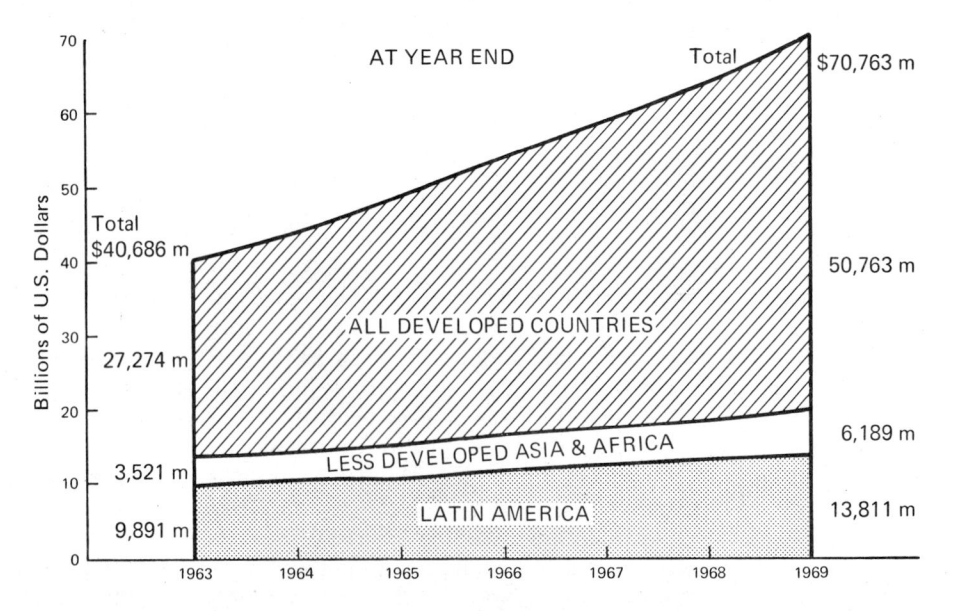

Figure 18-5. Book Value of Direct Investment. (*Source:* Adapted from *Survey of Current Business* 50 (September 1970: 21.)

zuela, Mexico, and Brazil. In Europe, approximately 35 percent of the investments are in Great Britain. In Africa, the Republic of South Africa has received the major share—over 40 percent of the money invested.

REGION AND TYPE OF INVESTMENT. The type of direct investment that is popular with the American businessman varies by region and reveals an interesting pattern, illustrated by Figure 18-6. The pattern in Third World nations is to invest heavily in extractive industries, such as petroleum, mining, and smelting; manufacturing has attracted less than one-third of direct investment there. This pattern reflects a concern in the United States for natural resources, which became especially acute with the development of the "energy crisis" in the early 1970s. Alternative sources of petroleum to fuel the growing energy needs of American industries and consumers became the object of extensive searches by U.S. firms.

Third World nations also are yielding higher profits for American investors than the more developed nations of Europe and Canada. The book value of direct investment in the developed nations is much larger than in LDC areas, but developing nations are yielding a disproportionately larger share of profits. While most of the investments are flowing into developed

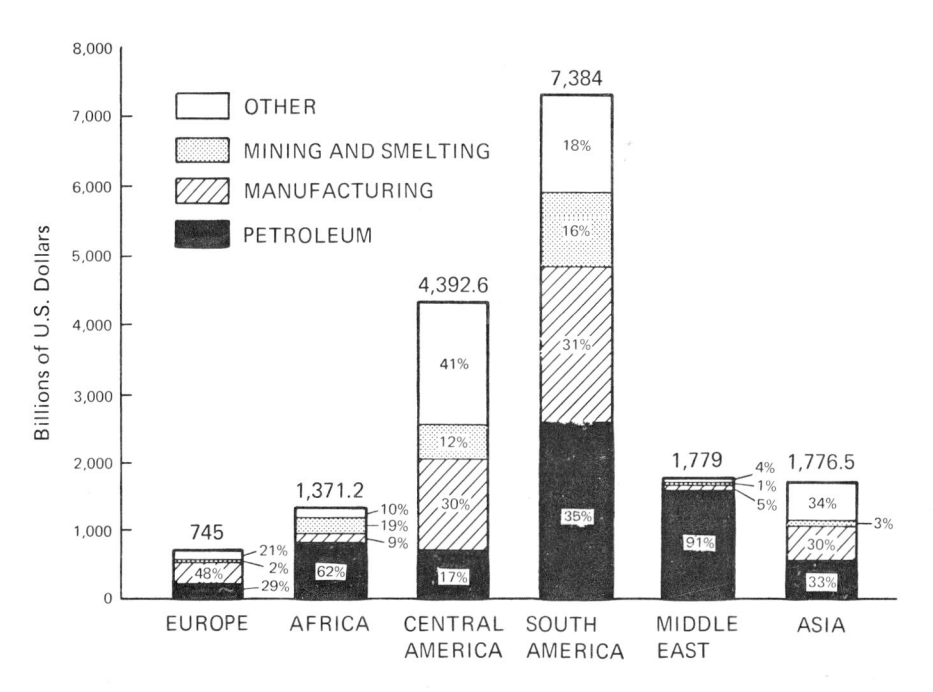

Figure 18-6. **Book Value of U.S. Direct Investment (1967) in the LDCs by Area and Sector.** *(Source:* "Private Direct Investments by DAC [Development Assistance Committee] Countries in Developing Countries" [Paris: Organization for Economic Cooperation and Development [OECD], 1971]).

countries, most of the income repatriated from investments is flowing from the Third World. In 1970, for example, American businesses invested 1,645 million dollars in the Middle East while repatriating 1,206 million dollars in income from interest, dividends, and branch earnings; thus, the amount of money flowing out of the Middle East is almost as much as the investment flowing in. Europe, however, received 24,471 million dollars and returned only 1,378 million dollars.[16]

One obvious reason for these divergent ratios of earnings to investment statistics is that the developed nations tend to attract capital-intensive industries that require large outlays of money for machinery. Moreover, the private investor in the industrialized Northern Hemisphere will leave his money in the country, reinvesting it in more capital-intensive projects. He is willing to do this because he does not fear confiscation of his long-term investments.

Occasionally, a multinational company (MNC) will undertake activities that are contrary to the expressed interests of the United States and are detrimental to the host nation. International Telephone and Telegraph allegedly approached the U.S. State Department with an offer to fund political activities against a socialist government in Chile in the early 1970s.

Not all MNCs are industrial giants; finance and banking are also important international economic actors. Chase Manhattan Bank, for example, has branches in almost every nation, including the People's Republic of China and the Soviet Union. Chase Manhattan's board chairman meets with heads of state when he travels abroad. International finance organizations and MNCs are transnational actors that possess incalculable economic and political influence.[17]

Problems Posed by Private Investment: Brain Co-option. The activities of private investors have several areas of concern for the host country, the first of which is the practice of hiring native talent and putting it to work in the interests of making profits for American-owned industries. In chapter 17, the problem of the educated Third World elite migration from their native land, where they were very much needed, to the United States was examined. This phenomenon was labeled the *brain drain*. A new term must be coined for the native scientist who finds employment with an American-based multinational firm in his country: *brain co-option*. The scientist, in this case, does not leave his country, but his talents are nevertheless put to use by a manufacturing or commercial business whose parentage is in the United States. Although his wages will be spent in his own country, he is a loss to his nation's economic development, except by the circulatory and dubious route of the American subsidiary. His skills, in other words, have been co-opted.

Problems Posed by Private Investment: Economic Domination. Although a Trojan Horse analogy to private investment is overly exaggerated, there is substantial foundation to the fears that investment abroad by American businessmen is creating an instrument for possible influence, if not domination, of the host country. In Canada, for example, American businesses own over half of the manufacturing, petroleum, natural gas, mining, and smelting industries. Over 80 percent of all non-Canadian investment in Canada comes from the United States. The French were nonplused when they discovered that their nuclear strike force, built over American opposition and to serve as a deterrent independent of United States policy, was very much dependent on computers built by American firms. Political independence does not necessarily mean economic independence.

Many Third World nations generally have come to view American investment abroad as neo-colonialism, or colonial domination in a different form. The foreign subsidiaries make inviting targets to nationalize. Nationalization is permitted by international law if the government ordering the action reimburses the owners.[18] Here, the nationalization process evolves into a tug-of-war; the investor estimates the worth of his equipment and business at a much higher figure than the host government is willing to pay. Most claims can be negotiated, although some linger on. Cuba's nationalization decrees were disputed because Castro wanted to reimburse American investors with bonds payable in pesos in the future. The American investors, suspicious of the present value of the Cuban peso and fearful of its value ten or twenty years hence, demanded dollars or gold. A few claims have been arbitrated, such as those arising out of Nasser's nationalization of the Suez Canal in 1956.

Traditionally, the flag has followed investments. Foreign governments who confiscated American-owned enterprises have frequently found themselves confronted with a political crisis with the United States government. Ordinarily, the State Department does not relish these confrontations; however, American businesses, especially large ones such as the United Fruit Company, have been able to gain a sympathetic hearing from certain congressmen. Consequently, the State Department has intervened on behalf of U.S. business interests in disputes with foreign nations. This problem may recede due to the International Bank for Reconstruction and Development's Convention on the Settlement of International Investment Disputes. This convention provides legal machinery for businessmen to use in disputes over confiscation or in other areas of contention. Not all countries, however, have subscribed to the convention. As an additional step, the State Department offers a form of "confiscation insurance" to companies investing abroad.

Problems Posed by Private Investment: Conflicts with American Foreign Policy. The final area of concern over American investments abroad deals with their conflicts with the stated aims of United States foreign policy. Often these conflicts occur in situations where the American government is following a policy of aloofness or even hostility toward a foreign nation, while the private investor is willing to ignore the official coolness because of attractive income possibilities. Two blatant instances of this development in the late 1960s were Greece and the Republic of South Africa. In 1967 a coup d'etat deposed the Greek king and brought a military junta to power. The American government reacted to the monarch's overthrow by cutting off military shipments under foreign aid. American investors, however, ignored the imbroglio and continued business as usual. In another affair, the American government in the early 1960s soundly criticized South Africa's policy of *apartheid* ("separateness"), or discrimination against blacks. The State Department admonished American businessmen to avoid the lucrative South African market (which offered one of the highest rates of returns in the world). The admonition was generally ignored.[19]

One frequent consequence of placing branches of American multinational firms in foreign countries is the development of a "dual loyalty." Does the American subsidiary abroad owe its allegiance to the foreign policy objectives of the U.S. or of the host country? Invariably, the American multinational subsidiary abroad will adhere to the dictates of United States foreign policy. The American firm, under these conditions, becomes an extension of American foreign policy in the host country.[20]

Economic Development and Cultural Identity

Development without Westernization. The Third World is striving to develop economically without losing its unique cultural identity.[21] Business and governmental personnel from industrialized nations tend to view culture-based mores and taboos as obstacles to development. Family ties, for example, may be stronger than the profit-making motive in LDCs. Nepotism is prevalent; members of the family are added to native businesses whether or not their services are needed and are retained whether or not they perform well. In some of the cultures of the emerging nations, the urge to take risks is lessened by traditions that frown on aggressiveness. Employers often find it difficult to offer constructive criticism to workers: to criticize an employee would result in his loss of "face" before his fellow workers.

The influx of American aid and industries into a developing nation often raises the problem of cultural identity. The LDCs are interested in the economic benefits of Westernization: the eradication of illiteracy and poverty, and the scientific and technological advances in health, food production, and other areas of the "good life." At the same time, the non-Western peoples are proud of their heritage and desire to maintain it. They fear that American culture will be brought in with American aid, trade, and investment. In short, can the Third World nations develop industrially and still maintain their traditional cultural identity?

Cultural Identity and Socialism. It is ironic that the non-West has tended to adopt an economic ideology, Marxism, that originated in the West and was primarily an explanation of an anticipated economic collapse of Western capitalism. Non-Western leaders have exhibited an inclination to mold a Western philosophy (Marxism) to conform to Third World circumstances. However, the socialism of Karl Marx has been screened through the prism of Russian Communism, and the colors that appear are not as Western as before.

Further transformation of Marxist ideology has occurred as it has been subjected to the economic realities of emerging nations, resulting in a highly practical blending of planned economic growth and private enterprise. This result cannot be accurately classified as a Soviet version of Communism, nor can it be called Western capitalism. This mixed approach to economic development should be viewed as an attempt by Third World nations to borrow from both East and West and to maintain their own identity in the international system.

The United States government has been unable to understand the Third World's attraction to socialism, to comprehend its differences with Soviet Communism or the classical writings of Marx, and to tolerate its existence in governments receiving U.S. dollars in foreign aid. In effect, the State Department wants recipients of economic assistance to politically duplicate the American system. Washington's insensitivity to the recipient's desire to walk its own ideological and cultural paths has resulted in needless diplomatic friction.

FOREIGN AID: AN EVALUATION

Success and Failure

The analysis of American foreign economic assistance presented in this chapter leads to the conclusion that the policy direction of foreign aid after the Marshall Plan has been deteriorating. After an outstanding success in reconstructing Europe after World War II, the United States has largely failed in its goal to close the gap between the rich and the poor nations.

The image of failure has reinforced the continual decrease in American interest in the economic problems of developing nations. As the United States has grown richer, its concern for foreign assistance activities has waned. From a high of over 2 percent of the GNP committed to foreign aid during the Marshall Plan, the U.S. aid program has fallen to approximately one-third of one percent of the GNP. In terms of percentage of the GNP, Washington ranks 12th among the 16 countries providing such aid, although the U.S. gives more dollar aid than other nations.[22] The oft-stated goal for developed nations is to contribute one percent of their gross national product for economic assistance. The United States is far from this goal which other states, such as Australia and Belgium, have achieved.

Lack of Evaluative Instruments

So many criticisms have been leveled at American foreign-aid programs that it is difficult to believe that economic assistance has any redeeming qualities. The criticisms come from two angles, one from orthodox economists and the other from revisionist economists.

To orthodox economists, foreign-aid programs have suffered from policy misjudgments and miscalculations that have brought about too many failures, if indeed failure can be determined. No reliable instrument to evaluate foreign-aid programs exists to conclude with certainty that U.S. economic assistance efforts in a specific nation are a "success" or "failure." Until valid procedures are developed to ascertain the success or failure of economic-aid programs, we are left with our instincts to judge whether foreign aid is worth the expense and effort.[23]

The mixture of political values with economic principles has contributed to the absence of evaluative instruments for foreign-aid programs. U.S. economic assistance programs have been, and continue to be, instruments for rewarding friends and for aiding states perceived as threatened by Communist expansion. While the theoretical purpose of American foreign aid is economic development, its real goal is support for governments whose continued existence is viewed with favor. In the perception of American decision makers, the alternatives to friendly governments in Jordan, Iran, South Korea, and South Vietnam were not acceptable. Concern for political values in American foreign policy has overshadowed basic economic standards that may be used to decide upon an equitable economic distribution.

The revisionist economists have no argument with evaluation; they believe that American foreign aid has been all too successful in perpetrating U.S. political interests abroad. The economic development of the recipients was never a major priority; therefore, to discuss "evaluation of effectiveness" is to dignify a program of selfish national interest that has worked against the national interests of recipient nations. In Brazil, for example, U.S. policies countervailed Brazilian efforts to modernize. The American program contributed to perpetuating Brazil's traditional oligarchy of special interests, rather than improving the lot of poor Brazilians.[24]

While the debate between orthodox and revisionist political economists rages, the gap between the rich northern and poor southern nations becomes larger. American foreign-aid efforts are hampered at home by lack of popular and congressional support, shortages and inflation, and buffeted abroad by adverse trade balances. The American economy no longer possesses the economic capacity or the will to lead the crusade to close the North–South gap through foreign-aid programs. Although suggestions have been proposed to reform foreign aid as an instrument of diplomacy,[25] American leaders in the 1970s are turning to trade as the solution, the subject of the next chapter.

NOTES

1. George D. Woods, "The Development Decade in the Balance," *Foreign Affairs* 44 (January 1966): 206–215.
2. For a general discussion of American aid programs, *see* Michael K. O'Leary, *The Politics of American Foreign Aid* (New York: Atherton, 1967); John D. Montgomery, *Foreign Aid in International Politics* (Englewood Cliffs, N.J.: Prentice-Hall, 1967); Max F. Millikan and

Donald L. Blackmer (eds.), *The Emerging Nations: Their Growth and United States Policy* (Boston: Little, Brown and Co., 1961); Edward S. Mason, *Foreign Aid and Foreign Policy* (New York: Harper & Row, 1964); George Liska, *The New Statecraft: Foreign Aid in American Foreign Policy* (Chicago: University of Chicago Press, 1960); Doris A. Graber, "Are Foreign Aid Objectives Attainable?" *Western Political Quarterly* 19 (March 1966): 68–84; Andrew F. Westwood, *Foreign Aid in a Foreign Policy Framework* (Washington, D.C.: Brookings Institution, 1966); Harry G. Johnson, *Economic Policies Toward Less Developed Countries* (Washington, D.C.: Brookings Institution, 1967); David A. Baldwin, *Economic Development and American Foreign Policy, 1943–1962* (Chicago: University of Chicago Press, 1966); H. B. Chenery and A. M. Strout, "Foreign Assistance and Economic Development," *American Economic Review* 56 (1966): 679–733; Milton Friedman, "Foreign Economic Aid: Means and Objectives," *Yale Review* 47 (June 1958): 500–516; and Herbert Feis, *Foreign Aid and Foreign Policy* (New York: St. Martin's Press, 1964). For a negative view of foreign aid, see Otto E. Passman, "Why I Am Opposed to Foreign Aid," *New York Times Magazine* (July 7, 1963): 16–17 and Eugene W. Castle, *Billions, Blunders, and Baloney* (New York: Devin-Adair, 1955).

3. Robert H. Jones, *The Roads to Russia: U.S. Lend-Lease to the Soviet Union* (Norman: University of Oklahoma Press, 1969); Warren F. Kimball, *The Most Unsordid Act: Lend-Lease, 1939–1941* (Baltimore: Johns Hopkins University Press, 1969); and George C. Herring, Jr., *Aid to Russia, 1941–1946: Strategy, Diplomacy, the Origins of the Cold War* (New York: Columbia University Press, 1973).

4. Harry B. Price, *The Marshall Plan and Its Meaning* (Ithaca, N.Y.: Cornell University Press, 1955); Hadley Arkes, *Bureaucracy, the Marshall Plan, and the National Interest* (Princeton, N.J.: Princeton University Press, 1973); and Geoffrey Warner, "Truman Doctrine and Marshall Plan," *International Affairs* 50 (January 1974): 82–92.

5. Finding consistent data on U.S. foreign-aid expenditures is not an easy task. For example, programs may be included in one year's figures and dropped in another, raising doubts about the validity of the statistics. In this chapter, the *Statistical Abstract of the United States* is the source for foreign-aid statistics. Another source is *U.S. Overseas Loans and Grants,* published by AID; occasionally, this publication's data will not correspond to those found in *Statistical Abstract*. A similar problem is encountered in chapter 19 when reconciling trade data published in the *Survey of Current Business, Federal Reserve Bulletin,* and the *Statistical Abstract.*

6. Harold A. Hovey, *United States Military Assistance: A Study of Policies and Practices* (New York: Praeger, 1965).

7. Harvey S. Perloff, *Alliance for Progress: A Social Invention in the Making* (Baltimore: Johns Hopkins Press, 1969); Martin C. Needler, *The United States and the Latin American Revolution* (Boston: Allyn

& Bacon, 1972); and Victor Alba, *Alliance without Allies: The Mythology of Progress in Latin America* (New York: Praeger, 1966). The reader may contrast the pessimistic views of these three authors with the earlier optimism over the alliance contained in John C. Drier, *The Alliance for Progress: Problems and Perspectives* (Baltimore: Johns Hopkins Press, 1963), and Lincoln Gordon, *A New Deal for Latin America: The Alliance for Progress* (Cambridge: Harvard University Press, 1963).

8. John D. Montgomery, *The Politics of Foreign Aid: American Experience in Southeast Asia* (New York: Harper & Row, 1964); Amos A. Jordan, Jr., *Foreign Aid and the Defense of Southeast Asia* (New York: Praeger, 1962); and Robert Scigliano and Guy H. Fox, *Technical Assistance in Vietnam: The Michigan State University Experience* (New York: Praeger, 1965).

9. Harry F. Waterhouse, *A Time to Build: Military Civil Action* (Columbia: University of South Carolina, 1964).

10. Helio Jaquaribe, *Political Development: A General Theory and a Latin American Case Study* (New York: Harper & Row, 1973), and Anibal Pinto, "Political Aspects of Economic Development," in Claudio Veliz (ed.), *Obstacles to Change in Latin America* (Santiago: Edit. Universitaria, 1965), pp. 9–46. Some of the literature on political development has been more general and not specifically related to foreign aid. This literature often looks at political and economic development in an historical perspective. See Edward Shils, *Political Development in the New States* (The Hague: Mouton, 1962); and Lucian W. Pye, *Aspects of Political Development* (Boston: Little, Brown and Co. 1966).

11. J. H. Davis, "Agricultural Surpluses and Foreign Aid," *American Economic Review* 49 (1959): 232–241.

12. Peter A. Toma, *The Politics of Food for Peace: Executive–Legislative Interaction* (Tuscon: University of Arizona Press, 1967).

13. Kingsley Davis, "The Political Impact of New Population Trends," *Foreign Affairs* 36 (January 1958), and Roy G. Francis (ed.), *The Population Ahead* (Minneapolis: University of Minnesota Press, 1958).

14. David B. Zenoff, *Private Enterprise in the Developing Countries* (Englewood Cliffs, N.J.: Prentice-Hall, 1969); Charles P. Kindleberger, *American Business Abroad* (New Haven: Yale University Press, 1969); J. N. Behrman, "Promoting Free World Economic Development Through Direct Investment," *American Economic Review* 50 (1960): 271–281; R. F. Mikesell (ed.), *U.S. Private and Government Investment* (Eugene: University of Oregon, 1962); and Paul O. Gaddis, "Analyzing Overseas Investment," *Harvard Business Review* 44 (May–June 1966): 115–122.

15. Raymond Vernon (ed.), *How Latin America Views the U.S. Investor* (New York: Praeger, 1966).

16. *Statistical Abstract of the United States,* 1972, p. 767.

17. Harvey D. Shapiro, "The Multinationals: Grants beyond Flag and

Country," *New York Times Magazine,* March 18, 1973, p. 20; Sidney E. Rolfe, *The International Corporation* (Paris: International Chamber of Commerce, 1969); Robert B. Stobaugh, Jr., "Financing Foreign Subsidiaries of U.S. Multinational Enterprises," *Journal of International Business Studies* 1 (1970): 43–64; Louis T. Wells, Jr., "The Multinational Business Enterprise: What Kind of International Organization?" in Robert O. Deohane and Joseph S. Nye, Jr. (eds.), *Transnational Relations and World Politics* (Cambridge: Harvard University Press, 1972); and John T. Wooster and G. Richard Thomas, "New Financial Priorities for MNCs," *Harvard Business Review* 52 (May–June 1974): 58–68.

18. Edward D. Re, *Foreign Confiscations in Anglo-American Law* (Dobbs Ferry, N.Y.: Oceana, 1951).

19. John Blashill, "The Proper Role of U.S. Corporations in South Africa," *Fortune* 86 (July 1972): 49–53; 89–91.

20. Raymond Vernon, "Multinational Enterprise and National Sovereignty," *Harvard Business Review* 45 (1967): 156–185.

21. This topic has generated a large amount of literature. A sample includes: Charles J. Eramus, *Man Takes Control: Cultural Development and American Aid* (Minneapolis: University of Minnesota Press, 1961); T. C. Cochran, "Cultural Factors in Economic Growth," *Journal of Economic History* 20 (December 1960): 515–530; George M. C. Foster, *Traditional Cultures and the Impact of Technological Change* (New York: Harper & Row, 1962); S. Herbert Frankel, *The Economic Impact on Under-Developed Societies: Essays on International Investment and Social Change* (Cambridge: Harvard University Press, 1959); James A. Lee, "Cultural Analysis in Overseas Operations," *Harvard Business Review* 44 (March–April 1966): 106–114; and Conrad M. Arensberg and Arthur Niehoff, *Introducing Social Change: A Manual for Americans Overseas* (Chicago: Aldine, 1964).

22. "Foreign Aid," *Foreign Policy Outlines* (Washington, D.C.: Department of State, 1973).

23. William and Elizabeth Paddock, *We Don't Know How: An Independent Audit of What They Call Success in Foreign Assistance* (Ames: Iowa State University Press, 1973).

24. Riordon Roett, *The Politics of Foreign Aid in the Brazilian Northeast* (Nashville, Tenn.: Vanderbilt University Press, 1972).

25. Some of the reforms suggested are developed in more detail in Robert E. Asher, *Development Assistance in the Seventies: Alternatives for the United States* (Washington, D.C.: Brookings Institution, 1970); Daniel Wit, "A New Strategy for Foreign Economic Aid," *Orbis* 7 (Winter 1964): 800–820; and Aurelius Morgner, "The American Foreign Aid Program: Costs, Accomplishments, Alternatives?" *Review of Politics* 29 (January 1967): 65–75.

19

Patterns of American Foreign Trade Policy

The post-World War II revolution in economics has been precipitated by several international factors: a weakened Europe, a stronger Japan, a strong United States growing weaker, and the emergence of Third World nations with their desire to develop industrially. As a result, the patterns of trading have undergone constant revision, and the stable international monetary system created at the end of World War II has gradually been eroded. These changes, some of them traumatic for American foreign policy, present the greatest challenge to the U.S. government in the 1970s.

The United States in 1945 was the primary source of manufactured goods and tools for businessmen of Western and developing nations. The "dollar shortage" that was created by Europe's large-scale purchases in the American market was solved by massive infusions of money under the Marshall Plan. As the world's economic giant, the United States produced 45 percent of the world's goods and claimed over 20 percent of the world's markets, while possessing only 6 percent of the world's population.

Today the "dollar glut," caused by U.S. consumers purchasing more foreign goods than U.S. businessmen are selling abroad, has replaced the "dollar shortage." By the early 1970s, the American economy's share of international production dropped to 30 percent and its claim on world trade to 14 percent. The reasons for this shift constitute the most complex topic in the study of American foreign policy.[1]

DEVELOPMENT OF POST-WAR TRADE POLICY

The Second World War disrupted the traditional patterns of international trade. In 1945, European and Japanese businessmen found themselves competing in an economic world devoid of their traditional customers. Their factories were largely destroyed and they lacked the financial capital to rebuild a viable economic system.

Three Solutions to Post-War Problems

The initial American attempt to solve the staggering problems of the post-war world was to establish a triad of organizations: the International Bank for Reconstruction and Development (IBRD), the International Monetary Fund (IMF), and the International Trade Organization (ITO). The first two were proposed and adopted before the Axis powers surrendered; the third came later in 1947 and was stillborn. The IBRD (or World Bank, as it informally has come to be called) was designed to handle Europe's reconstruction problems and the development needs of the rest of the world. The IMF was to establish order in international finance, and the ITO was to eliminate quotas and other non-tariff restrictions. This three-pronged approach was thought to be sufficiently potent to handle post-war economic problems, but obstacles developed that inhibited each of the three organizations from performing as well as their founders had anticipated. European reconstruction was too large a job for the IBRD to handle, and discontinuities in the international monetary system were too great for the IMF to be effective. Other nations did not have the dollar and gold reserves to purchase goods only available from the major industrial power unscathed by the war—the United States.[2]

ITO and GATT

Original and Substitute Proposals. Congressional reaction to ITO was negative. The Senate, especially, was reluctant to approve it because agreements for tariff reductions negotiated with other nations would have been effective without further congressional action. After the Senate failed to approve ITO, a substitute organization, the General Agreement on Tariffs and Trade (GATT), was founded in 1948. GATT is surprisingly simple in structure, compared to other international organizations. It is an example of bilateral tariff arrangements in a multilateral context. Many nations have "most-favored-nation" (MFN) clauses in their trade agreements, which means that more favorable terms of trade given to one country must be extended to all others. If the French tariff on wheat is reduced for the United States wheat grower, for example, it also must be reduced for the Canadian farmer. Since the MFN clause gave a multilateral dimension to trade negotiations, the international consequences of a two-nation agreement to reduce tariffs quickly could be ascertained and adjusted to (because all negotiating parties were present at the same GATT conference). Multilateral arrangements also are possible through arranging a series of bilateral agreements among several nations.

GATT negotiations have been conducted periodically during the post-war period (each series of negotiations being known as a *round*). Six rounds have been held since the founding of GATT; the last round (1963–67), named in honor of President John F. Kennedy, was the longest and most involved.[3] As a result of the GATT rounds, the United States no longer qualifies as a high-tariff country, a reputation that it gained from the prohibitive duties imposed by the 1930 Smoot-Hawley Tariff.

After the Kennedy Round. When the Kennedy round agreements were implemented in 1973, the critical condition of the American trade position became the primary concern in international economics. In the early 1970s, the United States began to import more than it exported; this situation encouraged a trend toward protectionism in American economic policy, reversing a forty-year trend toward free trade. When the GATT nations met again in Tokyo in September 1973 for the Nixon round, discussions centered on international monetary problems rather than on tariffs and nontariff obstacles to trade.

CONTEMPORARY PROBLEMS OF AMERICAN FOREIGN ECONOMIC POLICY

The contemporary problems in international economics centered on (1) American weaknesses in trade; (2) chronic U.S. balance-of-payments problems; and (3) the continuing needs for economic development of Third World nations (needs not met by foreign-aid programs). Finding workable solutions for these problems has been one of the most difficult tasks of contemporary American foreign policy.

The Balance of Trade: A Problem of Imbalance

The relationship of exports to imports is known as the *balance of trade*. A *trade surplus* (or "favorable balance") refers to an excess of exports over imports, and a *trade deficit* (or "unfavorable balance") indicates that more goods are being imported than exported. As Figure 19–1 shows, the United States enjoyed a trade surplus until 1971 when the American economy ran a trade deficit for two years.

Throughout the post-World War II period, the American economy exported more than it imported. In the 1960s, exports continued to rise, but at a slower rate than imports, until the amount of imported goods surpassed the amount that American businessmen sold abroad. Within this general pattern of exports and imports, several patterns have developed in American trade. They include trends in the location of trading partners, in the formation of regional trading blocs, and in the types of commodities exported and imported.

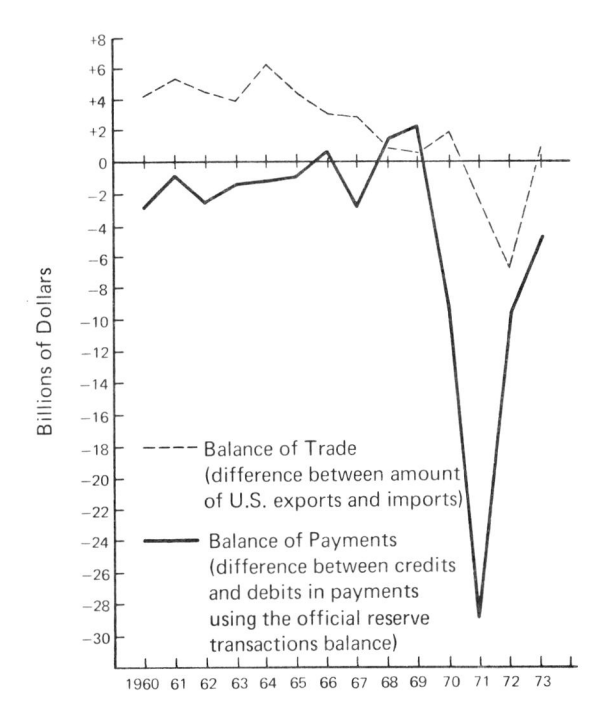

Figure 19-1. Patterns of Balance of Trade and Payments. *(Source: Economic Report of the President* [Washington, D.C.: U.S. Government Printing Office, 1974], pp. 350-351 and *Federal Reserve Bulletin* 6 [June 1974]: A60-A61. Data for 1973 are preliminary.)

Regional Trading Partners. In 1971, imports totaled 45.6 billion dollars and exports, 44.1 billion dollars. North America was the largest trading region for the U.S. primarily because Canada traditionally is the most active American buyer and supplier *(see* Figure 19-2). The United States also ran a trade deficit in 1971 with Europe, its second largest region for trade.

The major Asian trading partner for the U.S. in 1971 was Japan; next to Canada, it is the second largest customer of and seller to the American economy. Middle Eastern countries also are grouped in the Asian category. In 1971, the U.S. experienced a small trade deficit with Arab nations, a deficit that worsened after the 1973 Arab-Israeli conflict when the Arab oil-producing states raised their price of petroleum.

U.S. trade with Communist nations is not singled out in Figure 19-2. The Soviet Union and East European nations are grouped in the "Europe" category and the People's Republic of China in "Asia" because American trade with these nations in 1971 was quite small, a situation that Johnson's,

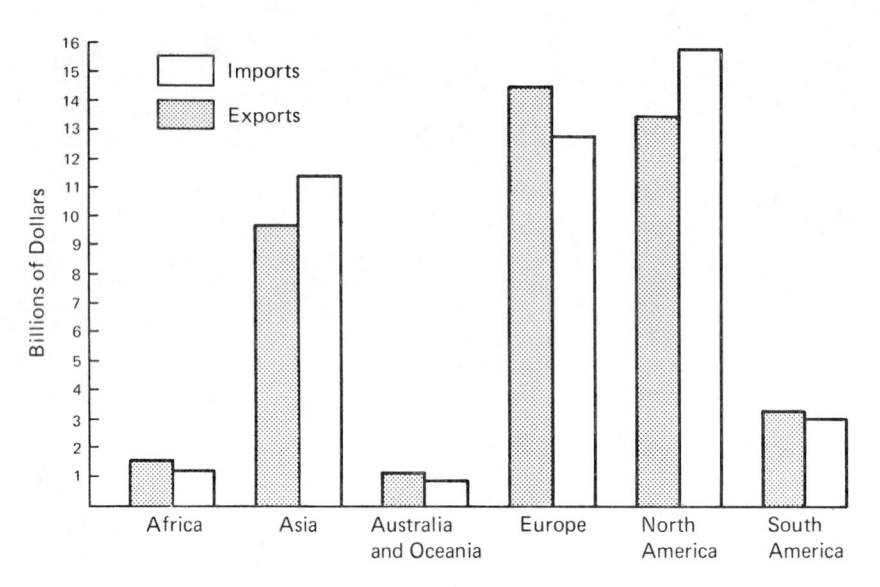

Figure 19-2. U.S. Exports and Imports by World Region, 1971. *(Source: Statistical Abstract of the United States.)*

and especially Nixon's administration set about to correct in the 1960s and 1970s.

Trading with Communist Nations. Washington's earlier policy toward East–West trade was substantially different.[4] Until the Cold War was replaced by a policy of detente, the State Department discouraged trade with Communist nations, a policy posture that often irritated European alliance partners. By the beginning of the 1970s, annual West German trade with the Soviet Union reached 2 billion dollars and Soviet–British trade, 1 billion dollars. The U.S.–U.S.S.R. trade was approximately 200 million dollars. Obviously, American industries were being excluded from profitable business ventures with Communist economies.

As a result of President Nixon's visits to Moscow and Peking in 1972, U.S. trade with the Soviet Union increased and official economic relations with the People's Republic of China were established for the first time in the post-war era. In 1973, the U.S.S.R. bought 1.2 billion dollars in American products and exported 214 million dollars to the U.S., an economic relationship that, on the surface, was overwhelmingly favorable to the American economy. American exports to China, composed mainly of agricultural products, reached 1 billion dollars in 1974.

Common Markets and U.S. Trade. Two regional economic organizations present peculiar challenges to U.S. foreign economic policy. The *common market* is an economic unit in which member nations agree to a common tariff wall to surround and protect the unit and to the reduction or elimination of tariff walls between themselves. In the early 1970s, the best-known common market organization was the European Economic

Community (EEC). The common market is distinct from the free trade association which has no common tariff wall around the unit, although tariff barriers are reduced or eliminated between nations within the unit.

Begun in 1958, the EEC originally consisted of six nations (Italy, France, Federal Republic of Germany, The Netherlands, Luxembourg, and Belgium); in 1972 Great Britain, Ireland, and Denmark also joined. The effect of EEC's common tariff wall on American exports is an obvious concern to Washington and to American businessmen. For example, it renders some parts of the German market inaccessible to Americans, and Germany was considered a low-tariff nation prior to the imposition of a higher, common EEC tariff. Although American exports to the original six European common market countries have grown since the community began, it is questionable whether American exports would have increased even more if EEC tariff policies were not in effect.[5]

Stimulated by the success of the EEC and the small Central American Common Market, Latin America established a regional common market as a goal. Constructing a regional common market among developing nations proved to be much more difficult than among developed nations. Consequently, the Organization of American States agreed to build two additional subgroups among South American states to supplement the Central American Common Market. The regional Latin American Common Market will have to wait until these subgroupings become viable organizations.[6]

The obvious danger to the American economy from both European and Latin American common markets is that the United States may find itself excluded from economic blocs composed of its traditional trading partners. American membership in regional groupings is not sought because of the size of the U.S. economy. The United States would cause major adjustment problems to other members and might dominate the group.

Types of Commodities. In addition to geographical distribution, the types of commodity groups exported from and imported into the United States are an important element in a profile of American trade.[7] Table 19–1 shows the largest category of exports as machinery and transport equipment.

Table 19–1. Selected Commodity Groups for Exports and Imports, 1971

Group	Percent of Total Exports	Imports
Food and live animals	10.0%	12.1%
Beverages and tobacco	1.6	1.9
Inedible crude materials, except fuels	9.9	7.4
Mineral fuels and related materials	3.4	8.1
Chemicals	8.8	3.5
Machinery and transport equipment	44.8	30.5
Other manufactured goods	16.4	32.7
Other transactions	5.1	3.8
Total	100.0	100.0

Source: *Statistical Abstract of the United States* (1972), pp. 782–87.

The American economy is the world's foremost supplier of industrial tools, construction equipment, and electronic computers. Automobiles, trucks, buses, aircraft, railway vehicles, and electrical equipment (such as household appliances) also are exported in large quantities. Among the food items, the United States exports grains (such as wheat and corn) and imports coffee, bananas, and sugar. Petroleum and petroleum products comprise a large part of the mineral fuels imported. If the "energy crisis" of the early 1970s continues, the United States economy will demand more of these products.

In short, the American nation is not a country that imports a large quantity of raw materials and sells finished products in return. The American citizen, as a member of an affluent society, buys foreign manufactured goods (or finished products) that usually can be made in his own country. The commodities that enter are competitive both in quality and price. Detroit, Chicago, and Pittsburgh may sell large amounts of machinery and transport equipment abroad, but foreign manufacturers of autos, television sets, motorcycles, calculators, and bicycles produce products that are competitive.

Agricultural Trade and U.S. Policy. While agricultural products represent only 10 percent of American exports, they are a vital part of U.S. trade patterns.[8] The agricultural yield from one out of every four acres in the United States is sold for foreign consumption. Some of the agricultural products exported represent a sizable proportion of the amount grown. Over 50 percent of the rice and soybeans produced in 1972 in the U.S. was shipped abroad, and over 40 percent of the American production of tallow, cattle hides, and wheat was exported.

So large is the export of American farm produce that the United States has been running a respectable balance in its agricultural trade, especially in 1973, as Figure 19–3 illustrates.[9] One reason for the agricultural trade surplus is the increasing demand for American food from nations that began experiencing a greater measure of affluency (e.g., Europe and Japan) and from nations encountering difficulty harvesting sufficient food for a growing population (e.g., U.S.S.R., People's Republic of China, and India). As a nation's standard of living increases, its population tends to eat more meat and less cereal. Although LDC's "purchase" American agricultural surpluses under the Food for Peace program, Public Law 480 funding accounts for only one-fourth of all agricultural shipments abroad.

The United States also imports food, some of which competes with that grown by American farmers and some that does not. The United States, a broad expanse of continental land, possesses a wide assortment of climates that permit a variety of crops to be grown. But most tropical produce is in short supply and must be imported in large quantities. The United States also imports produce that directly competes with American farmers, such as dairy products, meat, sugar, and wool. These products are subjected to a strictly enforced quota system.

The balance of agricultural imports and exports clearly favors the American economy. Domestic increases in the price of American agricul-

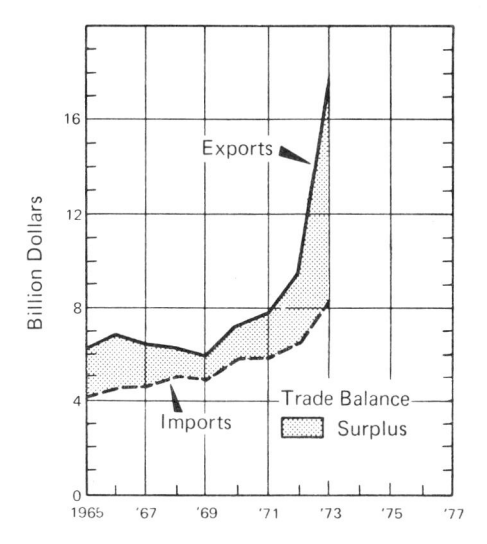

Figure 19-3. Balance of Agricultural Trade. *(Source:* Robert L. Tontz, "U.S. Agricultural Trade Balance Sets Alltime Record," *Foreign Agricultural Trade of the United States* [May 1974]: 4).

tural products similar to those that occurred in the early 1970s have both a positive and negative economic impact. Increased prices will have an adverse effect on U.S. economic health, fueling domestic inflation. At the same time, the positive effect on farmers' incomes and on the dollar are obvious. Higher prices for wheat, rice, and soybeans will improve the American trade position in much the same way that the radical increases in oil prices during 1973 helped the Arab oil-producing states; i.e., the U.S. may export the same amount of agricultural produce but at higher prices.

The Politics of Trade. Trade is a business with multiple points of political contact among farmers, interest groups, and government. The American government basically is interested in helping the businessman sell more of his products abroad. As a result, Washington performs a variety of services for the exporter, all justified by the need to bring about a surplus of exports over imports.

The Soviet–American grain deal of 1972 illustrates the interlocking relationship between businessmen, government decision makers, and interest groups.[10] Pushing the export of grain in 1972 were a variety of pressure groups, ranging from the Grain Sorgham Producers Association to the National Grain and Feed Association.

When the Soviet Union's wheat production dropped drastically in 1972 as a result of inclement weather, the Russian government began negotiating with large U.S. exporting companies for 19 million tons of grain at a cost of 1.14 billion dollars. The exporting companies, in turn, had to gain the Agriculture Department's permission to purchase the grain from farmers and to export it to the Soviet Union. Since the Agriculture Department controlled the number of acres producing wheat, the exporters had to know if the Soviet purchases would cause shortages and inflation of the domestic price of wheat. The price of wheat doubled in one year, adding to the spiraling cost of living in the United States; it is uncertain whether Soviet purchases were entirely to blame.

The issue of the *export subsidy* also prompted the Agriculture Department's involvement. The export subsidy is the difference between the high price of domestic wheat, supported by law, and the lower export price, competitive with prices charged by other grain-exporting nations. As long as the amount of grain to be exported was relatively small, the American government could satisfy the farmers who wanted a high price for their wheat and the exporters who wanted a more competitive price for their overseas customers. As matters turned out, the American government subsidized approximately one-fourth of the 1.14 billion dollars in grain sold to the Soviet Union.

The 1972 grain deal illustrates the relationship between trade and domestic economics, between business and the bureaucracy, and between foreign governments and business. The exporting companies made huge profits at the expense of American citizens whose tax dollars financed the export subsidy. Not all export sales are as large as the Soviet grain purchases, but they all involve political relationships that must be audited to ensure that American national interest is not being sacrificed to private or group profits.

The Balance of Payments: More Problems of Deficit

The balance of payments is the total accounting of a state's economic relationship with foreign nations.[11] It includes imports and exports, and much more: foreign aid, investments abroad, tourist expenditures, and expenditures by military personnel stationed on foreign bases. Thus, the balance-of-payments concept is much broader than the balance of trade.

Patterns of U.S. Balance of Payments. The United States has been running an adverse balance of payments since the end of World War II, a fact that did not generate concern until the late 1950s. The outflow of dollars was viewed as necessary to fund European reconstruction. Besides, the U.S. at the end of the war held more gold than it needed for reserves. By the beginning of the 1970s, the deficit in the balance of payments grew larger, and Washington no longer could justify the deficit's existence and, especially, its size (*see* Figure 19–1). Attempting to remedy this imbalance, the Nixon administration adopted policies previously unthinkable in American economic diplomacy, such as devaluation of the dollar. These policies, discussed later in this chapter, worked their own economic magic in 1973, and the United States experienced a favorable balance of payments.

The composition of the United States balance of payments is summarized in Table 19-2. Its largest item is the merchandise trade balance composed of exports and imports, but other entries are important as they illustrate the complexity of the American balance-of-payments problems in the 1970s.

Table 19-2. U.S. Balance-of-Payments Summary for 1972 in Billions of Dollars

Item	Amount
Merchandise trade balance	−6.8
Military transactions, net	−3.5
Travel and transportation, net	−2.6
Investment income, net	7.9
Transfer payments, net	−1.6
Economic grants	−2.2
U.S. government capital flows	−1.4
Private long-term capital flows, net	−1.4
Private short-term capital flows, net	−1.6
Errors and omissions, net	−3.8
Total	
Net liquidity balance	−14.0
Official reserve transaction balance	−10.3

Source: *Survey of Current Business*, March 1973, p. 31.

Military Transactions. The United States government engages in the lucrative business of selling arms to other nations.[12] The weapons are for conventional warfare, ranging from small arms to supersonic jets. Sometimes the weapons are obsolete by modern standards, but often they are current and in service.

Eighty-eight percent of American arms sales since World War II has been made to industrialized nations, with the remaining 12 percent sold to developing nations (e.g., Saudi Arabia and Israel). The figures for U.S. arms sales abroad are not easy to obtain. The amount is approximately 3 billion dollars a year, two to three times the amount of military grants under American foreign aid. The figures available for sales do not include arms manufactured in other nations under licensing agreements, U.S. equipment transsshipped by a second nation to a third, or sales by private merchants.

The United States sells its largest shipment of arms to Europe. Germany is our leading customer, which has precipitated a cluster of international problems. German purchases are intended to offset the costs of stationing American troops in Germany, but the expense of maintaining U.S. garrisons is approximately 1 billion dollars a year. The West German army could not absorb this amount of new equipment each year unless it were permitted to increase the size of its army, a prospect that neither the Germans, the U.S., nor the U.S.S.R. would welcome. As a result, the German government has been selling its surplus equipment to non-Western states, some of whom Washington does not wish to have American arms.

The sale of weapons to less developed nations has raised important issues in American foreign policy. Although the LDC's have received only 12 percent of the total sales since 1945, their portion has increased in recent years to between 25 and 30 percent. Third World nations have shown an increased interest in modernizing their armies. Modern conventional weapons are status symbols sought by governments of developing nations responding to their people's or their army's demands for more up-to-date arms.

The United States has been, and continues to be, the major supplier of weapons to the developing nations. Unlike sales to Western Europe that are largely for cash, credit constitutes the primary term of exchange for LDC purchases; this has led to congressional criticism and to several attempts by the Senate to restrict credit sales.

Transportation. "Transportation" (along with tourism) generates another deficit, more goods being shipped by foreign vessels than by the American merchant marine. American vessels, which carry only five percent of the world's total shipping are old and inefficient and should be replaced with more modern vessels.[13] To maintain its present rather lowly state among merchant nations, the United States must build 35 to 45 new ships a year to replace old ones. It costs more, however, to build ships in the United States than in other seafaring nations, such as Japan.

In part, the problems plaguing the American merchant marine are rooted in the Merchant Marine Act of 1936, which offered government subsidies to companies building vessels and to companies sailing them. If the vessel sails routes approved by the American government, stands ready to be pressed into national service during wartime, and is constructed according to specifications drawn up by the Coast Guard, the American government will subsidize its construction and underwrite 80 percent of the wages paid to its merchant sailors. Heavy government subsidies have desensitized American ship builders, ship owners, and labor unions to measures that would increase efficiency. Unable and evidently unwilling to trim down costs and to compete with other nations on the commercial high seas, the American merchant marine has not reflected the self-discipline and inventiveness of other aspects of American business. The American shipping industry needs to engage in intensive research on new ship design, to find less expensive ways to construct and operate vessels, and to discover alternatives to government restraints that inhibit its competitive position.

As a result of this situation, American businessmen who ship goods abroad tend to choose foreign carriers because of the significant savings in cost. The American government has attempted several policy initiatives to improve the situation, one of which was to require that foreign-aid shipments be carried in U.S. vessels (a policy often criticized by foreign governments). In the late 1950s and 1960s, the government subsidized the building of an atomic-powered merchant ship, in hopes that a nuclear-propelled vessel would prove more economical to operate. These hopes were never realized and the ship eventually was decommissioned.

Tourism. Travel abroad by Americans also contributes to the adverse balance of payments. Although foreign nationals are visiting the United States in increasing numbers each year, affluent (and not so affluent) American citizens are traveling abroad at an even greater rate. The American government has tried several policies to reverse the deficit created by tourism abroad, and perhaps make it profitable for the U. S. It reduced the amount of duty-free goods that could be brought back from an overseas trip; sponsored a "See America First" campaign to dissuade Americans from traveling abroad; and encouraged more foreigners to travel in the U.S.

Investment Income. Investment income represented the only surplus in the dismal U.S. balance-of-payments picture of 1972. These receipts were generated by private businessmen either purchasing foreign stocks and bonds or building company branches on foreign soil. Foreign investment in the United States is also growing, reaching 15 billion dollars in 1972. This figure paid off 5.8 billion dollars in repatriated income for the foreign investor; and the American businessman brought home 13.7 billion dollars. The net 7.9 billion dollars is listed in Table 19–2.

Transfer Payments. This category includes social security and veterans payments to Americans or to dependents of Americans living abroad.[14] Some Americans retire to countries with lower living costs so that their social security check will have more purchasing power. Few foreign nationals have retired in the United States.

Economic Grants and U.S. Capital Flows. The economic assistance aspect of foreign aid is reported separately from military grants. The "U.S. government capital flows" are the long-term loans that the Agency for International Development makes to developing nations (*see* chapter 18).

Private Capital Flows. Two types of private capital flow exist: (1) *long-term* or *direct investment*, which represents funds put into subsidiaries that the investor expects to remain abroad for more than one year, and (2) *short-term* or *indirect investment*, which the American businessman puts into stocks and bonds of foreign companies and which he usually can reclaim on short notice. Because American investments abroad are larger—and return more—than foreign investments in the United States, "investment income" is a credit and not a debit entry. Indeed, it was the only plus in the recent balance of payments accounting.

Since the mid-1960s, private investments have been criticized for contributing to the deficit in the balance of payments. Some argue that overseas subsidiaries reduce the need for American exports by providing products for foreign markets that might be manufactured in the United States. American labor union leaders have contended that foreign subsidiaries deprive U.S. workers of jobs and contribute to unemployment.

Proponents of foreign investment argue that their activity is an economic necessity. American businesses often cannot compete on the world market, given the cost of labor and materials in the United States. Furthermore, investment abroad becomes essential in common market areas because the tariff wall surrounding the market renders goods produced on the outside noncompetitive. For example, as the tariff walls of the European Economic Community have been raised, American businesses have attempted to circumvent the higher duties by establishing subsidiaries in the nine EEC member countries.[15] In this way, American branches take advantage of the low or nonexistent internal tariffs and ship their products to EEC countries where entrance directly from the U.S. would have been difficult, if not prohibited.

Trade as a Solution to the Problem of Development

As the industrialized nations of the Northern Hemisphere in the 1950s followed a policy of trade with each other and handouts to the developing nations, the rich grew relatively more prosperous and the poor, more impoverished. As the gulf between the rich nations and the poor nations grew wider, it was evident by the mid-1960s that a different approach was necessary. American economic problems also had an impact on the Third World's drive to receive trade concessions to replace foreign aid as a source for funding economic development.

The Shift from Aid to Trade. One of the more perceptible shifts in post-World War II American foreign policy has been the changing view of the role that trade should play in economic development. Emphasis on foreign aid as the primary thrust for economic growth has shifted to an emphasis on trade. The transitional stages between both policy approaches involve public controversy and disagreements with allies.

The United Nations Conference on Trade and Development, held in 1964 in Geneva, represented a benchmark in the change of official American attitude on trade with the LDC's. President Kennedy was in part responsible for the shift to foreign trade as a more effective means of supplying LDC's with sufficient capital for development.

Prior to 1964, a mixture of domestic politics and national interest created an American reluctance to employ trade for economic development. Foreign-aid grants were preferred because their impact on domestic producers could be controlled. Since most economic aid requires the receiver to spend the money in the United States, it tends to stimulate American production as well as eliminate the possibility of foreign competition. Foreign aid also has a controlled impact on the recipient. It can be used to bolster the power of the government in power, for example, by providing military hardware.

Trade, on the other hand, presents a threat of competition to developed countries with domestic industries. Normally, this fear is more mythical than real, because the LDC's account for approximately 10 percent of the world's trade. But the LDC's offer some competition, usually in industries that are labor intensive (i.e., hand labor rather than machines are used in the production process); textiles and shoemaking are good examples. Moreover, income from trade may be used by a government in a developing nation in any way that it, and not Washington, sees fit.

Other developed nations were reluctant to follow the shift in American foreign policy from emphasis on aid to emphasis on trade. U.S. proposals to lower tariffs on tropical produce and handcrafted items, and thus permit the LDC's to earn more money, found only a modicum of support among the European nations. The European reaction was influenced by preferential relationships between former colonies and former mother countries.

U.S. and Commodity Agreements. One of the most salient characteristics of a developing economy is its reliance on one or two major exports, a characteristic that has inhibited the shift from aid to trade as the primary instrument of economic development. A slight drop in commodity prices can cause disastrous economic losses for LDCs. For example, a reduction in coffee prices of one or two cents per pound can mean the difference of billions of dollars each year to the exporting nation.

In order to control wide price fluctuations, buyers and sellers have negotiated international commodity agreements on tin, sugar, coffee, olive oil, and wheat. In most agreements, the buyers pledge to purchase products at a set price and the sellers (usually the Third World nations) agree to sell at the same price. To control surpluses, the LDC governments agree to purchase and store excessive production. Then, in years of low production, the government will open its storage bins and place the products on the market.

Although the United States has exerted leadership in the industrialized North to reduce tariffs, it has shown only minimal interest in commodity agreements. In part, this posture stems from the concept of competition imbedded within American foreign and domestic economic policy; commodity agreements are thought to have inherent monopolistic tendencies. While commodity agreements are not the full answer to development problems, they do help to bring stability to Third World economies based on a single crop or single raw material. The agreements, however, are simply stopgaps; the ultimate answer is a diversified economy so that a bad year for one product can be offset by a good year for another.[16]

The Third World and the "Energy Crisis." Not all non-diversified economies are at a disadvantage. In the 1970s, the industrialized nations' need for energy fuels reversed the traditional rich–poor relationship in world trade, benefiting especially countries in the Middle East and North Africa with abundant oil reserves. Although the American economy's need for petroleum outruns its domestic reserves, the U.S. position is not as serious as that of Japan and Europe who normally would import 70–80 percent of their petroleum.

The United States began the 1970s with a 25 percent gap between energy needs and domestic energy production, a deficit that was made up by oil imports from Venezuela and the Middle East. Because American energy demands are growing at the rate of 4.5 percent annually, the U.S. must find and develop energy sources in 1980 that are 55 percent greater than in 1970.[16] The increasing shortage of energy fuel will have its influence on American foreign policy; reliable sources of oil must be found among the oil-surplus nations or the U.S. will be forced to develop other sources of energy. President Nixon's energy policy in 1973 was based on the objective of U.S. independence from outside sources of energy by 1985.

The energy crisis encouraged unilateral action among nations as they scrambled individually to approach the Arab states for deals in oil. The petroleum-rich nations in the Middle East demanded that nations seeking oil assume a more pro-Arab stance in the Arab–Israeli conflict, especially that they urge the Israelis to withdraw their forces to positions held before the 1967 war. The Nixon administration hosted a conference of oil-consuming states in 1974 in an effort to forge a common policy. The American effort met with only limited success. In the end, Washington paid the Arab price: the use of Secretary of State Kissinger's persuasive talents to bring about a truce and disengagement of forces in the Middle East.

THE SEARCH FOR A SOLUTION

An imbalance of trade and payments, growing demands for American agricultural products, Third World economic development, and the "energy crisis" all stimulated a search for a solution to the U.S. international economic position by American decision makers in the 1970s. Finding a solution is not an easy task; each problem is complex and the solution to one difficulty tends to increase strain in other areas. For example, any attempt to increase tariffs to bring about a balance in trade relationships militates against attempts to improve the Third World's economic position.

Moreover, American international economic problems cannot be approached with policies isolated from domestic considerations. The economic factors at work in 1958 illustrate the intricate relationship of domestic to international economy. To begin with, 1958 was a recession year; while exports fell 3 billion dollars, imports from other nations declined only 200 million dollars. Interest rates also declined (as they often do in a recession), so that American capital flowed elsewhere in search of higher returns, and foreign capital was discouraged from entering the American market because of low rates of return. Part of the large export surplus during the previous year was the result of the 1956 Arab-Israeli-British-French war in the Middle East which closed the Suez Canal and dictated that a portion of Europe's oil needs had to be met by shipments from American petroleum reserves. In 1958, the Suez was reopened and Europe returned to purchasing the cheaper Middle East oil. Finally, imports remained high in 1958 despite the recession because small, economy automobiles from Europe were in demand. Americans were inclined to turn to the less expensive imports in the midst of a recession year.

The deterioration of the American international position is characterized by many different stimuli, some of which are domestic. This explains in large measure why solving American economic problems is frustrating and difficult.

Reasons for Balance-of-Payments Problems

What appear to be the reasons for this shift in the international position of the American economy? By focusing on the factors contributing to the current U.S. international economic position, perhaps the solutions can be discovered.

Increasing Competition for Markets Abroad. Following World War II, the American businessman and farmer had a virtual monopoly on foreign markets, while European and Japanese competitors faced a major rebuilding task as a result of wartime devastation. The pattern of international trade underwent far-reaching structural changes. Where British, French, German, and Japanese traders had carved out pre-World War II markets for themselves, American merchants moved in as the only source of goods and services. In many areas, salesmanship skill was unnecessary as American exporters simply became order-takers. With no competitors to worry about, the American entrepreneur reaped profits with relatively little effort. Consequently, the American businessman failed to develop the kind of foreign market sensitivity and efficient sales organization needed to compete with the Japanese and European businessman in the 1950s and 1960s. The American manufacturer also tended to remain at the technological level that he had achieved while foreign businessmen were restocking their war-destroyed industries with the latest machinery.

Gold and Dollar Reserves. In addition to increased competition and inflationary tendencies, a "liquidity crisis" also contributes to American balance-of-payments problems. As the total volume of world trade surpassed the 300-billion-dollar level, the demand for additional gold reserves also increased at a time when the demand for gold for commercial uses multiplied. As a result, the gold-producing states of the world—primarily the Republic of South Africa and the Soviet Union—have been hard-pressed to mine sufficient quantities to fulfill both reserve and commercial needs. Often there is a hint that both states are holding back production in order to ensure a higher price for their product.

The immensity of the problem can be measured by comparing the total reserves available with the amount of imports that has been steadily declining. In 1954, gold and other reserves comprised 68 percent of the world's exports and in 1969, only 30 percent.[18] In other words, during the mid-1950s, nations had reserves available that amounted to two-thirds of the importer's demands; by the end of the 1960s, reserves had fallen to less than one-third of the importer's demands.

For the American government, the role of the dollar as a means of exchange and as a reserve currency resulted in ambivalent policy: all decisions on the dollar had to be made with consideration of the U.S. national interest *and* the good of the international trading community. The French government of President Charles de Gaulle in the 1960s contended that Washington often confused the two roles, making policy in the name of community interests when American self-interest was the motivating factor. The French government then converted most of its dollars into gold to show its distrust of American currency as a reserve instrument.

Gold Speculation. Individuals who speculated about the price of gold also contributed to the adverse balance of payments. Gold speculators (who prefer to be called "investors") read the signs as pointing to a greater demand for gold from governments to provide reserves and from industry for manufacturing processes. These speculators also thought that the dollar could not remain forever pegged at 35 dollars per ounce of gold, a figure set in 1934. At times the speculator's bidding ran to spectacular heights, reaching 180 dollars per ounce of gold at one point in 1974. Washington spokesmen had a tendency to blame most of the international monetary difficulties on speculators; it would be more accurate to say that they exacerbated an already tenuous situation.

Exchange Rates. Another contributor to American economic woes is the glut of American dollars held by foreign (especially European and Japanese) central banks. By 1974, 100 billion dollars in American currency was floating around the international monetary system. The dollar glut is caused by the adverse balance of payments that the U.S. has run throughout the post-war period. American businessmen, by buying more than they are selling abroad, place increasing amounts of dollars in the hands of foreign exporters.

The effect of the glut is to push down the value of the dollar vis-à-vis other currencies. Overseas businessmen are reluctant to hold on to the dollar because of the risk that it will lose more of its value. Central banks are willing to purchase dollars to support the price of their own national currency by artificially creating a demand for dollars. If the reason for the glut—U.S. payments and trade deficits—continues, foreign central banks will not be able to operate because they will not be able to purchase dollars indefinitely.

Internal Monetary Policy

In the Johnson, Nixon, and Ford administrations, internal monetary initiatives as well as external economic policies were examined in searching for a solution to the balance-of-payments problem. The outcome was a trial-and-error approach that seemed to produce more trials, more errors, and few successes. The Johnson administration generally approached the problem by revising only internal monetary policies. The attempt to restrict foreign investment and the Johnson administration's program to encourage foreign tourists to come to the U.S. and to encourage American tourists to stay home were discussed earlier. In 1968, President Johnson proposed and Congress approved the removal of a gold-reserve requirement for the domestic circulation of the dollar. The United States entered the 1970s with a gold reserve of 11.4 billion dollars, down from a high of 24.2 billion dollars in 1948. Part of this cache was reserved by law to support the currency in circulation. By removing the gold-reserve requirement on the dollar in circulation, the entire gold supply could be used as a reserve for world trade.

International Monetary Policy

The Two-Tier Gold System. An international monetary approach to U.S. balance-of-payments difficulties, the two-tier gold system, was begun during the Johnson administration and implemented in 1968. For official transactions, the official price of gold was set at 35 dollars an ounce, while the commercial price—reflecting the need for industrial production and speculation by investors—was permitted to fluctuate according to supply and demand. The two-tier system was conceived of to insulate official policy on exchange rates from the influence of speculative behavior. Speculators, betting that a specific currency was weak and overvalued, could bring pressure on that currency—and on that currency's government—by their buying and selling manipulations. In this way, speculators would sell their dollar holdings and drive down the price of the dollar in relation to gold (which would mean that an ounce of gold, for example, would increase to 37 or 43 dollars an ounce), in hopes that the American government would change its policy on officially exchanging an ounce of gold for 35 dollars. If Washington yielded to this pressure and *devalued* the dollar (or increased the number of dollars that would buy an ounce of gold), the speculator who sold his dollars for gold at the pre-devaluation exchange rate would then sell his gold for dollars at the post-devaluation rate and pocket the profit.

The philosophy of the two-tier system was sound, but it did not count on a continuation of American adverse balance of payments, and certainly not on an adverse balance of trade. In 1971, President Nixon suspended the conversion of dollars into gold, undermining the functioning of the two-tier system. In the end, it was American economic weakness, and not the speculators, that necessitated a change in the international monetary system that had stood since the end of World War II. The two-tier system was dropped officially in 1973.

Special Drawing Rights. As the dollar came under repeated attacks in the 1960s, primarily because the American imbalance of payments placed more dollars in the hands of foreign nationals and less of the foreign nationals' currencies in American hands, the question was continuously raised: How can the trading nations of the world find additional reserves to permit exchanges of goods and services, especially as the total volume of trade continues to grow? The answer was "paper gold" or Special Drawing Rights

(SDR), a reserve fund secured by gold from which nations running deficits in world trade could draw. Special Drawing Rights totaling 3.5 billion dollars were issued in 1970 by the International Monetary Fund. The United States had lobbied for a larger amount, but creditor nations, such as West Germany, Japan, and Italy, were reluctant to agree to a higher figure.

The creditor nations' reluctance to create more paper gold, however, was based primarily on uncertainty introduced in the international trade picture by American economic ills. Should inflation continue to dominate the United States domestic economy as it did in the late 1960s and early 1970s, prices on American exports would rise, thus eating up the reserves created by paper gold. SDRs, then, would only compensate for the United States' inability to set its economic house in order. Indeed, the creditor nations are afraid that SDRs, issued in too large amounts, would serve as an anesthetic to the painful task that the United States faces in reducing its economic commitments abroad and settling on a system of economic priorities.

At the beginning of the 1970s, it became apparent that inflation in the United States and a new development—an excess of imports over exports—were the central problems in the international economic system. The palliatives of a two-tier system and Special Drawing Rights were largely ineffective in light of American weaknesses. Major surgery was needed. The Nixon administration decided on devaluation as the instrument to bring economic health to the international system.

The U.S. Decision: Devaluation. In August 1971, as the United States faced an imbalance of trade and a chronic imbalance of payments, President Nixon announced controls on wages and prices, the imposition of a 10-percent surcharge on all imports, and nonconvertibility of dollars into gold. Eventually, the surcharge was removed and the dollar was devaluated by 8 percent in early 1972. The policy of nonconvertibility was continued; foreign banks could not demand gold for the dollars that they held on hand.

Nixon initiatives controlled inflation within the United States in 1972, but trade and payments imbalances continued. When the wage and price controls were removed in late 1972, the American economy experienced a renewed inflation. In February 1973, the American government devalued the dollar another 10 percent.

Nixon's decisions were motivated in part by the need to make American goods competitive in the U.S. market as well as in foreign markets. American goods were being priced out of their own domestic market by less expensive foreign imports. Foreign manufacturers in 1973 claimed 15 percent of the American automobile market; 17 percent of the market for steel; almost 30 percent of shoes and television sales; and nearly all of the market for bicycles, transistor radios, and smaller motorcycles.[19]

Devaluation of the dollar had ramifications in many segments of the world economy, increasing American gold reserves to over 1 billion dollars.[20] However, other nations with dollar reserves experienced the opposite effect. A 10-billion-dollar reserve in 1971 before the two devaluations of 18 percent was worth 8.2 billion dollars after the American action.

Exchange Rates. The devaluation of the dollar did not remove the problem of exchange rates. While the American dollar was overvalued (or worth less than its official price) in 1971, two currencies—the Japanese yen and the German mark—were undervalued (or worth more than their official price). Japanese and German exporters were thus given an advantage when competing with American goods. The Germans and especially the Japanese folllowed a policy of undervaluing their currency to stimulate sales abroad which, in turn, contributed to employment in their exporting industries. American leaders in 1972–73 tried to convince the Japanese and German governments to *revalue* their currencies vis-à-vis the dollar, i.e., to make the yen and mark more valuable.

At the Smithsonian Conference in December 1971, the currencies of the world were adjusted to reflect more of their true value. The American government's position has been that this agreement is temporary and a more permanent arrangement should be negotiated. As the world currencies were allow to float—some with restrictions and some without—the dollar hit new lows in currency exchanges. The Watergate affair in 1972–73 was partly to blame as it contributed to a lessening of international confidence in the Nixon administration.

In the Ford administration, Henry Kissinger, continuing in his capacity as Secretary of State, focused on reducing the price of Arab oil as the key to international economic stability. In effect, the "energy crisis" overshadowed American balance-of-payments problems in 1974.

POSITIVE DIRECTIONS TOWARD AN ECONOMIC SOLUTION

The greatest challenge to contemporary American foreign policy is economic. The answers and solutions are not readily available, but at stake is the survival of the American system as we know it. Traditional patterns of behavior are no longer applicable as the dollar is devalued, currencies are allowed to float, imports exceed exports, and the American nation appears to be moving to a debtor position in the international system. Traditional policies no longer provide answers to economic questions affecting American foreign policy in the last quarter of the 20th century.

Many of the options traditionally open to American decision makers have international ramifications that are unacceptable to either the United States or other nations. The U.S. economy can no longer retreat into an isolationist shell; isolationism became a nonviable option the first day of the 1973 "energy crisis." [21] A state that must import 25 percent of its energy needs cannot survive with a foreign policy of unilateralism.

A solution to the dilemmas of American economic policy will involve the development of a greater measure of restraint in diplomatic initiatives. The U.S. economy can no longer supply the resources to police the world, equip large numbers of foreign troops, and prop up friendly governments.

The claim of the Johnson administration that the American economy experienced a balance-of-payments deficit due to the Vietnam War is confirmation that the U.S. had overextended its resources.

To arrive at an economic solution, the American nation must begin by reordering its foreign policy priorities. To do so entails changing some of its traditional patterns of diplomatic behavior. This first step is a political solution to economic problems because the economic distress of the United States in the 1970s is rooted in political decisions that previously ignored the realities of limited national resources.

NOTES

1. For an overview of the American international economic position, consult Peter Kenan, *Giant Among Nations* (Chicago: Rand McNally and Co., 1964); Charles P. Kindleberger, *Foreign Trade and the National Economy* (New Haven: Yale University Press, 1962); Mordechai E. Kreinin, *International Economics: A Policy Approach* (New York: Harcourt Brace Jovanovich, 1971); and William Diebold, Jr., "U.S. Trade Policy: The New Political Dimensions," *Foreign Affairs* 52 (April 1974): 472–496.
2. Charles P. Kindleberger, *The Dollar Shortage* (Cambridge and New York: Technology Press of MIT and Wiley, 1950); Donald MacDouglas, *The World Dollar Problems: A Study in International Economics* (New York: St. Martin's Press, 1957); Fred H. Kopstock, *The International Status of the Dollar* (Princeton, N.J.: Princeton University Press, Essays in International Finance, 1957); Erik Hoffmeyer, *Dollar Shortage and the Structure of U.S. Foreign Trade* (Copenhagen: E. Munksgaard, 1958); Gottfried Haberler, "The Choice of Exchange Rates After the War," *American Economic Review* 35 (1945); 303–318; and Robert Triffin, *Gold and The Dollar Crisis: The Future of Convertibility* (New Haven, Conn.: Yale University Press, 1960); and *Europe and the Money Muddle: From Bilateralism to Near Convertibility 1947–1956* (New Haven, Conn.: Yale University Press, 1957).
3. Ernest H. Preeg, *Traders and Diplomats: An Analysis of the Kennedy Round of Negotiations under the General Agreement on Tariffs and Trade* (Washington, D.C.: Brookings Institution, 1970); and John W. Evans, *The Kennedy Round in American Trade Policy: The Twilight of GATT* (Cambridge: Harvard University Press, 1971). For a discussion of the economic agenda left after the Kennedy round, see John W. Evans, *U.S. Trade Policy: New Legislation for the Next Round* (New York: Harper & Row, 1967), and Frans A. M. Alting Von Geusau (ed.), *Economic Relations After the Kennedy Round* (Leyden: A. W. Sijthoff-Leyden, 1969).
4. Trading with Communist nations has generated an extensive dialogue.

See Theodore C. Sorensen, "Why We Should Trade with the Soviets," *Foreign Affairs* 46 (1968): 375–383, Harold J. Berman, "A Reappraisal of U.S.–U.S.S.R. Trade Policy," *Harvard Business Review* 42 (1964): 139–151; and Walter Krause and F. John Mathis, "The U.S. Shift on East–West Trade," *Journal of International Affairs* 28 (1974): 25–37. An extremely negative view of trade with Communist nations is expressed in J. Bernard Hutton, *The Traitor Trade* (New York: Ivan Obolensky, 1963).

5. The impact of the EEC on U.S. trade is discussed by L. B. Krause, "European Economic Integration and the United States," *American Economic Review* 53 (1963): 185–196; Francis K. Topping, *Comparative Tariffs and Trade: The United States and the European Common Market* (New York: Committee for Economic Development, 1963); Lawrence B. Krause, *European Economic Integration and the United States* (Washington, D.C.: Brookings Institution, 1968); Ernest H. Preeg, "Economic Blocs and U.S. Foreign Policy," *International Organization* 28 (Spring 1974): 233–246; and Werner J. Feld, "Trade Between the U.S. and the European Community: Differing Expectations in a Changing Power Relationship," *Journal of International Affairs* 28 (1974): 7–24.

6. The impact of the Latin American Common Market is discussed by James D. Cochrane, *The Politics of Regional Integration: The Central American Case* (New Orleans, La.: Tulane University Press, 1969); U.S. Senate Committee on Foreign Relations, *Survey of the Alliance for Progress: Foreign Trade Policies* (Washington, D.C.: U.S. Government Printing Office, 1967); and Joseph Grunwald, Miguel S. Wionczek, and Martin Carnoy, *Latin American Economic Integration and U.S. Policy* (Washington, D.C.: Brookings Institution, 1972).

7. Robert A. Baldwin, "Determinants of the Commodity Structure of U.S. Trade," *American Economic Review* 61 (1971): 126–146, and Robert E. Lipsey, *Price and Quantity Trends in the Foreign Trade of the United States* (Princeton, N.J.: Princeton University Press, 1963).

8. J. H. Richter, *Agricultural Protection and Trade: Proposals for an International Policy* (New York: Praeger, 1964), and Lucille Corder and Annette A. Parisi, *U.S. Import Duties on Agricultural Products* (Washington, D.C.: Foreign Agricultural Service, 1959).

9. The reader may perceive a discrepancy between Table 19–1 and 19–2. Table 19–1 shows that 10 percent of American exports are "food and live animals," as are 12.1 percent of its imports. Since the United States imported more than it exported in 1971, how can Figure 19–3 show a balance-of-trade surplus in agricultural products? The answer is found in the reporting system of the government. Soybeans, cattle hides, and tallow, for example, are not considered "food"; soybeans and hides are reported under "inedible crude materials" and tallow, under "animal and vegetable oils and fats," which in Table 19–1 is included in "other transactions." Taken together, these items produce a surplus of agricultural products.

10. Joseph Albright, "Some Deal: The Full Story on How America Got Burned and the Russians Got Bread," *New York Times Magazine* (Nov. 25, 1973): 36–7; 84–102, and James Trager, *Amber Waves of Grain* (New York: Arthur Fields Books, 1973).
11. John D. Hogan, *The U.S. Balance of Payments and Capital Flows* (New York: Praeger, 1967); Alfred E. Davidson, "Correcting the Imbalance in U.S. International Payments," *Orbis* 10 (1966): 213–222; D. A. Snider, "Capital Controls and U.S. Balance of Payments," *American Economic Review* 54 (1964): 346–358; Robert W. Stevens, "Wishful Thinking on the Balance of Payments," *Harvard Business Review* 44 (1966): 6–31; and Robert E. Baldwin et al., *Trade, Growth, and the Balance of Payments* (Chicago: Rand McNally and Co., 1965).
12. U.S. Senate Committee on Foreign Relations, *Arms Sales and Foreign Policy: A Staff Study* (Washington, D.C.: U.S. Government Printing Office, 1967); George Thayer, *The War Business: The International Trade in Armaments* (New York: Simon and Schuster, 1969); Lewis A. Frank, *The Arms Trade in International Relations* (New York: Praeger, 1969); and Stockholm International Peace Research Institute, *The Arms Trade with the Third World* (New York: Humanities Press, 1971).
13. For additional information on this subject, see Wytze Gorter, *United States Shipping Policy* (New York: Harper & Row, 1956); John D. Hayes, "Our Merchant Marine in Trouble," *The Reporter* 34 (January 13, 1967): 28–31.
14. M. C. Kemp, "Unilateral Transfers and the Terms of Trade," *American Economic Review* 46 (1956): 106–127.
15. Anthony Scaperlanda, "The E.E.C. and U.S. Foreign Investment: Some Empirical Evidence," *Economic Journal* 77 (March 1967): 22–26; Anthony Edwards, *Investment in the European Economic Community: A Study of Problems and Opportunities* (New York: Praeger, 1964); and C. F. Karsten, "Should Europe Restrict U.S. Investments?" *Harvard Business Review* 43 (September–October 1965): 53–61.
16. John A. Pincus, "Aid, Trade, and Economic Development: What Policy for Commodities?" *Foreign Affairs* 42 (1964): 227–241; Henry Brodie, "Commodity Agreements: A Partial Answer to the Trade Problems of Developing Countries," *Department of State Bulletin* (July 19, 1965): 111–117; and Raymond Vernon, "Foreign Enterprise and Developing Nations in the Raw Materials Industries," *American Economic Review* 60 (1970): 122–126; and Boris C. Swerling, "Sugar Policy for the United States," *American Economic Review* 42 (1952): 347–355.
17. Robert E. Hunter, *The Energy "Crisis" and U.S. Foreign Policy* (New York: Foreign Policy Association Headline Series, 1973); Gerald A. Pollack, "The Economic Consequences of the Energy Crisis," *Foreign Affairs* 52 (April 1974): 542–571; Walter J. Levy, "World Oil Corporation or International Chaos," *Foreign Affairs* 52 (July 1974): 675–689; and Cecil V. Crabb, Jr., "The Energy Crisis, the Middle East, and American Foreign Policy," *World Affairs* 136 (Summer 1973): 48–73.

18. *The New York Times* (June 4, 1970): 61.
19. Edwin L. Dale, Jr., "Why More Must Become Less," *New York Times Magazine* (March 11, 1973): 32.
20. *Economic Report of the President, 1973* (Washington, D.C.: U.S. Government Printing Office, 1973), p. 299.
21. George P. Shultz, former Secretary of the Treasury, argues for more cooperation between the trading nations. *See* his article, "The Need for Closer International-Financial Cooperation," *The Atlantic Community Quarterly* 12 (Spring 1974) 55–63.

SECTION 6

Conclusion

In the final section, the reader is invited to speculate about the permanency of the patterns discussed in this book. As the United States enters the last quarter of the 20th century, which of the patterns that evolved during 200 years of national history will remain a part of American diplomacy?

20

Patterns of American Foreign Policy: Continue or Innovate?

Thus far we have focused on American diplomatic patterns of the past and present. Patterns developed over the past 200 years of American history may survive intact or may be modified as new regularities of diplomatic behavior emerge. The four revolutions in warfare, international economics, Third World development, and statecraft have had their impact on traditional American foreign policy patterns of unilateralism, expansionism, legalism, and moralism. This chapter is organized around two questions: Which of the four traditional patterns have survived to the present decade? And, should the surviving patterns be replaced by a more innovative approach to future world challenges?

THE FOUR PATTERNS TODAY

Unilateralism

The United States emerged from World War II with a tenacious hold on a unilateralist foreign policy. The pattern had served American diplomacy in the past, and no reason appeared for it to be jettisoned. The world system in 1945 was characterized by three powerful actors — the Americans, British, and Russians—in a relationship that would permit Washington to play the "honest broker." The U.S. government would be able to maintain a free hand in formulating and attaining its goals and to act as a conciliating influence in disputes between Great Britain and the Soviet Union.

Loss of Freedom of Action. Prior to World War II, the United States could have both freedom of action and security. After World War II, however, the United States could not possess security without giving up some of its freedom of action. Alliances and the United Nations offered a promise of security, but both restricted the unilateral tradition in American foreign policy. The restriction placed on U.S. unilateralism by regional alliances and international organizations was more apparent than real. The American government had its way most of the time in its alliance relationships and in the UN General Assembly, at least in the earlier period of the post-war era.

Economic Weakness and Unilateralism. The diplomatic area within which the United States could maneuver, however, contracted due to economic difficulties imposed by an adverse balance-of-payments picture. The limited constraints of collective security and defense arrangements were outweighed by financial weaknesses both at the national and international level. The purse turned out to have a bottom after all; American leaders found themselves counting the costs of operations that in the past had been funded out of apparently unlimited resources.

Questions about American Leadership. Accompanying the financial and alliance difficulties of the 1960s were criticisms of American foreign policy, particularly by the French. The Gaullists argued that the Americans were not the most qualified to lead the Western nations. To them, the mantle of leadership had fallen on the United States by default, because no other Western nation was financially and militarily capable of giving direction at the time. The French were able to piece together a plausible and sometimes convincing case: the Americans were too naive for world leadership; they did not comprehend the principles of traditional world politics (particularly the balance of power); they failed to grasp the nuances of diplomacy; and they tended to build their own version of hegemony within the Western alliance when tolerance and diversity were required. The undistinguished termination of the Vietnam War in 1973 seemed to confirm the French criticism that the Americans had lost their ability to formulate policy that would bring peace and stability to the world system.

Suspicion of leadership capabilities tended to erode the American unilateralist pattern as the United States' ability to formulate policy without consulting other powerful states in the international system was questioned. While the U.S. continued to provide a measure of guidance in world politics, the American government was obliged to make more of its decisions in concert with other nations.

Expansionism

Will the American nation pursue less of an expansionist tack in the remaining quarter of the 20th century than it has in the past? The answer to this question appears to be "yes."

Economic Expansion. While the American nation has been vibrant and aggressive, engaging in numerous conflicts with other states throughout its history, its economic system has energetically reached out into almost all areas of the world. The Left-Wing Revisionists have highlighted this economic aspect of U.S. expansion.

What are the prospects for a continuing, aggressive economic foreign policy? Two factors mitigate against a perpetuation of economic expansion of the magnitude witnessed in the past. First, other entrepreneurs are now effectively competing with American businessmen for markets. The U.S. share of international trade is decreasing, not increasing.

The Third World nations, in the second place, are not unaware of the dangers that American multinational corporations present to their own independence. Instances of unfavorable (to the host nation) profit ratios largely have been reversed. American oil companies operating in the Middle East have had to settle for contracts that split profits from crude oil production on a more equitable basis. Third World nations, including those not normally classified as "socialist," have been less reluctant to nationalize American industries.

Political and Military Aggressiveness and Goals. The bellicosity of the United States is indelibly imprinted on the historical record of the post-war era. American forces have engaged in two conventional conflicts, funded numerous interventions by proxy forces (such as the abortive Cuban invasion in 1961), and intervened in several nations for brief periods of time (e.g., Lebanon and the Dominican Republic). It would appear obvious that political and military aggressiveness has remained a pattern of American diplomatic behavior.

Not so obvious, however, is the aimlessness of American aggression since 1945. In all previous conflicts, the American nation seemed to target its objectives with confidence and then apply its capabilities to achieve the stipulated goals. American aggression achieved a tangible result, usually territory. While World War I did not add to American holdings, ample opportunities existed for the United States to establish its jurisdiction over German islands in the Pacific or over Middle Eastern areas formerly controlled by the Ottoman Empire.

However, no specific territorial objective, no outstanding economic advantage, and no annihilation of an enemy has resulted from the armed conflicts and quasi-wars after 1945. Ironically, the United States has been aggressive without being expansive. No concrete payoff has flowed from American belligerency in the post-World War II period, despite the tremendous costs that an aggressive foreign policy has entailed.

The adverse reaction to overseas involvement that followed the withdrawal from Vietnam in 1973 militates against any attempt to expand into other areas of the world. How long this attitude will dominate American thinking remains to be seen. A period of withdrawal followed the 1898 Spanish-American War, but the United States found itself involved in a major war only two decades later.

Legalism

The modifications of the rule-of-law concept in American diplomacy were traced in chapters 2 and 16. By the time of the Cold War era, the concept was so nebulous and so infused with a phobia of Communism, it no longer was a viable pattern of American foreign policy. Of the four basic patterns, legalism was the first post-war casualty. It survived more as a superficial framework to justify American actions than as a source of regularities in U.S. diplomacy.

Moralism

In the post-1945 period, moralism has traveled a road similar to that traversed by foreign policy goals and international law: it has become more nebulous. In earlier stages of American history, moralism was abstract and general, but there were attempts to relate its principles to specific policies. The concepts behind Theodore Roosevelt's Peace of Righteousness and Woodrow Wilson's justifications for American involvement in World War I illustrate the application of moralistic principles to specific policy problems. For most of the 19th century, morality was associated with rights and duties and usually paralleled international law. To be morally right meant that the duties and privileges of international law must be honored.

In the post-World War II era, the principles and assumptions of moralism were never spelled out comprehensively, but were accepted *a priori* as a characteristic of American diplomacy. Moral principles were considered to be the guidelines of American policy, although they might be undefined or even undefinable. President Nixon, for example, insisted on a "peace with honor" in the Vietnam War. He justified American escalatory actions in Indochina, such as the mining of the North Vietnamese harbors and forays into neighboring Cambodia and Laos, as necessary to achieve his moralist goal. The United States government refused to accept a settlement with the North Vietnamese that appeared to "sell out" Saigon.

The Impact of Moralism. One of the foibles of American foreign policy in the post-World War II period has been the inability of the U.S. to order its priorities. The moralist pattern in American diplomacy, evolving to its most nebulous state when the U.S. became a superpower, has contributed to this weakness. A policymaker cannot place moral concepts in a rank order. Is "justice" more important than "honor"? Does "freedom" deserve more attention and more resources than "equality"? Because decision makers cannot distinguish among moralist principles, they make all of them equally important. Consequently, the process of separating goals and objectives that are *most* important from those that are *least* important is obviated by moralist considerations. *All* policy objectives are judged important and no priorities need to be established.

Failure to formulate goals in more specific, concrete terminology, another weakness of post-war U.S. diplomacy, can be linked to moralism. Effective foreign policy is founded on realistic objectives that are within a nation's capability to achieve. These objectives, specifically enumerated and defined, describe a condition within the international system that can be determined as existing when they are attained. In other words, objectives should be explained in language that can be used to judge whether or not the conditions the objectives envision exist. Herein lies the difficulty of evaluating goals encased in moralist verbiage. "Honor," "justice," and "equality" do not characterize international conditions that can be determined as existing at a specific time. Is the world community more "just" after the United States' pursuit of the goal of justice for 30 years? Specific objectives, such as negotiating an alliance, purchasing another state's territory, or defeating an opponent, can be judged as achieved at a given point in time. Moralist goals, however, cannot.

The Realists and Moralist Goals. It would appear that moralism is an anomaly in the period of American diplomacy apparently dominated by the Realist image. The Realists do not endorse abstract goals; in fact, they seldom miss opportunities to inveigh against them. Three explanations are offered for the apparent incongruence of a moralist pattern occurring during a period of Realism.

First, as pointed out in chapter 4, one analytical problem in the study of American diplomacy is to link an image with a decision maker (and then to link his image with the selection of a policy alternative). Besides Secretary of State Dean Acheson, George Kennan, and perhaps Henry Kissinger, no major American decision maker within the immediate administrative environs of the White House has been identified as a Realist. The Realist image may permeate the foreign policy bureaucracy, but this hypothesis is yet to be confirmed.

Second, the Realists inadvertently contributed to creating moralist goals in post-war American foreign policy when they designated the Soviet Union as an aggressive state that must be stopped. The Realist view that the Soviet Union must be contained underwent a modification as it was implemented; it eventually surfaced as a policy to contain Communism, shifting from containment of *national* aggression to containment of *ideological* aggression. The Realists cannot be blamed for any modification of their tenets, but the modification that occurred was the worst possible sort. However, while the Realists pointed out the influence of Communist ideology on Soviet foreign policy, they did not make it the object of American containment policy.

Finally, if the Realist image has had an impact on American foreign policy, that impact has been influential for only the past three decades. The diplomatic behavioral pattern of moralism, on the other hand, has characterized American foreign policy for two centuries. It is too early to determine whether the Realist impact has influenced U.S. diplomacy for the good (with "good" defined by the Realists).

American Sense of Mission. A further indication that moralism has continued to dominate contemporary American foreign policy is the reoccurrence of a sense of mission. President Nixon, for example, declared that the United States accepted "the responsibilities which *no other free nation* is able to meet in building a structure for peace."[1] The American nation has a singular role to play, which it must assume because other states lack the moral stamina or the military capabilities to do so. As long as this attitude pervades American foreign policy, innovative foreign policies will be difficult, if not impossible, to implement.

TRADITIONAL PATTERNS AND INNOVATION

The Breakdown of Traditional Patterns

The record of American foreign policy since 1945 is a chronicle of the erosion of the four traditional patterns of diplomatic behavior presented in this book. The United States has remained aggressive, but its imperialism has been aimless; the pattern of legalism has evolved into a nebulous rule-of-law concept; unilateralism has been diluted by "entangling" alliances and a weakened economic position; and moralism is a pattern that seems to have lost its mooring, drifting about without specific goals. It would appear that the four patterns have fulfilled their usefulness in American foreign policy and that now is the time for new patterns of behavior to be adopted.

The adoption of new patterns must be accompanied by engrafting a new worldview onto the American foreign policymaking process. Realism has come to a stage in its evolution similar to the one occupied by Liberalism in 1945: asking questions that no one is concerned about and giving answers to other questions that no one is asking. Questions such as, "How can we stop Soviet expansion?" are no longer relevant to American foreign policy. Realist assumptions no longer apply to the realities of international politics.

The Need for a New Image

There is a need for a new image in American diplomacy based on a different set of assumptions and prescribing alternative goals to the presuppositions and purposes advocated by Realism. The new image must take into account the present developments in world politics that Realism (or Liberalism or the Revisionist images) omits. The economic weakness of the United States, nuclear parity with the U.S.S.R., the emergence of the Third World, the impotency of the United Nations, the absence of a viable form of international law, the superiority of offensive over defensive weapons, and the development of regional economic actors are a few of the new realities in American foreign policy for which a new image must account.

The new worldview may be eclectic, borrowing from all of the four images. The obvious impact of the critique of American diplomacy propounded by the Left-Wing Revisionists especially must be taken into account. Before innovations can be built into U.S. foreign policy, the angle of vision must be changed with new assumptions and prescriptions.[2]

What Lies Ahead?

Since clairvoyance is not a refined human talent, projecting future events that will influence American diplomatic behavior involves a high risk of inaccurate judgment. However, thinking about the future should have a place in the foreign policy decision-making process. One of the functions of the bureaucracy is to engage in long-range prediction and planning. All too often the bureaucracy is burdened with managing immediate crises and does not have time to anticipate conditions that may breed imbroglios farther down the road.[3]

Four obstacles are encountered in speculating about the future of American foreign policy. (1) In projecting future events, the decision maker lacks control over domestic politics, where developments may destroy the best intentioned plans. The Nixon administration designated 1973 as the "Year of Europe," for example, but it sadly turned out to be the "Year of Watergate." Neither are world events predictable. International developments of the magnitude of the "energy crisis" obviously take years to evolve, but portents may be ignored until the event arrives in full bloom. A foreign policy leader who cannot see beyond his daily calendar may ignore the bureaucracy's warnings of impending crises. (2) Any social system has an option of revitalizing itself or of reversing a trend, making predictions of the future tenuous. The American economic system can be revitalized and the trends of trade and payment imbalances can be reversed. Such a turnabout would have an incalculable effect on world economics. (3) It is difficult to ferret out developments occurring beneath the surface of events. However, some aspects of the future appear obvious, and only conventional wisdom is needed to pinpoint them. One can assume as probable future events the rise of Japan to superpower status, the development of more sophisticated weapons, and the widening of the rich nation–poor nation gap. Less visible, but equally important, are population and food production trends, pollution of the oceans, and a worldwide depression. A President, however, might formulate policy with obvious future events in mind but be blind to other developments.[4]

(4) A bureaucracy tends to remain in the policy channel developed in handling past crises. To make radical departures from past recommendations is to admit that the bureaucracy was wrong in former cases. Once the bureaucratic pattern is set, there is a tendency to "leave well enough alone" and not disturb the accepted routine. Few individual decision makers, capsulated within the boundaries of their bureau or agency, can see the whole picture in diplomacy. They have their own bureaucratic interests to protect and their own bureaucratic viewpoint to argue. A pattern of policy with which they are satisfied can become comfortable, resisting efforts to change. To embark on a totally new policy path usually involves restructuring the budget and perhaps reorganizing the bureaucracy itself. The tendency is to not "rock the boat."

STEPS TO TAKE

American foreign policy since 1945 has not changed in its major content or orientation, although minor shifts, such as the erosion of support for the United Nations, have occurred. During this time, the substance of international politics has changed considerably. U.S. diplomacy must be attuned to transformations in world affairs and adjust objectives and operations to them. What steps must be taken to ensure that American foreign policy is responsive to international changes?

First, since foreign policy is made by *people,* the probability that innovations will be introduced in American diplomacy is increased if new faces with different ideas are elected or recruited. Men and women with innovative ideas should be welcomed into the federal bureaucracy or elected to office by a body politic dissatisfied with elements of the status quo.

American leaders must be responsive to these changes. They should be prepared to undertake policy innovations and to break with past traditions if the need arises. The opening of diplomatic ties with the People's Republic of China and detente with the Soviet Union during President Nixon's tenure illustrate the types of policy innovation that must occur in American diplomacy. These initiatives cleared away much of the political underbrush that had hindered American policy in the post-war period. They represent an attempt to try new tacks and to push American policy into a different channel. An equal amount of verve and innovative thinking should be applied to international economic development and the Arab–Israeli dispute, as well as to other crises that will sprout in years to come.

A second step toward innovation would be the formulation of foreign policy objectives in specific and concrete language rather than in general and abstract verbiage. Because American decision makers now recognize that U.S. resources are limited, they must order priorities carefully and choose directions that offer the best promise of fulfillment and that bring the greatest satisfaction to the American nation. After suffering frustration during the 1960s over chasing illusive objectives in Vietnam, the American people are ready for a more realistic approach to defining aims. Formulating foreign policy objectives with abstract concepts does not enhance their implementation; in the long run, it contributes to confusing allied and domestic opinion. Contradictions in foreign policy (e.g., supporting dictators and making the world safe for democracy) will be less troublesome if goals are framed in concrete and realistic terms.

A third step toward innovative foreign policy would be to recognize the limitations of power in today's political world. No change can be stymied by U.S. diplomacy; it may be beyond American capabilities to control a crisis in any way. Washington can influence only the direction of the change, not its generation or demise. To show alarm over Third World nations that adopt the trappings of socialism or over Soviet policy toward East European states is to fret over changes that lie outside the control of the United States.

Finally, the direction of our innovations is an important consideration. We must be on guard against changes that masquerade as innovations but are in effect regressions advocating a return to an old pattern that has fallen into temporary disuse. The Nixon Doctrine and the trend toward trade protectionism indicates that the U.S. may be turning inward and adopting a policy of isolationism. If American policymakers do become introspective, they will simply be returning to an isolationist stance of the past.[5] If U.S. policy is to move ahead, American leaders must not confuse a step backwards with a progressive solution to solve the problems that dot the international political landscape. If new patterns are to be effective in American foreign policy, they must provide solutions to contemporary problems—as well as to problems that will develop as the United States moves toward the 21st century.

NOTES

1. Richard Nixon, "1972: A Year of Historical Negotiations," *Department of State Bulletin* 68 (May 28, 1973): 674. Emphasis added.
2. Several possible images can be suggested. One is Donald Brandon's "moderationism," based on Judeo-Christian and humanist values that American leaders should use in making policy. See his *American Foreign Policy: Beyond Utopianism and Realism* (New York: Appleton-Century-Crofts, 1966). Raymond Aron and Stanley Hoffmann have proposed "historical sociology," a critique that questions one of the basic assumptions of Realism: that rational behavior is a characteristic of international relations. The decision maker is not irrational, but he must make decisions on the basis of incomplete information, increasing his risk of failure. See Aron's *War and Peace: A Theory of International Relations* (New York: Praeger, 1967) and Hoffmann's *Gulliver's Troubles, or the Setting of American Foreign Policy* (New York: McGraw-Hill, 1968). Finally, George Liska has argued that past empires should be used as models to study American foreign policy and not the national actors that have emerged in more recent times. The United States behaves more as an empire than it does as a nation. See his *Imperial America: The International Politics of Primacy* (Baltimore: Johns Hopkins Press, 1967). A follow-up study is Robert E. Osgood, Robert W. Tucker, Francis E. Rourke, Herbert S. Dinerstein, Laurence W. Martin, David Calleo, Benjamin M. Rowland, and George Liska, *Retreat from Empire? The First Nixon Administration* (Baltimore: Johns Hopkins University Press, 1973); and Raymond Aron, *The Imperial Republic: The United States and the World, 1945–1973* (Englewood Cliffs, N.J. Prentice-Hall, 1974).
3. Robert L. Rothstein, *Planning, Prediction, and Policymaking in Foreign Affairs: Theory and Practice* (Boston: Little, Brown and Co.,

1972) examines the State Department's planning mechanism and suggests improvements.
4. Several writers have attempted to project issues and outcomes for American foreign policy: Paul Seabury and Aaron Wildavsky (eds.), *U.S. Foreign Policy: Perspectives and Proposals for the 1970s* (New York: McGraw-Hill, 1969); Robert W. Gregg and Charles W. Kegley, Jr. (eds.), *After Vietnam: The Future of American Foreign Policy* (New York: Doubleday, 1971); Eugene V. Rostow, *Peace in the Balance: The Future of American Foreign Policy* (New York: Simon and Schuster, 1972); Donald E. Neuchterlein, *United States National Interests in a Changing World* (Lexington, Ky.: University Press of Kentucky, 1973); Henry Owen (ed.), *The Next Phase in Foreign Policy* (Washington, D.C.: Brookings Institution, 1973); James Chase, *A World Elsewhere: The New American Foreign Policy* (New York: Charles Scribner's Sons, 1973); Henry Brandon, *The Retreat of American Power* (New York: Doubleday, 1973); and Raymond Aron, "Richard Nixon and the Future of American Foreign Policy," *Daedalus* 101 (Fall 1972): 1–24.
5. *See* Robert W. Tucker, *A New Isolationism: Threat or Promise* (New York: Universe Books, 1972).

Subject Index

ABM agreements, 268–269
Acheson, Dean, 57, 62 n, 132, 143, 226 n, 253 n
AFL–CIO, 120
Agency for International Development, 334–337
Agreements, executive, 218–219
Agricultural attaché, 144
Agriculture:
　production, 341–344
　trade, 362–364
Alaska, purchase of, 29
Alliance for Progress, 339
Ambassador, 177
American Legion, 120
Anti-ballistic missile agreement. See ABM agreement.
Anti-ballistic missiles, 89, 212
Appropriations, 219–220
Arab–Israeli conflict, 109, 120–121, 133
Arms Control and Disarmament Agency, 261–262
Atomic Energy Commission, 148, 149, 198
Atoms for Peace Plan, 259

Baghdad Pact, 291–292
Balance-of-payments problems, 192
Balance of power, 21–23, 47, 229–301
Balance of trade, 358–364
Ball, George, 123
Barbary pirates. See North African pirates.
Baruch Plan, 256
Bay of Pigs invasion, 89, 285
Berlin Task Force, 159
Biological and chemical warfare, 270–272

Brain co-option, 348
Brain drain, 323–324
Byrnes, James F., 142, 309 n
Bureaucracy, 9, 93–94

Cambodia, invasion of, 108
"Campaign for Truth," 313
Caracas Doctrine, 284–285
Central American Common Market, 361
Central Intelligence Agency (CIA), 147–149, 171–173, 284–285
　director of, 147
Central Treaty Organization (CENTO), 290–292
Chapultepec, Act of, 283
China Lobby, 125
CIA. See Central Intelligence Agency
Citizen advisory committees, 91
Civil War, 25
Cold War, 233, 234
Colonies, American, 144
Commodity agreements, 369
Community-of-power concept, 47
Congo (Zaire), 302
Congressional investigations, 221, 222
Congressmen's ideology, 212
Consultantships, 154
Content analysis, 57–58
Cost effectiveness, 249–250
Council on Foreign Relations, 128
Country Director, 176
Country team, 178
Creel Committee, 312
Cuban missile crisis, 11, 165, 263
Cultural Affairs Officer, 319

Declaration of war, 215

393

Defense, Department of, 145–150
Defense Intelligence Agency, 149–150
Deterrence, 239–240
Devaluation of dollar, 374
Diplomacy (U.S.):
  and blacks, 90, 127
  citizen, 82–83
  professional, 81–82
  summit, 190–191
Dulles, John Foster, 58, 91, 143

Educational and cultural exchanges, 318–324
EEC. See European Economic Community.
Eisenhower, Dwight D., 119
ELINT (Electronic Intelligence), 150, 153
Energy crisis, 369–370, 389
Energy Research and Development Administration. See Atomic Energy Commission.
Espionage, 168–169
European Economic Community (EEC), 6, 360–361. See also Latin American Common Market.
Exchange rates, 372, 375
Executive agreements. See Agreements, executive.
Executive Offices of the White House, 199
Expansion (U.S.), 24–26, 29, 34–35, 385

Fall-out shelters, 111
Farewell Address, 4, 28
Federal Bureau of Investigation (FBI), 150
First-strike capability, 240–241
Florida, purchase of, 25
Food for Peace, 341–343
Ford, Gerald, 100, 237, 277
Foreign Affairs, 128
Foreign Agricultural Service, 144
Foreign aid and national character, 67
Foreign Intelligence Advisory Board, 202
Foreign policy, bipartisan, 131–132
Foreign Service Corps, 174–176
Foreign Service Information Corps, 316
Forrestal, James A., 103, 121
Forty Committee, 202, 222
Forward strategy, 52–53
Fulbright, J. William, 57, 62 n, 63 n, 78 n, 161 n, 216, 224 n, 228 n

Gatekeeper effect, 165–166

General Agreement on Tariffs and Trade, 357–358
Gladsden Purchase, 25
Goals (foreign policy), 5, 44–45, 387
Gold system, two-tier, 373
Goldwater, Barry, 53, 61 n, 134, 136
Good Neighbor Policy, 34
Great White Fleet, 38
Guatemala, invasion of, 284–285
Guerrilla warfare, 246–249
Gulf of Tonkin incident, 10, 179–180

Herter, Christian, 143
Hoover Commission, 200, 221
"Hotline," 279
House Foreign Affairs Committee, 210
House Un-American Activities Committee, 150
Humphrey, Hubert, 102, 136

Image, 10, 11, 44
Indians, American, 24
Information feedback, 14
Information Officer, 317
Intelligence:
  classification, 106–107
  community and Congress, 221
  doctrine, 170
Intelligence Checklist, 167
Intelligence and Research, Bureau of, 149
Interagency Classification Review Committee, 107
Interdepartmental Regional Groups, 158
Interim Agreement on Offensive Missiles, 265–267
International Commerce, Bureau of, 143
International law, 26–27, 30–31, 36–37, 49–50, 305–309, 386
International Non-Governmental Organization, 126–127
International Security Affairs, Bureau of, 146
International Trade Organization, 357
Investments, private abroad, 345–351
Isolationism, 33, 86, 391
Israel, 120–121, 133

Johnson, Lyndon B., 53, 134
Joint Chiefs of Staff, 146
Joint United States Public Affairs Office, 318

Kellogg-Briand Treaty, 33, 36
Kennedy, John F., 165, 189, 202—203
Kennedy round, 189, 358
King, Martin Luther, Jr., 90

Index

Kissinger, Henry A., 143, 159, 205, 207 n, 252 n, 253 n, 276 n, 298 n

Labor attaché, 144
Labor, Department of, 144
Latin American Common Market, 361
  See also European Economic Community.
Lavelle, Lieut. Gen. John D., 180
Law, international. *See* International law.
Left-Wing Revisionism:
  Cold War, view of, 233
  defined, 54–57
  mass media bias, 102
  and national values, 70
  Open Door policy, 55–56
  presidential power, view of, 209
  pressure groups, 115–116
Letterwriting, 87–88, 91
Lend-Lease program, 40, 43n, 333, 353 n
Liberalism:
  defined, 45–48
  and interest groups, 116
  and national values, 69–70
  and presidential power, 209
  and public opinion, 82–83
Library of Congress, 211
Limited Test Ban Agreement, 264
Limited war. *See* War, limited.
Liquidity crisis, 371
Lobbyist, foreign, 121–122
Louisiana Purchase, 25
Loyalty Order, 213

MacArthur, Douglas, 203–204
McCarthy, Eugene, 135–136
McCarthy, Joseph, 132, 201, 313
McGovern, George, 56
McNamara, Robert, 146, 236
Maneuverable Re-entry Vehicle (MaRV), 274
Manifest Destiny, 31
Marshall, George C., 132, 142–143, 149
Marshall Plan, 110–111, 333–334
Marxism, 350–351
Massive retaliation, 235
Maximilian affair, 25
Mexican–American War, 25
Military–industrial complex, 119, 153
MIRV *See* Multiple Independent Re-entry Vehicles.
Monroe Doctrine, 22–23
Moralism, 26, 31, 35, 386–387
"Most-Favored-Nation" clause, 357–358
Motion pictures and U.S. image, 325
Multinational companies, 348

Multiple Independent Re-entry Vehicle (MIRV), 266
Mutual and balanced force reduction, 270
My Lai atrocities, 105

National Intelligence Estimates, 170
National Intelligence Survey, 168
National interest, 5
National Military Command Center, 175–176
National Security Act, 145, 146
National Security Agency, 150
National Security Council, 156–159
NATO. *See* North Atlantic Treaty Organization.
Neutralism, 27, 30–31
Nigeria, 122
Nixon Doctrine, 236, 391
Nixon, Richard M.:
  defeat of McGovern, 56
  and Democrats, 132
  energy crisis, 153
  impeachment proceedings, 105
  personal values, 75
  race with Humphrey, 102, 136
  race with McGovern, 104
  "secret plan" for Vietnam, 134
  style of decision making, 198
  summit conferences, 190–191
  trip to China, 127
  view of press, 99
  visit to Latin America as Vice President, 285
Non-diplomatic representative. *See* Lobbyist, foreign.
Nonrecognition, Doctrine of, 37
North African pirate episode, 26
North Atlantic Treaty Organization (NATO), 14, 285–290
"Nth country" problem, 264–265
Nuclear sufficiency doctrine, 236
Nuclear Test Ban Treaty, 111
Nuclear weapons, 39–40

Office of Management and Budget, 159
Open Door Policy, 35, 55–56
"Open Skies" proposal, 259
Operation Camelot, 155
Operational code, 58–59
Operations Center, 175
Organization of American States (OAS), 281–285

Pan American Union, 283–284
Panama Canal Zone, 144
Paris Peace Pact. *See* Kellogg-Briand Treaty.
Patterns, definition of, 3–4

Pause theory, 288–289
Peace Corps, 189, 326–328
Peace of Righteousness, 35, 386
"Pentagon Papers," 108, 109, 155, 214
People's Republic of China, 89, 132, 294, 390
Planned program budgeting, 200–201
"Plumbers, the," 109
Policy:
 defined, 9
 stages of, 10–12
Policy Planning Staff, 179
Political development, 340–341
Political socialization, 74–75
Population control policy, 344–345
Private investment abroad, 345–351
Propaganda, 316–317
Public Affairs Officer, 317
Public Law 480. See Food for Peace.
Pueblo, 168
Pugwash Movement, 154

Quemoy and Matsu crisis, 89, 294

Rand Corporation, 155
Realism:
 and bureaucracy, 182, 200
 and the Cold War, 233
 and diplomacy, 50–51
 and international law, 49–50
 and moralism, 387
 and national values, 68–69
 and the presidency, 188–189, 209
 and public opinion, 81–82
 and special-interest groups, 116
 and the Third World, 50
Rearmament, German, 287
"Red Scare," 37
Religion and U.S. foreign policy, 31
Revisionist state, 49
Revolutionary War (American), 20–21
Right-Wing Revisionism:
 and the Chinese revolution, 51
 and the Cold War, 52, 233
 and disarmament, 274
 and presidential power, 209
 and the press, 102
 and public opinion, 83
 and special-interest groups, 116
Rio Treaty, 284
Rogers, William P., 108, 143
Roosevelt, Theodore, 35, 43 n, 386
Roosevelt's corollary (to the Monroe Doctrine), 33–34
Rule of law, 306
Rusk, Dean, 143

Samoa, 144
Schools abroad for American dependents, 325, 326
Science Advisory Committee, 153
Science and Technology, Special Assistant to the President for, 153
Second-strike capability, 240–241
Secretary of Defense, 146
Secretary of State, 142–143
Senate Foreign Relations Committee, 210
Senior Interdepartmental Group, 158
Situation room, 176
Southeast Treaty Organization (SEATO), 292–296
Soviet grain deal, 363–364
Spanish–American War, 29
Special Drawing Rights, 373–374
Subversive Activities Control Board, 150
Suez Canal, 29
Summit diplomacy, 190–191
Supreme Court, 213–214
Stettenus, Edward, 142
Strategic Arms Limitation Talks (SALT), 265–267
Strategy:
 counter-force, 241
 counter-city, 241
 military, defined, 234

Tariff Commission (U.S.), 143
Task forces and the intelligence community, 201
Tet offensive (1968), 93
Texas, annexation of, 25
"Think tanks," 154–155
Third World, 15 n, 40
Tourism, 325, 367
Trade:
 bureaucracy, 143–144
 with Communist nations, 360
 international law, 26–27
 party positions, 133
Trade Expansion Act, 189
Transfer payments, 367
Transportation, 366–367
Treaties, 216–218
Tripartite Declaration of 1950, 290–291
"Troika" arrangement, 303
Truman, Harry S., 88, 121
Trust territories (UN), 144
"Tuesday luncheon group," 158
Turkey, 202–203
Tunisia, 126–127
Two-tier gold system, 373

Index

Unilateralism, 20–24, 29–30, 32–34, 383–384
United Nations Conference on Trade and Development, 368–369
United Nations and U.S. policy, 14, 299–305
United States Information Agency (USIA), 314–318
United States Intelligence Board, 148
United States Mission to the UN, 305
U-2 incident, 12

Values, 6
Venezuelan boundary dispute, 29–30
Vietnam War, 12, 90, 93, 105, 192, 385
Virgin Islands, 144
Vladivostok agreement, 277

Wallace, George, 137

War:
    debts, interallied, 35
    declaration of, 215
    guerrilla, 246–249
    limited
        conventional, 244–246
        nuclear, 242–243
    powers limiting legislation, 222-223
War of 1812, 23–24
"Washington clearance," 177
Watergate scandal, 104–105, 187
Wilson, Woodrow, 32–33, 46–47, 75
Women:
    attitudes toward Vietnam War, 90
    Women's Activities Officer, 319
World Bank, 357
World Federalists, 125–126
World War I, 32

Zionists, 120–121

Author Index

Abshire, David M., 252 n
Acheson, Dean, 57, 62 n, 132, 143, 226 n, 253 n
Adams, Ephraim D., 42 n
Adler, Kenneth P., 96 n
Adler, Selig, 43 n
Alba, Victor, 354 n
Albertson, Maurice L., 331 n
Albright, Joseph, 378 n
Alger, Chadwick F., 183 n
Allard, Winston, 97 n
Allen, F.E., 228 n
Allen, Richard V., 252 n
Almond, Gabriel A., 76, 79 n, 95 n, 98 n
Alperovitz, Gar, 62 n
Ambrose, Stephen E., 43 n
Ameral, Marianne, 114 n
Anderson, Eugenie, 161 n
Arensberg, Conrad M., 355 n
Argyris, Chris, 184 n
Arkes, Hadley, 353 n
Arlen, Michael J., 114 n
Armacost, Michael H., 252 n
Armstrong, Hamilton, 138 n
Aron, Raymond, 207 n, 253 n, 391 n, 392 n
Aronowitz, Dennis, 276 n
Asher, Robert E., 355 n
Attwood, William, 113 n

Bacon, Eugene H., 252 n
Bader, William B., 277 n
Bailey, Norman A., 297 n
Bailey, Thomas A., 43 n, 95 n
Baker, Roscoe, 129 n
Baldwin, David A., 229 n, 353 n
Baldwin, Hanson W., 206 n
Baldwin, Robert E., 377 n, 378 n

Ball, W. Macmahon, 298 n
Barber, James David, 80 n
Barker, Sir Ernest, 77 n
Barnet, Richard J., 277 n
Barnett, Vincent, 183 n
Barns, William, 183 n
Barrett, Edward W., 329 n
Barzini, Luigi Giorgio, 79 n
Batten, James K., 276 n
Bauer, Raymond, 129 n
Bauer, Theodore, 161 n
Beale, Howard K., 43 n
Beard, Charles A., 43 n
Beauvoir, Simone de, 78 n
Beggiefer, Bernard C., 275 n
Behrman, J.N., 354 n
Beichman, Arnold, 310 n
Belknap, George, 138 n
Beloff, Max, 95 n, 128 n
Bemis, Samuel F., 41 n, 161 n
Bennett, John C., 60 n
Benoit, Emile, 276 n
Berger, Max, 78 n
Berger, Monroe, 78 n
Berman, Harold J., 276 n, 377 n
Bernardo, C. Joseph, 252 n
Bernien, F.K., 114 n
Berry, Karen, 80 n
Birky, Pauline E., 331 n
Black, Gordon S., 97 n
Blackmer, Donald L., 353 n
Blackstock, Paul W., 183 n
Blaisdell, Donald, 128 n
Blanke, W. Wendell, 183 n
Blashill, John, 355 n
Bletz, Donald F., 185 n
Bloomfield, Lincoln P., 276 n, 309 n
Blum, John M., 79 n

Index

Bobrow, Davis, 96 n
Bogart, Leo, 330 n
Bogen, David S., 310 n
Bohn, Lewis C., 276 n
Bolton, Roger E., 276 n
Boorstin, Daniel, 79 n
Borklund, Carl W., 161 n
Boulding, Kenneth E., 60 n, 276 n
Bowman, William W., 113 n
Boyd, Julian P., 228 n
Braeman, John, 183 n
Braestrup, Peter, 113 n
Brandon, Donald, 391 n, 392 n
Bremner, R.H., 183 n
Brennan, Donald G., 275 n
Bretail, Robert W., 60 n
Brodie, Bernard, 251 n, 253 n
Brodie, Henry, 378 n
Brody, David, 183 n
Brody, Richard, 97 n
Brogan, D.W., 78 n
Browder, Robert P., 43 n
Browne, Malcolm W., 113 n
Browning, Frank, 310 n
Brownlie, Ian, 276 n
Buchan, Alastair, 276 n, 298 n
Buckley, William F., 62 n
Bull, Hedley, 275 n
Bullit, William C., 80 n
Bundy, McGeorge, 252 n
Burnham, James, 61 n, 62 n
Burns, E.L.M., 276 n
Burns, James M., 138 n
Burt, Alfred LeRoy, 41 n
Burtness, Paul, 162 n
Burton, John, 277 n
Butterfield, Herbert C., 60 n
Byrd, Elbert M., 228 n

Calleo, David., 298 n, 391 n
Campbell, Angus, 138 n
Campbell, John C., 298 n
Cantril, Handley, 85, 96 n, 97 n
Carnoy, Martin, 377 n
Carroll, Holbert N., 226 n
Case, Lynn M., 42 n
Caspary, William R., 80 n
Castle, Eugene W., 353 n
Cater, Douglass, 129 n
Chace, James, 392 n
Chamberlain, John, 207 n
Chamberlain, L.H., 228 n
Chandler, Geoffrey, 95 n
Chenery, H.B., 353 n
Childs, James R., 183 n
Childs, Marquis, 61 n
Christiansen, Bjorn, 80 n
Clark, John J., 253 n, 276 n
Clark, Keith, 162 n

Clark, L. Pierce, 80 n
Clausen, Aage R., 97 n
Cleveland, Harlan, 60 n
Clotfelter, James, 184 n
Clyde, Paul H., 42 n
Coblentz, Gaston, 63 n
Cochran, T.C., 355 n
Cochrane, James D., 377 n
Coffin, Tristram, 63 n
Cohen, Benjamin V., 226 n
Cohen, Bernard C., 96 n, 98 n, 128 n
Cohen, Warren I., 42 n
Cohn, Fred, 227 n
Colegrove, Kenneth W., 226 n
Coleman, Lee, 73–74, 79 n
Collart, Yves, 275 n
Colligan, J., 329 n
Commager, Henry Steele, 79 n
Connell–Smith, Gordon, 297 n
Connett, William B., Jr., 184 n
Converse, Philip E., 97 n, 98 n
Cook, Thomas I., 60 n
Coombs, Philip, 330 n
Cooper, C.L., 183 n
Corder, Lucille, 377 n
Corwin, Edward S., 206 n, 227 n, 228 n
Cottrell, Alvin, 61 n
Cottrell, Leonard S., Jr., 95 n
Courtney, Kent, 277 n
Courtney, Phoebe, 277 n
Crabb, Cecil V., Jr., 78 n, 138 n, 378 n
Cronin, Thomas E., 206 n
Cross, James E., 253 n
Currey, Cecil B., 42 n
Cutler, Robert, 162 n
Cutlip, Scott N., 112 n

Dahl, Robert, 226 n
Dale, Edwin L., Jr., 379 n
D'Amato, Anthony A., 227 n
Dangerfield, Royden J., 228 n
Davidson, Alfred E., 378 n
Davies, David R., 60 n
Davis, Bruce E., 114 n
Davis, David Howard, 163 n
Davis, Elmer, 95 n
Davis, F. James, 331 n
Davis, Forrest, 43 n
Davis, Harry R., 60 n
Davis, J.H., 354 n
Davis, Kingsley, 354 n
Davis, Vincent, 252 n
De Conde, Alexander, 161 n
De Crèvecoeur, J. Hector, 70–71, 78 n
Deitchman, Seymour J., 253 n
Deohane, Robert O., 355 n
De Smith, Stanley A., 161 n
Destler, I.M., 206 n

Deutsch, Karl W., 276 n
Devine, Donald J., 96 n
Dexter, Louis A., 97 n, 129 n
Diebold, William, Jr., 376 n
Dinerstein, Jerbert S., 391 n
Dizard, Wilson P., 330 n
Doig, Jameson W., 206 n
Donovan, Frank R., 309 n
Doran, George H., 43 n
Dougherty, James E., 275 n
Doughty, James, 61 n
Dozer, Donald M., 41 n
Drier, John C., 297 n, 354 n
Drummund, Roscoe, 63 n
DuBois, Cora, 79 n
DuBridge, Lee A., 162 n
Dulles, Foster Rhea, 42 n
Duncan, W. Raumond, 41 n
Dyer, Murray, 329 n
Dyer, Philip W., 253 n

Eberhart, Sylvia, 95 n
Edwards, Anthony, 378 n
Efon, Edith, 113 n
Eisenhower, Dwight D., 309 n
Eisinger, Richard W., 113 n
Ekman, Paul, 97 n
El-Assal, 114 n
Elder, Robert E., 160 n, 183 n, 330 n, 330 n
Elliot-Bateman, Michael, 161 n
Ellis, Lavis E., 43 n
Elrod, J. McRee, 80 n
Emerson, Rupert, 129 n
Emery, Edwin, 113 n
Engstrom, Warren C., 114 n
Enthoven, Alain C., 253 n
Eramus, Charles J., 355 n
Esthus, Raymond A., 43 n
Evans, John W., 376 n
Evans, M. Stanton, 62 n

Falk, Irving A., 330 n
Falk, Richard A., 277 n, 310 n
Falk, Stanley L., 162 n
Farber, Maurice L., 78 n
Farnsworth, D.N., 226 n
Fedder, Edwin H., 298 n
Feinberg, Barry M., 113 n
Feingold, Harry L., 43 n
Feis, Herbert, 42 n, 43 n, 353 n
Feld, Werner J., 377 n
Fenno, Richard, 228 n
Ferrell, Robert H., 43 n
Fidler, Issac, 78 n
Filene, Peter G., 43 n
Finer, Herman, 63 n
Finkelstein, Lawrence S., 309 n
Finletter, Thomas K., 251 n

Fisher, Glen H., 329 n
Fleming, Denna F., 62 n, 228 n
Forbes, Henry W., 275 n
Forman, Dorothy, 310 n
Foster, George M.C., 355 n
Foster, H. Schuyler, 95 n
Fox, Annette B., 298 n
Fox, Guy H., 354 n
Fox, William T.R., 184 n, 298 n
Frances, Roy G., 354 n
Frank, Lewis A., 378 n
Frank, Robert Shelby, 114 n
Frankel, Charles, 206 n, 330 n
Frankel, S. Herbert, 355 n
Fraser, Henry S., 228 n
Frederich, Carl J., 138 n
Free, Lloyd A., 85, 96 n, 97 n
Freud, Sigmund, 80 n
Friedman, Milton, 353 n
Frisch, D.H., 277 n
Fulbright, J. William, 57, 62 n, 63 n, 78 n, 161 n, 216, 224, 228 n
Fyfe, Henry Hamilton, 78 n

Gaddis, Paul O., 354 n
Galbraith, J.K., 184 n
Gallagher, Charles F., 129 n
Gardner, Fred, 227 n
Gardner, Richard N., 309 n
Gavin, James N., 25 n
Gelber, Lionel M., 42 n
Gelber, Lionel M., 42 n
George, Alexander L., 58, 59, 63 n, 80 n, 207 n
George, Juliette, 80 n
Gilbert, Felix, 42 n
Gillin, John, 79 n
Gilpin, Robert, 162 n
Ginsburgh, Robert N., 185 n, 251 n
Gleeck, L.E., 97 n
Gleuson, S. Everett, 43 n
Glick, Edward B., 184 n
Goldsen, Rose K., 96 n
Goldstein, Walter, 275 n
Goldwater, Barry, 53, 61 n, 134, 136
Good, Robert C., 60 n
Goodsell, James N., 41 n
Gordon, George N., 330 n
Gordon, Lincoln, 354 n
Gordon, Rosalie M., 227 n
Gorer, Geoffrey, 78 n
Gorter, Wytze, 378 n
Gosnell, Cullen B., 228 n
Graber, Doris A., 353 n
Graebner, Norman A., 97 n, 161 n
Grassmuck, George L., 138 n, 227 n
Grattan, Clinton H., 42 n
Green, David, 41 n
Green, Philip, 252 n

Index

Greenberg, S.D., 206 n
Greene, Fred, 298 n
Greene, Theodore P., 42 n
Greenstein, Fred I., 80 n
Gregg, Robert W., 392 n
Griffin, Charles C., 42 n
Griswold, Alfred W., 42 n
Gross, Ernest A., 138 n
Gross, Franz B., 309 n
Grubel, H.G., 330 n
Grunwald, Joseph, 377 n
Gwertzman, Bernard, 63 n

Haas, Ernest B., 309 n
Habe, Hans, 78 n
Haberler, Gottfred, 376 n
Hachten, William A., 227 n
Hall, John A., 277 n
Halle, Louis J., 251 n
Halper, Thomas, 97 n
Halperin, Morton H., 97 n, 206 n
Hamilton, Richard F., 96 n
Hammond, Paul Y., 161 n, 162 n, 253 n, 276 n
Handberg, Roger B., Jr., 96 n
Hanes, John W., Jr., 95 n
Harland, Gordon, 60 n
Harr, John E., 183 n, 184 n, 206 n
Harris, Joseph P., 228 n
Harris, Seymour, 138 n
Hart, Jim A., 113 n
Hauser, William L., 185 n
Havens, Murray C., 227 n
Havighurst, C.C., 329 n
Haviland, H. Field, 160 n, 309 n
Hayes, John D., 378 n
Heibrunn, Otto, 253 n
Heinrichs, Waldo H., Jr., 183 n, 184 n
Henkin, Louis, 227 n, 276 n
Hennessy, Bernard, 129 n
Hero, Alfred O., 96 n
Herring, George C., Jr., 353 n
Hersh, Seymour M., 113 n, 276 n
Hertz, Frederick, 77 n
Hertzog, Arthur, 162 n
Herzog, Herta, 97 n
Hickey, John, 226 n
Higgins, B.J., 309 n
Hill, Norman L., 205 n
Hilsman, Roger, 161 n, 185 n, 226 n
Hitch, Charles J., 161 n, 253 n
Hitchens, Harold L., 114 n
Hoffmann, Stanley, 77 n, 391 n
Hoffmeyer, Erik, 376 n
Hogan, John D., 378 n
Hohenberg, John, 113 n
Holsti, Ole R., 58, 59, 63 n
Holt, Robert T., 329 n
Holt, W. Stull, 228 n

Hoopes, Roy, 331 n
Hoopes, Townsend, 206 n
Horney, Karen, 72, 79 n
Horowitz, David, 62 n
Hovey, Harold A., 353 n
Huff, Earl D., 129 n
Hunter, Robert E., 378 n
Huntington, Samuel P., 151 n, 185 n
Hussein, 331 n
Hutton, J. Bernard, 377 n
Huzar, Elias, 229 n

Inkeles, Alex, 77 n
Irish, Marian D., 97 n
Irwin, R.W., 42 n

Jackson, Henry, 162 n
Jacobson, Harold K., 162 n
Jaquaribe, Helio, 354 n
Javits, Jacob K., 227 n
Jewell, Malcolm E., 138 n, 227 n, 228 n
Johnson, Harry G., 353 n
Johnson, Haynes, 63 n, 206 n
Johnson, Richard A., 161 n
Johnson, Robert H., 163 n
Johnstone, John W.C., 113 n
Jonas, Manfred, 43 n
Jones, Arthur G., 183 n
Jones, Robert H., 353 n
Jordan, Amos A., Jr., 354 n

Kahn, David, 162 n
Kahn, Herman, 253 n
Kaplan, Lawrence, 298 n
Karsten, C.F., 378 n
Kash, Don, 162 n
Kaufmann, William W., 252 n
Kegley, Charles W., 60 n
Kegley, Charles W., Jr., 392 n
Kellerman, Don, 227 n
Kemp, M.C., 378 n
Kenan, Peter, 376 n
Kennan, George F., 43 n, 49, 57, 61 n, 63 n, 78 n
Kennedy, Robert, 183 n, 206 n
Kent, Sherman, 162 n
Khadduri, Majid, 298 n
Kilson, Martin, 129 n
Kimball, Warren F., 353 n
Kin, Young Hum, 206 n
Kindleberger, Charles P., 354 n, 376 n
Kintner, William R., 61 n, 161 n, 253 n
Kissinger, Henry A., 143, 159, 205, 207 n, 252 n, 253 n, 276 n, 298 n
Kittler, Glenn D., 331 n
Kline, Carl L., 73–74, 80 n

Klingberg, Frank I., 76, 80 n
Kluckhohn, Clyde, 79 n
Knorr, Klaus, 183 n, 277 n, 298 n
Koch, Adrienne, 42 n
Koen, Ross Y., 129 n
Koening, Donald, 96 n
Kofmehl, Kenneth, 226 n
Kohn, Hans, 79 n
Kolodziej, Edward, 162 n, 252 n
Kopstock, Fred H., 376 n
Kotok, Alan B., 113 n
Kosselman, Mark, 206 n
Kramer, Daniel C., 62 n
Kraus, Sidney, 114 n
Krause, Lawrence B., 377 n, 377 n
Krause, Walter, 377 n
Kreinin, Mordechai E., 376 n
Krieghbaum, Hillier, 113 n
Kriesberg, Martin, 97 n

Lafever, Ernest W., 275 n, 309 n
Lane, Thomas A., 61 n
Lang, Daniel, 253 n
Langer, William L., 43 n
Lapham, Lewis H., 113 n
Larrabee, Eric, 79 n
Lasch, Christopher, 62 n
Laski, Harold J., 78 n
Lasswell, Harold D., 80 n
Laves, Walter H.C., 330 n
Lawler, Justus George, 253 n
Leacacos, John P., 160 n
Lee, James A., 355 n
Lee, Muna, 330 n
Legere, L.J., 162 n
Lehman, J.F., Jr., 275 n
Leiss, Amelia C., 276 n
LeMay, Curtis E., 61 n
Lepper, Mary Milling, 114 n
Lerche, Charles O., Jr., 78 n, 227 n, 298 n
Lerner, Max, 79 n
Levine, Robert A., 251 n
Levinson, Daniel, 77 n
Levy, Walter J., 378 n
Licklider, Roy E., 162 n
Lindzey, Gardner, 77 n
Ling, Dwight L., 129 n
Lippmann, Walter, 49, 60 n–61 n, 103
Lipset, Seymour M., 61 n, 79 n
Lipsey, Robert E., 377 n
Liska, George, 297 n, 353 n, 391 n
Liston, Robert A., 331 n
Longley, Charles H., 252 n
Lowe, George E., 252 n
Lowenthal, Abraham F., 297 n
Lukacs, John, 62 n
Lynd, Staughton, 62 n
Lyons, Gene M., 162 n

McBride, James H., 277 n
McCamy, James L., 160 n, 161 n, 184 n
McClelland, David S., 128 n
MacCloskey, Monro, 161 n
McClosky, Herbert, 80 n
McClure, Wallace, 228 n
MacDouglas, Donald, 376 n
McEvoy, James, III, 61 n
McGarvey, Patrick J., 183 n
McGovern, William M., 183 n
McKean, Roland N., 253 n
Maclean, Malcom S., Jr., 114 n
McLellan, David S., 77 n
McLeod, J.H., 42 n
MacMahon, Arthur, 160 n
McMurray, Ruth E., 330 n
McNamara, Robert C., 252 n
MacVane, John, 310 n
Madow, Pauline, 331 n
Magdoff, Harry, 62 n
Maggs, Peter B., 276 n
Mann, Dean E., 206 n
Markel, Lester, 113 n
Markham, James W., 112 n
Marshall, James, 95 n
Martin, Laurence W., 42 n, 275 n, 391 n
Martineau, Harriet, 78 n
Mason, Edward S., 353 n
Mathis, F. John, 377 n
Mazlish, Bruce, 80 n
Mead, Margaret, 72, 79 n
Mehling, Rouben, 114 n
Melman, Seymour, 276 n
Mennis, Bernard, 184 n
Merrill, Maurice H., 228 n
Mesick, Jane L., 78 n
Meyer, Karl E., 206 n
Michael, Donald N., 98 n
Mikesell, R.F., 354 n
Milbrath, Lester W., 128 n
Miller, August C., Jr., 298 n
Miller, Warren E., 97 n, 138 n
Millikan, Max F., 352 n
Millis, Walter, 113 n, 129 n, 184 n, 251 n, 277 n
Minor, Dale, 113 n
Modelski, George, 298 n
Mollenhoff, Clark R., 161 n
Monet, Pawel, 183 n
Montgomery, John D., 227 n, 352 n, 354 n
Moore, Ben T., 298 n
Moore, John N., 310 n
Moos, Malcolm, 60 n
Morgan, John H., 183 n
Morgenstern, Oskar, 251 n
Morgenthau, Hans J., 48, 49, 60 n, 162 n

Index

Morgner, Aurelius, 355 n
Morris, Richard T., 331 n
Morrison, Elting, 79 n
Morrow, William L., 226 n
Morton, Louis, 162 n
Mosher, Frederick C., 206 n
Moulton, Harland B., 252 n
Mueller, John E., 96 n
Muirhead, James Fullerton, 78 n
Munsterberg, Hugo, 78 n
Murphy, Robert D., 183 n

Nafziger, Ralph O., 114 n
Nelson, Randal H., 228 n
Newhouse, John, 277 n
Nicholson, Harold, 183 n
Nie, Norman H., 97 n
Niebuhr, Reinhold, 49, 60 n
Niehoff, Arthur, 355 n
Nigro, Felix, 228 n
Niland, John R., 330 n
Nimer, Benjamin, 63 n
Nogee, Joseph L., 275 n
Norwood, William R., 161 n
Nostrand, Howard Lee, 330 n
Nuechterlein, Donald E., 298 n, 392 n
Nye, Joseph S., Jr., 355 n

Ober, Warren U., 162 n
O'Connor, Raymond G., 252 n
O'Leary, Michael K., 352 n
O'Neal, Robert, 227 n
Osgood, Robert E., 253 n, 297 n, 298 n, 391 n
Owen, Henry, 392 n
Owen, Jean, 113 n

Packard, George R., III, 113 n
Paddock, Elizabeth, 355 n
Paddock, William, 355 n
Paige, Glenn D., 253 n
Parisi, Annette A., 377 n
Parker, Edwin B., 97 n
Passman, Otto E., 67, 77 n, 353 n
Patterson, Samuel C., 227 n
Pauker, Guy J., 298 n
Peeters, Paul, 252 n
Peffer, Nathaniel, 298 n
Perkins, Bradford, 41 n
Perkins, Dexter, 95 n
Perkins, James A., 229 n
Perlmann, M., 298 n
Perloff, Harvey S., 353 n
Pincus, John A., 378 n
Pinto, Anibal, 354 n
Pollack, Gerald A., 378 n
Polsby, Nelson W., 97 n, 226 n
Pool, Ithiel de Sola, 98 n, 129 n

Possony, Stefan T., 61 n
Potter, David M., 77 n, 78 n
Pournelle, J.E., 61 n
Powers, Patrick W., 161 n
Powers, Thomas S., 253 n
Pustay, John S., 253 n
Pratt, Julius W., 42 n
Preeg, Ernest H., 376 n, 377 n
Price, Don K., 161 n
Price, Harry B., 353 n
Princus, Walter, 129 n
Pruitt, Dean G., 161 n
Pye, Lucian W., 354 n

Qualter, Terence H., 329 n

Raab, Earl, 61 n
Rainey, Gene E., 98 n
Ramsey, Paul, 253 n
Ransom, Harry Howe, 161 n
Re, Edward D., 355 n
Real, James, 277 n
Reinhardt, George C., 251 n
Reston, James B., 61 n, 112 n
Reynolds, Mary T., 163 n
Rice, Andrew E., 331 n
Richter, J.H., 377 n
Rider, Katharine, 80 n
Ries, John C., 161 n
Rieselbach, Leroy N., 227 n
Riesman, David, 72, 79 n
Riggs, Robert E., 309 n, 310 n
Ripley, Randall B., 163 n, 226 n
Rippy, James F., 41 n
Rivers, William L., 113 n
Roberts, Chalmers M., 207 n
Robinson, Edgar E., 205 n
Robinson, James A., 226 n, 229 n
Roett, Riordon, 355 n
Rogers, William C., 96 n
Rogow, Arnold, 80 n
Roherty, James M., 252 n
Rolfe, Sidney E., 355 n
Roosevelt, Theodore, 43 n
Roper, Elmo, 97 n
Rose, Steven, 276 n
Rosenau, James, 80 n, 95 n, 98 n, 112 n
Rosenberg, Milton J., 96 n, 98 n
Rosi, Eugene J., 96 n
Ross, Thomas B., 206 n
Rossiter, Clinton, 61 n
Rostow, Eugene V., 392 n
Rothstein, Robert L., 279 n, 391 n
Rourke, Francis E., 391 n
Rubin, Ronald I., 330 n
Russell, Bertrand, 277 n
Russell, Ruth B., 309 n
Russett, Bruce M., 43 n, 253 n

Russo, Frank D., 114 n
Rustow, Dankwort, 298 n

Salvadori, Massimo, 298 n
Sapolsky, Harvey M., 252 n
Scaperlanda, Anthony, 378 n
Schelling, Thomas C., 251 n
Schilling, Warner, 253 n
Schlesinger, Arthur M., Jr., 207 n
Schlesinger, James R., 253 n
Schooler, Dean, Jr., 162 n
Schulman, Carol, 114 n
Schwarz, Fred, 62 n
Schwarz, Urs, 251 n
Scigliano, Robert, 354 n
Scott, A.D., 330 n
Seabury, Paul, 392 n
Seed, Philip, 277 n
Sessions, Gene A., 297 n
Shannon, Fred A., 78 n
Shapiro, Harvey D., 354 n
Shapiro, Martin, 138 n
Sherrill, Robert, 227 n
Shils, Edward, 354 n
Shriver, R. Sargent, 331 n
Shultz, George P., 379 n
Sigal, Leon V., 114 n
Singer, Benjamin D., 114 n
Singer, J. David, 80 n, 251 n, 275 n
Skolnikoff, Eugene B., 162 n
Skousen, W. Cleon, 62 n
Slater, Jerome, 297 n
Slawski, Edward J., 113 n
Smith, Dale O., 61 n, 251 n
Smith, George H. E., 138 n
Smith, K. Wayne, 253 n
Smith, M. Brewster, 96 n
Smith, Paul, 96 n
Smithies, Arthur, 227 n,
Smuts, Robert W., 78 n
Snider, D.A., 378 n
Snyder, Glenn, 253 n
Snyder, Richard C., 228 n
Sorensen, Theodore C., 98 n, 377 n
Sorenson, John, 330 n
Spanier, John W., 206 n, 275 n
Spencer, Warren F., 42 n
Spicer, George W., 227 n
Spiller, Robert E., 79 n
Stanley, Timothy W., 251 n, 298 n
Stein, Eric, 162 n
Steiner, Zara S., 184 n
Stephens, Oren, 330 n
Stevens, Richard P., 129 n
Stevens, Robert W., 378 n
Stevenson, Robert L., 113 n
Stillmann, Edmund, 63 n
Stinchcombe, William C., 41 n
Stobaugh, Robert B., Jr., 355 n

Stoessinger, John G., 309 n, 309 n
Stolberg-Wernigerock, Otto, 42 n
Stone, Jeremy, 277 n
Strausz-hupé, Robert, 61 n
Strickland, Donald A., 162 n
Strong, Sir Kenneth, 161 n
Strout, A.M., 353 n
Stuart, Graham H., 160 n, 206 n
Stubbs, William B., 228 n
Stuhler, Barbara, 96 n
Stupak, Ronald J., 62 n
Suchman, Edward A., 96 n
Suderland, Riley, 183 n
Sullivan, George, 331 n
Swerling, Boris C., 378 n
Syed, Anwar Hussain, 61 n
Szulc, Tad, 206 n

Tannenbaum, Frank, 60 n, 78 n
Tarr, David W., 251 n
Taylor, Maxwell D., 251 n
Teller, Edward, 277 n
Terrell, John U., 160 n
Textor, Robert, 331 n
Thayer, Charles W., 183 n
Thayer, George, 378 n
Thomas, Ann, 297 n
Thomas, G. Richard, 355 n
Thomas, M. Ladd, 298 n
Thomson, Charles A., 330 n
Thomson, Charles A.H., 330 n
Tocqueville, Alexis de, 70–71, 78 n
Toma, Peter A., 354 n
Topping, Frances K., 377 n
Torrielli, Andrew J., 79 n
Trager, James, 378 n
Triffin, Robert, 376 n
Tripathi, K.S., 252 n
Truman, Harry, 97 n, 309 n
Tucker, Robert W., 60 n, 62 n, 252 n, 391 n, 392 n
Twining, Nathan F., 253 n

Unger, Irwin, 62 n
Urban, George R., 330 n

Vagts, Alfred, 252 n
Van Deusen, Glyndon G., 95 n
Van de Velde, R.W., 330 n
Varg, Paul A., 42 n
Velvel, Lawrence R., 227 n
Verba, Sidney, 79 n, 97 n, 98 n
Vernon, Raymond, 354 n, 355 n, 378 n
Von Alting, Frans A.M., 376 n

Wade, Richard C., 95 n
Walther, Regis, 184 n

Index

Warner, Geoffrey, 353 n
Warren, Sidney, 206 n
Waskow, Arthur I., 252 n
Wasserman, Benno, 183 n
Waterhouse, Harry F.. 354 n
Watson, Richard A., 138 n
Weiss, Alan, 331 n
Welch, Robert, 62 n
Welch, William, 79 n
Wells, Benjamin, 206 n
Wells, John M., 227 n
Wells, Louis T., Jr., 355 n
Wells, Sumner, 128 n
Westcott, Allan F., 42 n
Westerfield, H. Bradford, 138 n, 183 n, 229 n
Westwood, Andrew F., 353 n
Whitaker, Urban, 114 n
Whittlesey, Susan, 331 n
Wilcox, Francis O., 226 n, 309 n
Wildavsky, Aaron, 392 n
Wilhelm, John, 112 n
Williams, Benjamin H., 138 n
Williams, Robin M., 79 n
Williams, Robin M., Jr., 96 n
Williams, William A., 62 n
Willoughby, Charles A., 206 n

Willrich, Mason, 277 n
Windmuller, John P., 129 n
Windsor, Philip, 276 n
Wingenbach, Charles E., 331 n
Wionczek, Miguel S., 377 n
Wise, David., 206 n
Wit, Daniel, 355 n
Wohlstetter, Roberta, 162 n
Wolf, Wayne, 79 n
Wolfers, Arnold, 42 n, 297 n
Woodhouse, Charles E., 128 n
Woods, George D., 352 n
Wooster, John T., 355 n
Wright, L.B., 42 n
Wright, Quincy, 228 n, 310 n
Wriston, Henry, 183 n
Wyant, Rowena, 97 n
Wyeth, George A., 162 n

Yarmolinsky, Adam, 184 n, 251 n
Yglesias, Jose, 41 n
Yoshpe, Harry B., 161 n
Young, Wayland H., 275 n
Younger, Kenneth, 276 n

Zenoff, David B., 354 n